The
Problem-Solving Approaches
in
NO-FAULT PARENTING

The five basic approaches to problem solving, which are summarized here and detailed in the Appendix, underlie the organization of the text itself.

CLARIFY OBJECTIVES. What are the child's objectives? What are specific parental objectives and how can they be clearly conveyed?

CHANGE THE ENVIRONMENT. What physical, social, or time factors can be altered for the better?

CHANGE ATTITUDES. How appropriate are parental attitudes? Does the child feel understood? Can humor or fantasy alter the child's attitude?

CHANGE PARENTAL RESPONSE. Don't just talk—act. Is this a time to attend more to parental needs or children's needs? What rewards and/or punishments might be effective?

ADOPT TOLERANCE. Put up with the current situation because it cannot be changed, it is too difficult to change, or it will improve by itself with time.

NO-FAULT
PARENTING

NO-FAULT PARENTING

Helen Neville
&
Mona Halaby

Facts On File Publications
New York, New York • Bicester, England

NO-FAULT PARENTING

Library of Congress Cataloging in Publication Data
Neville, Helen.
  No-fault parenting.

  Includes index.
  1. Child rearing.   2. Parent and child.   I. Halaby,
Mona.   II. Title.
HQ769.N416   649′.1   82-2525
ISBN 0-87196-671-9

Printed in the United States of America

10 9 8 7 6 5 4 3 2 1

To all parents—
who live with total dependence,
then surging independence;
and yet, despite frustration and challenge,
nurture the bonds of mutual love.

Contents

Preface

One cannot speak realistically about child care without also discussing parent care. *No-Fault Parenting* addresses both. The task for today's parents has become increasingly difficult. More and more families function without the traditional support of grandparents or even two live-in parents. Values and standards we once accepted may no longer apply when we raise our own children in a changing world. For example, we hear parents talk less about music and nature, more about academic pressure and teenage sexuality. Through it all, we compare ourselves with TV's sit-com families, who are lively and funny and who handle all their dilemmas in twenty-four minutes. Parenting doesn't fit such a time frame. One can buy homemaker services, for a price, but not a mother, who looks after a child fifteen or more hours a day, seven days a week, twelve months a year, and *cares* what happens to the child during that time.

Our children watch us minutely, day by day: not only what we do, but how we do it, and their cumulative observations will have an effect for years. What a responsibility! Unless we want to raise our children by knee-jerk responses and folklore, we have to *learn* new techniques. There is a tremendous volume of technical data about what helps and hinders the development of children, but how are parents to learn this vital information? How many ''family-life'' classes hold the respect of classes in economics or English literature? In my experience, few pediatricians are as well versed in child-rearing practices as in physical illness. Even the most concerned doctors are generally too swamped to spend much time teaching parents. Many of today's high-quality nursery schools are run by child-development specialists, but patterns of family interaction have evolved, and crucial developmental stages have passed, long before children start nursery school. Furthermore, many books increase rather than relieve anxiety, because they imply that, whenever anything goes wrong, the parent is at fault.

Ideally, every mother and father would have a knowledgeable, sensitive, supportive, and trustworthy consultant available whenever questions arise concerning child behavior. Since this ideal is generally unattainable, *No-Fault Parenting* capsulizes, in some detail, the kinds of responses that a responsible, professionally trained person might offer. From my experience in psychiatry, pediatrics, child development, education, and social work, I believe this book can be trusted and referred to again and again for information and support.

Why do people become parents anyway? It's certainly a biological drive. It can also be cultural and emotional, as in the desire to complete one's sense of family, to have a child because everyone else does, or because there's nothing else one wants to do. Further, a baby assures our own perpetuity, assures an eternal companion in our own home. (This latter dream is, needless to say, hard for our children to live up to.) Having children is also a chance to do things better: a new generation gives us hope for mankind and the world. Thus the conscious decision to become a parent contains the seed of idealism. Though we don't talk about it much, those of us who are child psychiatrists, pediatric nurses, child-development specialists, and loving, caring parents are idealists. There is a tender, sensitive child within us, and we want to nurture other such children as well. The positive thrust of *No-Fault Parenting* makes it an investment in idealism in an era when it is popular to be cynical. For each problem listed within its pages, there are ways to enlarge, develop, and magnify, rather than close off, the growth of parent and child. We are not merely talking of avoiding harm, but of strengthening personal development. Though we no longer believe people's psyches enter the world as blank slates, we do believe they can be influenced not only negatively, but positively.

Existential issues are an integral part of child rearing. We want our children to develop some sense of where they are in time and space, some concept of what really matters. Through a hundred thousand interactive experiences with what we, their parents, care about and believe, our children decide what is important to them. A book such as this can help parents believe in the child-rearing process, and that in itself is a kind of idealism. The child is the parent of the next generation, and we, as the guides, provide influence toward hope or cynicism, through our own idealism or lack thereof.

On the other hand, in a practical way, this book also addresses such issues as maternal depression. It gives permission to be discouraged, angry, sad, or afraid, by acknowledging the universality of such feelings among parents, and by relating how others respond to such emotions. I am struck by how many mothers are alone, physically, emotionally, or both. It is an awesome responsibility to be a lonely parent. Even reading about similar feelings in others can provide a measure of comfort.

The energy shortage doesn't apply only to petroleum and electricity. It takes a lot of energy just to live, especially for those with small children. A book such as this can help conserve parental energy, by helping parents sort priorities and funnel their efforts economically.

If we talk more of mothers than fathers, it is because in *most* families today, mothers are still more involved in early child care. Historically, fathers weren't involved at all, and, in some of our subcultures, are still not involved. I am impressed by the number of families I see in my practice in which there isn't any father at all. Certainly among the most positive trends today is that toward the increasing involvement of many fathers with their young children.

Children have a right to develop without being hampered by the prejudices and scars of our own past. That's easy to say and hard to accomplish. To free our children from our own difficulties, we need to pursue our own personal growth. If the parent is depressed, the child is not going to feel as well as if the parent is not depressed. When couples come to me about problems with their children, the parents are often in conflict with each other but are fighting *through* the children. In such situations, my task is to help them see the issue with the child as meaningful but separate. The child can thereby be freed to grow, and the real battle, which is not with the child, comes to the surface where it can be dealt with.

Much of what I hear these days has to do with parents who have lost touch with their growing adolescents. It is my belief that if parents have developed good communication with their offspring from early on, those means of relating will continue to be available as the child matures. In many families, children are not allowed to speak for themselves about what they think and feel, or if they do speak up, they have to pay for it later. I see the lack of ability and freedom to communicate as one of the major roadblocks to emotional growth. To cope well, children need a quite detailed awareness of their own feelings.

Another great need I see is for consistency. Children need consistent support and contact with an ongoing bearer of knowledge. Some consistent plan for educating children is very much in order. *No-Fault Parenting* not only provides such a consistent attitude and approach toward child-rearing, but also provides needed support, education, and help that can enable parents to be consistent.

Though to own this book is to strike a blow for freedom, it is not that simple. Unfortunately, the material won't seep into one's head if the book lies under a pillow. The information must be easily accessible and useful. Indexing and cross-referencing make it easy to locate an array of issues. And because theoretically sound information is expressed in terms of parental experience, it is a distillation of practical information that is easy to read, understand, *and* apply. By enabling parents to respond appropriately to children's needs as well as to respect their own needs, this book provides a myriad of opportunities for the growth of parental self-confidence.

HAROLD MANN, M.D.

Acknowledgments

Our grateful acknowledgments belong to all those who helped turn this dream into reality.

My appreciation begins with my children, Sonya and Eric, who not only provided firsthand knowledge of the excitement, joy, fear, and pain of parenthood, but also endured the frustration of a mother who was often glued to the typewriter. Terri Denis is the friend and fellow parent whose creativity and down-to-earth practicality provided the first inspiration to compile a book. Jose Silva, founder of Silva Mind Control, broadened my perception of reality and made such an undertaking seem possible. My husband, John, not only provided encouragement and child care, but endured my desertion to the typewriter, time-pressured bitchiness, and sleepless nights. Sylvia Adler Schmidt, LCSW and skilled family therapist in Berkeley, enabled our family to grow rather than disintegrate amid the pressures of work and living together. Writing would have been impossible if Ruth Craig, R.N., my supervisor at Kaiser Hospital in Oakland, hadn't been flexible in arranging my work schedule there. My mother, Kay Fowler, remained continually enthusiastic about the project even as she retyped endless drafts. Many other family members and friends supported me throughout the last seven years, despite my neglect of personal relationships.

HELEN NEVILLE

I wish to thank David, my husband, for his love and support. I also wish to thank my sons, Jason and Alexander, for all they have taught me and for their patience during the long and sometimes agonizing process of writing this book. Needless to say that with two small children, writing would have been unfeasible had it not been for all those who helped with child care, especially my friend Bari Nelson.

MONA HALABY

We are also grateful to Roni Wong, whose interest and expertise was essential in compiling a productive questionnaire; Elizabeth Fishel, author of

Sisters, for her interest in our work, her encouragement, and her willingness to give us advice and direction; Elizabeth Lay, literary agent, who perceived our intent long before we could write it coherently, and without whose uplifting hope, hard-nosed practicality, and dedication, our effort would have gone unnoticed by big-city editors; and Harold Mann, M.D., adult psychoanalyst and child psychiatrist in private practice in Berkeley, who most importantly is a warm and delightful human being. As our consultant, he was concerned not only with our project, but with all the children entrusted to us, as a nation. His knowledge and experience helped us write with more confidence on even the most perplexing issues.

We are indebted to all those who helped us collect background information: Jeannine Dupuis, Lynn Dille, Judy Calder of Bananas Child Care Information and Referral Service in Oakland, and Jim Mead of For Kids Sake in Brea, California.

We wish to thank all the professionals: nurses, pediatricians, therapists, educators, and others who through their own writings laid the theoretical base on which our parenting is based. Others, through their discussions with us, improved the quality of our manuscript. Mary C. Tall, Ph.D. in clinical psychology, taught us to look for underlying patterns in parental experience. Barry Hunau, D.D.S. in Berkeley, reviewed sections on dentistry. Sue Haskell, LCSW, instructor and clinical supervisor in psychology at John F. Kennedy University in Orinda, and in private practice in Richmond, California, constructively reviewed the entire manuscript. Carole Dwinell's illustrations added life and clarity to the text. David Laskin skillfully edited the text and John Thornton, Editor at Facts On File, pushed the project to completion despite an inauspicious beginning. Many thanks to all others whose efforts large and small were crucial to this endeavor.

Finally, we appreciate all those who attended parenting classes, as well as support and discussion groups, thereby expanding our knowledge of the challenges of modern parenthood. We especially extend our heartfelt appreciation to all the following parents who made this book possible, by completing lengthy interviews and laborious questionnaires. They candidly related their concerns and defeats, shared their joys and inspirations, and detailed their experiments and hard-won victories in order that others might benefit from their experiences: Ann Alderman, Dorothy Bauer, Bonnie Bouey, Charmaine Boulmay, Jackie Brand, Jan Brown, Sharon Brunetti, Lanny Campbell, Jane Carpenter, Barbara Collins, Judy Dadak, Terri Denis, Lynn Dille, Jeannine Dupuis, Kim Edel, Agatha Elmes, Ana Fenesik, Ziona Frankel, Paul Fransella, Karen Fraser, Peter Freedman, Linda Fujikawa, Roberta Gould, Etta Hadley, Joanne Hahn, Gail Harris, Sue Haskell, M.C. Haug-Boone, Betsy Honiky, Bea Huah, Pam Jacobs, Denise Joganic, Rose Jue, Gay Keiser, Jackie Kirschbaum, Janice Krones, Nancy Kunitsugu, Betsy Lamoureux, Stephanie Leonard, Jane Liu, Margaret Lopez, Cynthia Lozano, Kathy Lucas, Sheila Luengen, Bernadette Mele, Barbara Meyers, Juli Moscovitz, Pam Ormsby, Meida Pang, Marchelle Patrick, Joe Ann Patton, Jeannie Pharies, Ann Poage, Linda Powell, Caroline Purves, Jill Putt, Caren Quay, Connie Real, Sherry Reinhardt, Pat Rivera, Joy Rodriguez, Judi Rogers, Sandy Rogin, Janet Sachs-Weintraub, Kris Samuelson, Bonnie Sanders, Julia Schoon, Carolyn Scott, Geraldine Seid, Sargam Shah, Beryl Shaw, Kristin Shepherd, Roberta Shomon, Rhoda Slagle, Diane Smith, Marika Smith, Althea Soldano, Susanne Spiersch, Donna Stefanek, Sunny Stevenson, Leila Tassano, Jan Taylor, Mary Ann Todd, Lindy Tuttle, Jo Anne Waldron, Mary Weinstein, Charlene Wells, Robin Wolf, Roberta Wong, Roni Wong, Claudette Zinnerman.

Introduction

Why *another* parenting book? Because others have major shortcomings that we have attempted to overcome. To begin with, many such volumes are either pro-child, or pro-parent, in that they advise us either to be patient and accepting or to be firm and take care of ourselves. The real issue, however, is how to *balance* the needs of different beings living in the same household. To consider the parent without the child, or vice versa, is to consider a shoreline without water.

Many books imply there is one "right" solution for a particular problem (while other books declare a *different* "right" solution). Given the variations of personalities, the individuality of children, and the diversity of parenting circumstances, we found no solutions that were helpful to *all* parents in our study. What works miraculously for one child proves useless for another, is impossible for a different parent to carry out, and is unworkable for a family in dissimilar circumstances. The purpose of this book is to present *a range of potential solutions* that they can choose from or, alternatively, that will fire their imaginations into dreaming up still more unique possibilities.

In addition to providing a range of concrete solutions, a further goal is to suggest a *problem-solving process*. Although parents use a surprising number of different approaches to the same issue, we eventually realized such alternative solutions could be grouped into five essential categories: CLARIFY OBJECTIVES, CHANGE THE EN-VIRONMENT, CHANGE ATTITUDES, CHANGE PARENTAL BEHAVIOR, and ADOPT TOLERANCE. When we find ourselves in a problem-solving rut, it is generally because we are stuck in one or two of the above modes. By broadening our perspective and considering the full range of possibilities, we can *usually* find a constructive solution. These five approaches are summarized inside the front cover and detailed in the appendix. Throughout the text, possible solutions have generally been listed in the same sequence in the hope that readers will gradually find it easier and more automatic to consider all the options.

This book supports parents. Unfortunately, many excellent books about parenting explore only *one* necessary component of our problem-solving repertoire—e.g., communication, behavior modification—and therefore, inadvertently, imply that parenting is far simpler than it is. Although there are books on toilet training, creativity, money matters, discipline, sex, death, and more, only a volume that recognizes *all of these concerns* can fully acknowledge the weight of responsibility we feel as parents and can stand as a ready reference whenever needed. Furthermore, in recent years, an abundance of new child-rearing theories has evolved, giving the impression that experts are more able to raise our children than we are. The experts, however, face many of the same dilemmas as the rest of us when they are home with their own children. Though research and theory are extremely important, it is from the experiences of other parents that we can learn how to apply abstract theory to the hundreds of minute but crucial issues which form the essentials of living with small children.

Our unfortunate legacy, as well-read parents of the 1970's and 80's, is the belief that we should be model parents, confident of our decisions, consistent, and firm yet loving, and that raising children should be easy and problem-free. Realistically, parenting is a series of problems. We pull through the present one, then slide into the next. But with our overall concern, our growing experience, and the inherent development of our children, we can gradually become more confident that we will also make it through the next round. It is from other parents that we find out about the inherent difficulties of our job. To be a firm *and* loving disciplinarian sounds fine in theory, but often *feels* like a contradiction in terms. And problems almost always get worse before they get better. "Either the children act worse while I'm trying to change their behavior or my life is more complicated while the change is in process.''

It is also from parents that we learn others are as fallible as we are. Such a truth is not surprising when we consider that the role of ideal parent is always assigned to flesh-and-blood human beings. There are as many individual parents as individual children. While some jump in to wrestle with each new problem as it arises, one parent sighed, ''Often, I don't solve problems with my kids, I endure them.'' Most parents agree that the biggest challenge of child-rearing is the personal one: as one mother reports, ''You have to get to know yourself, your strengths, and your weaknesses. When you're able to deal with them in yourself, *then* you're ready to deal with them in your children.'' Another mother laughed at the mention of consistency, then concluded, ''I'm consistent. There are two of me, the tired me and the regular me, and the kids, age two and a half, know the difference.'' While the experts confidently quote the results of their statistical samples, we as parents struggle with the knowledge that we never know how this *particular* child-rearing venture will turn out. One father concluded philosophically, ''If my kids only need a couple years of therapy to straighten out my mistakes, I'll consider myself a successful parent.''

Some readers may wish to know how this book came about. Having lived on four continents before my child-rearing days, I, Helen, had long been intrigued by a wide range of child care techniques. I enjoyed reading ahead in preparation for the arrival of our first baby and felt generally successful in caring for him. But when he suddenly became a vivacious two-year-old, turning our child-proof apartment into Disastersville, while his new sister screamed with the mysterious agony of colic, I searched for a volume that would ease my survival, rather than erode my plunging self-confidence. There was no such book. In desperation, I inquired of other parents and became increasingly impressed by the triumphs of creative genius that enabled them to live more easily with their offspring. Gradually, I became convinced that someone ought to collect all those inspirations for the benefit of other struggling parents.

At first, I wrote down ideas that worked for my friends and me. Realizing more sources of information were needed, I asked others to recommend parents whose techniques they admired. With time, participants in parenting classes and support groups also volunteered to undergo interviews or to complete questionnaires (a number of the latter being repeated semiannually over a period of three years). Thus, rather than being taken from a random sample, input came from over ninety mothers and fathers who had time to share their experiences and in addition were particularly concerned about the quality of their parenting and/or were considered by others to be creative in their approaches. For the most part, they were well educated and well versed in the modern child-rearing theories they were learning to put into daily practice.

When it was time to begin writing, I enlisted the help of Mona Halaby, who was anxious to pursue a career in writing, had a master's degree in comparative literature from the University of California in Berkeley, and was also a mother. Born in Egypt and educated in Switzerland, she too was interested in a broad view of parenting. She honed my writing skill with her forthright criticism, provided guidance with both intellect and intuition, shared the inevitable drudgeries, and held my hand as we clambered over numerous stumbling blocks.

While writing, I returned to my career part-time. As a Pediatric Advice Nurse at Kaiser Hospital in Oakland, California, as well as an instructor in parenting classes and a leader in parent support groups, I became aware of concerns that were common to many. Gradually, my interests extended into the intricate relationship between mind and body, and I began to teach classes in stress management. In doing so, I became increasingly aware that early attitudes toward exercise, food, and emotions affect physical health for decades, and I looked for ways to include this finding in the book.

We hope the material contained herein proves as useful to you as it has been to us.

1

Eating

We look forward to nurturing our newborns with both the calories of milk and the warmth of our mealtime attentiveness. And there are moments of joyous contentment just like those we imagined. But sometimes, though hungry, our little ones scream instead of eating. They spit up foul-smelling formula or bite tender breasts. We feel frustrated if they won't stop nursing when we want them to, and sad when they stop for good. We can't stand their fussiness when deprived of the bottle, yet fear it will accompany them to high school graduation.

As if milk didn't give us enough problems, at some point we have to cope with self-feeding as well. Toddlers approach our tidy tables with the glee of a kid at Christmas. Mashed potatoes for play-dough, milk for blowing bubbles, and apricot puree for finger paint. Meals end with strings of spaghetti glued to the floor and pools of spilled juice on the table. We can tell when snack is over by the half-eaten apple on the floor.

We are told that if exposed to nutritious food and left on their own, youngsters will be reasonable eaters. Unfortunately, some children seem to prefer junk food.

We had such good intentions about maintaining a pleasant mealtime atmosphere. Just because eating is essential, doesn't mean it's easy.

DRINKING FROM BREAST, BOTTLE, OR CUP

BREASTFEEDING

Anyone who thinks nursing is natural, and therefore simple the first time around, probably hasn't tried it. In fact, it's easier for a newborn to get milk out of a bottle. However, patience and persistence, along with sufficient information and support, can almost always overcome the complexities of getting started. Once both Mom and baby have discovered how the system works, there's nothing that can beat it for convenience and a healthy start in life.

Increasing numbers of doctors and nurses are well informed about breastfeeding and will help support new mothers through problems. La Leche League is an invaluable source of guidance and information—to find them, check with your phone book or medical staff.

Tips for Nursing

Alternating the starting breast assures even milk production. Many mothers move a safety pin from one side of their bra to the other to remind them which side is next, while some who go bra-less slip a bracelet from one wrist to the other.

Caution: Some nightgowns may be dangerous. When nursing an

infant in bed, be sure your nightgown doesn't have long bows or ties that might wrap around baby's neck.

Unlike the bottle, the breast doesn't always deliver milk immediately. A few seconds to a minute or more of sucking may be needed first. Any baby, but especially those accustomed to a bottle, may become frustrated and cry instead of sucking persistently. To ease a difficult transition, try one of the following:

Karo® *syrup.* Put a dab of Karo syrup on the nipple so the baby's immediate reaction to the breast is positive. (Do *not* use honey, as it can cause botulism in infants under one year of age.)

Eye dropper. Dribble formula or expressed breast milk onto the breast with a boiled, plastic medicine dropper to attract the baby. If the baby is very hungry and upset, put several dropperfuls directly into the baby's mouth first. Caution: The baby is apt to gag unless wide awake when this technique is used.

Nipple massage. Before putting baby to breast, lightly rub or roll your nipple to induce milk let-down.

Lact-Aid®. Lact-Aid allows the baby to suck at the breast and simultaneously drink formula or expressed breast milk. The baby associates the breast with food, and sucking provides the necessary stimulation for increasing milk production. See illustration. Lact-Aid is available through La Leche League.

Holding or massaging the baby's hands may prevent embarrassing exploring in public. Otherwise, wear an enticing but *sturdy* necklace, or make one of old spools and bits of ribbon.

Sometime between six and twelve months, a number of babies seem frustrated by eating with their back to the rest of the world. With any noise, they yank away from the breast to see what is going on. If you can't nurse in a secluded room without interference you may choose to substitute a bottle or cup during the exciting daytime hours and nurse only during periods when the baby is tired: early morning, naptime, or bedtime.

Although most newborns will take milk from either breast or bottle, such open-mindedness may not continue. After several weeks of delightful, exclusive breastfeeding, many babies would rather diet than change. Plans to enjoy a well-deserved night out alone or return to work may be compromised by a hungry baby who refuses the bottle.

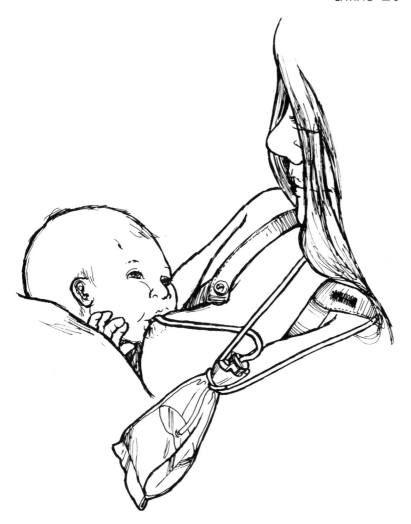

Parents employ a number of different solutions. Sometimes babies especially resent a bottle when they know the breast is nearby, so have your spouse or a sitter offer a bottle when Mom is not around. Try an assortment of differently shaped bottle nipples, or offer juice instead of milk. Some parents avoid the problem by giving an ounce or two of formula or expressed breast milk once a day or several times a week to preserve their newborn's willingness to take a bottle. Such an insignificant amount of formula doesn't compromise the overall supply of breast milk.

Lori, five months, refused all bottles, but was starting to drink from a cup with the help of a patient sitter by the time her mother returned to work.

Carolyn screamed when offered a bottle until she was five and one-half months old. But then, because she was teething and chewing on everything, she discovered that a bottle delivered milk as well, and started sucking.

A baby who bites the breast can take all the joy out of nursing. While some babies try it only once, a few are so persistent that mothers are forced to wean. There is an inevitable conflict between providing an atmosphere of total love and giving a clear message that biting is unacceptable. Most mothers who handle the problem successfully use some form of mild punishment (unpleasant response) consistently enough over several days or weeks that the baby is able to relate the cause and effect. Mom's unrestricted yelp of pain or a sudden loud "No!" is usually enough to frighten the baby out of continual biting.

Babies may be more apt to bite at the end of a feeding, so stop nursing early if necessary. If biting seems to be due to teething discomfort, soothe the baby's gums *before* nursing. (See Teething, p. 163.)

More drastic measures include setting the baby down immediately and walking away for a few moments, or flicking your middle finger against the baby's chin.

EASIER BOTTLE-FEEDING

To avoid lengthy crying while waiting for a bottle to warm, try one of the following. Heat an ounce or two of milk first, then warm the remainder while the baby drinks the first "course." Powdered formula mixes instantly with lukewarm tap water. (Some pediatricians recommend that tap water be boiled during the baby's first three months.) Individual prepackaged bottles of ready-to-feed formula can be stored and served at room temperature. A microwave oven heats a bottle in a few seconds. Some babies are content with formula right out of the refrigerator.

If you're tired of hunting for nipples, try placing an extra silverware drainer only for nipples on the kitchen drying rack. If nipples are becoming clogged with orange juice pulp, strain the juice first with a tea strainer.

SPITTING UP

Spitting up, which is generally harmless, is often confused with vomiting, which can, if it persists, cause dangerous loss of fluids. The milk looks the same in either case. If it has curdled, it merely shows that normal digestive processes have started, not that the baby is sick. Babies often spit up a tablespoon or two of milk, which dribbles out of their mouths. In vomiting, on the other hand, milk comes out more forcefully and in larger amounts. If vomiting occurs more than twice within a short time, call your doctor.

Overfeeding is a common cause of excessive spitting up. Offer an ounce or two less. An open milk carton will spill less if it is upright, and the same is true of a baby's full stomach. Try holding or propping the baby up after feeding. Spitting up will be less likely in twenty minutes to an hour once the milk has passed on to the intestine. Also, spitting up is less likely to occur if the baby lies on the right side, because of the anatomical shape of the stomach.

Allergy to the formula or foods in the diet of a breastfeeding mother can cause excessive spitting up in some babies.

Burping won't prevent spitting up, but at least you know when to expect it. If you don't get immediate results, try again in ten to fifteen minutes, keeping baby semi-upright in the meantime.

A sponge dipped in water and baking soda helps absorb both spit-up and odor. When visiting, carry one in a plastic bag and choose your wardrobe to minimize stain visibility. In the crib, put a diaper under the baby's head.

Spitting up generally ends around eight months of age when the ring of muscle around the entrance to the stomach develops sufficient strength to keep food in the stomach, even when baby bounces.

STARTING A CUP

Many parents offer a cup when the baby is between four and eight months of age. While a few started "because my baby started reaching for my cup," much more common reasons were to prepare for weaning and to give juice to a breastfed baby without introducing a bottle. Early introduction of the cup seems to reflect our discomfort with bottles, as discussed on p. 22.

To avoid spills try:

- *A rubber band* around a small plastic cup to keep it from slipping out of the baby's grasp.

· *A measuring cup,* a one-quarter cup measure with a long handle is easy to hold.
· *Tupperware sipperseals®* drinking cups that don't spill when dropped.
· *Tommee Tippee®* training cups have a spout with little holes, and tip back upright automatically.

APPROPRIATE QUANTITY AND QUALITY OF FOODS FOR INFANTS AND CHILDREN

Many of us worry a great deal about how, what, and how much our children eat. Much of this worry is needless. No child starves to death in a loving environment with ample food. The ultimate test of an adequate diet is health and activity.

The most common and serious nutritional deficiency in the United States is iron-deficiency anemia, which occurs between nine months and three years of age, and can easily be avoided through the use of iron-fortified formulas, *or* fortified baby cereal, *or* iron drops for infants, *or* vitamins with iron. Children's bodies have the ability to extract most other needed elements from surprisingly small amounts of nutritious food. Rather than fret because children skip meals now and then, we can keep track of their intake over the course of a week. Often one day's undernourishment will be balanced by a feast the following day.

There are simple and reliable methods for determining the basic eating requirements for infants. To estimate the number of ounces of formula a newborn needs in a twenty-four-hour period, multiply the baby's weight by three (give or take a few ounces). Thus a seven-pound infant needs approximately twenty-one ounces of formula in twenty-four hours. An infant drinking only breast milk (that is, no water) and wetting at least six to eight diapers every twenty-four hours is generally getting enough milk. Unless the baby is jaundiced or the weather is extremely hot, water is generally not necessary after the milk is consumed. Regular pediatric check-ups will further verify whether youngsters are gaining adequate weight.

Many infants simply *won't* eat for one reason or another, so parents need to figure out why before attempting solutions. Some newborns just aren't very hungry for a day or two, and others need time for the effects of the labor medications to wear off. Babies who are too sleepy to eat may have to be awakened for feedings, and this can be accomplished in a number of ways: cuddling or massage, holding the baby upright and patting gently on the back, talking and playing for ten minutes before eating, changing the diaper, giving a bath, tickling the feet, rubbing the nipple on the baby's cheek. Mothers of sleepy babies who breastfeed may want to switch to the opposite breast after the first five minutes of nursing to maximize milk intake before the baby falls asleep again. Also, nursing mothers should remember that excessive alcohol and sedatives can pass through the breast milk and cause sleepiness in the infant.

An infant with a stomach full of air will need to be burped before he or she will continue sucking. Teething pain can be aggravated by sucking, and in this case the baby may do better on a cup temporarily. Bottle-fed infants may be unable to get milk because the bottle cap is on too tight to let air in, or because the nipple hole is too small.

Appetite naturally decreases with illness. If the baby is warm or listless, or you suspect illness for other reasons, take the baby's temperature and call the doctor.

All children develop their own signals to let you know they're not hungry—disinterested sucking, closed mouth, turned head—and parents quickly learn to respect these.

EATING TOO LITTLE OR
AVOIDING CERTAIN FOODS

We want our children to eat sufficient amounts and varieties of nutritious food to grow and to stay healthy. Furthermore, if we make the effort to cook it, we want them to eat it. Finally, we want to encourage their social adaptability through an open-minded attitude toward different foods. How do we go about it?

The environment is one factor to keep in mind in feeding children. Changes in the environment and special equipment can encourage indifferent eaters. Of course what works for one child may be a disaster for another, so experimentation is essential.

Some children, for example, eat better with the TV on: They will unconsciously spoon the food into their mouths while absorbed in ''Sesame Street.'' Others are distracted by TV and forget all about the plate in front of them. For some, a secluded room is best, while others prefer to be with the whole family. Kevin, age three, eats better when given a choice of eating in the kitchen or dining room. Amy likes to eat standing: she wanders off and then returns for more. The key is to be flexible without getting caught in too elaborate a ritual.

Revising our own attitudes about eating can also relieve our distress about children's eating habits. One mother who was concerned about her two-year-old son's small appetite, reminded herself that she weighed four times as much as he, and that she was accustomed to quantities four times as large. She therefore multiplied what he ate by four: his meager two ounces of milk suddenly became equivalent to a substantial eight ounces for her. Another mother decided to stop pressuring her daughter to eat certain foods. Her daughter's eating habits are still erratic, but at least the mealtime fighting has stopped.

Emotional atmosphere can also be an important factor in a child's eating habits. Tension before or during meals can decrease the appetite, and parents who realize this can look for ways to change it. For example, parents of five-year-old Jennifer devoted mealtimes to discussing their incompatible in-laws. Jennifer became aware of the tension and picked at her food. The couple decided to keep dinner conversation on lighter topics, and their daughter's appetite improved noticeably.

Most children are as curious about food as about everything else, and this can be used to advantage at the dinner table. In one family the parents will point to a new food and tell their three-year-old, "Don't eat any of that!" She can't resist.

Encouraging children to like a wide variety of foods can be approached in different ways: Some parents require children to taste a little of everything, and others let youngsters experiment at will. In both systems, most children retain a few long-term food dislikes, but still eat a wide range of foods in general.

Rewarding children for eating, common as this practice is, carries two possible hazards. First, adults who have a weight problem are generally less aware than the average person of their body's signals of being hungry and full. Thus when we reward children for eating more food, we teach them to ignore their body's message to stop. Second, if a child is rewarded with dessert for eating meat and vegetables, desserts become more attractive because of their association with love and approval. The body's need for a well-balanced diet can thus become distorted by the child's emotional need for tokens of acceptance. As Dr. Spock pointed out, if children had to eat ice cream before eating carrots, many would hate ice cream and love carrots.

Despite the potential drawbacks of food rewards, a number of parents use them, but with distinct variations from the traditional "No cake unless you eat your vegetables." Alex, age four, must eat some meat and potatoes before he gets the fruit he loves. If Elena, age three, eats everything on her plate, she can have seconds of whichever foods she prefers. For Beth, age three, a tiny dessert follows a tiny dinner, and a larger dessert follows a larger dinner.

For the most part, parents are tolerant of the erratic and picky appetites of their two-year-olds, and wisely so. There are plenty of other issues to spice up *that* year. Once youngsters reach three, we realize that they thrive despite picky eating, or they are eating more broadly by their own choice, or they are more able to tolerate some pressure to expand their horizons.

Parents generally choose from four basic systems of food service and may alternate plans as the needs of a growing family change.

1. Separate meals. Prepare separate meals to suit the individual preferences of adults and children.
2. Simple alternatives. Children can eat a predetermined simple alternative, such as bread, cheese, or fruit, if they don't want the family fare.
3. Veto power. Children may decline any food on the table, but no special food is prepared.
4. Same for everyone. Children are required to eat at least a taste of everything.

Problem Foods

Milk

Older babies and toddlers who fill up on milk have little room left for solids. Such youngsters are likely to be deficient in iron, as regular milk contains almost none. After the first birthday, sixteen to twenty-four ounces of milk per day is plenty.

To decrease milk intake, keep bottles out of sight during mealtime, gradually decrease the amount in each bottle, or *gradually* dilute milk with increasing amounts of water without increasing the overall amount of liquid.

If, on the other hand, the child drinks too little milk, there are a number of possible solutions:

- Milkshakes. Add a banana or other fruits or juices to milk in the blender.
- Cheese. Yogurt and most cheese (except cottage cheese) contain significant amounts of calcium.
- Powdered milk. Add extra powder to soups, sauces, puddings, casseroles, meat loaf, and so forth.
- Calcium supplement. Even if children don't drink milk directly, "disguised" milk and leafy green vegetables generally provide enough calcium. If your child is allergic to milk products, discuss a possible calcium supplement with your doctor.

Gregory, age two, drinks more milk with a Fun Straw© (clear plastic straw bent into loops, available at variety stores) because he has so much fun watching the milk whooshing around.

Meat
Thanks to our increased understanding of protein, we know that meat is not essential to children's diets *if an appropriate variety* of milk products, vegetable protein, and iron sources is included instead. Adequate nutrition is more complex if the child is allergic to milk. For more information about vegetarian diets check with your doctor or see *Laurel's Kitchen: A Handbook for Vegetarian Cookery and Nutrition* by Laurel Robertson (Bantam, 1978).

Nathaniel, age four, watched intently as I cut up a fryer for dinner one night. He asked, "Where is the wing?" "What happened to its head?" "Why did it die?" That night he just picked at his dinner. When I commented that he didn't seem very hungry, his eyes filled with tears, and he responded, "It was mean to kill it. It got cold without its feathers. I don't like dead chickens." The following nights there were more questions about the meat I served, and his portions went untouched. There seemed no point in pushing the matter. After a number of weeks, he timidly started eating meat again, though a friend of his stopped for good.

Vegetables

Youngsters are more apt to dislike foods their parents dislike. On the other hand, if we can restrain our personal opinions, they may like foods that we do not.

Some children prefer vegetables separately, others prefer them mixed together. Try adding extra vegetables to favorite foods such as omelets, stews, vegetable soups (as vegetable pieces or pureed), spaghetti sauce, and meat loaf. For spoon feeding, try mixing apricots with squash, applesauce with peas, peaches with carrots, and so forth.

Some children like to snack on raw vegetables and can meet their vegetable requirements while Mom chops carrots for dinner. For youngsters who won't touch them at all, a daily vitamin may be the easiest way to avoid worry.

Desserts

Refuses all but cookies? Take a basic cookie recipe, substitute iron-fortified baby rice cereal for half the flour, cut down the sugar, and add dry milk powder and peanut butter, sesame seeds, chopped dried fruit, grated carrots, and so forth. In a few weeks or months, youngsters will be ready for new foods, and have gotten a lot of good nutrition in the meantime.

Putting Up With Puny Appetites

Many difficulties are avoided by the assumption that youngsters know more about their own appetites than we do. Sometimes children are wolfish and sometimes they just pick at their food. It generally all balances out as long as we don't make a problem out of it. Many parents find it helpful to consider the reasons for the irregular eating patterns and apparently small food intake of most young children.

Body Rhythms Vary

If left to ourselves in a relatively unchanging environment, our bodies tend to develop fairly regular patterns of sleeping, eating, and so forth. However, appetite naturally varies with activity level, emotional state, size and content of the last meal, and growth rate. Thus, variations in appetite are to be expected, especially during childhood.

Exercise *does* burn up calories, so the relatively quiet, sedate child naturally eats less than the one who is always vigorously active.

Growth Rates Fluctuate

An infant's appetite does not increase gradually and evenly but in spurts that occur around six weeks, three months, and six months of age. (Exact time varies with each child.) Formerly content babies may become much hungrier. Frequent nursing for several days increases milk supply, and feeding times spread out again.

Conversely, growth rates decline dramatically between the first and second birthdays. Our former good eaters go on a relative hunger strike. If growth continued at the earlier rate, the average six-year-old would weigh nearly one hundred pounds.

Different Sizes Require Different Amounts

There is a tremendous difference in the energy requirements for short and tall children the same age. Between two and four, the petite girl in the third percentile for both height and weight needs about six hundred calories less per day than the strapping boy in the ninety-seventh percentile.

Children Just Don't Like All Foods

When newborns are offered a variety of foods to smell, they smile at some and wrinkle their noses at others. What better evidence that food preferences are innate? Furthermore, our sense of taste is most acute in early childhood. Rather than having "learned to like" grapefruit, for example, we may no longer perceive its bitterness so intensely as when we were young. Accepting the fact that most adults as well as children dislike certain flavors and textures can save a lot of struggles.

EATING TOO MUCH

Eating too much wasn't considered a problem in the old days because a chubby youngster was considered proof of good parenting. But studies now indicate that overweight youngsters, especially chubby preschoolers, are more prone to become overweight adults. They may, in fact, develop extra fat cells that gobble up and store too much fat.

Eating too much means different things. To parents it may mean that a baby still seems hungry after the "proper" amount of formula, or wants to nurse or snack all the time. To the doctor, it generally means weighing more than is recommended for one's height.

Hunger comes in many forms. What appears to be hunger for calories may be hunger for something else, often a simple need to suck or a craving for attention.

The baby's need to suck is instinctive and essential to survival. However, the need to suck and need for calories are not always well matched. Many infants need more sucking exercise than they can get from drinking milk from a bottle. Thus babies may still fuss after the appropriate number of ounces. The most common way to satisfy this need to suck is with a pacifier. For more information, see p. 52.

Sometimes babies are thirsty, not hungry, though their cry will sound the same. Try plain water or diluted noncitrus juice, which contain fewer calories than does milk. Hunger for interesting things to look at and do are as instinctive as hunger for food. Babies and children are less apt to overeat in interesting surroundings.

It's a rare infant who gains too much on breast milk, and an even rarer one who doesn't thin out with increased exercise of crawling and walking. But if overfeeding really is a problem, nurse on just one breast per feeding, or only two to three minutes on the first breast and as much as the baby wants to suck on the second breast.

If the baby is genuinely hungry and not gaining weight too fast, offer more to eat in the form of more frequent nursing, which will increase milk supply, or add extra formula. Check with your doctor, however, before starting solids.

Some children do overeat and will need firm, direct limits on the amount of food they are allowed. Some overweight toddlers and preschoolers can become locked in a power struggle. One mother solved this issue by stocking a small table with low-calorie foods. Her two-year-old overate tremendously for several days, but once the novelty wore off and the family atmosphere was no longer electrified by the power struggle, he became more able to respond to internal cues.

The newborn's need for food and love are filled simultaneously through feeding, but in order to establish lifelong attitudes toward healthy eating, we need to gradually help our children distinguish between the need for food and the need for love and acceptance. It may be an especially difficult task because youngsters pick up our attitudes toward food.

Parents who lavishly praise a child for eating, or who unconsciously hand a bottle to a fussy child instead of identifying the cause of the upset, are setting up patterns and expectations that are difficult to change.

Too Much Salt

Tape some of the holes of the salt shaker, so less pours out. Better yet, don't put the shaker on the table.

LIMITING SPECIFIC KINDS OF FOODS

Though few of us want to give up our refrigerators or central heating, there were some advantages to the primitive life. Except for an occasional beehive, fruit was the sweetest thing around, and it was eminently nutritious. We, on the other hand, have to trek past bushels of candy to get to the fresh produce, to say nothing of the candy bars and gum-ball machines that besiege us at checkout counters. Even our homes are invaded with ads for soda pop and potato chips.

There are various issues to consider in regulating the consumption of junk food, each with its positive and negative aspects. For example, if no junk food is allowed in the house, the prohibited foods may take on the aura of forbidden fruit. Children may learn to sneak candy at school or in friends' homes. If junk foods are permitted only at certain specified times, for example, sodas at restaurants, chips on picnics, candy at Grandma's, or sugar-coated cereal for Sunday dessert, continual conflict may be avoided. Some parents allow sweets and chips only as rewards for good behavior, but this may increase the emotional value of such foods. Making objectives clear to our children is important in establishing patterns of good nutrition.

Bad for Teeth. We tell Greg, age three, that candy causes cavities, which are like little cuts on your teeth that hurt.

Lots of Vitamins. We tell Karen, age three, that vitamins make her strong. In the grocery store, I point out which foods are nutritious. I praise her for both identifying and eating nutritious foods, and her new knowledge affects her choices.

No Saturday TV. The Saturday-morning cartoon commercials make it seem as though sugar-coated cereal is essential for life. After years of invasive TV advertising, I forbade Saturday-morning viewing and started taking the kids to the park instead.

Many parents try to instill a *healthful* attitude toward sweets rather than the *high-status* one with which they were raised. The methods seem bizarre, but they are effective. For example, instead of serving desserts regularly, serve them infrequently but *with* the main course rather than a special addition. Or, serve leftover birthday cake at every meal, including breakfast, until it's gone. Struggles over food may cover up many basic emotional issues.

Precious Sweets. When I was growing up, desserts were a daily prize for eating vegetables and there were sweets for every family occasion. Like myself, Ricky, age five, and Gina, age three, were learning to measure their goodness by sweets, and I couldn't bring myself to deny their requests for more. One day, I'd suddenly had it with tantrums for more cookies. I went home with two screaming kids and no cookies, and stopped making desserts. The kids almost stopped eating for several days, but then even meat and vegetables looked good to them. I missed the sweets more than they, but the peace was worth the price.

Unusual Special Treats. We stuff stockings with fancy crackers, banana chips, beef jerky, and olives. For birthdays we serve ice cream cones with jello and give favors, not candy. At Easter, we stick with real eggs; and at Halloween give pennies, balloons, raisins, or stickers.

Feeding a Marriage. My husband and I had lots of battles about givin sweets until it became clear in therapy that candy wasn't the real issue. Whenever I felt distant from my husband, I started a fight about sweets. Negative contact was better than none at all. As we discovered positive ways to make contact, it was easy to find compromises for candy.

Despite the best intentions, some families have to contend with an obsession with sugar: one mother finally put the cookies under lock and key. In some households, cookies filched during the day mean no dessert that night. Parents who were raised with sweets as proof of love are trapped between their own sweet-dependent pasts and their nutrition ideals for their children. Some such parents overcome their own sweet tooth through the necessity of modeling behavior for their children. Others store a secret bag of cookies in a back cupboard or pick up a candy bar when away from the youngsters. Better a double standard, they affirm, than passing on the longing for sweets to the next generation.

SNACKS: PRO AND CON

Some parents believe in snacks and others don't. In some families, struggles about food relate as much to *when* children eat as to *what* they eat. In fact, parents serve snacks for many different reasons, and each family is likely to develop its own eating policy.

Families who permit eating only at three regular meals do so to establish regular eating habits, to avoid fixing time-consuming snacks, to assure mealtime appetites, and to emphasize the social aspect of eating together. The opposite extreme is unlimited snacking at any time, a policy some parents adopt because it gives maximum regard to a child's internal hunger signals and encourages eating according to body need rather than the clock.

Most families will find a method in between these two, such as permitting limited snacks if the child ate well at the last meal or serving only dull snacks (bread, for example) so that meals are more enticing. Many parents minimize frustration and fighting by setting limits on the kinds of foods kids may snack on, the times of the day when snacking is permitted, or the size of snack portions.

Before-meal snacks of fruits, vegetables, or low-fat proteins have less impact on appetite than will sweets and starches, which quickly break down into sugar and enter the bloodstream.

If we are hungry and don't eat, the body raises our sagging blood-sugar level by pulling calories from storage into the bloodstream. The rise in blood sugar temporarily decreases the sensation of hunger. The child who is hungry at five o'clock but not allowed to eat till six o'clock may no longer feel as hungry, and therefore may eat poorly. Thus a small, nutritious snack at five o'clock may do more than abstinence for overall nutrition.

Three meals a day is a cultural preference, not a physiological necessity. Metabolic studies suggest that our bodies may more easily handle small frequent meals than large, infrequent ones, assuming the total quantity and quality of food are appropriate.

The key to successful snacking is convenient, nutritious food. If your child is cavity-prone and snacks frequently, dentists recommend avoiding sugar, acid food such as fruit juices, and foods that stick to the teeth, such as dried fruits and crackers.

The possibilities for snacks are limited only by your imagination: cottage cheese in ice cream cones, bagels because they don't crumble, Spoon Size Shredded Wheat, cubes of cheese, pitted prunes, last night's leftovers, extra pancakes from breakfast, popcorn, crunchy mung bean sprouts, slightly defrosted frozen green beans, split bananas spread with peanut butter and raisins, and yogurt popsicles made of yogurt and orange juice concentrate.

Many families opt to make snacks readily available. Store crackers in a low cupboard so youngsters can help themselves. Or, set out a day's ration of crackers and dry fruit. When it's gone, it's gone. For more variety and nutrition, stock a corner of the refrigerator with celery sticks and cheese slices. Turn leftovers into snacks by putting the remainder from each serving dish in topless plastic boxes and placing them in a drawer of the refrigerator. Family members can just open the drawer for an instant array of snacks.

To make liquids accessible, put a stool by the kitchen sink or a picnic jug of juice within youngsters' reach. Decrease cleanup by providing *one* distinctive cup for each child. For milk, keep a small, easy-to-manage pitcher in the refrigerator.

WEANING

While few babies are weaned from the bottle before one year of age, the use of bottles steadily declines thereafter. On the other hand, there are three periods when weaning from the breast is more common.

1. Birth to five months. Mothers who have difficulty breast-feeding, those who don't enjoy it, or those who face imminent long hours back at work may wean in these early months.
2. Eight to eleven months. Enjoying the excitement of exploring and self-feeding, many babies show less interest in nursing.

3. Two to two-and-one-half years. A number of mothers wean their offspring during this period, and a similar number of babies self-wean.

Though weaning from the breast is initiated almost as often by youngsters as by parents, weaning from the bottle is usually initiated by parents. With nourishment and a reminder of Mom in hand, a bottle is as exciting to a two-year-old as car keys to a teen. No wonder it's the rare child who voluntarily surrenders it. Interestingly, one youngster whose mother always held him while he drank his bottle weaned himself to a cup by fifteen months.

The tremendous range in ages at which children are weaned from breast and bottle is indicative of current flux in child-rearing trends. "Old-school" infants were expected to grow up as soon as possible, so early weaning was the rule. A bottle-toting toddler was scorned, and a nursing toddler disgraceful. The "new school" accepts that it is a long, slow road to adulthood and support groups like La Leche League hold meetings for mothers of nursing toddlers. Unlike mothers of traditional cultures, for whom weaning time was automatically established by the regular arrival of another baby, most of us must make a personal decision about timing.

WEANING FROM THE BREAST

Here are some of the reasons mothers give for weaning their children from the breast:

> *Personal preference.* I nursed Alice because everyone said I should. "Breast milk is better," "It insures physical and emotional closeness," and on and on. But I *felt* degraded and like a cow. No matter how good nursing might be for some babies, I knew it wouldn't be good for mine because I hated the process. So I weaned Alice at three weeks, and she is doing fine.
>
> *Rejection by baby.* I really wanted to breastfeed, but Kristin, age one week, simply refused. My feelings were terribly hurt and I felt like a failure. Then my best friend pointed out that in the past she would have died or been nursed by someone else. Realizing that bottles allowed her to survive and me to care for her, I could appreciate the alternative.
>
> *Fatigue and resentment.* Erin, 17 months, was getting me

up several times at night not so much from hunger as from wanting me as a pacifier.

Husband's jealousy. My husband resented being left out of feedings. Changing diapers is inherently less satisfying. He was relieved when I quit nursing, because we became equal parents. [Some husbands also have difficulty sharing their wife's breasts with a baby, as our culture places such emphasis on breasts as sexual adornments.]

Nursing must end sometime. I can't but feel sad on the nights the twins, age two and one-half, say they'd rather have a bottle than nurse. I've really enjoyed nursing, and I know I'll never have another chance. Fortunately, the fact that we now enjoy so many other activities together makes it a little easier to make this transition in their life *and* mine.

In discussions with various mothers, the most obvious fact to emerge is that there is no way to predict how weaning will take place. It may be initiated by parent or child, may be gradual or sudden, easy or hard. In general, weaning is a process in which one nursing time after another is gradually replaced by bottle, cup, physical closeness, or even an extra story for older toddlers. Many parents make a point of giving their children lots of extra physical attention, such as rocking and snuggling, to ease the weaning period.

While gradual weaning is more common, sudden transitions don't necessarily cause prolonged distress. One mother, after 17 months of nursing, decided she'd had enough. Her daughter threw a tantrum when handed her bottle, but the mother announced that nursing was over. When this single tantrum had run its course, her daughter never asked to nurse again. Children who show no particular preference for breast over cup or bottle are the easiest to wean, and some children will decide on their own to quit nursing. For those who don't, patience and a consistent policy are important in smoothing the transition.

About two-thirds of the children in our survey were weaned from breast to bottle. Since the bottle still provides both calories and sucking pleasure, this transition generally goes easily. For babies who refuse a bottle, see p. 5.

Youngsters often become attached to a pacifier when weaned, or to a blanket with lace, reminiscent of Mom's nursing nightgowns.

One mother bought a nightgown for her daughter similar to the ones worn during nursing.

WEANING FROM THE BOTTLE

For some children, a bottle provides mere nourishment and cups are an easy substitute. Others, for whom fulfilling an intense need to suck is as important as filling the empty tummy, find cups obviously second-rate. For a third group of children, the bottle also holds the emotional significance of a security object. It may be years before this last group is able to give up a bottle easily.

Parents give a variety of reasons for weaning from the bottle, the most common of which are the ability to drink from a cup, social pressure, fear that the child will never surrender the bottle, the desire to keep the child dry through the night, and the child's own loss of interest in the bottle.

Among the most important reasons parents cited is our cultural belief that bottles are "bad." We are embarrassed by childish behavior from children. We feel an underlying sense of panic at being caught in public with a bottle-bearing preschooler. It would not only be indecent, as being caught outside in our underwear, but would also broadcast our incompetence as parents in failing to train our two-, three-, or four-year-old to act like an adult. Furthermore, we joke about weaning "cold turkey," as though discussing a drug habit, forgetting that the instinct to suck, on which the newborn's very life depends, fades only gradually over the course of years.

We assume that what children *can* do, they *must* do. If they can drink from a cup, they ought to. We, on the other hand, *can* live without the modern conveniences of "Sesame Street," frozen vegetables, umbrella strollers, and permanents, but appropriately enough choose to indulge ourselves. Tolerance will help both parents and children through the weaning process. Bottle-free children are not a measure of our success as parents.

There is tremendous variation in the age at which youngsters are able to give up the bottle with minimal or short-lived distress. Only a few toddlers are ready. Two-year-olds are apt to protest long and bitterly, and besides, their parents generally appreciate the solace bottles afford during an otherwise rocky period. At this age, the struggle may be waged more successfully in the opposite direction:

One mother announced to Grandmother, "If you keep taking Andrea's bottle away, I'll stop coming to visit." If three- and four-year-olds are still very attached to bottles, some parents merely wait, or, if overwhelmed by embarrassment in public, restrict the bottle's use to home or bedroom.

Weaning some children from the bottle is a snap. A few literally toss the bottle out of the crib and are ready to move on. Others forget to ask for the nighttime nipple, and if the parents don't give it to them automatically, the deed is effortlessly accomplished. One mother told her eighteen-month-old, "Please, Roma, no bottle tonight," whereupon Roma handed over the bottle and never asked for another. Not everyone is so lucky!

As with weaning in nursing, weaning from the bottle is basically a process of substitution. No matter how accustomed the child is to drinking from a cup, the first night without a bottle is sudden, and it takes some time to adjust. For several nights, Scott was offered warm milk from a cup; Ann was allowed to stay up late with her parents; Bruce snuggled with Mom until he fell asleep. Janice took a bottle with a blind nipple to bed, and Nate was presented with a Teddy bear. One mother gave her son plenty of warning that there would be no bottles once he turned four, and to her relief, he gave up the bottle on his birthday, without a struggle.

STARTING SOLIDS AND SELF-FEEDING

WHEN TO START

Reflecting the changing opinions of parents and pediatricians, babies don't start solids as early as they used to. One mother noted that each of her five children began later: the first at two months and the last at six months. Among those we talked with, only one family started solids before two months and one waited until one year. Most started in the fifth or sixth month.

Naturally, physical development determines feeding options to some extent. Tiny babies can't manage lumpy foods, and early feeders can't manage spoons. Between six and fourteen months, eating is accomplished through a variety of methods. Many youngsters can start self-feeding with their fingers around six months. In feeding decisions, three opinions must be considered: the parents', the doctor's, and the baby's. Of course, friends and relatives will offer their opinions as well.

Medical concerns about starting solids include:

- Preventing allergy. Certain families are allergy prone, and certain foods are apt to cause an allergy. The earlier high-risk foods are introduced, the more likely they are to cause an allergic reaction. Discuss this topic with your doctor before introducing solids.
- Weight control. To prevent overweight due to overfeeding, many doctors advise against solids before five or six months of age, when babies can lean forward if still hungry and turn away if full.
- Iron needs. Around six months, full-term babies run low on the iron they had stored before birth. Iron-fortified formula and iron-rich solids (such as baby cereals) provide the necessary iron. *Regular cow's milk does not supply adequate iron for children of any age.*

Historically, many parents have been anxious to start solids as a sign of baby's progress, but others fear the likely mess and how long the new meals will take. In one home, Mom *feeds* with one spoon while her daughter "plays" with another spoon.

For feeding to go smoothly, parents must ultimately consider not only their own and their doctor's opinions, but the child's as well. Some children are slower than others at self-feeding, and some will refuse to take a spoon but will pick food up and feed themselves. Parents find they get best results by matching objectives to the temperament and aptitude of the child.

One little boy started feeding himself at about nine months, to the delight of the cats who circled under his high chair. But when he turned two, and the twins arrived, he suddenly wanted his parents to feed him about half the time. They did so without complaint or comment, confident that he'd eventually want to do it himself again. Right then he needed the additional contact.

SIMPLIFYING SOLIDS

By the time we have nursing down pat and are able to prepare formula in our sleep, it's time to move on to the next phase of infant feeding. No wonder we want to know how to do it easily. We each have more or less tolerance for the inevitable gooey mess of self-feeding. Cereal, patiently mashed onto the arms of a high chair, does make a mess, but not nearly so much as an overturned bowl of soup. Thus many parents control the situation by careful selection of foods for self-feeding.

Pureed foods may be bought commercially prepared for convenience, or you can make your own by mashing foods with a fork or in a blender. Freeze the latter in ice cube trays for later, individual servings. You can also prepare junior foods using a potato masher or a grinder.

Some parents, however, avoid all of the above and start directly with finger foods.

Here are a few samples of less messy finger foods:

· Cubes of cooked vegetables.
· Fresh and canned fruits.*
· Rice cereal mixed with applesauce, yogurt, cottage cheese, or finely chopped chicken, to the consistency of thick mashed potatoes.
· Baby cookies. You can make nutritional baby cookies using half cup of iron-fortified rice cereal, half cup flour, half tea-

---

Preventing Choking

Most babies occasionally cough or gag because a speck of food or a dribble of milk starts down the windpipe. Because of the baby's automatic response, such occasions are startling but rarely dangerous. On the other hand, peanuts are slippery, hard to chew, remain solid when wet, and are the perfect size and shape to lodge firmly in lung passages. Therefore, peanuts and similar foods are unsafe until children reach age three. However, *foods that mash easily between your thumb and finger when moist generally don't present a hazard,* as they can also be mashed by the gums of an average six-month old.

---

*Because minute amounts of lead are transferred from the seams of cans to the contents, pediatricians caution against canned fruits and vegetables as a major source of infant nutrition.

spoon baking powder, two tablespoons cooking oil, and half cup applesauce. Spread rounds quarter inch thick at 350 degrees for twenty minutes.

· Dried cereals. Easy-to-grasp cakes made of pressed puffed wheat are available at health-food stores.

· Cubes of cheese or soybean curd (tofu).

· Pancakes fortified with extra milk powder and chopped fruit.*

· Spinach and other vegetables added to scrambled eggs.†

TABLE ETIQUETTE?

MAKES A MESS

Nine-month-olds drop peas over the edge of their high chairs with the scientific intensity of Galileo dropping objects off the Tower of Pisa. And alas, what we call orange custard toddlers believe is body paint. Life was so simple with breasts and bottles! Fortunately, although a certain amount of mess must be tolerated, there *are* things you can do ahead of time to avoid some of the inconvenience. A mother of two-year-old triplets shrugged: "I just plan my menus to match what I'm wearing, so the spills won't show." Our objective is to fill a hungry tummy with minimal work and exasperation and without destroying a youngster's delight in food.

Planning ahead can diminish the mess made by novice eaters. High chairs with large trays will minimize the amount of food on the floor. If walls and rugs begin to look like a dinner plate, put some easy-wipe plastic over them.

Thicken applesauce and yogurt with flakes of baby cereal so they are less drippy.

Draw or tape a spot on your two-year-old's high-chair tray or placemat to show that the cup belongs away from the edge.

If your youngster drops apples because they are too big to hold, stab the handle of a tablespoon all the way through the core, until the end emerges from the other side, and serve the apple as a two-handled popsicle.

Parents deal in a variety of ways with children who purposely

*See footnote on p. 25.
†Because eggs have high allergy potential, check with your doctor before starting egg whites.

throw and spill food. Some require their kids to help clean up the mess they've made, others withhold privileges, along the lines of "No refills if juice is dumped," or else send the child away from the table (on the assumption that children who throw their food must not be hungry anymore).

HIGH CHAIRS, BIBS, AND UTENSILS

What do parents do when a baby who was delighted to sit in the high chair a week ago now climbs out determinedly, to teeter on the brink of a colossal fall?

- Harness. If the high chair strap is insufficient to keep a vigorous toddler in place, use a toddler walking harness instead.
- Walker. "At eight months, Alice kept climbing out of her high chair. I fed her in her walker instead, with the seat raised so that her feet couldn't touch the ground."
- High chair at table. "Andy, age two, struggled and screamed when we put him in his high chair. But when we dispensed with the tray and slid his high chair up to the table with us, he felt more a part of the family and no longer objected."
- Own table. "At nursery school, the twins, age two, loved sitting at their own little table with small chairs, and they resented coming home to high chairs. So we bought them a small table and set of chairs for meals at home."
- Standing guard. "David, age one, climbs and stands up even if I buckle him in. Now I just stay within arm's reach and let him stand up. He's never fallen. When he puts his foot in his plate, I take him down."

There comes a point when many youngsters scream at the sight of a bib as if it were a pair of handcuffs. Such an affront to personal independence! Parents solve this one by picking out bibs with char-

---

Baby Slides Down

To stop a small baby from sliding out of the high chair, put a nonslip rubber sink mat or bathtub daisies on the seat, in addition to using the safety strap.

acters children like, such as Cookie Monster. Some little ones prefer a cowboy bandana. Buy or make a bib that youngsters can put on and take off by themselves, or tuck a kitchen towel in at the neckline. As soon as Laura, age two, pulled off her bib, her parents removed all the food from in front of her. After several repetitions, she learned to leave it on until she was finished.

Some children are naturally (or can easily learn to be) neat eaters and don't need bibs at all. Others will always look like piglets, and the parents must just get used to it.

Our two objectives regarding utensils are that our children eventually learn to eat in a socially acceptable way and that we not be unduly embarrassed in the meantime. There are six important variables to consider.

1. When to introduce eating utensils. The age at which children can manage utensils varies tremendously. Pushing too soon frustrates everyone. One mother teaches table manners, including the use of utensils, at lunchtime, because it is less chaotic than dinner time.

2. Equipment. High edges on a plate keep food from being pushed off. If the child's dish doesn't have a suction cup to hold it in place, use a suction soap holder. Short-handled utensils are easier, as is the twisted Tommee Tippee® spoon, which gets food to the mouth at just the right angle. Once youngsters switch to flat plates, they may find it easier to eat European style, holding the knife in the right hand to push food against. Soup is easier to manage with Chinese soup spoons (some are made of plastic rather than ceramic), or allow toddlers to pick up the bowl to drink it Japanese style or serve it in a cup. Some youngsters more easily manage paring knives or pizza cutters, which cut better than table knives.

3. Food. We all struggle with skittish peas and slippery fried eggs. To assure early success, start with foods that almost stick to the spoon, such as mashed potatoes.

4. Emotional development. Independent youngsters would rather pick up waffles, drippy syrup and all, than ask for help. Cut food before passing the plate to the child.

5. The social situation. If you expect behavior in public or with guests that is different from that at regular family meals, notify the children ahead of time.

6. Parents' sensitivity.What makes one parent squirm goes unnoticed by another. At times we must question which is more in need of control, our expectations or the child's behavior. Some youngsters are expected to eat consistently with utensils at two and one-half, others not until four and one-half or five. Furthermore, the desire to touch with the fingers persists long after children are capable of using utensils. We wouldn't expect them to satisfy their curiosity out-of-doors by investigating with just a stick.

COMPLAINTS ABOUT FOOD SERVED

One important way parents minimize complaints is to allow youngsters to make some choices about food. This is particularly effective because children are often as unhappy about what we *don't* serve as what we do. However, there comes a point when parents want to put a cap on criticism. Here is how they do it.

Indecision. For children who have difficulty with decisions, or are inclined to say no automatically, see pp. 277 and 402.

Junior menu planner. "I let Lee, age three, plan the family's Sunday lunch menu, and he helped prepare as much as he could. He loved being in charge of a meal and having a chance to pick foods he liked. At age four, he started planning one dinner per week, and I gradually taught him how to choose something from each food group—protein, starch, fruits, and vegetables. Soon he was noting whether I was including all four in my meals. He's also come to appreciate the cook's experience of positive and negative criticism, especially from his sister, who has her own night to cook."

Parental feelings. "When the girls, age three, five, and eight, complain about my cooking, I tell them exactly how I feel. After working hard to plan and prepare meals, I feel hurt and angry. If they don't like something, they can eat just a small amount and be silent."

LEFTOVERS

To avoid the problems of overweight, we want our children to heed the stomach's warning to stop eating, yet many of us feel uncomfortable dumping good food in the garbage. Some of our leftover problems relate not so much to quantity as to the eating abilities and habits of small children.

Here are some easy and effective ways to avoid wasting leftovers:

- The last of the cereal. When children are anxious to move on to a new box of dry cereal, collect the remainders of several weeks into a "mystery" box, which will be interesting and fun.
- Milk after the cereal is gone. Serve dry cereal in a cup instead of a bowl, so it's easy to gulp down the last of the milk.
- Bottled baby meats. Use them as sandwich spreads.
- Bottle baby vegetables. Add to creamed soups.
- Bottled baby fruits. Eat them plain yourself, or add to fruit juice.
- Bread crusts. Save them for the ducks or pigeons, fry them for croutons, blend them for breadcrumbs, or bake them into a bread pudding.

Be careful with leftover formula. What the baby doesn't drink from the bottle within one hour should not be offered again. Once opened, formula stored in the refrigerator for more than forty-eight hours should be disposed of. To avoid leftovers, use small cans of formula or powdered formula so you can mix just what you need.

To dispose of formula: Throw it away, or add it to pet food, keep it refrigerated and use within a day or two in cream sauces, cream soups, or cooked puddings, but be sure it is boiled during preparation.

Most parents agree that the basic solution to leftovers lies in serving small portions, so that if the child doesn't finish, a minimum of food is wasted. There are, however, some additional considerations.

One father doesn't insist that his four-year-old daughter finish her first serving, which is automatically put on her plate. But if she asks for seconds of anything, she is required to finish the second portion. This encourages the child to take responsibility for food she requests.

Eric, age two and one-half, loves to serve himself but sometimes gets carried away. If he serves a lot more than he can eat, he isn't allowed to serve himself at the next meal. (Because he loves serving so much, his parents often let him serve one dish to the whole family.)

CHAOTIC DINNERS

Many of us imagine a relaxing dinner, basking in family closeness. Our dreams are dispelled by squealing infants, two-year-olds drumming on their plates with the silverware whenever the conversation intensifies, and four-year-olds practicing obnoxious burps. What happened to the peaceful dream?

The problem lies in our multiple objectives for the dinner table, only one of which concerns nutrition, and all of which are contradictory.

How simple it would be if mealtime were just for eating! Over the course of several years, we must teach increasingly complex rules: Peas are not for tossing; butter is served in small portions; no fingers in serving dishes; take only what you can eat. All these instructions would be fine in a classroom, but they hardly make dinner relaxing. And when we come down hard on rules, the food may not be eaten.

From the end of newborn colic till youngsters learn to talk, dinner time is relatively peaceful. Adults can share the day's experiences or discuss important issues as they did before the baby's arrival. But once children realize that disruption puts them in the spotlight, it will be a long time until they can participate in the delicate give-and-take of social conversation, or sit patiently through boring adult discussions.

One mother, judging herself and her little ones harshly for chaotic mealtimes, sat down to recall in detail the congenial family meals of her childhood. She was startled to realize her memories dated from about age ten. "I don't remember *what* meals were like when I was *two*," she mused. "Chances are they weren't much better than this three-ring circus." Viewing the present mealtimes as a stage of family development, rather than a sign of failure, she felt much more relaxed.

Given the complexity and contradictory nature of our dinner-time objectives, it is well to consider whether we want to attempt them all at once. The basic decision is whether to have the family eat together or separately, given the ages of the children. (For those parents who give up talking to each other during dinner, see p. 224. For more about teaching table manners, see p. 301.)

Many parents find that dinner goes better when the children eat first. After a full meal, the little ones are often in good spirits and more able to entertain themselves while the adults eat.

Kathy comes and goes while her parents eat, tasting here and there. It's much less disruptive than having her squirming in her high chair.

One husband has a snack when he gets home, and then he and his wife have a late but peaceful dinner after the children are in bed. The dishes are done the next morning. On the other hand, if the working spouse arrives late, everyone may be too hungry to be sociable, and meals together may be overwhelming. One mother solved this by eating early with the kids, when she could concentrate on their needs. Her husband eats when he gets home, and she keeps him company with a cup of tea.

Starting the meal together works well if children eat quickly and play elsewhere while the adults finish. They can be called back if dessert will be served later, so adults can enjoy a few quiet moments in the meantime. A variation on this is having children eat early and then come back to the table to join Mom and Dad for salad. The children have even come to revere the leafy greens they associate with their ten to fifteen minutes in the family limelight.

As shown in the above examples, you don't have to choose between adult-oriented and family-oriented meals. Furthermore, in some households, weekday meals go one way and weekend meals the other.

If children eat an early dinner, they can have a preview of what will be served to adults, leftovers refrigerated from last night or frozen in TV trays from last week, canned or frozen convenience foods, or nutritious snacks if they have eaten well earlier in the day.

To deal with a fussy baby at dinnertime, try an infant swing; an infant seat that rocks can be put beside the table and rocked with your foot; Jolly Jumper® (a bouncing swing) can be used once the baby has good head control; prop the baby on a pillow on your lap (with breast, bottle, or pacifier in his mouth) while you eat one-handed. It's awkward, but relatively peaceful.

The image of stimulating family conversation is hard to maintain in the face of an incoherent nine-month-old, a self-centered three-year-old, quarreling siblings, and exhausted parents. However, in this regard, the possibilities definitely go from worse to better.

To increase awareness of others' desire to talk, and to help little ones break in at appropriate moments, some families require members to raise their hands before speaking. In one household, the kitchen timer is set at a minute or two, and must be passed to another speaker when it rings. Some nights, the only solution is to sit down together and watch 3-2-1 Contact during dinner.

With boys eight, six, and four years of age, a couple tried to gear conversations around the day's low and high points, or something in the news of interest to the children, like the eruptions of Mount St. Helen's. Sometimes one member is designated as a guest, and is "interviewed" by the others.

When Amber, age two, finishes eating before her parents do, she brings some books to the table and "reads." In a few minutes she's lost in her books and reads quietly to herself while the grown-ups talk and finish eating. Her parents are luckier than most!

From the time Alan was one year, if he was too noisy at the dinnertable, his parents gave him one reprimand, then put him in his room if he continued. He was free to return whenever he was able to behave. Now he's three, and it's rarely necessary.

2

Sleep

E veryone talks about sleepless youngsters, when the real issue is sleepless parents. If someone would tuck us into bed and care for the household while we slumbered, we wouldn't care *how* little our youngsters dozed. As it is, their inability to quiet down, their refusal to go to bed, let alone go to sleep, their nighttime hunger, their nightmares and loneliness, their bright little eyes at the crack of dawn, all impinge on *our* need for sleep, to say nothing of our needs to relate to other adults or have a few quiet moments to ourselves. Sleep deprivation can turn anyone into a monster or a zombie.

The simple question, "When shall bedtime be?" is often our first introduction to ongoing conflicts of interest between our own needs and those of our children.

When an infant is inconsolable or a two-year-old *knows* there is a tiger in the closet, we suddenly find ourselves in the realm of the irrational where all our years of proper, logical education come to no avail. We need to learn whole new ways of relating to our little ones and whole new ways to care for ourselves in order not to be overwhelmed by a sense of helplessness. Even if we don't encounter opposition from our little ones, we may well encounter it from neighbors and self-appointed experts.

The subject of sleep includes the most controversial question in parenting today: whether to share the parental bed with our offspring. And no discussion of sleep is complete without considering the famous security blanket. Few items are more essential to household serenity, or cause more consternation when the precious tattered remnant hasn't been seen since the morning trip to the store.

Will the days of household calm and full night's sleep ever return? And how *do* parents get the sleep they need?

SCHEDULES

WHEN SHOULD YOUNGSTERS GO TO SLEEP?

"When *should* David go to sleep" often obscures an underlying question such as "When will I get some time to myself, time with my spouse, or catch up on *my* sleep?" Parents who spend ten to fourteen hours with youngsters each day are often relieved to get them settled into bed by seven or eight-thirty. On the other hand, if parents have been away all day, and aren't exhausted, they may enjoy evening time with youngsters, who may stay up until 9:00 or 11:00. Finally, youngsters too have their opinions. Like adults, some are innate larks and others owls, some need a lot of sleep and others too little for parental comfort. Newborns may tend to be up late, while on-the-go preschoolers may turn in comparatively early. With today's broad range of life-styles and acceptance of individual differences, there is no such thing as *an* appropriate bedtime. There are, however, ways of settling on bedtimes that take the needs of both adults and little ones into account.

Most babies and children have an innate inclination toward regularity, which we can encourage with consistent timing and bedtime rituals until a pattern develops. The key to developing routine bedtime is consistency, especially early on.

We recognize tiredness in children by their yawning, droopy eyelids, rubbing of eyes, and, in some cases, fussiness. Most youngsters go down comparatively easily at this point, though some still need a few minutes of crying to wind down.

Unfortunately, it's not always so easy. Children's sleep needs can vary from day to day, and some youngsters are irregular in everything. Rather than pressuring such little ones into a regular pattern, some parents allow them to choose their own bedtimes. When left on their own, most such youngsters fall asleep within the same one- or two-hour period each night, which is a broad but consistent pattern of its own. In households where children are permitted to choose their bedtimes, parents appreciate the lack of nightly struggles and find that over the years many such children continue to fall asleep easily, perhaps because they have become accustomed to responding to their own internal cues of tiredness.

Once youngsters pass infancy, some parents combine the ease of letting children choose their own bedtime with the pleasure of a regular schedule for themselves. To do so, children are required to stay in their own room after a certain hour, but can go to sleep whenever they want. In her evening solitude Sasha, age three, delights in trying on all her clothes.

Naturally, each scheduling system has its own advantages and disadvantages. For example, children who become hyper rather than sleepy when they're tired cannot be allowed to choose their own bedtime: They simply won't settle down. And parents who prefer to keep the youngsters on a tight, regular schedule will inevitably encounter some nights when they break the routine because children aren't tired at all.

GETTING YOUNGSTERS TO SLEEP EARLIER

There are several strategies for making bedtime earlier, the simplest being the direct approach: Put youngsters in bed earlier.

The basic decision in this method is whether to implement change in small increments or all at once. Our sample of babies suggests that the smaller the change in bedtime, the less the baby cries. How rapidly to change the bedtime depends on how eager parents are for a reasonable bedtime, how much change is needed, and how much crying is acceptable. Parents in a great hurry to move an infant's bedtime up by several hours should expect long stretches of crying at first; parents who are willing to wait longer for the ideal bedtime to become established can minimize crying by putting the child down five, fifteen, or thirty minutes earlier over a period of several nights.

Another way of implementing earlier bedtimes involves shortening naps, or dropping them altogether. Or, in order to get youngsters tired earlier, wake them earlier in the morning.

One mother, whose one-month-old would never fall asleep earlier than 2:00 A.M., decided out of desperation to try the opposite approach. She made sure to get plenty of rest during the day and then started *keeping her daughter up half an hour later,* both in the middle of the night and at naptime. Thus, over the course of two weeks, her 2:00 P.M. naptime evolved into a 9:00 P.M. bedtime, and her previous 2:00 A.M. bedtime turned into a morning nap at 9:00 A.M. It was an exhausting two weeks, but well worth it.

DELAYING SLEEPTIME

Sometimes we want to keep youngsters up later, and there are two basic strategies for readjusting schedules in this way.

Food perks up droopy children, so plan snacks and meals accordingly. When Lisa became droopy at 10:00 A.M., her mother gave her a snack instead of a nap and gradually delayed the calorie boost until morning snack had become lunchtime. The morning nap had disappeared.

Plan quiet activities, like reading, while children are still wide awake. As they become tired, move their arms and legs for exercise, take a tour of the house or a trip to the park, have a bath, play outdoor games, or dance to the radio.

If the purpose of delaying bedtime is to get youngsters to sleep later in the morning, don't expect immediate results. It may take a week of staying up late before they begin to wake at a correspondingly later hour.

YOUNGSTERS WHO NEED LITTLE SLEEP

Heaven help us if our youngsters need less sleep than we do. Such is often the case when a mother is pregnant the second time around. According to various studies, the amount that different youngsters sleep varies tremendously and therefore has an astonishing effect on the size of our work load. Some youngsters sleep as much as forty fewer hours per week than others, the equivalent of another full-time job for their parents.

Because drugging wakeful youngsters into oblivion is unacceptable, we are forced to accept their meager sleep needs. It may be some consolation, however, that many such babies are smarter in the long run. That's not surprising, as each year they have hundreds of additional hours to study the world around them. Research shows they also tend to have higher energy levels and as adults can study longer, work more, and more easily go without sleep to care for their own active children.

In the meantime, there are ways to ease survival, including giving ourselves credit for a parenting job that is more difficult than average. See How Parents Get Enough Sleep, p. 71, and Waking Too Early, p. 50.

NAPS AND THEIR ALTERNATIVES

Everyone knows that youngsters need to sleep at night, but daytime slumber is not so clear-cut. Some babies take regular long naps from day one, but others keep parents on their toes by taking only catnaps or refusing to nap at all. As with bedtimes, we have some control of the napping habits and schedules of our children, but we will have to take into account the energy level and tractability of the individual child.

Further complications arise because youngsters are almost always ready to give up their naps before we are prepared to give up that extra hour of semi-freedom. When some children stop napping, they still need the same total amount of sleep. Thus, there may be some compensation in a voluntary earlier bedtime.

For parents who still need midday solitude for work or a nap, one solution is "quiet time," in which youngsters take care of themselves in quiet activity such as looking at books, listening to music, coloring, or building with blocks. On occasion they may even fall asleep. Depending on the household, quiet time can last between one-half hour and an hour and a half. Good places for the child to be during quiet time are crib or bed, bedroom or a section of the house secured with a baby gate, the living room sofa, or— as a special privilege—a visit in the parental bed while Mom relaxes (or works) elsewhere. Reliable three- and four-year-olds might play by themselves in a secure backyard. It's often best to separate siblings and distribute them among the various quiet-time locales.

Some parents use one sibling's nap time to give individual attention to the other. Other parents make a point of coordinating nap times so they themselves won't be wiped out by 5:00 P.M.

GETTING YOUNGSTERS TO BED

Getting youngsters to bed is the toughest test of the day for some of us, and it comes when scant patience remains. Little ones fight getting their pajamas on, lose the essential teddy bear, imagine creepy-crawlies on the ceiling, plead for water as though lost in a desert, and, when we think they are finally settled, tiptoe out to the living room to see what the adults are up to.

From the youngsters' viewpoint, however, they are not only deprived of stimulating entertainment, coveted mobility, and beloved company, but are often plunged into darkness as well. Having tolerated the bathing and dressing of bedtime preparation, no wonder they now resist with the indignation of the unjustly punished. How do families make a smooth transition at the end of the day?

As adults, our lives are often so regulated by clocks and habits that we forget we used to live by whim. But our impulsive children can become accustomed to a bedtime routine.

· Clear objectives. Many parents use props or games to help establish a bedtime ritual and make their objectives clear.

After the initial warning, a kitchen timer can be set to go off at the "exact" bedtime. A parent might announce "last chance" (for water, trip to bathroom, and so forth) as the child is led to bed. And one toddler jumps into his crib to the tune of "Humpty Dumpty Had a Great Fall." Here are additional helpful hints.

· Picture list. Cut out and post pictures of each step of the bedtime ritual, such as bath, brushing teeth, and bedtime story.
· Pajamas on early. "Lisa, age two and one-half, struggled so much about getting her pajamas on that she was wide awake at bedtime, until we started putting them on her right after dinner and letting her play."
· No pajamas. "I just let Sandy sleep in her play clothes and put on clean ones in the morning."

There are a variety of techniques for dealing with infants who, having been walked to sleep, wake again when set in bed:

· Warm water bottle. Warm the bed first with a water bottle, so the baby isn't startled by cool sheets. Remove the water bottle just before putting the baby down.
· Pacifier. Walk the baby to sleep with a pacifier. She may wake just enough to notice it, and suck herself back to sleep.
· Don't move the baby. Feed, nurse, or pat babies to sleep wherever you want them to remain, so they don't have to be moved. One mother left her newborn in the baby carriage after being walked to sleep during a tour of the house.
· Sleep cycles. Newborns alternate between two kinds of sleep and parents can learn to distinguish them. Light sleep, during which they wake easily, lasts for the first fifteen to twenty-five minutes of each cycle. It can often be identified by movements of the eyeballs underneath the eyelids and sometimes gentle facial and body movements. In deep sleep, during which they can often be moved without waking, eyes stop moving, and the face and body are generally limp except for occasional jerks.

BEDS CHILDREN LIKE

A first step toward avoiding or ending bedtime battles is to arrange, if possible, a bed to the child's liking. At some point youngsters may be ready for something more grown-up, and resent the confinement of a crib. Sarah was happier with her bed once it was moved next to the doorway so she could see the family down the hall. Some children fall asleep most easily on the living-room sofa, in the parental bed, or in a sleeping bag in the family room. Others might prefer a large mattress they can share comfortably with siblings. There are children who seem to be able to fall asleep anywhere *but* their own beds. After these little ones are sleeping soundly, parents can pick them up and tuck them in. Also see Why Parents Choose Different Sleeping Arrangements, p. 57.

FAVORITE BEDTIME STORIES

In addition to whatever bedtime storybooks we or our children might choose, personal stories often add a special sense of completion to the day. One mother tells her son a story about his day: What went well, what didn't, and what she imagines was important to him. Or make up a story based on what you imagine the child would love to do: own a candy store, fly like a bird, be an only child, or whatever.

REWARDS AND PUNISHMENT

Rewards, adeptly used, can help assure that youngsters will go to bed, stay there, and not disturb parents after bedtime. Evening stories may best be read *after* youngsters are in bed, and Jack-in-the-box David, age two and one-half, now stays in bed because Mom or Dad lies down with him while he falls asleep.

Certain coveted privileges can be offered as rewards, and withheld as punishment, if necessary. If Stefan, age two, doesn't get to bed on time, there will be no lullabies. When Allison climbed out of her new youth bed, she was put back in her crib for the night. Sharon can keep her transistor radio on *as long as* she stays in bed. Paul can have his bedroom door open and Willie can keep his light on, *as long as* they stay in their rooms. And when Ryan, age three, said he had to go to the bathroom *again,* he was put back in "baby diapers."

FUSSINESS AND FALLING ASLEEP

What parent hasn't wished for a magic wand to wave little ones instantly to sleep? Whether we are trying to calm an infant's midday fussiness, return to sleep after a 2:00 A.M. feeding, handle daily bouts of infant upset, cope with a colicky baby, or ease youngsters of any age into slumberland, there's a technique which may help. Many of the same methods will work in different situations and can be combined in a multitude of ways.

SOOTHING FUSSY INFANTS
AND SLEEPLESS YOUNGSTERS

Infants may cry differently depending on what they want, but in the early months, most of us can't tell the difference. Generally, we are reduced to trial and error to discover what will calm our little ones. Many parents work out a cycle of techniques to employ one after another, because what doesn't work now may do the trick a few minutes later. If crying persists, get help from family, friends, or pediatrician, and see Surviving Children's Crying and Tantrums, p. 223.

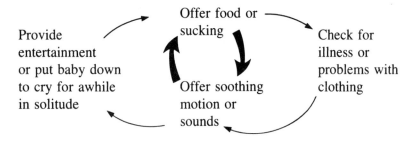

Foods and Chemicals

In general, there's nothing like a full tummy to help little ones drift off to sleep. One mother saves an extra bottle of breast milk for bedtime. But sometimes filling up is not the answer and can actually make the problem worse. If, for example, babies have colic or undergo a regular period of evening fussiness, then small frequent feedings may be better.

According to Doris Rapp, M.D., and Claude Frazier, M.D., in their respective books on allergies—*Allergies & the Hyperactive Child* (Cornerstone, 1980) and *Current Therapy of Allergy* (Med Exam, 1978)—certain chemicals and specific foods, including cow's milk and even soy formulas, may cause fussiness and difficulty in sleeping for some infants and children. Breastfeeding infants occasionally react to specific foods in the mother's diet. Experimenting is the only way to conclusively identify the cause.

Because of children's smaller size, it takes smaller amounts of caffeine to affect them. Caffeine in beverages, including breast milk, can cause sleeplessness, as can certain common medicines for colds. Check with your doctor if the latter is a problem.

Beware of Bedtime Bottles

Dentists warn that children *whose teeth are in* can be more prone to cavities if they take bottles to bed, because teeth may be continuously bathed in milk or, even more harmful, acid fruit juices. Research suggests that breastfed babies rarely have this problem because the breast fills the mouth completely, so less milk reaches the teeth, and it doesn't drip unless baby sucks. What are the alternatives to the bedtime bottle?

Remove the bottle from the crib after youngsters fall asleep.

Pacifier. For more about pacifiers, see Security Objects, p. 51.

Gradual dilution. Once toddlers no longer need a bottle for nutrition, gradually dilute the milk with increasing amounts of water over a period of several weeks. They can't distinguish *slight* changes in taste. Once the bottle holds plain water, there's no need for concern.

Ways to Rock a Baby

Just as we find the gentle rocking of a boat or hammock very soothing, so do many youngsters. Some have specific preferences for one kind of motion or another; some are particular about the position in which they are held. The standard rocking position is cradled in one's arms for easy eye contact. Holding the baby up over your shoulder so that it gently presses into baby's abdomen can be especially soothing for gas pain. The "airplane position," as shown in the illustration, is preferred by some fussy babies.

There are many kinds of baby carriers that are useful for rocking fussy babies. See also Chapter 7, Travel, for further discussion. Other devices and strategies for soothing little ones include rocking chairs and infant swings; cradles or infant seats that rock; stroller

rides, indoors or out; vibration from a washing machine if baby is placed nearby; rides in the car; and water beds that wiggle.

Many babies prefer patting to rocking, but grown-ups should exercise caution when doing so. What seems a gentle pat to us may be a startling wallop to a tiny infant. If you are inclined to get over-enthusiastic when holding a baby, rub instead of pat.

Sounds That Soothe

Lullabies or any music you sing or play on record or tape soothes infants and later preschoolers because of pleasant familiarity. Low-pitched, slow sounds are generally more calming. Or lie on your back with baby on your chest listening to your heartbeat for a reminder of the good old days back in the womb. Some stuffed animals come with a heartbeat sound.

Physical Relaxation

Swaddling babies can sometimes help soothe and relax them. Wrap baby gently but firmly in the familiar fetal position so arms and legs meet resistance reminiscent of the womb, instead of flailing around in midair. Some babies are calmed by gentle pressure against the tops of their heads: Use the palms of your hands, or place the infant snugly against the padded end of the crib. An allover body massage with warm baby oil will frequently do the trick. To help relieve gas pains, rub the tummy in a clockwise direction.

Restless toddlers can be helped to relax in bed by first wiggling then dropping different body parts to the bed. Start with the toes and work toward the head, body part by body part.

Provide Warmth

Unless the weather is already hot, providing warmth generally promotes drowsiness. Besides warm baths and warm drinks, try the following:

- Fireside story. Tell a story before bed for toddlers and pre-schoolers.
- Warm Face. While walking baby, place a diaper between the two of you to warm it. Place the diaper in the crib first and put baby's face on it instead of on cool sheets.
- Warm tummy. Place a warm, *not hot,* water bottle under the abdomen of a colicky baby to relax stomach muscles, or warm a toddler's pajamas for a moment in the dryer.

Simplicity and Solitude

Solitude and a simple, undistracting environment will aid many youngsters in falling asleep more easily.

With the clarity of hindsight, one mother reported that with three mobiles on the crib, a room full of educational gadgetry, and a mob of attentive relatives, it was no wonder her little one was often too hyped up to sleep.

In order to fall asleep, or to figure out what they want next, some babies need to be left to themselves to cry for five to fifteen minutes, or sometimes longer. To endure their noisy distress, see Surviving Children's Crying and Tantrums, p. 223.

Get Help

Faced with an inconsolable youngster, we often need to hear the comparatively calm voice of another adult, if only for reassurance that what we are doing is appropriate. Our own frustration can add to our infant's distress. Alerted to parental distress by the faster heart rate and greater muscle tension, infants may be soothed more readily by someone who is calmer.

Brandon, three weeks, cries for several hours a day no matter who holds him. Taking turns at least reassures his mother that Brandon is the problem, not her.

Provide Interesting Sights for Infants

Infants cry for many reasons, among them sheer boredom, especially before they are able to crawl and explore on their own. Holding babies upright, with eyes peering over parent's shoulders, encourages them to pay attention to their surroundings and may help relieve boredom.

Newborns can focus only on objects that are within eight to twelve inches, while the sense of hearing is well developed. Keep this in mind when planning entertainment.

Check Clothing

Not only do babies still get poked by errant diaper pins, but toes may get tangled in the unclipped threads inside the feet of little suits. Fans and air conditioners help when temperatures are high, and blanket sleepers and sleeping bags keep little ones warm on cold nights.

Overdressing is a common mistake that can interfere with sleep. It's all right if the baby's hands and feet feel cool, as long as thighs and back are warm. Normally, little ones need the same amount of clothing and covering as do adults at the same temperature.

Provide Sufficient Daytime Activity

There's nothing like physical exhaustion to get children to go to sleep easily and to sleep well. Exercise, indoors or out, is important.

Finally, when all else fails, exhausted parents may just have to wait out sleep difficulties and fussiness.

Siblings or Friends Keeping Each Other Awake

Siblings or visiting friends keeping each other awake may be a problem at nap time, bedtime, or both. Sensible solutions include:

Different bedtimes. Get one tucked in and asleep before putting the next one down. This also allows each child some important individual time with parents. Who goes to bed first may be determined by age, tiredness, or taking turns.

Different rooms. Even if youngsters generally sleep in the same room, have one go to sleep elsewhere and be carried to bed later. Or, if possible, rearrange the house to turn a den or alcove into a separate bedroom.

Records. Buy an inexpensive record player, and let each child choose one long-playing record. They'll be asleep by the time they've listened to both.

PROBLEMS WITH WAKING

WAKING DURING THE NIGHT

A few lucky parents have little ones who sleep through the night from the time they are born. Most of us, however, find that interrupted sleep is one of the most difficult adjustments of parenthood. Though we might not have slept well during later pregnancy, at least it was our own bodies that roused us from the slumber we used to take for granted. Now, we're apt to feel more resentful because someone *else* disturbs our nighttime quiet. Once babies no longer need midnight snacks, we assume we're in for regular sleep, so we feel doubly tricked when youngsters start waking again for other reasons. But wake at night they probably will, at one time or another. Our objectives are to endure while we must, and reclaim our rest as soon as we reasonably can.

Periods of nighttime wakefulness occur in many different situations, often reflecting change *or* stress, as in the newborn period, during and after illness, and on family vacations, as well as at the time of developmental milestones such as learning to crawl or walk. Furthermore, infants absorb parental worry like a sponge soaks up water. Thus some sleep problems reflect parental concerns and disappear when parental anxiety is resolved. Often we can solve such sleep problems only by waiting them out or dealing with other aspects of the change or stress.

Parents may find it comforting to know that it is easier to wake during certain phases of our natural sleep cycles than during others.

There is some evidence that the nursing hormone prolactin may tend to synchronize mother and baby sleep cycles so that they wake about the same time.

Many nighttime disturbances, especially during the early months of a child's life, are related to feeding. In this regard, breast and bottle-feeding each have their pros and cons. Parents who bottle-feed have the advantage of being able to take turns holding the bottle; also, formula is digested more slowly than breast milk so parents will be interrupted less frequently. On the other hand, once infants are nursing well, many mothers find a safe, comfortable place where they can doze while the baby drinks. This could be a reclining chair, hide-a-bed, the parental bed, or a sleeping mat. If you are nursing *and* giving a supplement, offer the bottle in the evening to take advantage of the longer digestive period for formula.

Of course, the ultimate solution to this problem will be to eventually cut out night feedings altogether. One approach is to arrange the longest possible sleep before midnight refueling, then eliminate the remaining feedings one at a time. Another technique to speed the process along is to wake the little one for a late evening snack just before you go to bed. Or try gradually reducing nighttime bottles by half an ounce every few nights. Eventually, the baby won't bother to wake up for so little. Shorter nursing (five minutes, then four minutes, and so forth) can accomplish the same goal.

Some parents offer a cup of warm water instead of milk, which eventually isn't worth waking up for. Others, especially during hot summer weather, leave several bottles of water in the bed at night so toddlers can quench their own thirst.

Instead of food, offer brief companionship during the transition to nights without calories. Fathers often play a crucial role here.

Crying is often an inevitable part of the transition. I thought you weren't supposed to let babies cry. When Davie was twelve months, the pediatrician told me that hunger during the night was a mere habit, and that Davie needed to learn to sleep through. He cried for two hours on two consecutive nights, and an hour for the next five. Even my husband woke and asked, "Shouldn't you get him?" The doctor was perceptive in seeing that *I* needed my sleep. Without her support, I wouldn't have been able to tolerate Davie's distress in making this necessary change.

Another mother chose a different approach

> Tommy, twelve months, still wakes two or three times each night. I always lie down while I nurse him back to sleep. He's our fourth child, so I've been up almost every night for the past ten years. It simply doesn't bother me any more.

An interesting fact in this area is that by six weeks of age, some babies will be roused from light sleep just by the *smell* of their mothers. The solution here may be for mom to resist the impulse to check up on the baby frequently and stay out when the little one is peaceful.

Sleep studies show that babies naturally have several periods of sleeping and waking during the night. Around eight months, some babies who had previously remained quiet begin to fuss, possibly due to more intense dreams. Overall our objective is to help them learn how to get back to sleep by themselves.

Here's how one mother dealt with her son's waking up:

> When Gerald started waking at eight months, I went in, patted him, and talked to him, but didn't pick him up. After a few nights, I just talked to him across the room, then for several more I reassured him from just outside the door. Finally I stopped getting up and he was able to return to sleep on his own.

LIGHT SLEEPERS

The average infant sleeps anywhere. We watch with envy as they snooze in strollers along bustling sidewalks. Some parents carefully cultivate this natural asset. Their babies take afternoon naps in the living room, and the nursery door is left open to keep them accustomed to sleeping amid different sounds in a variety of places. But some innately sensitive babies seem to wake at the drop of a cotton ball. How do parents adapt their household to such a newcomer?

The doorbell is quieted by putting a paper towel between clapper and bell, or disconnecting it entirely. A note tells visitors to knock.

The telephone is adjusted to flash a light or to ring quietly or not at all. (Check with the telephone company if you have questions.)

Soft music or vaporizer in the baby's room can block out more disruptive sounds.

WAKING TOO EARLY

A youngster who wakes with the roosters suits those who get up to milk the cows, but for most of us, morning sleep is precious. Given the tendency of small fry to wake early, bleary-eyed parents have several choices.

To induce children to sleep later, put a heavy blind over the window to keep the room dark longer. Or let them have an hour or so of morning sleep in the parental bed.

You can plan ahead for early birds by leaving a bottle of juice (not milk which may spoil) within reach of the crib. Put a bowl of dry cereal and a bag of orange slices on the kitchen table for a three-year-old, and have a "snack corner" in the refrigerator for children four and over.

Provide early morning entertainment in the form of a "new" collection of toys or books on a shelf or dresser within reach of the crib. Set out a project on the kitchen table for a three- or four-year-old, such as dot-to-dot pages, water colors, magnifying glass and something to look at.

TV may leave a lot to be desired, but for parents of a four-year-old, it functions as the extended family that makes it possible to sleep in on Saturday morning.

It's hard to keep entertained in pitch darkness. Put a night light near the crib. For an older child whose siblings sleep later, put a night light in the hall or another room.

A crib will confine an infant, and a baby gate a toddler, but to keep preschoolers in their rooms, put green dots on a clock to mark where the hands will be at a respectable hour.

Parents can safeguard their early morning privacy by making their bedroom off limits. If the rest of the house is adequately childproofed, and youngsters are safe around the house alone, put a stop sign on the parental door, or a lock if necessary.

When Jessica, age three, comes into her parents' room on Saturday morning, they pretend they're sound asleep. After a few minutes of waiting, she goes out and amuses herself.

One working mother tried everything to get her baby to sleep later in the morning, until she realized those early hours were in fact their best time together. This realization helped her enjoy a period that formerly created resentment.

SECURITY OBJECTS

Thank goodness for changing opinion. It used to be that security blankets were ridiculed, pacifiers unavailable, and thumbs daubed with hot sauce, while, ironically, parents puffed on cigarettes! Now we have come to accept not only our children's need for security objects, but *our* need to promote their sense of security. We realize that such objects are substitutes for us during the many moments each day when we are unavailable, and security objects are substitutes for the live-in relatives of yore, who were the extensions of our love. Tattered blankets and dowdy teddy bears have become essential to our small family life-style. Far from ridiculing the fabled blanket, we encourage such attachments to ease bedtime, car rides, the discomfort of illness, evenings with the sitter, and transitions to child care. Security objects also support youngsters' budding ability to care for themselves, help soothe the hurt of parental reprimands, and soften moments of grumpiness. Some youngsters, however, get along just fine without any particular security object.

HOW TO SELECT SECURITY OBJECTS

The most common group of security objects includes bottles, pacifiers, and thumbs, with their obvious connection to the essential early pleasure of sucking. The next most common group includes bedding and soft blankets, especially those with satin bindings. Tots have selected even rabbit fur, nylon ski jackets, and feather dusters. Some parents hypothesize that such silky textures may stir memories of mother's hair or nursing nightgowns.

Though many parents assume security objects are chosen solely by their offspring, we can often influence the decision: Objects that are repeatedly associated with comfort and parental presence are likely choices. Thus one mother regularly put a diaper in her infant's hand while she fed him, and placed one under his head when she sang him to sleep. Not surprisingly, he became very attached to diapers. Another mother always made sure a favorite teddy bear was conspicuously present for bedtime stories and then carefully tucked into bed.

We don't however, have the final word. Wendy, two months, thought her thumb was fine. Her parents, preferring a pacifier, repeatedly replaced the former with the latter. Wendy determinedly spit out the pacifier and returned to her thumb, until her parents finally accepted her decision.

THUMBS, PACIFIERS, AND THEIR ALTERNATIVES

While Joseph's parents are unsuccessfully urging him to take a pacifier, Michelle's parents are upset because she *wants* one. Reluctant babies don't tell us their objections, but parents have several concerns. Not the least of these is our Puritan heritage, which suggests there is something slightly immoral about pleasure for pleasure's sake. Others worry that youngsters will go off to kindergarten with the precious pacifier clenched between their teeth.

Before forbidding thumb or pacifier, consider the following: Muscles of the mouth are the only ones baby can reliably control, and thus the only available form of exercise. After a sufficient amount of exertion from sucking, babies naturally relax. Like some adults, some infants don't particularly like exercise and they get quite enough at mealtime. Others, especially before they develop alternative outlets for physical energy, need to suck for hours a day, much more than Mom's tender breasts can tolerate, or so much they would quickly become overweight if a bottle of milk accompanied all their efforts. A pacifier or thumb sucking are the obvious solutions.

Before trying to influence a baby's choice between thumb and pacifier, we'd do well to ponder the pros and cons of each:

Thumbs won't get lost or left behind; a child has more incentive to take it out of the mouth because it ties up a hand needed for crawling and playtime; a thumb gives the child control and independence in choosing when and if to suck.

Pacifiers, on the other hand, are good for infants under three months who can't reliably find or keep their thumbs in their mouths. Pacifiers are more conspicuous than thumbs, a fact that may induce pre-schoolers to stop due to peer pressure; and they may be easier for children to give up because they're not always available and because the pleasure they provide is limited to the mouth alone, as opposed to mouth *and* hand.

Parents who worry that thumb sucking and pacifiers might harm tooth alignment can relax. Now, not only have pacifiers been designed to minimize possible effects, but more and more dentists believe that thumb sucking is rarely detrimental if it has pretty much ended by the time permanent teeth come in. Almost all children, given ample opportunity to suck in the early years, will have stopped on their own by then.

The problem remains that despite parental acceptance or active encouragement of thumb sucking and pacifiers, some upset babies won't take either. What are the alternatives?

A *correct bottle nipple,* one with a nipple hole that isn't too large, will assure vigorous sucking at mealtime. Milk should drip out slowly when the bottle is upside down. Too small a hole, however, will cause frustration.

A *bottle of water* will give baby plenty of sucking opportunity without adding excess calories. If a baby won't take this either, try sugar water; then, over the next few days, dilute sugar with greater and greater amounts of water until you omit it altogether.

A *parent's thumb* may be an acceptable alternative. Gently massage the roof of baby's mouth with the fleshy part of your thumb to induce sucking.

More acceptable pacifiers may be found in different sizes and shapes. Or put a dab of Karo syrup on the end for the first few times to encourage baby to try it.

MAKING SECURITY OBJECTS MORE AVAILABLE

A security object that is unavailable in times of need is useless. Thus many parents look for ways to maximize practicality and accessibility.

It is often the familiar *texture* that attracts youngsters to a security object, which explains why an "identical" new blanket may be an unacceptable substitute for the scruffy old one. One mother bought two identical blankets to begin with. Because they "aged" simultaneously, their textures remained the same and both continued to be acceptable.

Frustrated by the forever grubby blanket, one mother cut a hole in the middle of it so her son could wear it like a poncho! It no longer trailed on the ground, and his hands were free for play.

The scraps of rabbit fur to which one toddler was attached were getting smaller and harder to keep track of. His mother pinned one to his bed and one to his car seat, and kept several to pin on his shirt for outings.

One ingenious parent put a collar of reflective tape on her child's teddy bear so it was easier to find during the night.

GIVING UP SECURITY OBJECTS

A security blanket is as dear to the heart of a child as the old home town is to us, and like the old home town, it is easier for some to leave behind than others. One mother silently observed her teenager nostalgically clutch his old blanket when he discovered it in the back of the hall closet.

There are predictable times when separation from security objects is likely to occur. Some babies give up sucking in order to explore: Thumbs are needed for holding blocks and it's hard to taste a toy with a pacifier in your mouth. Some youngsters, however, adeptly manage such complexities.

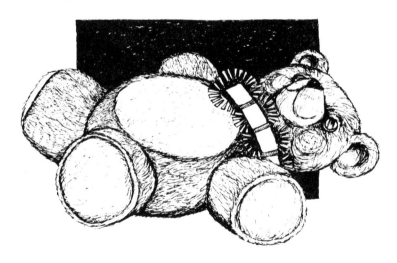

Generally speaking, the tumultuous twos or periods of emotional strain are poor times to try to get children to give up security objects. Everybody is better off if you wait for a calmer time.

Few parents take issue with the blanket of a two-year-old, but many become uncomfortable in public when youngsters turn three. A common solution to this is to restrict the use of security objects to certain times or places after age three. One advantage is that they are not so subject to loss. If the treasure does get lost, and youngsters don't protest or are overly picky about a replacement, chances are they are ready to give it up. Around age five or six, peer pressure often provides the impetus to give up security objects, or at least substitute more "grown-up" alternatives.

After one kindergartner, for example, made the effort to conceal his nightly thumb sucking when friends were sleeping over, he finally quit entirely. Two other boys in families we interviewed stopped surreptitious thumb sucking at ages seven and nine respectively, without parental intervention. One little girl switched from thumb sucking to more socially acceptable nail biting.

Some of us are startled, after a bit of introspection, to realize that *we* need our children's security objects more than they do. Sticking a pacifier in a youngster's mouth may be easier than giving personal attention, or easier than tolerating a toddler's need to cry out some frustration. Mothers have also discovered that if youngsters are well supplied with playmates and activities, the need for security objects may diminish.

Here are insights gained by two different mothers into the roles that security objects play in the lives of children. Both learned not to hurry the little ones out of habits that were obviously serving good purposes.

> In addition to my own children, I started taking care of Tanya, age two, for day care. Every day she brought a giant stuffed dog: She wouldn't go anywhere without it and talked to it all the time. Her mother wanted to take it away in order to end her "excessive" attachment. But I convinced her that just after a divorce was no time to have another "person" disappear from Tanya's life. After a month or so, she started leaving the dog while she played in another room, and one day she left it on the sofa while we went to the park. Needless to say, she's talking to it less.

My friends all have active boys who go full speed ahead all the time. Sean, age four, is a quiet child who spends a certain amount of time sucking his thumb and contemplating his next creative project. I think that quiet time is important to him, and I'm not about to disrupt it by saying he can't suck his thumb.

CO-SLEEPING: PRO AND CON

OPTIONS AND ARRANGEMENTS

Sooner or later almost all of us face the decision of whether to share beds with our little ones. Parents who have successfully avoided bed sharing when the child is an infant may find themselves confronted with a vocal toddler who walks right up and demands admission because he's lonely or afraid. This issue is probably the most controversial in parenting today, with ardent proponents of each side. Those who think children should never sleep with parents argue that no child will leave the parental bed without a fight and that co-sleeping can be emotionally damaging. On the other hand, those who think young children and especially infants should sleep regularly with parents point out that physical closeness is part of the natural state of affairs between mother and child and that co-sleeping provides needed emotional security and warmth. It is important to realize that millions of healthy children have grown up each way.

As with most controversial issues, a middle-of-the-road stance seems to suit the majority of parents. This middle view allows that there are certain situations and periods of development during which everyone may get more sleep if parent and child are together.

An important factor to take into account is the wide variety of options in who sleeps where, with whom, how frequently, and for how long. Co-sleeping does not necessarily mean youngsters in the parental bed all night, every night, for years. A number of parents share their beds to ease the newborn period and later to comfort a youngster's fears. After nightmares, youngsters may spend the remainder of the night with parents, or be carried back to their own beds once deeply asleep again. Though babies and toddlers may need the body contact of a back rub or a snuggle when upset, frightened preschoolers may feel reassured merely by sleeping in the same *room*. Separate beds in the same room avoid the more intense attractiveness of bed sharing and can therefore be easier to give up eventually. Some parents protect the privacy of their bedroom by staying in the *child's room* when needed. "Furthermore," such parents reason, "I want Peter's *own room* to take on an aura of warmth and companionship when he needs it, rather than his bedroom seeming cold and isolated compared with ours."

Any of the above arrangements can be used for part of the night, all night, short term, or long term. In many families, flexibility is the key. As one mother explained, "Sometimes we play musical beds, because all three of the boys, ages two, four, and six, pile into our bed the same night. When it gets that crowded, my husband and I go stretch out in their beds."

Some families provide foam mats, sofa pillows, quilts, or sleeping bags so youngsters can curl up on the floor of the parents' room or vice versa. To provide a safety rim at the edge of a family bed, fold a pillow inside an extra sheet, as shown in the illustration, or tuck a pillow between the box spring and mattress. For extra width, beds can be tied together. Alternatively, chairs or a crib with the inside rail left down can be tethered against the parental bed. Or, place a picnic bench between the bed and the wall.

Why Parents Choose
Different Sleeping Arrangements

In most cases, co-sleeping arrangements arise out of specific needs. We found four basic situations in which parents were more likely to choose co-sleeping. (1) The younger the child, the more likely the child is to sleep with parents, especially if nursing during the night. Parents who bottle-feed have to fetch a bottle and stay awake to hold it, so are more apt to put the baby back in the crib. (2) Co-sleeping is also more likely when youngsters are ill. Studies in pain perception suggest that children may experience less discomfort from the same physical cause when with parents than when alone. (3) When youngsters are under emotional stress, they are more likely to sleep with parents. Knowing that children are, in fact, safe and not alone with their distress, we may be more relaxed and, therefore, transmit less disruptive anxiety to them. (4) The larger the family, the more likely is co-sleeping. With the first child,

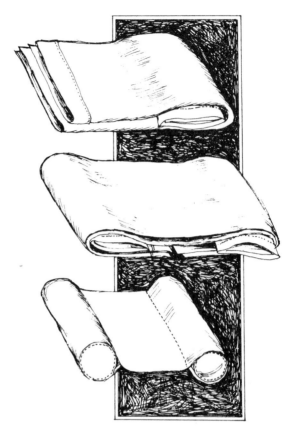

believing we will never be liberated from day-in, day-out dependence, we may guard our bed as the last refuge of personal freedom. Or, all too aware that eventual separation *will* come, especially with an only child, we may fear overattachment to such an absorbing, cuddly bed companion. But with multiple small children, such fears decrease, while the number of likely nighttime interruptions increases. Thus co-sleeping becomes a practical way for parents to avoid chronic sleep deprivation. In addition, toddlers and pre-schoolers generally find it easier to eventually move *out* of the parents' room if they can move *in* with a sibling.

On the other hand, many parents avoid co-sleeping because maintaining the peace and privacy of their own bed and bedroom is essential. These mothers explain why:

I wanted my new baby in our bedroom, but with all her

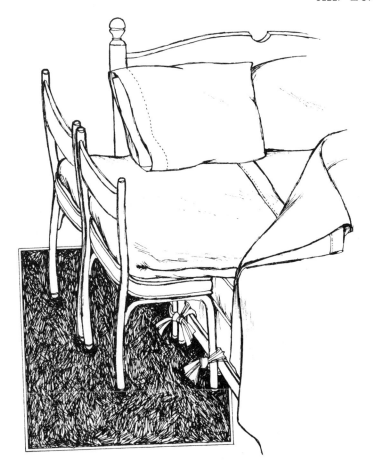

gurgles, snuffles, hiccoughs, and funny breathing, I couldn't sleep. From another room, I could only hear her cry when she was hungry.

I can't sleep with a wiggle worm, and I need *some* time off!

My husband is on the tense, quiet side: He needs time to relax before he can talk. If the kids were in our bed, I'd never hear from him, and our marriage would just fade away.

Having children start the night in their own beds has much to recommend it. (1) Parents get some time to themselves. (2) Youngsters become accustomed to sleeping in their own beds and bedrooms. (3) There is a gradual transition because co-sleeping occurs less and less often as the need for closeness diminishes.

Here is how some different families worked it out:

> We became zombies, constantly dragging ourselves out of bed to settle one or another of the triplets. Finally, when they could crawl, we put them on the floor on sleeping mats. Now my husband and I go to sleep and they come when they need us. We wake up with all three of them in our low bed without even remembering their arrival.

At three months, Lee was moved from a bassinet in his parents' room to a foam pad on his bedroom carpet. His Mom could snuggle with him whenever needed, then slip away without waking him. At night, she closed the baby gate at his doorway, so when he woke, he could play in the safety of his room. He needed her less and less, and not at all after he turned three.

> Kevin slept through the night in his own bed from six weeks of age. Then at eight months, he started waking frequently and continued to do so, despite our efforts to soothe him back to sleep with minimal fuss. Finally, at fourteen months, my husband and I steeled ourselves and let him cry it out. He cried hard, though intermittently, for eight hours the first night and seven the next. The following seven nights he woke and cried hard for forty-five minutes, sometimes to the point of vomiting, then finally slept through. During the next two years, we went through repeated heart-rending cycles of sleep disruption and readjustments after illness, a family vacation, a new baby-sitter, his best friend moving away, and my going away on a trip alone. Occasionally, when we were exhausted to the point of desperation, we took him to bed with us, where he not only slept better but longer. Finally, after he turned three, we decided to let him come sleep with us whenever he woke during the night, which was about five nights out of seven. This pattern continued until he was five, and a baby sister arrived. We put her crib in his room, at his request, and he stopped coming to our room at night.

Sharing a bed with children while one's spouse is away needs to be balanced by how much resentment they may feel when they must return to their own rooms.

WHEN AND HOW DOES CO-SLEEPING END?

We are cautioned not to bring youngsters to our beds because "it will never end without a struggle." But in fact, we found co-sleeping arrangements end smoothly more often than not. There seem to be three key factors.

1. Lack of parental ambivalence. If, even deep down, we feel painfully insecure or lonely when our little ones sleep elsewhere, they may well cling to protect *us*.
2. A flexible sleeping arrangement. Usually, after the first few months of newborn adjustment, or after night feedings have ended, most youngsters are easily able to sleep by themselves some nights or at least part of some nights. Little by little, they will become able to spend more time sleeping alone.
3. Perceptiveness. If we assume children grow naturally but gradually toward independence and if we are attentive to their needs, we can alternately support them when they backslide and encourage them when they are ready to move ahead. But if bringing a fearful youngster to our bed brings no improvement or makes the problem worse, we need to look for other solutions. There is no substitute for attentiveness to the individual needs of children.

Unfortunately, the decision to end co-sleeping isn't always easy to make or carry out. One mother found it took longer and longer to get her lonely twenty-month-old to sleep and with increasing frequency she was sleeping with him on the living-room sofa to calm him after terrifying nightmares. She increasingly resented the chaos and lack of time wih her husband until one day she realized she couldn't always cater to her son. She decided to begin by being very firm about bedtime and was even prepared to go for a drive while her stronger-willed husband endured the inevitable screaming. To their amazement, he cried only five minutes for several nights, started going to bed without complaint *and* sleeping through the night.

Kenny, age two and one-half, was lonely and therefore allowed to sleep on a sofa in his parents' room. But soon he was waking them as often as six times a night with the same complaint. They said he must either sleep in their room without disturbance or return to his own room. When he woke them again, he was carried back to his own room, where he screamed and banged his feet against the wall for half an hour. He repeated this performance the next night, but after that he slept through the night in his own room, without complaint.

WHY THE WORRY
ABOUT SLEEPING TOGETHER?

There is no doubt that physical contact with someone who cares has a magical effect. We all know the relief, security, and hope that an embrace can provide, so it *does* seem natural to comfort our little ones in our bed when they are hungry, lonely, or frightened and *we* are tired. Why all the controversy?

One source of concern stems from evidence presented in various psychiatric studies that co-sleeping can be harmful to children, particularly in the form of emotional turmoil and later sexual maladjustment. The crucial term here is *can be,* because studies on sleeping patterns in normal families, scarce as they are, offer no clear evidence that such practices alone adversely affect emotional health. (The same is true for sharing bathrooms and for family nudity.) *However, when parents are experiencing emotional difficulties, co-sleeping can clearly intensify the child's experience of the problem.*

As conscientious parents, we must ask, ''Who is this co-sleeping arrangement really for?'' We need to examine our motives, not merely accept surface appearances. ''Is Michelle's difficulty sleeping her very own problem, or a reflection of *my* anxiety?'' ''Is my need for closeness and security hampering David's growth toward independence?'' Are there inappropriate overtones between parent and child? ''Am I at a loss for how to handle my dissatisfaction with my spouse?'' If the answer is yes to any of these questions, the most important thing we can do for our children is to find support for ourselves *from other adults.* Such burdens are too heavy for small children, especially in bed.

Despite all the concerns and controversy, a majority of American infants spend some time sleeping with parents as do almost half the toddlers and 20 percent of kindergartners. Most suffer no harm from the arrangement. When damage *is* done, there are often clear warning signals. The hazards of co-sleeping are real. What are they?

Prolonged Dependence

In many ways, our culture places excessive emphasis on independence, and many of us therefore arrange for our wee ones to sleep alone long before it is necessary. To take a helpless babe, lonely toddler, or frightened preschooler to bed with us is one thing. But to take a content child to bed because *we* need his or her physical closeness to reassure us that the world is good and to protect *us* from loneliness is a different issue. *If we need the child, the child may become needy in order to accommodate us.* Children may even develop fears and nightmares so we can take them to bed without having to examine our own anxieties. A child caught in such a web finds it difficult to respond over the years to natural urges toward independence and may thereby be condemned to dependence as long as *our* need persists.

When our own concerns about loneliness surface, we not only need to decide how much distance to maintain from our children, but ultimately we need to consider how to diminish our own loneliness and isolation.

One mother became aware of a potentially difficult situation:

> One night, when my husband was away, I kept Sean with me after a late night nursing. His warm little body filled an aching loneliness within me. I knew I could easily become addicted to such closeness and find it very hard to give up. Thereafter, I put him back in his bassinet as soon as he finished nursing.

A Cover-up for Marital Problems

"We can't, dear, because Junior is here" can be a better cover-up than "I have a headache." However, the former is far more destructive because children can become trapped pawns if parents consciously or unconsciously allow children to share the bed in order to avoid issues of intimacy. For example, a wife might unintentionally encourage special closeness between father and daughter to reduce personal pressure for intimacy, and a husband might come to rely on the child for emotional warmth that is not available in the marital relationship. Children are not able to turn down such permissions and expectations, yet involvement in such a triangle clearly leads to difficulties unless parents face their differences.

Excessive Sexual Stimulation

Once children reach age two, three, or four, they become very sensitive to sexual undertones. They sense the spark that may flicker when we climb into bed with our spouse, they pick up the slightest seductive nuances we may direct their way, and they sense what is behind an older sibling's requests for intimate physical exploration. With their vivid imaginations, they may fantasize about, distort, or exaggerate anything they perceive. Thus, a child may experience the quasi-sexual intimacy of the parental bed as a way of actually participating in something much more intimate. In their naiveté and dependence on their elders, children are easy to seduce. Most youngsters who become sexually overinvolved with someone they know well like it, in part. Yet this closeness, while attractive at first, is also frightening and soon proves to be more than they can handle. With either the fact or the fantasy of sexual encounter, young children have very limited capacity to deal with the emotional intensity of their own or another's sexual feelings. To pressure them to face directly what may be their natural inclination toward incest is to rob them of their right to a relatively carefree childhood. There is ample evidence that not just excessive intimacy, but also serious worries about it, can cause anxiety at the time, as well as hamper normal sexual adjustment years later. Bed, of course, is not the only place children can be exposed to excessive sexual stimulation; it is merely one of the more likely.

Children's anxiety in such matters may be obvious, or may emerge only in therapy. Symptoms may be general, such as tics, stuttering, trouble with eating, or as specific as an unusually intense interest in where babies come from, dreams of nude parents, or worries about sleeping pelvis across pelvis with a parent. Unfortunately, such anxiety can also produce fears and nightmares, creating a vicious cycle of difficulty sleeping, visits to the parental bed for comfort, too much intimacy, and therefore more fear. Not surprisingly, preschoolers caught in such a circle cannot clearly explain the basis of their fears.

Some parents fear that sleeping with a same-sex child may ultimately incline their offspring toward homosexuality. There is no reliable evidence that this is the case.

PARENTAL LOVEMAKING DESPITE THE CHILDREN

Once youngsters are mobile, there is always the possibility that they will interrupt parental lovemaking. Small children are easily frightened by events they don't completely understand—parental arguments, for example. Thus we can imagine why a child silently observing the sounds and motions of passionate lovemaking might be confused and concerned. If the same child were angrily ordered from the room by startled parents, and thus picked up an unspoken message not to question the earlier events, we can imagine worry increasing. Finally, consider the terror a child would be likely to feel if such a scene was reminiscent of actual physical violence previously witnessed in the family. It is not difficult to comprehend why certain adults have recalled in therapy frightening memories of adult sexual activity. Parents who engage in sexual intercourse when they know the child is present can cause damage, particularly if there is an edge of exhibitionism or seductiveness that invites emotional involvement.

Some traditional cultures casually mix little ones and lovemaking, while others require that parents go elsewhere. Parents in the close quarters of cold-climate cultures may not even have the option of privacy. Preferences in *our* culture are to avoid whenever possible both the interruption of personal moments and the potential for misinterpretation. How do parents arrange privacy and handle the interruptions when they occur?

Lock. Once our youngster turned three, we put a lock on our bedroom door. When Aaron bangs on the door, we just tell him we want some time alone and will be out soon.

Freeze. When we have been interrupted on rare occasions by our two- or four-year-olds, we just freeze, answer whatever they came in to ask, and continue after they leave.

Restrained lovemaking. When we lived in such tight quarters that it was a matter of make love with youngsters around or not at all, we waited till they were asleep and kept our activities on the quiet side.

NIGHTTIME FEARS

LEFTOVER DAYTIME WORRIES

Like us, our children can have difficulty settling down for sleep if they are still tense about events of the day. These three mothers have developed their own ways for alleviating their children's worries:

> *Personalized bedtime stories.* Kier, age four, doesn't talk easily about his feelings. So if he's tense at bedtime, I make up a story about Iggy the Allosaurus, for example. (Kier likes dinosaurs these days.) Iggy just happens to have the same difficulties I suspect Kier is having. Sometimes Iggy finds solutions, and sometimes he just wonders what to do. Some nights Kier gets even more tense, but more often I can see the relief on his face as he hears his concerns expressed.
>
> *"Good days–bad days."* This is a regular time for each of our children, now three, six, and eight, to share any special events of their day, or discuss any of their frustrations. There's never any punishment for secrets shared. They really look forward to it.
>
> *Worry bag.* Brian, age four, and I play an imaginary game at bedtime. I hold out my hands and he tells me all the day's worries that he is dropping into my palms. We imagine tying up the bag and I tell him I'll lock it in my desk drawer for the night. We also have another imaginary bag, which he keeps under his pillow after filling it with happy and peaceful moments from his day.

FEAR OF BEING ALONE

Fears of loneliness are common in fairly predictable stages and circumstances. Sometime between six and fourteen months, most youngsters fear separation from their usual caretakers and their sensitivity lasts from a few weeks to months. Rebellious two-year-olds, aware of the frustration they cause us, are understandably fearful that we might abandon them. In fact, it isn't until about age four that children easily grasp the notion that a relationship can endure despite physical separation. Regardless of age, when the family undergoes stress or change, children need more closeness than usual for reassurance that their entire world isn't falling apart. On the other hand, there are times to encourage them to cope with their loneliness, in order that *we* can get some time for ourselves. Because bedtime is in fact a kind of separation, see also Planning and Preparation, p. 341 in Chapter 10.

Mom and Dad are nearby. When Luke, age three, calls out that he is lonely, we call back to him that we are nearby.

Imaginary company. When we tuck William, almost three, into bed, he lists all the people he wants to have stay with him, including us, his grandfather, Superman, and so forth. We tell him to describe just where in his room they should be. By the time we leave, there's hardly space for the real us.

FEAR OF THE DARK

Children may express fear of the dark in specific terms, as a general fear, or as loneliness. If youngsters wake from bad dreams alone and in darkness, where it is difficult to recognize the surroundings, they may come to fear darkness at all times. Parents take opposite approaches as far as leaving children without light. One mother left her youngsters in a dark room from birth "so they wouldn't become afraid" and they never did. Another mother remembered her own disorientation and panic at waking in pitch blackness while traveling overseas as a young adult, and so she provided night lights for her children from early on. If children do become afraid of the dark, there are two basically different approaches to take.

1. *Provide light,* in the realization that children eventually outgrow their fear of the dark. Parents use night lights; open doors to let in hall light; or provide a flashlight to go to sleep with, taped closed to protect its innards from small explorers. Some arrange a wall switch that is safely within reach if youngsters wake during the night. Put a stool under it, or check local baby supply and hardware stores for a "light switch extender," which allows little ones to operate it while standing on the floor.

2. Help children overcome their fear of the dark. A dimmer switch will allow you to lower the lights gradually to ease through a period of fear. Some parents reward their children with special treats, first for entering, then gradually staying longer, and ultimately sleeping in a dark room.

These parents invented an ingenious story to help their son overcome his fear:

> Because Jack, age five, was afraid of the dark and greatly admired Luke Skywalker of *Star Wars,* we decided to use his hero to help his fear of the dark. We asked him to close his eyes and imagine that Luke was calling him on a secret computer. To answer the call, Jack was supposed to imagine going into a dimly lit room. Whenever he started to feel afraid, we stopped. After several evenings, Jack was able to imagine himself alone in his bedroom with the lights off, waiting for a message from Luke. Gradually he was able to transfer his newfound bravery to his real bedroom.

NIGHTMARES AND SCARY CREATURES

Sleep researchers tell us that babies dream from the day they are born. Nightmares, however, through which our minds process the upsetting events of our lives, seem to first appear between six and twelve months of age or later. There are three probable causes for the emergence of upsetting dreams at this time: (1) Newly mobile little ones begin to encounter our necessary ''no-no's'' for the first time; (2) the development of walking skills leads to inevitable bumps and falls; (3) during this period babies make an emotional commitment to their primary caretakers and may develop nightmares related to separation anxiety. Throughout the childhood years, physical and emotional distress may turn sweet dreams into nightmares. Even explaining to preschoolers what dreams are can be a challenge. Thoughtful parents have described dreams as being ''things you imagine during the night instead of the day,'' ''a way of working out problems,'' and ''something like you and people you know dressed up in a play.''

Nightmares are a common cause of otherwise unexplained crying during the night. Because children gradually connect fearful experiences with the location in which they occur, nightmares can cause fear of beds and bedrooms as well. Fearful monsters in the bedroom are often those of the dream world and can often be handled similarly.

Night terrors are different from nightmares in that children are inconsolable, and if awakened show no sign of recognizing their parents. Eventually youngsters cry themselves back to sleep and have no memory of the incident in the morning. Opinions vary as to the cause. Some people see them merely as a passing phase, and others advise that if such episodes recur the child may need professional help with emotional issues.

Because children's fears and nightmares are usually a code for genuine but unconscious worries, it is a waste of time to deny that there is a creature in the closet. To young children who can't clearly distinguish between fantasy and reality, the bear in the dream is as real as a pet cat that unpredictably appears and disappears. Before our little ones can talk, we have no clues about the contents of their nightmares, and even verbal youngsters may not be able to say much that we can understand. Fortunately, we can help despite our lack of information. With preverbal youngsters, bolstering their sense of security with our presence is usually sufficient. With two-year-olds and preschoolers, an effective technique is to enter the land of fantasy with them, armed with inspiration and imagination, and take on the dragons.

Props can often help in providing protection. Amanda's teddy bear becomes the invincible watchdog who will protect her from monsters and company. Ken, age three, keeps a pair of magic Chinese chopsticks under his pillow to fight off threatening intruders.

One mother uses a special bedtime ritual whenever her three-year-old son wakes her too early, has nightmares, or is sick. At bedtime she runs her hands all over his body and repeats, "I'm wrapping you in a safe blue cocoon. This is your special, safe place. I'm near, but don't wake me unless you really need me. You have your own safe space." She then chants, "All the gods and fairies will protect you through the night."

Another mother tells of how she literally disposed of her daughter's personal demon: "Night after night, when Nia was two, I had to calm her down after finding her screaming and pounding the floor beside her bed with her fists. One day I told her to draw a picture of the monster. After she scribbled all over the paper, we put it in the garbage with a brick on top until the garbage man took it. No more nightmares.''

Yet another mother invented a very effective deterrent to the beast that plagued her son: ''One night, amid Ben's terrified cries about the owls in his room, I held up the can of Lysol and announced firmly, 'This is owl spray. Owls hate the smell so they go away and stay away.' As I sprayed here and there, Ben settled down with immense relief. On the way to the store the next day, he reminded me to buy more owl spray.''

Some dreams are triggered by frightening real-life events, and can be handled accordingly. David had nightmares after seeing a store burn down. His parents therefore demonstrated their home fire alarm, practiced an escape routine, *and* encouraged David to imagine that he was a fireman who saved buildings from burning. After being frightened by a raccoon, Sonya was invited to imagine the raccoon and ask what it wanted. It wanted food, which Sonya imagined giving it. Soon she was dreaming of a friendly raccoon, rather than a frightening one.

Other dreams originate in the day-to-day emotion of family living. For example, a youngster may show little daytime resentment of a new sibling, but suddenly start having nightmares. Many fearsome dreams, especially among boys, originate in the normal love triangle among mother, father, and child, which is described in Competition between Parent and Child, see p. 225. Children can be immensely relieved to learn that their angry, jealous wishes won't cause harm to themselves or others.

Stefan dreamed repeatedly that an angry bear was pushing him out of his bed. His perceptive mother made up a story about a little boy named Jackie, whose new sister was crowding him out of his house and his mother's attention. Jackie didn't like the baby and while out one day, both hoped and feared the garbage man would take her away. The baby was still there when Jackie returned and they continued to live all together. Stefan was overheard the next day, talking to himself about having bad dreams because he hated his new sister. His mother was amazed, because he himself had made the connection between his nightmares and the story. However, because his feelings had been brought into the open and accepted, they were no longer so scary, and the nightmares stopped.

Jason, age three, who showed obvious jealousy of his parents' relationship, also had repeated nightmares about spiders. Indicating the connection between his dreams and ambivalent feelings toward his father, Jason announced one morning, "Papa, *you* are scared of the spider, too." His father replied, "No, the spider won't hurt me, you won't hurt me, and I won't hurt you." Thus reassured, Jason had no more nightmares.

HOW PARENTS GET ENOUGH SLEEP

Though some two-year-olds push themselves to exhaustion in order to avoid sleep, children generally get all the sleep they need. The same cannot be said for us. Nor is there any way to prepare for the sleep deprivation of parenthood. One mother, whose two children are eighteen months apart, remembers that when they were little she was tired all the time. Many parents have the same experience.

No parental objectives conflict more directly than the desire to keep infants content and the need to get enough sleep for ourselves. Buoyed by the exhilaration of our new role, and pressured by books that urge us to establish baby's sense of security, we jump to quiet every whimper of our fragile newborns. However, as the weeks pass, many of us become exhausted. We resent walking Jennifer until midnight each night, but dread putting her down at 10:00 P.M. to cry herself to sleep. Having focused entirely on our infant's needs in the beginning, we must now acknowledge our own needs as well, and look for compromises. One of the most difficult tasks of parenthood is to realize that the ultimate objective is to live *with* rather than *for* our children. Parents take several different approaches to getting the sleep they need.

When we need a rest as much as or more than our restless little ones, we may have to make special arrangements for napping. Toddlers may rest more easily when snuggled with Mom on her bed, or Mom's nap might be scheduled while preschoolers watch TV. One mother stretches out on sofa pillows on the floor of her two-year-old's room. Because she is dozing nearby, he plays contentedly. Jason, age three, earns a star if he doesn't disturb his mother during her nap. If Sonya gets a late morning catnap in the car, she skips her hour-long afternoon nap. Thus Mom plans her day to avoid sleep-inducing car rides after 11:00 A.M.

When napping is not possible, there are other tricks that parents develop to compensate for interrupted sleep.

With four kids, I've trained myself to stay half asleep, no matter how many times I get up at night. I always keep my eyes half closed, use a flashlight rather than bright lights, and lie down with whichever child needs me.

I've never been able to sleep during the day, but twenty minutes of meditation is as good as a nap.

Finally, exhausted parents learn to be less severe and demanding with themselves. It's enough to endure life with less sleep than we need without expecting ourselves to be in top shape despite fatigue. We *will* have a shorter fuse, and *will* be more prone to feeling depressed until we catch up. Fortunately, lack of sleep, the disease of early parenthood, ends eventually, and its symptoms are reversible.

3

Clean and Clothed

We are so accustomed to bathing, brushing our teeth, and dressing ourselves that we can do each in our sleep. But once youngsters join the household, the amount of time and attention that each of these details of daily living consumes can be staggering.

All too soon, after a fresh diaper is secured, it is wet again or sagging off our pot-bellied toddler. One year we're trying to keep diapers on, and the next we're trying to get them off, as we launch the great toilet-training campaign. Unfortunately, youngsters catch on quickly to our various ploys for freedom, and have a way of turning the simplest routine into a power struggle. The increasing parental acceptance of late toilet training hasn't solved all the problems because messy diapers are still with us, and unfortunately many nursery schools won't let diapers in the door. Just as we congratulate ourselves on *our* success and Jennifer's *control,* she demonstrates she can let go *exactly* where she pleases, and it may not be in the potty. What about dry nights? Return to square one.

Oh, for a whiff of general anesthesia to gain the limp cooperation of the angry two-year-old we must dress. Then, as soon as we've mastered the complexity of dressing them, they want to do it themselves, especially when we are in a hurry. They are as frustrated by putting on a pair of underpants as we are by operating a computer. And it's a rare preschooler who has a chic sense of color. Kids outgrow their clothes in all directions, crawl through puddles, wipe drippy noses with yogurt-coated sleeves, decorate themselves with permanent marking pens, and experimentally pat glue and gum into their hair.

We are frightened at the prospect of touching sharp scissors to the minute, fragile nails of our newborns. The bath brings gurgles of delight one day, elicits squalls of anger on another. When we apply shampoo to a grubby scalp, or move a brush toward snarled hair, our little ones scream as if they were being tortured. They are terrified of slithering down the drainpipe, of being hurt when their hair is cut. And the toothpaste stings the tongue. How did *we* ever come to delight in leisurely baths and having our hair brushed?

While we are anxiously getting clothes on, our youngsters are anxiously taking them off. At first they are casual investigators of *all* their body parts, while we face the larger issues of what to name each one. As the months go by, they delight in physical sensations, even in public, while a wild red blush spreads to our faces. Sensing our embarrassment, they choose quiet rooms and dark closets to investigate the differing bodies of their little friends.

Keeping youngsters even partially clothed and moderately clean is a challenge and a half.

SIMPLIFYING DIAPERING

Before our youngsters graduate to the potty, we'll spend three hundred to five hundred hours per child *changing* diapers, to say nothing of washing them. No wonder parents want to find the easiest, most convenient ways to cope with soggy diapers, mushy bowel movements, and wiggly bottoms.

Places for easy diaper changes include: any sturdy table or dresser top of convenient working height, kitchen or bathroom counters near a sink, or in the crib or on the floor to avoid falls. In a large house, it is best to have several fully equipped diapering locations.

Types of diapers will depend to some extent on your pocketbook and your attitude toward the environment. Diaper service and disposables are comparable in price in many locales; if you can afford to spend the extra money, they save time and trips to the laundry. Environmentalists recommend diaper service. Disposables, with their tapes, are easier to put on.

Leaky diapers can be prevented by folding extra material to the back for girls and to the front for boys. Fold an inner diaper lengthwise several times. Avoid dribble of newborn's runny bowel movements by sewing several tucks around the legs of the rubber pants. Snip them as the baby grows.

To help keep diapers on, dress small children in overalls (pants tend to pull diapers down) or use suspenders. One mother taped the disposable diapers all the way around with adhesive tape so her two-year-old couldn't pull them off.

TIPS FOR DIAPER EASE

· Store diaper pins in a bar of soap to keep them slippery.
· Diaper clips are an alternative to pins. They take practice at first, but you avoid the risks of stabbing the baby or yourself.
· Flushable diaper liners make cleanup easier.
· If you know that certain foods (raisins or creamed corn, for

example) cause messier stools, don't stock them for your two-year-old.

Wiggling and squirming seem to be favorite activities during diapering time, and once kids have learned to stand or walk they often try their best to escape. One way to deal with this problem is to minimize the time it takes to diaper the little one: Keep equipment handy. Some changing tables come equipped with a strap to hold down a squiggly infant. Parents also soothe unruly youngsters by providing entertainment in the form of animal sounds, songs, mobiles, pictures from magazines taped nearby, or special toys.

A child who gets involved in the diapering process is more likely to be cooperative, and many parents encourage their children to do their "favorite" parts themselves—such as fetching the diaper or holding the ointment. Some little ones will tolerate diapering better only when they are on their stomachs; others prefer to stand up, holding onto a chair, a window sill for an interesting view, or the toilet seat for convenient clean-up.

When all else fails, punishment may be the only method to get the diapering time to go smoothly. When Kier squirmed during diaper changes, his mom held him firmly in place with both her arms for a moment and then let go and tried diapering him again. He got the message after a number of repeats. Shauna's mother pinned her daughter momentarily to the floor with her legs.

Two-year-olds who vigorously resist diapering *may* be ready for toilet training.

TOILET TRAINING

GENERAL GUIDELINES

There is a tremendous range in both the age at which toilet training is started and the length of time it takes. We found no rule that held consistently. A girl may or may not be easier than a boy. A second child may or may not be faster than a firstborn. Bowel training may precede urine, or vice versa. Some children seem to be perfectly trained for a few months and then revert. Others will gradually train themselves over a long period of time. In our sample, only those children trained after age two trained rapidly (in less than a month), but later training did not necessarily guarantee quick results. There is no single time to begin and no single method to employ. Toilet training requires as much flexibility as patience from parents. To a large extent, children will each accomplish it at their own speed and in their own way. Our job as parents is to encourage, guide, and accommodate.

GETTING STARTED: TIMING, EQUIPMENT, AND CLOTHING

Many parents find that a good time to start toilet training is when youngsters first show an interest in it themselves. Summer is a good time to undertake the project, because clothes are minimal. Some families feel they *have* to begin because of pressure from friends or relatives or because a nursery school bars diaper-wearers. But if you really want to wait, you can almost always find a different nursery school or one that will make an exception. And there are certain circumstances in which waiting is the best decision. If a new baby is due soon, if you're moving, if you're too busy with other children, you will probably be better off postponing the toilet-training process until things settle down.

It's generally a good idea to get children familiar with the equipment before you begin. Many parents buy a potty chair when their young ones are between one and two years of age. Youngsters enjoy sitting on the potty both fully clothed and when naked at bathtime. Such familiarity creates a sense of ease. (An extra potty chair at the far end of a big house may increase opportunities for success.) Training seats make the large toilet feel more secure and yet allow the kids to use the same equipment as Mom and Dad. Spend some time teaching children how to flush the toilet: They will probably think it's fun and it will accustom them to the loud whooshing noise. A footstool helps little ones to get on and off the toilet and provides a footrest for added security while they're doing their business. Some youngsters feel safer if they sit backward so they can see the drain.

Training pants are the traditional apparel for toilet training, but there are other possibilities. When it's warm enough, you may want to let the kids run around in nothing at all, especially outdoors. One little boy who was ready for toilet training during the winter wore just socks and a jacket in the house. He stayed warm despite his bare bottom. When in the midst of toilet training, it helps to avoid overalls as pants are simpler, put girls in dresses, and skip underpants while they're wearing slacks. A few mothers choose to keep children in diapers until they are consistently dry, and some put plastic pants over training pants, to avoid drips.

THE THREE BASIC APPROACHES TO TOILET TRAINING

Parents choose from three basic approaches to toilet training: (1) Let children train themselves, (2) remind and catch, or (3) teach body awareness. We decide according to our beliefs about toilet training, the degree of our eagerness to be done with diapers, and the personalities of both our children and ourselves.

Letting Children Train Themselves

Easygoing parents who really aren't bothered by changing endless diapers may opt for the first approach. Because youngsters see others use the toilet, and gradually become aware of their own body sensations and products, they simply pull off their diapers and head for the toilet or ask for pants and manage them successfully henceforth, all on their own initiative. It's the simplest of the three methods and it minimizes struggles between parent and child. The disadvantage is that it frequently takes a long time. Occasionally toddlers as young as eighteen months will train themselves, but it is more likely to occur between the ages of two and one-half and three and one-half.

Reminding and Catching

In the remind-and-catch approach, parents observe the child's routine behavior and use it to estimate when to take the child to the toilet. Parents take full responsibility for initiating every trip to the toilet, for a period of months. This system has been termed "toilet training the parent," but it *can* decrease the number of diapers. It does, however, have two essential requirements: (1) Children must be willing and cooperative, because otherwise they can't "let go" until after they leave the potty and relax; (2) they must have predictable bowel movements or sufficiently developed bladder control to hold the urine for an hour or two. One mother caught her nine-month-old's BM's this way, and some ready-to-please eighteen-month-olds take readily to this system, but most two-year-olds are too self-determined to take such parental guidance kindly. A kitchen timer can help parents remember the next trek to the potty.

Teaching Body Awareness

Most parents use an alternative to the above approaches, namely, teaching body awareness and encouraging youngsters to respond to internal sensations. As with the remind-and-catch approach, the muscle at the bladder outlet must be sufficiently strong to hold back a full bladder. Furthermore, the child must be able to understand the process, convey needs, and exert conscious control over bladder and bowels. Some eighteen- and twenty-month-olds are ready to respond to this approach and many are not. With this method, children learn to initiate trips to the toilet because of parental encouragement to do so, not because of a personal decision to dispense with diapers.

Some families prefer gradual transitions and others choose to make them quickly. Heather, two and one-half, started wearing panties for an hour a day, and the time was gradually extended. Aaron, almost three, was given the choice of pants or diapers each morning, and gradually chose pants with increasing frequency. One mother describes how she made an intensive bout of toilet training fun:

> Having read Nathan Azrin's book *Toilet Training in Less than a Day,* I decided to train Alice, just two, during the week of my vacation. I explained and demonstrated the whole procedure, gave her lots of praise and rewards, including her favorite liquids so she'd have more opportunity to practice. We stayed home and did projects together, with the toilet nearby. By the end of the week she was trained, and we'd had a good time together.

HOW TO CONVEY OUR OBJECTIVES TO CHILDREN

If only our goals were as obvious to our children as they are to us! How, in fact, do parents convey what toilet training is all about?

Teach Vocabulary

Choose words you're comfortable with, but keep in mind the child's language ability. Embarrassed by the usual idioms, one family talked only of bowel movements, which their toddler quickly shortened to "bums."

Give Demonstrations

Most of today's youngsters see their parents or older siblings use the toilet, and they naturally want to imitate what they see their elders do. But the process can also be demonstrated with a doll that wets, or an older child who spends the weekend with an agreement to show off his or her potty prowess.

Let Children Experience Wet and Dry

Without plastic pants, wet diapers quickly become cold and uncomfortable, so youngsters may ask to be changed.

> On a family camping trip, I dressed Norman in light shorts so he could feel the pee running down his leg. He soon began stopping to take his shorts down instead.

Develop the Desire to Learn

> As soon as Kyle could understand, I prepared for future toilet training by building positive associations. Grandmother, Superman, and your friend Jeffie all pee and go poop in the toilet. Someday you'll be able to do that too.

Give Rewards

The most common and frustrating dilemma of toilet training stems from the fact that most youngsters are physically and intellectually able to use the bathroom long before they are *willing* to do so on a regular basis. Given that they all spent their first nine months in an amniotic hot tub, it's not surprising that so many of them *like* warm, wet diapers. Furthermore a portable potty pinned to one's bottom *is* wonderfully convenient: It avoids interrupting "Sesame Street" and sand castle construction. The challenge for us as parents is to find incentives that are worth more to our children than convenience.

Many children like company while sitting on the pot. Jenny will call in the family dog for bathroom companionship if everyone else is busy.

Anne loves to flush the toilet, so Mom requires that she urinate first. Peter likes to "make bubbles" in the toilet, which also encourages him to aim for the center. (Some days Dad adds a drop of liquid detergent for greater effect.) Pieces of toilet paper become targets to shoot at, and are even more fun if decorated beforehand with a crayon bull's-eye. An ice cube dropped into the toilet will shatter excitingly when deluged with warm urine.

Some parents offer treats such as bits of dried apricots for potty success, or stars on a chart. Ruffled pink panties, Super Hero Underoos, and a belt like Dad's have all provided sufficient incentive for self-training.

Ron, almost four and one-half years, had been urine-trained for two years, but no matter what we tried, he still had BM's in his diapers. Finally, an article in *Redbook* pointed out that he *was* trained; he had never had an accident; he had perfect control and *chose* to go in his diapers. I followed the article's recommendations, and they worked. I bought a bunch of small games and toys, wrapped them, and set them in a basket on the kitchen table. When Ron asked about them, I said, "Yes, you *could* have a surprise if you had your poops in the potty today, but there's no need to hurry." That day he tried every hour to have a BM in the pot, and within several days was doing so regularly. Once the routine was well established, we gradually tapered rewards to every fifth BM.

Punishment

Many parenting books advise ignoring undesired behavior and all condemn spanking and humiliation as punishment for toilet-training accidents. But some of us have gone to such lengths to avoid toileting disapproval that our little ones may not even know that we want them out of diapers. Thus there is a time and a place for "I don't like changing messy diapers."

Once youngsters are easily able to use the toilet, some parents set up consequences for repeated, careless accidents. Jamie, age two, has to help wipe up the puddles. Byron, age three and one-half, has to wear diapers (Mom puts his overalls on backward and pins them so he can't take them off). Rather than going outside with the big kids, Tina, two and one-half, has to stay inside if she wets her ''one'' pair of slacks. Sheila, age three, has to walk from the place of the accident to the toilet three times.

RESISTANCE TO TOILET TRAINING

For every toilet-training method, there is a child who will subvert it. When offered rewards, some children delight us by going in the pot in grown-up fashion while others confound us by learning to urinate every five minutes and demanding a goodie each time.

Occasional accidents are, of course, a routine part of learning. However, frequent accidents or refusal to go to the potty may reflect inability or resistance to training. Under such circumstances, it is generally better to pull back for awhile and minimize emotional strain while you contemplate a different course of action.

COMMON TOILET-TRAINING PROBLEMS

Understanding children's resistance is the key to discovering a more successful approach. Are they not yet ready physically or emotionally to respond to our expectations? Are they getting conflicting messages from two parents? Is the household under a lot of emotional strain? All these factors may operate in causing resistance to toilet training. How can we best deal with them?

Training for or by the Wrong Person

Many a toilet-training venture has started because Grandmother said it should be so. Frustration is inevitable as the child is caught between differing expectations of mother and grandmother.

Children are remarkable in their ability to pick up adult attitudes and conflicts. Parents who are inconsistent or unsure of their goals are much less apt to get cooperation from little ones than parents who are clear and straightforward.

Especially for three-year-old boys, father's participation may be crucial. One mother struggled with her son without success until Dad stepped in with encouragement, praise, and rewards.

Concerns about Flushing Toilets

Given our elation about successful performance, many children regard bowel movements as gifts to us, and therefore feel hurt when we flush them so unceremoniously. Parents may, therefore, wait until little ones leave the bathroom. In one family, however, everyone waves bye-bye to "Poopie going home through the tunnel," and another mother declares enthusiastically, "The toilet loves poop!"

Many children, watching their BM's disappear so mysteriously, fear they too will be gobbled up by the toilet. One mother in response to this fear, demonstrated that a kickball wouldn't flush, and another stuck her foot in the toilet to make the point.

Emotional Stress and Strain

More commonly in toilet training than in any other area of early child-rearing, parents sigh, "I'd do it differently if I had another chance." When faced with the odorous diapers of a youngster who can sort peas from carrots, name eighteen animals, climb a jungle gym, and put a puzzle together, we can't but think that this kid should be able to manage something as elementary as toilet training. But such is not necessarily so, and the detrimental effects of pushing too hard are many.

First, training may not work and family relationships can suffer. Despite our enthusiasm and praise, our carefully chosen presents, our cajoling or angry looks, the potty may go unused. Trying to make children do something our way when *they* have the ultimate sphincter control is the perfect setup for an escalating power struggle: entrenched resistance on their part and outraged helplessness on ours. One mother related with regret, "My six-year-old *still* wets her pants when she is angry at me."

Constipation is another common side-effect of toilet training when children are not ready. As soon as one mother saw her fourteen-month-old start to strain, she'd carry him to the potty: "He'd scream, hold it in, and inevitably develop an impaction." Fortunately, this mother was wise enough to set toilet training aside for the time being. The anus automatically clamps tight when we are under stress, so it is not sheer perversity but normal physiology that causes pressured children to go in their diapers *after* they get off the pot. Because hard, large, constipated stools are uncomfortable to pass, fear of pain increases resistance. (Constipation can also be caused by general emotional upsets, dietary changes, and other circumstances. Discuss such problems with your doctor.)

Another effect of high-pressure toilet training *may be* smaller bladder capacity and therefore more difficulty learning to stay dry at night. The normal bladder is a muscle with a lot of potential to stretch, a trick it learns by gradually holding increasing amounts of urine. The child who is forever taken or reminded to go to the toilet at frequent intervals or, worse yet, the child who is very fearful of having an accident is less likely to "hold on" often enough to maximize bladder capacity. (Unfortunately, relaxed toilet training does not assure a large bladder capacity and easy night training.)

As most of today's parents are aware, self-esteem and personality can be adversely affected by overly harsh toilet training. We are our bodies, so if things that come out of our bodies are bad and nasty, then we ourselves must be bad and nasty too. Children who are condemned for lacking control they don't yet have cannot feel positive about themselves. Thus it is that humiliation and shaming are inappropriate to the toilet-training repertoire. Realistically, more than one modern parent has given an instinctive swat of frustration when a resistant youngster lets loose on the new sofa. Such an event, if rare, doesn't cause lifelong trauma. What *is* damaging is *recurrent* or severe punishment.

Many youngsters lose their earlier control when a new baby arrives (or even beforehand), during or after a hospital stay, when the household routine is interrupted by visitors or travel, when parents experience intense emotional conflicts, and for similar reasons. Emotional stress may cause just an accident or two or may lead to weeks of regression. Parents who continue to apply pressure at such times often regret it. Backing off for a while is the most satisfactory strategy.

If, on the other hand, a child had been trained for some time and starts having accidents for no apparent reason, or if you are concerned because a preschooler is not making any progress toward training, discuss the matter with your doctor.

BM versus Baby

What grows big in your tummy and is pushed out when it is ready? Because young children live in the misty world between fact and fantasy, some of them confuse babies with bowel movements. Youngsters, both male and female, can wish to have a miraculous baby growing inside, and who would let something so precious plunk into the toilet? Youngsters in particular who are urine-trained but resist bowel training may be reacting to discussions about babies. Draw simple anatomy pictures and sympathize with the disappointment at not having a baby. Fortunately, fantasy helps escape the pain of reality, and many children get over this issue if you make a game out of it. It's more fun to carry dolls under one's shirt, and make them be born, than to hold on to plain old BM's.

Refusal to Wipe

Bobby, age four, was toilet trained, but didn't yet wipe himself. I hadn't pushed because he had always avoided messy things like finger paints and mud, even though they were often available. When he started nursery school the teacher was adamant that he ought to wipe himself both at home and at school. Informed of the new policy, Bobby stopped having BM's at school and instead had them in his pants at home. I felt trapped until I realized I had the freedom to backtrack. I told him I'd continue to wipe him if he needed it, and he stopped having "accidents." As for school, Bobby just never had BM's there, which eliminated the problem.

Intentionally "Doing It" in Inappropriate Places

This may not be so much a form of resistance as sheer curiosity. To the child who has just learned the joy and power of sphincter control, the pot soon seems quite dull compared with a flowerbed or the sandbox.

Some parents simply hide their smile and walk away when they see two three-year-old boys checking out who can hit the side of the house from varying distances. Some parents silently clean up the pile after the child is out of sight and find no reoccurrences. Others calmly clarify their instructions: "The potty, not the lawn." Some youngsters are required to help clean up, and one persistent little boy had to be removed several times from playing with his friends in the neighborhood sandbox.

BED-WETTING

What we want is clear enough: an end to diapers and wet beds. When to expect it is more problematic. A few youngsters stay dry at night as soon as they are daytime trained; for many more, night-time dryness just happens within eighteen months of toilet training. Most youngsters are daytime trained by age three and one-half, but fewer than two-thirds are dry at night at that age. By age five, 75 percent are dry at night. The problem generally disappears by age eight, when 94 percent are dry (as compared with 98 percent of the general adult population). However, if we wait until age eight and the problem still isn't resolved, we may wish we had worked on it sooner. Age five is often a promising time to undertake this task, given the general intellectual development, emotional equilibrium, and social awareness of children at this time of their lives. Bed-wetting, it should be pointed out, is twice as common among boys as among girls.

There's no point in expecting youngsters to stay dry when they're asleep at night if they can hardly stay dry while awake. Bed-wetting is much more complex than toilet training and may test parental ingenuity, patience, and forbearance to the limit. There's no fool-proof approach, but there are techniques that may be used singly or in combination. Here are a few that parents have used with success:

- Wake the child up to go to the bathroom before you go to bed yourself. Such an approach doesn't necessarily teach nighttime control, but it does avoid wet beds until children are old enough to learn how to get up by themselves. Some parents gradually wake youngsters, earlier and earlier, until they are making it all the way through the night.
- Regulate liquid intake in the evening hours.
- Keep a potty chair and night light near the child's bed if the bathroom is far away.
- Minimize *your* workload by making the bed with two sets of rubber mats and bottom sheets, so midnight changes are simple. Or buy large diapers and plastic pants from medical supply stores or Sears for use until youngsters are dry at night.

· Find out if bed-wetting is caused by allergy to certain foods. Milk, citrus, and eggs are common causes of allergy that *may* affect the bladder's capacity to hold urine.

In general, chronic bed-wetters don't hold as much urine in their bladder as do their dry peers. According to a study, "Nocturnal Enuresis: The Importance of Small Bladder Capacity" by Anne Zaleski in *Bladder Control and Enuresis* (Lippincott, 1973), four-year-old bed-wetters pass an average of one-fourth cup of urine at a time during the day; non–bed-wetters average twice as much. By age five, bed-wetters usually pass about one-third cup at a time, and non-bed-wetters about ⅔ cup. Fortunately, we *can* help little ones to increase bladder capacity. Encourage youngsters to drink lots of liquids, and to hold on as long as they can after feeling the first urge to go. Unless the bladder is completely full, the urge fades after about two minutes of holding back. With practice, youngsters can gradually wait longer and longer.

Children need lots of parental encouragement along the way, for even the smallest of gains. Some parents have their preschoolers urinate into a plastic measuring cup; then they post a chart in the bathroom to keep track of increases in volume. The sheer competitive joy of measuring out more urine than ever before provides incentive for some youngsters. Most do better with additional rewards.

Terry, age five, wasn't much interested in measuring bladder capacity until we told several of his friends we were doing a scientific study and wanted to know how much each of them could urinate. Terry was impressed that his friends could hold three times as much as he could. After just ten days of copious drinking and resisting the urge to go, he almost doubled his capacity.

Another mother tried a different approach. She drew a graph for her son, age five, to illustrate that bedwetting usually occurs during the total unconsciousness of the deepest phases of sleep. Then, as he settled into bed, she quietly repeated, "If you'll need to go to the bathroom soon, you'll get up and go *before* you go deeply to sleep again." Nightly repetitions of this suggestion brought gradual success.

Alternatively, some stores carry a buzzer system that sounds when the bed gets wet. Thus alerted, many children eventually gain control and get up instead.

REWARDS

When choosing rewards, keep in mind that learning to stay dry *automatically* is often a long, slow process. It is common for a preschooler to stay dry for several weeks to win a coveted pair of fancy pajamas, only to revert to bed-wetting once the incentive is gone. Therefore, choose rewards you'll be willing to repeat for a period of months, such as having a friend stay over on the weekend, visiting relatives overnight, or going out for lunch after a week or two of staying dry.

For some children, the reward of self-esteem is sufficient:

While Brent was four, I kept a rubber sheet over the mattress and did laundry every day; sometimes quietly and sometimes complaining loudly. One night after he turned five, he stayed dry all night. We rejoiced for days, telling him how excited we were that he was growing up. He told us that he didn't want to be wetting his bed when he started school. Once he realized he could actually do it, he made good progress.

PRESSURE AND PUNISHMENT

Intense pressure to stop bed-wetting can often backfire. Spanking, a common "remedy" in the past, is definitely *not* recommended. Many parents feel that if they had to do it again, they would exert less pressure and let the problem take care of itself, as it so frequently does. The natural consequence of bed-wetting is a cold, wet bed: this unpleasantness is enough by itself to get some youngsters to stay dry. Then of course there are those who don't notice! Some five-year olds dislike the required chore of remaking their own beds, and others *love* to run the washing machine.

Bed-wetting, like regression in toilet training, is sometimes a sign of emotional stress, and therefore a signal to pause and review what is happening in the child's life. Some families opt for family therapy when problems appear, and as family conflicts resolve, so does bed-wetting.

A very small percentage of bed-wetting is due to a medical problem. If the difficulty persists, discuss the matter with your doctor.

One mother, who realized that her daughter's bed-wetting was correlating directly with the illness-related emotional strain in the household, chose a positive and supportive approach. She reassured her daughter that she *would* outgrow the bed-wetting with time. At about age eight, she did.

DRESSING

CLOTHING AND DRESSING PROBLEMS

Many children surprise their parents with peculiar notions of what to wear (or not to wear). Winter coats and sweaters are shunned like the plague, while the same filthy pair of blue jeans is requested, or demanded, day after day. Some children prefer to go naked at all times, while others think nothing is more fun than putting on as many articles of clothing as possible.

Here's how parents have dealt with some common and stubborn clothing problems.

Refusing to Allow Dressing

Many youngsters act as though the clothing we offer were shackles. How does one dress a struggling, resistant youngster?

Lisa must either cooperate with dressing or wait in her crib for awhile. Brent is content getting his shoes on if he's strapped in his high chair with a snack at hand.

Eric's Mom found the straddle position, as illustrated, was the only way to get shoes on amid two-year old tantrums. If all else fails, it may be time to start helping youngsters get dressed by themselves.

Many a child is a stripper at heart and would simply prefer to go naked. Depending on the child's age and parent's comfort, such natural displays may be restricted to the house, the yard, or the beach.

Refusing to Self-Dress

There is a tremendous difference in the age at which children dress themselves. Refusing to get dressed may be a way of obtaining

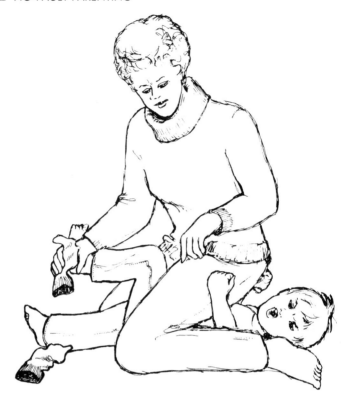

more of the direct physical care and contact that the child needs. Kier has younger twin brothers, so dressing time assured some precious time with Mom or Dad, and both willingly obliged. Some self-sufficient two-and-one-half-year-olds do most of the job themselves, while some four-year-olds receive help from parents. Most five-year-olds generally dress themselves, but may still need help with shoelaces, back zippers, tight snaps, and so forth, or when things are rushed.

Some youngsters are cunning enough that instead of refusing outright, they drive us to distraction by dawdling instead. If decision making is hard, and mornings are rushed, have children pick out the next day's clothes before they go to bed. Anya puts on all but a clean dress and shoes at bedtime, so in the groggy early morning there is little left to do. On cold mornings, Donald warms his underwear inside his bed covers before putting it on, and as soon as he's *all* dressed, he can go sit by the heater. Sharing the work can also help: Dad puts on the left shoe and Beth the other.

Jennifer's Mom gets her started on each successive item of clothing, then does her own hair, teeth, or makeup while the job is being completed. And on mornings when John's mother is really rushed, she saves time by dressing him herself.

Choosing and Changing Clothes

Some young descendants of Tom Sawyer would rather fight than switch to clean clothes. However, if there is someone in the family as inventive as Tom, a solution can often be found. Here are a few that seem to work:

> Rather than fight with Greg, age two, every day about putting on a clean shirt, I bought several more Superman shirts just like the one he loved. Thus equipped, he changed without a fuss.

> Rosalie, age four, resisted changing clothes, especially underpants. So I bought her a set with the days of the week on them. When I told her, "Today is Monday, and it says here that these are Monday's panties," she put them on without a fuss.

Can't give up a favorite shirt or dress? Choose a colorful iron-on design or embroidery patch to cover a stain that won't come out.

On the other hand, some youngsters enjoy changing clothes as much as building with blocks or doing puzzles. Parents of such children may choose to be firm in setting limits. Jennifer was restricted to two sets of clothes a day, so she could alternate back and forth.

And what about the child who chooses outrageous clothes? The day Susie triumphantly pops out of her boudoir in an orange dress with pink socks pulled over purple tights, we know our objectives are incompatible! We want her to dress herself *and* look well put together. How do we convey a sense of appropriate clothing to our youngsters? One mother talks about color combinations when she sorts the laundry with her three-year-old.

Compliments. I compliment Sean, age two, whenever he picks a good color combination: "Those pants and that shirt look nice together. The stripes in the shirt are the same color as the pants.''

Limited choices. One mother offers her two-year old a choice between one coordinated *set* of clothes and another. Another parent generally buys limited colors that automatically go together: His daughter likes pink and blue, his son brown and green.

Special occasions. Lee and Marie, age three and five, usually pick their outfits, outlandish or not. If I'm going to visit a friend, I may make a suggestion, but if they resist they can do it their way. For places that really matter to me, like Christmas dinner at Grandma's or a wedding, *I* pick the clothes. Because they get to decide the rest of the time, they don't object when I choose.

Refusing Warm Clothing

The decisions are all ours when we dress our *infants* for appropriate warmth. But once Beth and David can tug off their clothes, life is no longer so simple. Many children grow up believing a sweater is what you put on when your mother is cold. Children feel the cold less than we do, because physical activity produces tremendous amounts of body heat, and goodness knows they are more active than we are. How can we judge if our youngsters are warm enough and convey our concern to them?

Mom lets Lee, age two, go out without a jacket because she's discovered he'll come back and ask for one if he's cold. Dwayne can dispense with a jacket as long as he doesn't have goose pimples. Beth's mother installed a thermometer just outside the window, and *it* decides whether it's a jacket day.

Jason hates having his arms covered up, but he's willing to wear a quilted vest instead of a jacket. Shauna will wear a jacket if she doesn't have to have it zipped. Lisa objected to her bulky nylon jacket because she hated to carry it when she became warm. Her mother stitched an elastic belt near one pocket (for storage) so Shauna could carry her jacket around her waist.

MAKING IT EASIER TO GET DRESSED

Almost all one- and two-year-olds like *undressing* themselves, and many, but not all, two- and three-year-olds want to get dressed as well. Dressing is not just about clothing, but also about independence. Children have three main hurdles to contend with in learning to dress themselves.

1. Complexity of clothing. Children are as frustrated by the "simple" tasks of dressing as we are by trying to hook nursing bras single-handed, disengaging stuck zippers, and threading shoelaces after the ends come off. Fortunately we can teach them some basics about bundling up.
2. Adult expectations about proper dress. We don't merely want our youngsters dressed; we want clothes right side out, front to front, weather-appropriate, color-coordinated, socks to *match*. No wonder it's a struggle and many children give up in frustration. We all hate being criticized on our hard-won accomplishments. Thus, Sonya often wore her shirts inside out or backwards, until her Mom found an appropriate low-key time to teach her about seams, labels, and such.
3. Time pressure. Remember how difficult it was when we first shaved, put hair in rollers, threaded a needle, or used a saw? We never attempted such challenging tasks without *lots* of time. Yet our two- and three-year-olds are often learning to get dressed "right now," before eating breakfast, going to the park, or packing for nursery school. No wonder they feel overwhelmed!

Tips for Easier Dressing

- Big hole first is the way to put on all pants and shirts.
- Direction markers. Sew patch pockets on the front of pants. Or mark the inner front hem of skirts and waistband of pants with embroidery thread or laundry marker so the mark faces the child who is getting dressed.
- Easy closures. Front openings with large buttons, zippers, or toggles. Or avoid closures entirely, with slip-on clothes.
- Galoshes. To slip feet in more easily, slide them into a plastic bag first, or keep a piece of waxed paper in each boot.
- Jackets and coats. There are three easy ways to get them on: (1) Zip first, then slip the jacket on like a pullover shirt; (2) place the coat against the back of a chair, have the child sit in the chair and slip it on; and (3) lay the jacket out on the floor or bed; kneel in front of the neck; slip hands into sleeves; flip jacket over head. (See illustration.)

- Larger-than-necessary sizes are easier to put on.
- Shoelaces. If laces get pulled out of shoes, tie a knot after lacing the first pair of holes, or tie a tight single knot at the ends of each lace so they won't pull back through the holes. For easier tying, dye half of each lace with food color to demonstrate tying more easily. One father tells about a bunny who runs around a tree and ducks into a hole. To avoid tying, tie laces permanently just halfway up, or use elastic instead of shoelaces, so shoes slip on. Or, buy tennis shoes with Velcro or have a shoe repair shop stitch some Velcro on sandals to replace the buckles.
- Shoe tongues. Stitch out-of-place shoe tongues to one side of the shoe or put two slits through the top and lace them in place.
- Socks. Tube socks have no heel to misplace; put a laundry-marker dot on regular socks to go under the ball of the foot.

PROMOTING BODY CARE: OBJECTIVES AND STANDARDS

Before the children came along, our main concern with body hygiene was where to find a hair stylist we liked and could afford. We took nail cutting, tooth brushing, hand washing, and bathing for granted. But with youngsters, each of the above becomes a major issue. Though we all cringe at excessive grime, Americans very often go overboard in an obsession with cleanliness. Making children wash hands before every meal, brush teeth after every

meal, brush hair several times a day, bathe daily, and shampoo frequently can easily turn a parent into a full-time child scrubber. Many parents have made their own lives easier and the lives of their young ones happier by adjusting hygiene standards to suit the pressures and demands of busy schedules.

Jenni, age three months, gets a bath every two or three days. At two, Brian gets his bottom wiped with a washcloth each night, and a bath once a week. Gareth usually has a nightly bath, but on nights he doesn't want one, his parents don't push "unless he's tremendously dirty." Joseph's mom sprinkles a few soap flakes in the tub and lets him play; sometimes he gets all clean and sometimes he doesn't. (Some babies are prone to "cradle cap" unless they get a daily shampoo, and in hot weather, a few youngsters may feel skin irritations from accumulated sweat if baths are infrequent.)

Matthew, age three, stopped fighting shampoos when Mom let him do his own hair. She just passes supplies. Squeaky clean may not be worth a screaming match.

On the other hand, one difficulty of parenting is lack of support for pursuing appropriate goals. Our children think we are the only ones in the world who think hair and teeth should be brushed, so they pass our ideas off as rather strange. One mother, therefore, arranged with a family friend to comment on her four-year-old's appearance, and gave a high sign about whether teeth had been brushed. Her friend commented accordingly, "Your hair is nicely brushed today," or "Looks like the fuzzy germs are growing on your teeth." Susan became much more cooperative about body care.

The basic areas of child hygiene, with general discussion and specific helpful hints, follow.

BATHING AND WASHING

Traditionally a slippery, squirming infant is balanced against one hand and washed with the other. Not easy! No wonder so many parents and infants feel insecure about baths, and no wonder babies scream. Bath time *can* be made more secure, more fun, or at least less stressful.

To free both hands, strap the baby into an infant seat that you set in the bathtub. Or fill the tub with just an inch of water so the baby can lie on his back. For softness, baby can lie on a large molded bathsponge or a towel. The kitchen sink is often the most comfortable working height.

A number of parents in our sample bathe *with* their infants and small children. Infants can thus be supported securely from underneath and physical closeness in the strange bath environment is reassuring. For safety, be sure tubs or showers are adequately slip-proof and be especially cautious about getting in and out. If possible have one parent wash, and the other pass kids in and out.

Contrary to old wives' tales, water doesn't harm baby's ears unless there's an ear infection and, therefore, a possible ruptured ear drum. After all, those little ears have been soaking in amniotic fluid for nine months.

To make bath time more fun, add food coloring to the water, bubble bath plus an egg beater, "soap crayon" for drawing on the tub; check your local toy store for a multitude of other ideas.

Tips for Cleaning Ease

- Hang a low mirror so *youngsters* can see the grime.
- Choose a *soft* washcloth. Some youngsters prefer a sponge on their tender skin.
- It's more fun to be washed by a puppet than a parent: Make one by sewing a pair of washcloths together around three sides.
- Put a step stool by the bathroom sink so youngsters can wash "by self!"
- Bring home mini bars of soap from motels—they're easier for little people to hold; or tie soap ends in an outgrown sock.
- Dad and Chris wash each *other's* hands before dinner. Use dark towels so you don't notice what comes off in wiping rather than washing.
- Let siblings keep each other company in the bathtub, once they're old enough. They have more fun and you do two at once.
- If evening baths are a struggle, try earlier in the day.
- Put Dad in charge of bath time. Instead of a boring bath, it's special time with father.
- Get washing over quickly, then let youngsters play.
- Tell youngsters how clean they look and how fresh they smell after a wash or a bath.

Fear of Baths

Sometimes we never know why children come to dread the bath. At other times it's obvious because they've been hurt by hot water, soap, or a fall in the tub. A few youngsters are afraid of whooshing down the drain. Whatever approach you try, patience is the main ingredient.

Stefanie, age one, stuck her hand under the hot water faucet while I was fixing her bath. It took months to overcome her fear. She was afraid of all running water anywhere. For several weeks, I gave her sponge baths in her bedroom. Then I sat beside the empty bathroom sink and held her on my lap to play. Several days later I filled the sink first, then held her. The next step was to let the cold faucet drip while I brought her in to play. Eventually she was splashing in the sink and filling cups from the faucet. We went through the same procedure with the bathtub, starting with holding her in the empty tub to play with her toys. After a long three months, she was enjoying her bath again.

HAIR: WASHING, CUTTING, AND BRUSHING

With fear of both water and shampoo to contend with, no wonder hair washing is a struggle. One mother reported, "Hair washing is a two-person ordeal. I only do it when my husband is on hand to help." But for those who have to do it alone, here are some tips to ease the strain.

- Use a "no-sting" shampoo. Also, a strip of vaseline around the forehead or a dry washcloth that the child holds in place helps keep water out of eyes, as do swim goggles or a plastic "hair washing halo" available in some children's supply stores.
- Rinsing hair may be easier with a water sprayer attached to the bathtub faucet. With just an inch or so of water in the tub, youngsters can comfortably lie on their backs for rinsing. Some preschoolers prefer to rinse on their own, in the shower or by "swimming" through a full tub.
- More body contact can help. Have youngsters lie on their backs on the kitchen counter for a simultaneous hug, or climb in the tub with them for more support.
- A time limit makes it easier for youngsters to endure the ordeal. Judy's mom brushes until she finishes singing "Baa Baa Black Sheep," and Tim fills the jug ten times for Dad to rinse his hair. Tim learned to count that way.
- If the child is really frightened, skip hair washing for a few weeks, then rinse off tiny dabs of shampoo with a wash cloth.

Some children find the very *idea* of a haircut frightening, while others submit placidly. One family talks about *trimming* hair, rather than cutting it. Distraction often proves helpful for a restless youngster. Stock up on favorite foods, have books or family photo albums on hand, or turn on the tape recorder or television. One youngster is permitted to watch cartoons *only* during haircuts. One mother cleverly turned haircuts into a reward: "Instead of taking your nap today, you can stay up with me and get a haircut." William, two and one-half, gets his hair cut outside so he can wander around when he needs a break. Steven, also two and one-half, has sittings on three consecutive days.

When choosing a barber, try to get recommendations from friends with children. Some barbers just seem to have a way with little ones. On the other hand, children who are put off by a visit to the barber may be more willing thereafter to put up with haircuts at home. If you're doing it yourself, use blunt-tipped scissors so you won't poke the child while cutting hair. A diving mask or a Halloween mask will hold hair off faces while you trim bangs and may amuse the reluctant "victim" of your ministrations.

A few words of advice about hair brushing: Short hair is easier to care for than long hair; it doesn't tangle as much and it's quicker to brush. Minimize snarls by using a cream rinse. For occasional bad tangles, cut *parallel* to the hair, rather than across it, as shown in the illustration. Good old-fashioned braids save loads of morning time *if* you braid the night before.

CUTTING FINGER NAILS

It's frightening to cut a newborn's nails, but we have to do it anyway. Best time is when baby is sleeping deeply or sucking on breast or bottle.

TOOTH BRUSHING

In bygone days, diseased teeth were yanked out, and if all were gone in twenty-five years it didn't matter because death was probably just around the corner. Our modern hope that teeth will last near a century comes with a price tag: more complicated and time-consuming care.

With the best of intentions, dentists remind us to rinse after every snack; brush after every meal once teeth come in; and floss daily

once teeth are close together. Someone has to point toward the ideal, but we found almost no parents who met today's high standards for children's dental care. Many started later than recommended, were baffled by the complexity of flossing someone else's teeth, and felt unable to make the necessary time commitment. As in so many areas of child care, compromises will be worked out to suit the needs of parents and children.

Especially while children are too young to manage a brush effectively by themselves, parents are likely to brush once a day. The evening brushing is most important because it removes food before the long night.

Once youngsters are brushing pretty well by themselves, twice a day is easier to manage.

We didn't meet any parents who got their children to brush three times a day, but some encouraged rinsing with water after lunch, and a few after snacks as well. This habit is more likely to be carried off to school and on visits to friends than is midday brushing.

Though baby's toothy smile generally appears between six and eight months, youngsters may be six or eight *years* old before they are physically coordinated and persistent enough to clean all surfaces of their teeth thoroughly. To ensure adequate teeth cleaning,

First Dental Checkup

Today's pediatric dentists advise the first checkup between eighteen and twenty-four months. Such an early visit avoids the possible chaos of introducing two-year-olds to the dental office. If one waits until three, there's a chance children will already have cavities. Some children are physiologically more cavity prone than others.

parents often let children start by themselves and then finish up for them. Rosalie, age two and one-half, brushes her front teeth, then Mom does her back ones. Alex, age four, cleans his teeth both morning and evening, but Mom brushes after him at night. Once or twice a week, Mom brushes after Roma, age five. Brushing youngsters' teeth may be easier if you stand *behind* them, or have them lie down. Be careful that children don't swallow excessive amounts of fluoride toothpaste, as it can cause mottling of teeth.

Tips for Toothbrushing

- Baby's first new teeth may be easier to clean with a piece of gauze than with a brush.
- Post pictures in the bathroom of shiny, cared-for teeth, and unhappy dirty ones.
- Use brushing time for dental education: Review which of the day's foods have been good, and which not so good, for teeth.
- Ask your dentist about "diclosing tablets" so youngsters can see what areas need more thorough brushing.
- Strongly minted toothpaste may taste painfully "hot" to children. Try a different brand, use less, dispense with it entirely, or use mouthwash instead.
- Flossing may be easier with a dental-floss holder. Ask your dentist.
- Make brushing a family ritual that everyone does together.
- Have Mom read a story while Dad brushes the youngster's teeth.
- Brush right after dinner instead of at bedtime when little ones are tired.

- Use a three-minute egg timer to measure adequate brushing time.
- If Junior keeps dropping toothbrushes down the drain, keep a long wire, hooked at the end, in the bathroom.

Reward and Punishment

The struggle to get teeth brushed regularly lasts well into elementary school. With young children, brushing often precedes story time, so the story provides ample reward. Later, stars might be earned for brushing without protest. In addition, punishment might be restriction to the bathroom until the job is done. As youngsters approach age six, some are impressed to learn that a judgmental tooth fairy pays more for good-quality teeth. And some youngsters this age are required to pay a token sum if fillings are required.

SEXUALITY

Questions relating to sexuality are often first raised when we are washing naked little bodies or, alternatively, when our youngsters observe us in the bathroom. Adult-style sex is not part of a child's life, but modern psychological theory suggests that sexuality is. By sexuality we mean the general awareness that bodies feel pleasure and the awareness of the desire for physical as well as emotional closeness to others. With time, sexuality also brings the realization that we are constructed differently from half the people in the world, and beginning around age two, it is common awareness that the genital regions provide more intense physical pleasure than other parts of the body.

Parents used to teach that sexuality was evil by ignoring the body's sexual apparatus and suppressing their children's natural pleasure in curiosity and genital exploration. Shame and guilt were encouraged. Most of today's parents, on the other hand, accept curiosity as natural, and foster a healthy acceptance of bodies as a whole, including inherent sexuality. We therefore give our children the freedom to explore, the vocabulary to talk, and the openness to ask about bodies. However, acceptance of sexuality does not mean acceptance of all sexual activity. We don't want our four-year-olds obviously masturbating in public or inviting more sexual intimacy than their emotional maturity can handle. To the best of our ability, we want to keep the way clear for the child's future growth into fulfilling adult sexuality.

MASTURBATION

We are fortunate to live in an enlightened era when the pleasure of masturbation is generally accepted as a normal biologic function, rather than an innate evil. In general, toddlers no longer get their hands slapped for exploration; and emerging teens no longer face humiliating confessions in church or threats of acne, impotence, and insanity for masturbation. Our culture has also progressed in realizing that both males and females are sexual beings, and thus it is no surprise that while Davie, age two, thrusts his hands inside his pants, Natalie, age two, wiggles against the teddy bear she places between her thighs.

Some youngsters are so discreet about masturbating that parents never see them do it. Others are more carefree. Observing Nick's hand clutched to his groin while they were shopping, Mom asked unobtrusively, "Do you need to go to the bathroom?" Nick, age three, replied brightly for all to hear, "No, I'm just holding my pecker." Masturbation may be acceptable, but that doesn't make it simple. How in fact do today's parents handle masturbation?

Ignore. I don't pay any attention when Lydia, age two, touches herself, unless she has something in her hand that could hurt her.

Distract. When Tony, age ten months, plays with his penis in the bathtub, I give him a toy. Chris, age four, masturbates more when he's bored, so I get him started on a project.

Acknowledge. When I come upon one of the kids masturbating contentedly, I say, "That feels good, doesn't it?"

Adult behavior. We tell Ricky that if he wants to masturbate, he's to do it in his bedroom, because that's where big people do it.

Therapy. Ted, age four, began masturbating more, and in preference to playing with friends and toys. When he was taken to a therapist, it gradually became apparent that he was worried about the increasing conflict between his parents. Several months later, his parents separated, and the therapist continued to work with Ted during the difficult months of adjustment. Once the emotional tension settled, Ted spent less time masturbating.

Naming and Understanding Body Parts

There are two schools of thought about teaching children the names of body parts. Given children's lack of social *savoir-faire* and adults' susceptibility to acute embarrassment, some families prefer to use nicknames rather than risk youngsters' asking the boss, the grandparents, and the gas station attendant whether they have a penis or a clitoris.

On the other hand, there are those who believe it's important to be as direct and casual about sexual apparatus as about fingers and toes. They call a penis "a penis." Interestingly, many such parents avoid the analogous term "clitoris." A few use "vulva" or "labia," but most refer instead to the unseen "vagina." Lest little girls feel slighted by their less showy equipment for aiming urine, it's important that they know about the uterus, that "little bag in which a baby can grow."

Four-year-olds can understand that different words are appropriate for different social situations, though they won't necessarily abide by the usual social conventions.

Understanding Different Bodies

Watching small children cope with the complexities of male and female bodies can be both amusing and painful.

Sara, eighteen months, stares at her vulva, obviously looking for the penis she expects to match her brother's.

Beverly, eighteen months, insists her Daddy's penis is a tail. When Ellen, age two, insists she's a boy and has a penis, her parents say she has a clitoris-penis and let the topic drop. When informed that her Daddy didn't have a clitoris, she suggested he go to the store and buy one.

Kara, age two and one-half, announced defiantly that *she* would grow up to have a uterus *and* a penis. Noting her sudden sadness,

Mom asked, "Do you wish you had a penis now?" Further questioning revealed that Kara assumed she used to have one that had been cut off. Asked who would do such a terrible thing, she replied with heart-rending resignation, "Probably you." It was time to explain that babies come in two different styles!

Little boys, suddenly noticing that a playmate lacks a penis, have been known to wonder, "Will I lose mine too?" The difference between circumcised and uncircumcised boys also calls for delicacy. If people cut off the ends of penises, what all is in the cards for me, and when? A two-year-old may best be answered with partial truth: "Some boys have one kind and some another." A four-year-old might need to know that the skin is only "trimmed on a *new* baby."

The best approach in dealing with children who are confused or concerned about anatomy is reassurance that bodies are different from birth, that nothing will get lopped off in the future, and that we love them just as they are.

Playing Doctor

Fortunately the days are past when playmates were banished for the crime of sexual curiosity. However, some parents still fear that allowing preschoolers the freedom to explore will lead to teenage pregnancy, homosexuality, excessive interest in sex, or an overly casual attitude toward relationships. Such is not the case. Preschoolers check out each other's similarities and differences from sheer curiosity. The intense adult need for sexual satisfaction and release does not yet exist; we can save that worry for later.

When two four-year-olds, undressed and peering at each other with flashlights, dive for cover when we open the closet door, one reaction is to ignore it. One mother gulped back her surprise and said as calmly as she could, "It's time to get dressed and play in the playroom." Another acknowledged the situation, saying, "I see you want to know what each other looks like" before she left.

Answering Awkward Questions

Ryan, age three, has normal curiosity. He and his friends, both male and female, love to go to the bathroom together, and he's noted the difference between Mommy and Daddy as well. We discuss his findings and questions in a simple, mat-ter-of-fact way—at least we try.

One of the great challenges of parenthood is to think up simple, informative answers, in three seconds or less, on the most tender of topics. If youngsters want more than a one-sentence answer, they'll ask another question, as long as the first was comfortably answered. Books and anatomically correct dolls can help parents explain sex differences. How do parents answer when confronted with "What's this?"

> *Birth control pills.* Pills that I take because we don't want to have another baby. [To Aaron, age two.]
> *Condoms.* A cover that goes over Daddy's penis because we don't want to have another baby. [To David, age three.]
> *Sanitary napkins.* They are part of a lady's underwear. [To Justin, age three.]
> *Menstrual blood.* [Not wanting to alarm her daughter Alice, age three, by talking about blood when questioned about the bright red color on the sanitary napkin, Mother replied] It is food that would be there for a baby if one were growing in my uterus.
> *Sanitary napkin dispenser in a public restroom.* A place to buy cotton pads. [To Lisa, age four.] I'll tell you when we get home. [To Diana, age five. Mother later explained:] Every month extra blood stays in a woman's uterus in case a baby needs it to grow. If there isn't a baby, the blood comes out. The cotton pads keep the blood from spilling on clothes. It doesn't hurt when the blood comes out.

Child and Adult

Many of today's parents are relaxed about their own bodies and automatically convey acceptance to their offspring. Youngsters may sleep part-time in the parental bed and see their parents nude while bathing and dressing. Preschoolers are as curious about different bodies as about different breakfast cereals, and fortunately neither bathing with their peers nor touching each other causes unwanted pregnancy.

Although we casually handle exploits among preschool friends, we are naive to mistake our youngsters for sexual innocents. Some children engage in provocative sexual behavior that can become difficult, to say nothing of dangerous, when directed toward adults or teenagers who allow it to continue or progress. One little girl, age four, welcomed each father to the nursery school picnic with a stroke on the penis. A snuggly three-year-old liked to sit on Daddy's lap and caress his penis. A theatrical five-year-old, announcing he was Dracula, became suddenly intent on ripping off Mom's blouse.

In cultures where everyone is bare, nudity is no more arousing than a naked forearm is to us. But when everyone else is dressed, children may respond more strongly to beloved relatives in the buff, especially if nude adults provoke sexual feelings through their behavior. In *The Flight of the Stork,* (Dell, 1980), Anne Bernstein focuses the issue this way: "Seductiveness, not nudity, is what overstimulates children. Parents can be seductive without being nude, and nude without being seductive."

Most important, as responsible parents we need to be aware of what either we *or our children* perceive as arousing behavior on our part. Most parents sense a need for more discretion in the presence of opposite-sex children beginning between the ages of two and one-half and seven. Some parents may back off because of the child's sexual forwardness, or in response to the child's newfound interest in privacy. Some parents intuitively sense that it is time to become more discreet, and others conclude intellectually that children should now be acknowledged as responsive sexual beings. If we don't accept both our young children's growing sexual awareness and their limited capacity to handle sexual exposure and stimulation, they may develop signs of emotional overload such as recurrent sleep disturbances, clinginess, bed-wetting, or masturbation to the exclusion of other activities. Similar symptoms can arise from a variety of emotional problems. Somewhere between the extremes of prudery and provocation there is an appropriate path to follow through the changing stages of children's development.

In these two examples, parents were sensitive to potential problems and acted to avert them:

Mother and Son. I'd started bathing with my infant son for sheer convenience, and we continued to enjoy the closeness of a shared bath. But one day, when he was almost three, I was startled by the realization that he was rhythmically thrusting his erect penis into my belly button. I hardly knew whether to laugh or cry. The innocent pleasure ended for me. I finished up the bath as casually as I could, knowing that life had pushed us forward on a path we couldn't retrace. It was our last bath together.

Brother and Sister. As my youngsters approached ages five and seven, I became uncomfortable with their regular baths together. I told Elise that when she turned six, she would be old enough to bathe by herself. I gave her some fragrant pink bath oil for her birthday, which I knew her brother wouldn't want to share. It was an easy, comfortable transition.

Youngsters are at the mercy of both their own needs and those of the adults around them. Boisterous two-year-olds may fill their need for attention by pouring paint or kicking the baby. Older, more sophisticated children *may* seek attention through sexual advances. Adults whose own lives are emotionally satisfying are able to set appropriate limits on such invitations. One parent gave a gentle, firm ''No,'' another father picked up and held his daughter's inappropriately wandering hand, and still another announced it was time to play a game of cards together.

Unfortunately, a few adolescents and adults who lack appropriately fulfilling relationships press their needs for emotional closeness on children. Such encounters generally revolve around touching of genitals. Children are often afraid to speak up because they have been threatened not to tell, or because at the time they enjoyed or felt frightened by the intensity of such special attention. They frequently report the situation obliquely: by expressing a sudden dislike or fear of a particular acquaintance, relative, or baby-sitter; commenting on offensive body odors, or strange underwear; or— in the case of one little girl—fearfully declaring, ''Lollipops are yucky.'' Some adults who genuinely care for the child take apparent receptiveness at face value, without realizing that even ''pleasant'' relationships can lead to deep conflicts that may surface only years later, with the approach of sexual maturity.

Regardless of the circumstances, children assume *they* are at fault. Intense, frightened reactions and questions from parents can increase the child's sense of guilt. On the other hand, parents who pass off such accounts as "sheer fantasy" may well be leaving their youngsters on their own to cope with very difficult situations. If you are concerned that your child *may* be sexually involved with an older person, talk with your child's doctor or a mental health professional for information on how to proceed. Appropriate counseling can usually help both the children and the adults involved.*

---

*For additional information see The Study Group of New York, *Children and Sex. The Parents Speak* (New York: Facts on File, 1983).

4

Housework

W e expect to have additional work once a baby arrives, but we don't expect that all the *routine* chores will take longer than ever before. The vacuum cleaner wakes up two-month-old Susanna; Eric, nine months, pulls over the bucket of water for mopping the kitchen floor; Jessica, age two, unpacks the cupboard as fast as we put away the groceries; and David, age five, cuts his finger while dinner preparation is under way. On top of all this, there's a load of dirty diapers in the hamper, spit-up on Daddy's business suit, crayon marks on the wall, muddy footprints in the hall, and toys crowded on the floor of every room. Because we aren't granted an extra four hours in every day for each new baby, something has to go: Usually it's our housekeeping standards or our sleep.

Because we *expect* to do everything for our helpless infants, we often cater to them willingly. But once Alisha can stack a set of nesting cups, express herself with a paintbrush, and make a bed for her dolly, we begin to wonder why she can't set toys back on the shelf, use a sponge to wipe up orange juice, and drop her clothes in the hamper. Why is she so much more willing to make the doll's bed than her own? Is it worth the effort to teach and persuade her to help?

While our toddlers want to copy our every move, our preschoolers scorn the routine of housework for the excitement of making a new Lego truck or putting together another puzzle. Yet when they return from nursery school and kindergarten announcing proudly that they baked pretzels, cleaned the blackboard, matched the colored squares, were allowed to use the broom, and joined in the school litter cleanup, we may wonder why *we* still butter all the toast, clean all the doorjambs, sort all the colored socks, man the broom alone, and pick up all the gum wrappers. How long, a small inner voice asks, will we be their servants?

HOW PARENTS GET
THEIR HOUSEWORK DONE

DECIDING HOW MUCH TO DO

Only parents know how difficult housework becomes with children around. One mother found it impossible to explain to a childless therapist (who thought she was overconcerned with housework) that her bathroom became a disaster in two minutes when her two-year-old washed up after chocolate pudding. We not only work harder at housework, but also drop our standards to the point where our self-esteem becomes precarious.

Given the amount of time required by child care, we must of necessity simplify our menus and skimp on housecleaning. One mother rephrased President Lincoln's statement about fooling people: "You can keep all of the house clean some of the time, and some of the house clean all of the time, but you can't keep all the house clean all of the time." With a newborn, a sick child, or a flock of little ones to tend, we may not be able to keep *any* of the house clean for a time.

To clarify objectives regarding housework, it helps to think of degrees of cleanliness. We must balance the desire for neatness against the time and effort required to get the work done. Rather than trying to keep the whole house sparkling and clutter-free all the time, parents generally think in terms of particular rooms (living rooom? kitchen? play area?) being cleaned at particular times, such as once or twice a day, once a week, before company, or whenever.

If we merely change what we *do*, without changing our attitudes about what we *should* do, we are bound to feel guilty about the remaining housework. Parents who make the transition comfortably review their priorities consciously and conclude that housework isn't as important as having time and energy to love a priceless child. They understand that regular gourmet meals are as out of place on a busy parent's menu as on an Arctic expedition.

> *Educational clutter.* I was a perfect housekeeper before Timmy started playing on the floor. After weeks of feeling guilty about the clutter, I finally realized that he'd never learn to nest cups if he could only play with one at a time! It was hard for me to accept that he needs clutter in order to learn, but that realization helped me overcome my compulsive cleanliness.

> *Personal life.* I get most upset about the clutter in the house when I've let things go in my own life and I start to feel overwhelmed.

> *Babysitter's lesson.* I was really annoyed to return home one day and find the new sitter had left the house in the same shambles it was in before I left. Instead of cleaning up, she was having a wonderful time with Andy. Suddenly I felt jeal-

ous, and promised myself some "babysitting" time each day when I, too, would turn off the demands of housework.

Cleaning day. After I chose just one day a week for housecleaning, my internal struggle ended. Every day except Tuesday, I'd say, "This is *not* my day for housecleaning." If the baby was ill and fussy on cleaning day, the work had to wait until the following Tuesday. Having a *rule* made it possible for me to let go. Once Benjii was crawling, and putting things in his mouth, I did have to keep the floor reasonably clean.

DECIDING WHEN TO DO IT

The decision about when to do our housework will be affected by tolerance for interruptions, whether we work best in the morning or at night, whether in long stretches or short bursts, whether alone or with other adults around. These factors will also influence our basic approach to getting the housework done. Most parents use one of three models:

1. Do whatever job is most pressing. Tackle the piles of essential laundry before cleaning the stove. The rationale for this approach is: Why plan ahead when everything is bound to change and will have to be planned all over again?
2. Plan and accomplish chores in a specific order. One mother usually keeps to this routine: She washes breakfast dishes first, so the kitchen looks orderly; then she makes the beds (children's moods permitting). She showers and dresses last because she *knows* she'll tend to those before leaving home.
3. Plan to do chores at regular intervals; for example, Tuesday clean the bathroom, Wednesday mop the kitchen, Thursday vacuum. Once the appointed task is done, it's easier to ignore the remainder of the mess.

Before they have children, many parents promise they will never use precious nap time for such unfulfilling tasks as housework. They don't yet realize how long it takes to vacuum with Jeremy clinging to their ankles, or to load the washing machine after Priscilla has dumped all the detergent on the floor. Thus many parents take careful note of what chores are particularly difficult while children are awake, such as mopping or mending, and use nap time only for those. That way they still have some time to themselves.

HOW TO GET WORK DONE
WITH YOUNGSTERS AROUND

Because children are more content when close to parents, work may be done more quickly by keeping youngsters close. If children spend their early years watching and copying us in the kitchen, they may be a real help by the time they're four or five. But when we're rushed, or when we must perform a task that requires concentration and skill, children are often a nuisance. Safety is also an important factor in many household chores. For these reasons, little ones are often restricted from the immediate work area or confined nearby.

Infant seats, a Jolly Jumper, a bassinet on wheels, or a walker will all keep the little one out of your way while working but allow conversation and intermittent eye contact. Many parents these days cook dinner, vacuum, and mow lawns with babies riding in a backpack. Alternatively, one father installed a sturdy hook by the kitchen table to hold up baby and backpack while he cooked.

Toddlers in a high chair or playpen can eat or play with toys while we iron, garden, or sew. One mother puts her daughter in a wheeled play table and pulls her from room to room while she cleans. Another puts her son in his crib for brief periods when there are hazardous chores to be done.

Dinner preparation provides a special challenge, given worn-out youngsters, hot stoves, and preparing the most substantial meal of the day. Some parents put a baby gate at the kitchen doorway. Others feed youngsters a finger-food dinner while cooking for the rest of the family. Mothers may prepare dinner in the early morning or during late-afternoon ''Sesame Street.'' Try storing some emergency meals in the freezer for days when youngsters are especially fussy. In many households, Dad does some or all of the evening cooking.

If youngsters are buzzing around the kitchen while you work, entertainment is a great help. Reserve a bottom drawer for plastic kitchenware, old spools, and other such ''toys.'' Attach an unbreakable mirror or a felt board to low cupboards or paint the doors with chalkboard paint. If you're tired of picking magnetic letters off the kitchen floor, tie a water-soluble marker to the refrigerator door handle and tape up a large sheet of paper. Supply youngsters with an egg beater to whip soap bubbles in the sink and an extra set of measuring cups and spoons. Reserve Play-Dough for use in the kitchen when you are cooking. Set up a play-kitchen within talking distance, or let youngsters close their eyes and guess what ingredients you are using.

To keep youngsters busy while you clean, hide toys for them to find. Or ask them about what you are doing. "Am I dusting the top shelf or the bottom one? Am I sweeping fast or slow? near the chair or far?"

Two-year-olds usually want to do whatever we do, so it's often helpful to let them have first go at whatever equipment we're about to use. But they are also pleased with parallel play as long as it *looks* as though their job is similar to our own.

When cleaning floors, let Melissa play with the vacuum cleaner for a few minutes before you start, and supply her with a small broom of her own. One mother puts her little boy in swim trunks, gives him a bucket with an inch of water, and lets him "mop" before she starts the kitchen floor. Another mother decks her youngster in a plastic apron and seats him in his high chair with a bowl of water to splash in. Not only is he out of her way, but by the time she reaches his corner, the spilled water has loosened the dried food below his chair.

While Mom cleans the bathroom, two-year-olds may stack plastic bandages back in the box, weigh things on the bathroom scale, or "spray" the bathtub with a spray bottle of *plain* water.

While Mom or Dad is putting away groceries, youngsters enjoy being asked what foods they like and where they belong. Let them trace around cans and boxes to make designs on shopping bags. Tape old labels on low shelves so youngsters can put things away by matching pictures.

If you have mending to do, let youngsters string macaroni or cut up straws. Some youngsters use giant plastic darning needles and burlap so they can embroider with yarn, or sew on giant buttons that Mom cut from an old Clorox® bottle. Willie, age three, pins scraps of cloth together with safety pins, and Miranda, age five, makes herself a play skirt by stapling the seams.

Some household chores can be eased by planning ahead. Put a high chair in the shower for a few minutes to loosen the goo. Turn on the stereo and gradually increase the volume if the sudden noise of the vacuum cleaner will wake a sleeping child. Teach preschoolers to remove their clothes without turning them inside out, so laundry folding takes less time. Keep mending supplies in a handy basket that you can carry when you visit friends or attend a discussion group.

Then there are the special cleaning chores parents are bound to encounter at one time or another. Crayon comes off nonporous surfaces with a dry, chemical-stick suede cleaner available at shoe stores, or wax-removing furniture polish. Permanent-pen marks can be safely removed from certain surfaces with nail polish remover. And gum can be cooled down with ice or slicked up with cooking oil to make removal easier.

In addition to all the above, consider getting help. More and more fathers are pitching in: Many wash dishes while Mom bathes the kids. Arrange a work exchange with a friend: Cook and clean together so one can tend to youngsters as needed and the job isn't so lonely. And consider hiring help. If you can't afford a full or part-time housekeeper, hire a teenager to clean once a week, or even an elementary schooler for a nominal fee, to play with your preschoolers while you fix dinner. One mother hires a cook one afternoon a week to prepare a week's worth of entrées.

Through a senior citizen's center, one mother found a wonderful grandmother who comes twice a week for a small fee. Mom can cook and clean in peace, then steps out alone to shop for *both* herself and "Grandma."

HOW TO PREVENT UNNECESSARY MESS

No parent has any idea of all the ways to create a mess until children begin their endless demonstrations. Fortunately, minutes of preparation can often prevent hours of cleanup. Here are some ways that parents have developed to keep homes and clothes cleaner:

Eating and Diaper-Changing Areas

·. Put a plastic tablecloth, piece of vinyl, leftover piece of linoleum, or plastic floor mat (for use under rolling office chairs) under the baby's high chair. It will be a lot easier to wipe off or toss in the washing machine than your wall-to-wall carpet. When the child moves to the dining room table, put the protective mat under the chair. Similar protection can be used under the changing table.

- Attach a roll of paper towels to the back of the high chair and changing table for instant use.
- Provide trays if children are allowed to snack on the carpet in front of the TV.

Drawers, Cupboards, and Shelves

- Childproof them so they won't be continually dumped or else attach a bell to the handles so you'll know what's about to happen.
- Move all the books off the lower shelves of your bookcase, or wedge the books in very tightly.

Toilet and Toilet Paper

- Avoid water play in the toilet by keeping the bathroom door closed, or a baby gate across the doorway.
- Position the paper so it rolls off the back of the roll. Toddlers generally spin the roll down in front, which will roll the paper up. Or put a large stiff letter clip on it.

Aprons for Painting and Pastry Making

- An adult T-shirt makes a complete cover-up for a child.
- Some youngsters want aprons they can put on by themselves. Start with a hand towel and sew on a tape to slip over the head. Sew a tie on each side, and attach a clothespin to the end of each tie, so the child can pass it behind her back and clip it to the opposite side.
- Save a set of old clothes for messy projects.

Artwork

- To keep counter tops clear, set aside a folder or box for all those works of art from home and school until there's time to hang some up.
- Put toddlers in their high chairs with crayons so they *can't* write on the walls.
- Cut a hole in the center of a sponge and insert the container

of paint or glue. The sponge keeps the container from tipping and absorbs drips.

· Use a plastic placemat or an ample piece of vinyl to cover the table or floor for projects with paint or glue.
· Let children fingerpaint on the tiles above the bathtub.

Mud

· If youngsters are muddy, give them a bucket of *warm* water and a sponge rather than a cold hose, so they will wash more thoroughly. Remove faucet handle from the outside water spigot (if available) and tie it to a high nail with a piece of elastic so adults can maintain control.

HOUSEHOLD RULES AND RESTRICTIONS

Limits on what, when, and where activities are allowed will reduce the amount of mess. Initially, such restrictions are made by and for parents. "I don't want to fish for rattles in the applesauce, or scrub graham crackers from the crib bumpers, so Elsie sleeps in her crib and eats in her high chair."

Once children start walking, they become involved too. Children may learn the necessary rules more easily if we state both the general concept and the specific limitation, such as "Food doesn't go in the living room, so eat your cracker here in the kitchen." Restrictions stated in negative form, such as "don't write on the walls," may invite defiance. Therefore, many parents phrase limits as positive choices instead: "You can write on this paper or I will put the crayons away." Enforce such limits by taking away crackers and crayons, if necessary. Though stating alternatives may seem awkward, especially at first, it is usually more effective to direct children's energy positively.

Location Restrictions

Adept parents manage to turn even simple commands into *apparent* choices. For example, Ann may sit still and let her mother wash her sticky fingers now, or wait a while in the high chair, because her mother doesn't want sticky marks on the walls. Barry may continue playing outside, or wash off the mud and come in. When *parents* need children to come in, the choice becomes, "You can wash the mud off, or I will."

Another good way of preventing the spread of mess is to restrict toys to certain rooms or parts of rooms. Susanna may play with the blocks in her room, or on the coffee table in the living room. Jackie may play with dolls on the sofa, or in the corner behind the big chair. (Toys left out of bounds are put out of reach for a while.)

Similarly, be aware of times when you can and cannot tolerate certain messy activities, and devise rules accordingly.

Despite all our precautions, we will of course spend more time cleaning up in a day than we used to spend in a week or a month. No one likes it, but since we have to live with it, we may as well try to adjust.

Dealing with mess is a matter both of our tolerance and of the personalities of our children. Some youngsters are just born more messy and unruly than others. Less coordinated children *will* spill more, very active youngsters *will* speed through more play equipment. With strong-willed youngsters, we must either tolerate more messy antics or tolerate the extra time and effort it takes to get them to accept limits, one or the other. It helps if we can accept these givens in our children's personalities and work with them. Finally, our own personalities and where we live also affect how tolerant we may be. One parent reported, "We've ignored the fact that the children have crayoned on their bedroom wall. Rather than hassle every day, we'll repaint the room once they are older."

ALLOWING AND PERSUADING CHILDREN TO HELP

HOW REALISTIC ARE OUR EXPECTATIONS?

It's a rare child who innately prefers neatness to clutter. Though a fifteen-month-old may plop toys back into the toy box, this game doesn't hold nearly the fascination of pulling them all out again. We, on the other hand, tire of toys strewn through every room. We want the mess cleaned up. And, after months of picking up toys, we want our children to help. Eventually, we want children to take responsibility for their own possessions and manage cleanup on their own. Alas, this final objective, according to our sample, is not reached within the first six years. Gradually, between ages two and six, children do an increasingly large proportion of cleanup, but few volunteered or did the job entirely.

There is much variation from family to family in participation in cleanup, especially as children approach age six. In some families, parents still do the majority of pickup; in others, it is almost always a cooperative venture; and in still others, children do most of the work. Parents are more inclined to help for occasional thorough room cleaning and after other children visit.

Household neatness is an emotionally loaded topic, which often has more to do with our own backgrounds and other adults than it does with children. Becoming aware of the motivation behind our standards of neatness can help us to evaluate our expectations more realistically.

Some parents never learned to be neat, either because their childhood homes were always a mess or because someone else did all the picking up. Others react against the oppressive neatness of their early childhood and now prefer to let the clutter build. "I value children's projects more than vacant floor space," one mother commented. "This house is usually cluttered, and often a mess, but it's a great place for active, eager children to play and learn." Other parents reason that when the mess gets out of control it's difficult to find things or think straight. They feel that it's worth the time getting things in order, and it's worth the time teaching the children to pitch in and do their share.

If Mom and Dad each hold to a different attitude toward household neatness, children will be confused by the discrepancy or use it to their advantage. It's often helpful to get issues of this sort out in the open and resolved in some way before putting pressure on little ones to pitch in.

Parents tend to hold one of three basically different philosophies about whether to include children in general housework.

1. Children should have regular chores in order to foster a sense of responsibility. Furthermore, self-esteem flourishes when small children feel important and appreciated for bringing in the morning paper, dumping the trash, sweeping the kitchen, or polishing furniture. In today's society, housework is often the most available grown-up job. Par-

ents who follow this philosophy readily admit that they don't want to do all the work themselves, and point out that they start at an early age because converting children into household helpers isn't apt to get any easier as the years go by. Indeed, one mother reported, ''Roma used to like vacuuming and mopping but I didn't often let her because she was so slow. Now's she's five and *able* to help, but when I ask her, she won't.''

2. Children should pitch in when asked to do so as a means of developing cooperation. Parents who want to foster cooperation do not assign regular tasks, but expect children to help when needed. Thus, youngsters may set the table if dinner is late, clean the bathroom sink before Aunt Jane arrives, hold the broken toy while it is being glued, or dust while Mom vacuums so story time can begin sooner.

3. Children need not do housework unless they want to. Reasons include the following: The children are too young; since *they* don't care about household cleanliness, it's not fair to push adult needs on small children. One mother wants her daughter to enjoy housework: ''I love it when she helps and praise her, but I don't want her to dislike it because it's something she has to do.'' Parents who hire help to clean their homes don't usually expect their kids to perform tasks they don't do themselves.

HOW TO BEGIN INVOLVING CHILDREN

If we want our children to participate, we have to make a time commitment for both teaching and enforcement. To help assure success, it's best to institute new household obligations when children's overall behavior is in a generally positive phase. In the beginning, when youngsters say they can't do a particular job, or they do it very poorly, chances are that we gave inadequate directions or that our expectations are too high. Teaching can accomplish what orders cannot. Gradually, as the months pass, instruction time is offset by the real contribution children can make.

The chart that follows outlines the various chores that children can help us with at eighteen months, two years, and three to four years. In general, we have used the *youngest* age reported to us. Even though many children may not yet be sufficiently adept or self-controlled to perform these tasks at such an early age, often *we* need to remind ourselves how capable our little ones *might* be if given the opportunity. For the most part, these are chores that our children will do *with* us; in time, they will be able to carry some of them out alone, or with minimal supervision.

How Children Can Help			
Household Tasks	18 Months	2 Years	3 to 4 Years
Laundry	Pass clothespins. Collect and carry wash. Load and unload machine.	Sort by color, type of clothing, or who it belongs to.	Put away clothes and hang towels on racks.
Iron		Sprinkle for ironing, even if things don't *need* sprinkling; tape over most of the holes in the sprinkler.	Iron handkerchiefs on a towel or carpet, not ironing board. Use low setting and close supervision.
Shoes		Polish with saddle soap or neutral polish.	
Beds	Pull up blankets and smooth wrinkles.		Change pillow cases.
Wastebaskets	Collect litter.	Empty into garbage can.	
Mirrors and windows	Wipe with dry cloth.	Child sprays, parent wipes.	Clean windows alone.

Household Tasks	18 Months	2 Years	3 to 4 Years
		How Children Can Help	
Dust	Especially baseboards, with feather duster for sheer delight.		Hide some buttons, dimes, to encourage a thorough job. Polish furniture.
Floors		Sweep with a small broom. Help polish wax by skating with rags tied to feet.	Mop small sections.
Woodwork		Wipe with damp sponge.	Use cleaning solutions.
Sink and bathtub			Use cleaners.
Toilet bowl		Clean with brush.	Can clean alone.
Food preparation	Stir juice. Mix ingredients with a fork.	Butter bread. Make bread crumbs. Decorate cookies. Wash vegetables; put items in pots. Fill a designated measuring cup.	Make simple recipes, written out with large numbers and pictures. Mark measuring implements clearly with paint or nail polish.

How Children Can Help

Household Tasks	18 Months	2 Years	3 to 4 Years
Kitchen equipment	Electric blender, push buttons under close supervision.	Hand grater for soft cheese. Flour sifter. Vegetable peeler. Hand egg beater. Electric can opener and mixer with close supervision.	Scissors to cut chives. Hand can opener. Sharp knives, see Sharp Objects, p. 149.
Cooking		Pour juice from small pitcher. Help fix own school lunch. Set table, draw proper positions of utensils on inexpensive place mats, including one for center of table, for serving spoons, trivet, salt and pepper. Fry French toast, under close supervision.	Heat own hot chocolate in microwave oven. Pour boiling water for Jello, under close supervision (five years). Fix simple breakfast for self and others.

How Children Can Help			
Household Tasks	18 Months	2 Years	3 to 4 Years
Kitchen cleanup	"Wash" plastic dishes. Unload dishwasher, handling one plate at a time. Preliminary wipe-up of spills and high chair tray.	Rinse dishes parent has washed and put them in drying rack. Wipe own placemat. Help polish silver.	Actually wash a few dishes. Sweep crumbs into a bowl while wiping table. Clear off own place setting; a bread pan on the sink counter collects silver neatly and assures dishes stack better.

Here are some suggestions to keep in mind when starting children on housework projects:

- Obvious results. To promote a sense of accomplishment, choose jobs in which the "before and after" difference is obvious, like setting the table or washing fingerprints off doorways.
- Divided tasks. Break big jobs into segments. Vacuuming the house or washing all the dishes may be overwhelming, but vacuuming the hall or rinsing the lunch dishes may be just right. Several small jobs are more appealing than a single large one.
- Variety. If the child's attention span is too short to complete a task, give two jobs to alternate between, such as straightening a bookshelf and cleaning a couple of windows.
- Companionship versus independence. Do children work more effectively if you are both working on the same job, in the same room, or if you are elsewhere? Plan accordingly.

In order to avoid discouragement, standards must be appropriate to the child's ability and experience. One five-year-old cleared up only 50 percent of the dirt the first time he swept, but his mother resisted the temptation to make him do it again, or do it over herself, because she didn't want to dishearten him or devalue his efforts. As the work routine became established, she pointed out missed spots and gradually required a better job.

Who will do which task? Children may choose which jobs they wish to do for the day, week, or month. Or else leave it to chance: Each household member draws his job from a hat. Some families write names on a rotating wheel and turn it regularly to new tasks.

HOW TO MAKE THE WORK
PHYSICALLY EASIER

- Store toys on shelves rather than in a toy box so children don't have to take everything out to find what they are looking for.
- Individual containers assure that everything has its place. Use assorted containers, including plastic dishpans, cardboard boxes reinforced with tape, plastic bottles with tops cut off, old purses and lunch boxes from rummage sales. A clear plastic shoe bag on the wall holds lots of little treasures.

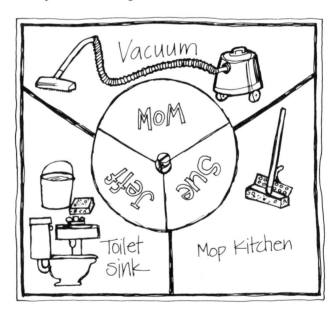

- Encourage youngsters not to spread puzzles and other multipiece toys by giving them a placemat, a carpet remnant, or two pieces of cardboard taped together to work on. At cleanup time, tip pieces toward the center and pour them back into the box. Or, keep an extra dustpan on the toy shelf to scoop up little parts and pieces.
- The Lego® company sells a circle of cloth with a drawstring, so it spreads out for play and pulls together for storage. Or, donate an old sheet. Spread it out for play, then pick up the whole bundle and plop it in a cardboard box.
- Six-year-old Eric proposed a "sandbox" for his Lego® blocks, so his parents blocked off a corner of his room with cardboard boxes. He could sit among his blocks to build, display his creations on several boxes that were turned upside down, and skip pickup entirely.
- Trikes are more rapidly put away if paint or strips of tape mark their parking spaces.
- A low dresser allows children to put away their own clothes. Label drawers with pictures of their proper contents.
- A stepstool allows preschoolers to hang clothes in their closets.
- Put laundry hampers and wastebaskets in preschoolers' rooms.
- Put a box for shoes by the front door if that's where they take them off and put them on.

Beds

- Stitch blankets together so they can be pulled up all at once or use quilts or indoor sleeping bags, which look neat with less effort.

HOW TO MAKE THE WORK
EMOTIONALLY EASIER

Once we've set realistic goals, we have to translate them into language our children can understand. "Go clean your room" is so general that it baffles most children. It helps to explain the purpose of our actions in general, as well as specifically what needs to be done: "If we put things away, we can find them more easily. Let's put all the doll clothes together here." Or, "We need room to sit on your bed and read a story, so let's clear off the toys."

No amount of nagging will raise our children's standards above our own and how we talk to them about cleanup will greatly affect their attitudes as well. Some children resist being told to clean up, but will pitch in when asked to help. One little girl who repeatedly claimed she was too tired to clean up her room worked enthusiastically whenever her mother asked her daughter to "surprise" her.

A wise mother told her children that they would be "allowed" to care for their rooms all by themselves when they turned six. Before that, they could "practice." With such status attached, children looked forward to taking full responsibility.

Children love games. Some parents change the family attitude toward cleanup time by using a light spirit that captures the imagination and subtly gains cooperation. Here are a few that kids seem to respond to:

Use a bucket or basket to go "shopping" for toys. Children pretending to be mail carriers, garbage collectors, or dump truck drivers can "drive" a wagon, a cardboard box, or a laundry basket around the house to accomplish the task. Jeffery prefers a space shuttle.

Once the child puts away one toy, you do the same, copying his or her actions. Children delight in playing "copycat" and in the sense of power they get from making you put away one, two, or a whole handful of toys.

"Belongs" is a matching game in which each thing has its proper place. You can adapt it for laundry too.

Line boxes along the wall, and toss blocks and toys into the appropriate box. Whether or not anyone keeps track, yell out a score for each "basket."

Choose a lively dance or march record and watch the toys disappear, thanks to ballerinas and robots.

Hold a clutter contest! Set the kitchen timer as you announce, "On your mark, get set, go." It's amazing how much can get picked up in five to fifteen minutes. Be sure to stop when the timer rings, or the contestants will lose interest. If you want to score this race, give one point for each item put away, or score the family as a whole by counting how many things are left out. Because game time is limited, even reluctant husbands have been known to join in.

Cleaning up more often, or less often, or at different times of the day may get the job done more easily. The most obvious time for cleanup is at the end of playtime, or at the end of the day. However, experience shows that it is not always the easiest or most effective.

Finally, many children respond more positively to a regular set of chores than to sporadic requests. It give them a sense of responsibility and relieves the suspicion that they're being "singled out" for extra duties.

In desperation, one mother told her three- and five-year-old sons they would have to stay in their room until they chucked all the toys in their closet. "Until then, you can only come out to go to the bathroom," she announced. To her astonishment, and horror, they waited for thirty-six hours before doing the fifteen minutes worth of work. They finally emerged at breakfast time. Thereafter, she required they clean their room before breakfast; as their appetites provided the necessary incentive, the cleanup battles ceased.

A perceptive mother realized that her children resisted cleanup because it always signaled the end of playtime. When she changed to, "It's time to put away some toys, and then you can play longer," the children were much more cooperative.

A cluttered room may look as overwhelming to our children at 5:00 P.M. as a sink of dirty dishes looks to us at midnight. Plan cleanup earlier in the day and ignore or put away yourself what remains at the end of the day.

Require that visitors help pick up before they go. If you are afraid of alienating Ronny and his mother, take courage. He very likely *will* come back, and his mother will probably be relieved to make the same request of your child.

What To Do When Siblings Fight About Cleanup

There are two basic approaches to cleanup when more than one child is involved. One is individual responsibility: Whoever takes it out puts it away. The other is family cooperation: Everyone played together so everyone helps clean up. Each can have its drawbacks. When an item is in dispute, we may not know *who* took it out. And if Jenny took it out, then Brian played with it, whose responsibility is it? On the other hand, Beth may produce much more clutter than her brother and it's unfair to expect him to clean up regularly after her. The essential key is perceptiveness and flexibility as the months go by.

If children resist individual responsibility, you can divide up chores. Assign a portion of toys to each child, or have one make beds and collect dirty clothes while another puts toys away.

If one child always denies responsibility and the other is more inclined to be honest, have the trustworthy one do pickup first and then have the other youngster put away the remainder.

Some parents resort to the tactic of drawing a truce line down the center of bedrooms with yarn stitched into a rug, or tape on the floor, or, as a final resort, they build a wall to split a large bedroom into two rooms. With each child in a separate room or separate play space, only the toys left in the family areas will be subject for contention.

What To Do When the Job Gets Too Big

Sometimes the volume of toys, ancient art projects, and bottle-cap collections, to say nothing of just plain junk, reaches overwhelming proportions in a child's room. Restoring order can be mind-boggling to both parents and children. What do parents do?

- Work together. Even five-year-olds who are able to do routine pickup still need help with major cleaning.
- Provide suitable storage. Evaluate whether the child has suitable shelf and drawer space, as well as assorted containers to keep possessions in order. Make necessary additions or alterations.
- Divide into sections. Divide the area to be cleaned into sections such as the bed, the dresser top, the floor, and so forth, so the job isn't so overwhelming. Draw lots to see which gets cleaned next.
- Rotate toys. Divide toys in two or three groups. Return one pile to the playroom and store the others in a back closet. Rotate batches of toys every few weeks. Not only will there be less cleanup, but the "new" toys will be more interesting.
- Start from scratch. When the children aren't looking, take all toys and junk out of their room, and let them have back whatever they want. You'll be amazed by how little they ask for, provided they haven't seen you clear the room. Keep the remainder out of sight for a month. During that time, return any further items the children request. After that, your

conscience is free. Divide the booty between Goodwill, the garbage, and a bag *you* want to keep.

How to Get the Work Finished

The most common reward offered for pickup is praise, but eventually praise alone becomes as meaningless to a child as a nickel to a millionaire. More appealing rewards become necessary, since it will be a long time before youngsters find aesthetic reward in an uncluttered room. Even attractive rewards, however, are sometimes insufficient motivation to get the job done, so backup punishment may become necessary.

Rewards

Typical rewards that parents offer for completion of household chores include shared activities such as a game, story, or outing; stars on a star chart; or money. To pay or not to pay is a question that has troubled many parents eager to involve youngsters in housework. Some reject the idea because they see cooperative housework as a basic element of living together. Others believe incentives are important, and that money is as legitimate as any other. Still other parents want their children to learn about the relationship between work and money, and they think housework provides the most available job for small children. One mother considered hiring a cleaning person until she decided it was more practical to hire the children to help instead.

Many families blend concepts about family responsibility and money by paying for some jobs, but not others. Parents are less apt to pay for routine chores and those directly related to the child's own possessions and activities, and more inclined to pay for jobs that need to be done only occasionally.

How much to pay? Most children are paid by the job, though some are paid according to how long they work. For picking up books and helping carry in groceries, Brian, age three, gets a few pennies. Some parents calculate payment according to the kinds of things children want to buy (an approach that is usually only effective until age six, after which most parents won't be able to afford it!). Deborah, age five, earns a dollar for her weekly hour of housework because she works with about one-fourth the efficiency of a hired cleaning person.

Some parents apportion rewards according to how much work

has been accomplished. Thus if Marie has cleaned only a small corner of her room, only the introductory paragraph of Marie's favorite story will be read. In another family, preschoolers can either pitch in or sit on the sofa during the hour of Saturday morning family housework, but of course they are paid only for the amount of time they work.

Punishment

What happens when Junior tosses a token toy in the box and smugly waits for Mom to do the rest? What happens when money fails to convert preschoolers into regular household helpers? Many youngsters lose interest after the novelty wears off, or after they have bought the object of their heart's desire. Certain parents are content to have children work sporadically, when moved to do so by a spirit of sheer goodwill or by an empty piggy bank. Other parents want help they can count on and need the means to assure that the children will do their share, if rewards don't do the trick. One mother clarified the issue this way, to her three-year-old: You didn't help me bring in the packages from the car so I won't help you with your train now.

The most common punishment is withholding privileges: no leaving the room, no playing outside, no TV, or no new projects until the required work is done. Another parental ploy that has proved useful in many households is the "put-away box." When children fail to put toys or belongings away by the specified deadline, parents impound them. Toys are kept out of children's reach for a few hours when they're very young, up to a week for older children. In some families, youngsters may buy back toys for a penny or by doing ten jumping jacks.

If Rita, age two, doesn't pick up her blanket when Mom tells her to, Mom holds her hand and manipulates her fingers so they pick it up and put it away together. Older children might benefit from "practicing" chores that they consistently neglect; for example, when Randy sheds his jacket by the front door, he not only has to hang it up, but he must take it back to the door and practice hanging it four more times.

Offering children choices is often helpful: Let's divide the job. Do you want to pick up the cars or the dirty clothes? Or: Either you can do your pickup before we read or we can do pickup together and read if there is still enough time. Or try: Either you can put the blocks away and then you can paint, or else you can just continue playing with the blocks. Because children never quite picked up all the clutter, one mother made them sit on the sofa for one minute for every toy, article of clothing, or whatever they passed over. She appointed one child "inspector," on a rotating basis, to check up on the work of others, including the child's own work. Within a few days, everyone became meticulous about cleanup and children loved their turn as inspector.

5

Motor Development and Safety

W|hen our babies cry with frustration because their un-
coordinated arms and legs won't obey the urge to crawl,
stand, and walk, we join their yearning for liberation
from the immobility of infancy. Yet as their mobility
increases, so does the complexity of our job. What a shame we
didn't fully appreciate the simple safety of life during the endless
months of pregnancy. There were no falls from the sofa, no blis-
tered little fingers, no wild dashes into the street.

Once little ones are mobile, suddenly nothing is safe from eager
exploring hands, and we live on the edge of constant concern that
they will discover some unavoidable or overlooked danger. This is
the first test of parental ingenuity: matching our wits against the
enticing environment and the indomitable curiosity of our offspring.
Life would be much simpler if we could raise them inside great,
safe plastic boxes, shielded from all hazards. But such all-encom-
passing safety would carry a high price: Enveloped with overprotection, surrounded by a fear of impending disaster, their self-esteem and independence would suffer greatly. Though we once forbade
knives and electric cords, there comes a point where we must teach
our youngsters to use them safely.

Despite the best of parental care, there's hardly a youngster who
doesn't have at least one or two close calls. When any child is
injured or has a narrow escape, we are reminded of the often fine
line we walk between safety and disaster. Maybe there are some
lessons of faith to be learned here: for some a growing belief in
guardian angels, for others awe for our children's instinctual will
to survive. As time passes, our confidence grows in their basic
common sense, and we sigh with relief when we realize our safety
teachings have finally taken hold. Such faith, whatever its origins,
will undoubtedly serve us well in years to come, as our youngsters
move beyond home in ever-widening circles.

PROBLEMS IN ACQUIRING
BODY CONTROL

Given how little a young tree changes in eighteen months, it is
awesome to contemplate a baby by comparison—from immobility
on tummy or back to lurching confidently and with surprising speed.
But this progress doesn't occur without some rough spots.

Little ones often experience a period of frustration and general fussiness just before they accomplish a new task such as learning to crawl or walk. To appreciate the frustration, we have only to imagine being seated in the middle of the floor with everyone else mobile around us and everything new just beyond our fingers' grasp! Accepting these difficult periods as temporary and looking forward to the approaching accomplishment help many parents endure.

Meanwhile, there are ways that we can help our children as they move from stage to stage of motor control.

Sitting up can be made easier if we pad a baby bathtub or laundry basket with firm pillows.

When babies want to crawl but can't, try putting them in a walker or Jolly Jumper door swing for exercise and practice that will assist standing and walking. One family gave their five-month-old swimming lessons when she got frustrated trying to crawl. It was a great outlet for her physical energy.

When baby stands and can't sit down again, you can teach the knack by supporting baby's back with one hand while you swipe at knees with the other. This may last about a week. If you are tired of waking up every night to help baby sit again, you can try a sleeping harness that restrains such a baby from standing up during the night. Buy a comfortable one that can't choke the baby and *never* strap a baby on its back: This can cause choking if the child vomits.

When baby wants to walk but can't, you can help by arranging chairs, toy boxes, ice chests, and so forth, around the house so little ones can pull themselves hand over hand all around a room. A mesh playpen is often the first thing that youngsters use to pull themselves upright. One father whose back was aching from leaning over and holding up his pre-toddler came up with a good idea: He unhooked the Jolly Jumper swing from the door and held his daughter up in it to walk. The child got the support she needed, and Dad could stand up straight. When your child is using a walker, you can make things easier by rolling up the rugs or laying down a piece of rubber stair tread to bridge carpet to floor.

PROTECTING CHILDREN AND PROPERTY IN THE HOUSE

We don't have to worry that our youngsters may be carried off by lions, but modern childhood is risky nonetheless. Given that we are not always within arm's length of our little explorers, child-proofing is essential to our peace of mind. Furthermore, keeping our precious possessions safely beyond their reach assures us that they won't be crushed, dropped, or otherwise destroyed.

Not surprisingly, childhood accidents most often occur when we are less than normally attentive. High risk times include periods of emotional stress and exhaustion of illness, marital difficulties or job loss, the busy chaos of a move, the interruption of routine when we have guests, or visiting in homes less familiar or less child-proofed than our own. Finding ways to acquire the sleep we need, seeking emotional support from other adults, and obtaining sitters to free ourselves momentarily from our toddlers and two-year-olds are all important in assuring their safety.

PUTTING OBJECTS IN THE MOUTH

Thanks to modern sewage systems, ample wash water, and a high level of general public health, our children are not exposed to the multitude of potentially dangerous germs that afflicted children in the past and, unfortunately, still endanger children in many other countries today. Our current state of health is reflected in changing opinions about what children are allowed to put in their mouths. Most contemporary parents acknowledge that testing things with the tongue is a basic form of learning that children will use and mostly outgrow by two or three years of age. Since crawling infants have already developed immunity to our common household germs, we may feel more relaxed than our own parents did about what our children pick up off our floors and put into their mouths.

We are not, however, free from all concern. During the first three months of life, even healthy babies have a relatively low resistance to infection. (Thanks to Mother Nature, they can't put much in their mouths at first.) Once they are moving about on their own, we do have to protect them from poisons, things they might choke on, and certain germs as well.

All parents agree that clean food and teething objects are fine for babies to put in their mouths, and nearly all parents permit baby bottles and pacifiers, but there is a large area that must be defined by personal standards and comfort levels. Many parents will allow fingers and toys to go into mouths, pacifiers picked up off the floor at home and used again once the baby is three months old, and food to be eaten off the kitchen floor after six to nine months of age. Toddlers in many homes drink out of cups and bottles used by other healthy family members. There are some parents who feel comfortable with their children's tasting grass, sand, bits of paper, rocks that are too large to go all the way into the mouth, and, in certain surroundings, the potato chips Junior just dropped on the ground. One mother was relieved to learn that thirty seconds of direct sunlight will kill most of the germs on the surface of an object. Note that some *colored* inks are poisonous, so if youngsters are paper-eaters, watch their selections.

All parents forbid their children to put near their mouths anything sharp, poisonous, or with the potential to get caught in the windpipe. Likewise, things that could cause illness are forbidden. These include: human and animal feces, straws and cups from the street, second-hand gum, used tissues, and cups or utensils used by a family member who is ill.

Certain objects are dangerous because of their *size*. Most hazardous of all are objects that can block off major breathing passages. Peanuts, hard candies, pebbles, marbles, pennies, dimes, small buttons, plastic eyes from dolls, and tiny parts of toys are all in this category.

Even smaller solid and relatively heavy objects such as sunflower seeds can enter the lungs, especially of children under three, who not only laugh and cry suddenly, but who still lack the back teeth and coordination for careful chewing and swallowing.

Also of concern are items that are apt to get stuck even if they bypass the lungs and go to the stomach; these include nickels, straight pins, small open safety pins, and so forth.

On the other hand, a bit of paper will probably be coughed up if it goes down the wrong way, and a standard-size checker from the gameboard may cause a toddler to gag momentarily if it touches the back of the throat but is too big to go where it shouldn't.

Emily, age two, loved to put her Dad's cigarette butts in her mouth. Because *even small amounts of tobacco are poisonous to children,* Dad switched to a pipe, and also kept an unused one for her to play with. Another father taught his son to stomp on cigarette butts instead of picking them up from the street. Some parents quit smoking when faced with their children's interest in cigarettes.

One mother frequently played the game ''show me your tongue'' with her toddler. When she was concerned about what he might have in his mouth, her playful invitation to show off his tongue revealed what was inside.

Poisons and Medicines

Modern households abound in hazardous substances. How children get into them, despite our customary care, is a statement about human fallibility, and a frightening tribute to the curiosity and ingenuity of young children. Close calls occur with startling frequency even in the homes of conscientious parents who regularly lock away medicines and poisons: Suzanne lurched her way across the room in her crib and reached a bottle of aspirin; Nany, age two, discovered the bleach that was left out while Mom was involved in a family emergency; Ricky pulled an open bottle of nail polish remover over into his face; Eric jimmied the lock on a storage chest and found mothballs to play with; and youngsters have discovered endless dangerous delights while visiting relatives and friends, even those who have children.

Hazardous chemicals need to be kept out of children's reach; they include medicines, cleaning fluids, cosmetics, paint and paint thinners, insect and rodent poisons, lighter fluid, gasoline, and fertilizers.

The definition of a "safe" place to store medicines and poisons changes rapidly as youngsters grow. A low cupboard, even one with a safety latch or lock, is *never* safe, as someone might accidentally leave it open. A high shelf may provide adequate safety for a crawling infant, but not for a climbing toddler. The hall cupboard kept poisons out of Jerome's reach until, at twenty-two months, he pushed a chair down the hall so he could reach the medicine shelf. A *high* safety-latched or locked cupboard ultimately becomes necessary.

As soon as children can understand, begin to explain the hazards of certain substances to them. Show children the insignia for poison, either the old skull and crossbones or the new "yuck" face. Keep such labels on all household poisons. Check and see if your local hospital or Red Cross has films for children about the hazards of medicines.

Plants

The biggest childproofing challenge for those of us who aren't botanists is to find out which of the many common household and

> ## Poison Emergencies
>
> Immediate first aid is to dilute any poison with water. The American Academy of Pediatrics recommends that parents keep Ipecac syrup on hand to induce vomiting after certain kinds of poisoning. NEVER USE IT WITHOUT CALLING YOUR DOCTOR OR POISON CONTROL CENTER FIRST. If used inappropriately, it can cause more harm than good. Check with your doctor.

garden plants are poisonous. Check with well-informed friends, local library or nursery, and poison-control center to learn whether there are any hazardous plants in your child's environment, and get rid of them, if possible.

Some parents need only to protect their children from harmful plants, but the plant lovers among us also want to protect our greenery from the children. Also, we hope they will some day enjoy plants as much as we do. Rules about plants vary according to the child's general level of understanding and ability to recognize specific plants. For example, a one-year-old might not be allowed to touch plants at all, or might, *if* supervised. A two-year-old might touch plants at home, where all are safe, but not elsewhere unless supervised. A three-year-old might know never to touch mushrooms, but be allowed to pick daisies any time at home.

Teaching children to touch plants gently and allowing them to help care for plants are two good ways of increasing their appreciation and decreasing the risk of damage. Encourage youngsters to smell and touch rather than taste plants.

When children are very young, plants may be put up high out of reach (on top of shelves or high chests of drawers, for example) or fence off a section of the garden. Even a small fence helps little ones remember to stay out.

TOUCHING FORBIDDEN THINGS

Having catered for months to the needs of our immobile infants, we suddenly step into a whole new world of limits and discipline once they learn to crawl. How do we protect our favorite possessions and preserve a little household orderliness, not to mention the very lives of these fearless explorers who don't yet understand that lamps fall, glass cuts, and fire burns? How do we safeguard both our little ones and ourselves without making them neurotically afraid of their environment or curbing the instinctive curiosity that underlies intellectual growth?

Childhood mobility changes family life almost as dramatically as birth itself, and parental challenge increases in proportion to the child's adeptness. One mother sighed, "Given the way Dean sailed through the house on all fours, I didn't think learning to walk would make any difference. But once he learned, we were monitoring a speedboat instead of a sailboat. I couldn't believe how fast he could get from one end of the house to the other!"

There are a number of options we can choose from to prevent children from touching forbidden objects. We can childproof, block off sections of the house, distract youngsters, institute rules, and if necessary punish when rules are broken.

All of us childproof our homes to some extent, so the first question is not *whether* to childproof but *how much*. There are two schools of thought on the matter—partial and complete—and each has its rationale.

Partial childproofing means that dangerous objects are put safely away but that other adult possessions are declared off limits. Some homes are so large or contain so many things that it may be easier to supervise a child for a year or two than to childproof the entire place. Another reason some parents choose partial childproofing is to expose children, early on, to the need to accept certain limits.

In complete childproofing, everything that the child is not to touch is secured out of reach. This method gives the parent maximum freedom of mind while youngsters have freedom to roam through the house. There is no need to get into confrontations or arguments over objects with the child, and there are no limits on exploration.

Parents, of course, choose which approach or combination of approaches best suits their homes, needs, and children.

When youngsters *do* touch forbidden objects, it's often helpful to identify their reasons for doing so. Do they merely want to satisfy their curiosity about something new or newly within reach? If so, we may be able to help them explore carefully, or, in the case of a knife or electric cord, may declare it a "no-no" for this stage of development. Is touching a matter of learning? Most rules take time to learn, so we can expect repeated efforts to touch. Furthermore, when rules *are* broken, we must repeat the consequences with sufficient consistency that youngsters can learn the limits. If children are touching forbidden objects in order to get attention, try to figure out how to better meet their needs. Have we brushed aside other less dangerous bids for attention? Next time, if possible, meet their needs for attention sooner.

What are our options when our little ones reach for a vase, the stereo, or an electric cord?

Depending on the object and child in question, the answer may be as simple as moving the stereo to a far corner of the living room to decrease the temptation to touch.

Distractions work well in keeping many toddlers from touching things, though some are much less distractible than others. Lead or carry them elsewhere or offer an alternative, saying "Let's trade." As youngsters approach the self-determined twos, distraction often becomes less effective. However, alternative but *similar* merchandise may satisfy their curiosity, such as an old, nonfunctional typewriter or second-hand necklaces instead of Mom's best.

Another approach is to teach youngsters *how* to explore rather than *not* to explore, so fewer household items have to be defended. For example, a delicate knickknack might be handled "just *with* Mommy."

Shouting "No!" is usually our instinctive response when toddlers reach for a forbidden object. Those who study child behavior report that even up to age three, youngsters react more to the emotional tone of such a command than to the meaning of the word itself. Thus Jeffy, age eleven months, pulls his hand away from the electric cord because he is *frightened* by our loud, sharp sound. With experience, he may learn to ignore his startled reaction and continue exploring unless parents follow through with some further instruction or punishment. Our determined toddlers even seem able to count. They quickly learn how many times we shout before we act. If we want them to *respond* after just one command, we have to *act* after just one command. Some parents also reinforce their wishes by praising youngsters for *not* touching. Even after youngsters can themselves recite, "No-no, don't touch," it may take several years before they have the self-control to follow their own instructions consistently.

Some children easily respect a parental no and distraction while others will test repeatedly. Thus punishment may be necessary. If no and a stern look are followed with punishment when necessary, children eventually learn to stop on the basis of mere command and frown. A single slap on the hand is a common method of backup. Or, youngsters may be restricted to cribs or playpens for a minute to two.

When parents have to fetch the laundry from the basement or the mail from the sidewalk, baste a turkey or jump into the shower, they may put youngsters in a Jolly Jumper swing, a walker from which the wheels have been removed, a crib, or a safely gated room. During such moments, one mother placed her climbing toddler underneath an overturned playpen. Children cannot safely have all the freedom they want, so sometimes we have to accept their angry cries and assure them that we know how frustrated they are.

COMMON SAFETY CONCERNS

Falling

In the early months of life, babies are most likely to fall off things *we* put them on. Amazingly young and "immobile" infants have edged off changing tables and ample-appearing sofas and beds. Unfortunately, they don't announce ahead of time the day they will take the first great roll. With early mobility, the lack of reliable muscle control and balance makes falls likely, and once little ones begin to climb on their own, the risk escalates. Though growing experience helps youngsters respond appropriately when crawling or climbing, they are so easily distracted they may simply forget that they are teetering on a household precipice.

Some youngsters are content to explore the world at floor level, and assuring their safety is comparatively easy. Certain cautious, well-coordinated youngsters with mountaineering mentalities climb but almost never fall. But heaven and very attentive parents must help the fast-moving, impulsive, or unstable youngster who aspires to be a climber.

Falls while learning to walk and climb are as inevitable as pronunciation errors while learning to talk. Our job as parents is not to prevent falls entirely, but to assure as best we can that they are not serious. Fortunately, there are many ways to reduce the likelihood of serious falls.

Because tired children are more accident prone, some activities are more risky at certain times than at others. The following rules have proven helpful:

- Just before nap time, no slides and jungle-gym climbing.
- In the late afternoon, no skating.
- Just before bedtime, no roughhousing.

Prevent falls from the changing table by strapping babies down or holding them. Babies as young as five days old have been known to flip from front to back, proving that they can never be trusted to stay in place. As soon as baby's feet can reach the supporting surface, an infant seat is no longer safe on a table or counter, as a baby can easily push it over. Once youngsters seem likely to climb out of cribs, move them to a youth bed or sleeping mat on the floor. If you're worried about their falling off a youth bed, pad the surrounding floor with blankets or pillows or attach a rail to the edge of the bed.

Recent studies suggest that because babies *feel* secure in walkers, they are less likely to avoid a potential drop-off when in a walker than when crawling. Be especially cautious about stairs and curbs.

Slippery shoes and floors cause many falls. Abrade new leather soles with sandpaper, use tennis shoes for first walking shoes (pediatricians now approve of this), or let children go barefoot while learning to walk. One mother knit tiny leg warmers for her wintertime toddler. Some wood-floor waxes provide a less slippery surface. Put your throw rugs away until toddlers are steadier on their feet, or else put non-slip padding underneath.

Because chairs serve as stepladders to counter and table tops,

---

Save That Tooth!

Teeth that get knocked out can often be reimplanted, thanks to modern dentistry. Don't wash the tooth off because doing so may damage the roots. Keep it moist, preferably in saliva. If necessary, carry it under your tongue. For best results, get to a dentist within half an hour, though chances are still fair in an hour. Even baby teeth may be reimplanted to hold proper spacing if they accidentally come out long before permanent teeth are due.

some parents use folding chairs, which they can put away after meals. So rocking chairs won't fall over backward, nail a block of wood under the back of each runner so it can't tip over.

As in so many other things, it often helps to *be positive* when warning children about the danger of falling. One mother, seeing her son pause to consider his next move on a playground structure, would say, "Lee is being *careful* not to fall." Now, at age nine, Lee is a good climber who has never had a serious fall.

As a general matter, it's a good idea to avoid threats. When we caution, "Don't run, you'll fall," we're also conveying a hidden message that you *will* fall when you run. It would be better to caution, "This path is slippery so it is for walking," or to clarify, "This hallway is a walking place, not a running place."

Stairs

For those who climb home via a staircase or live in split-level houses, coping with stairs is a major concern. Some of us know firsthand the fears of ancient Indian cliff dwellers. Lucky are parents of the plains who can ignore the whole issue.

Teaching little ones to navigate stairs is time-consuming, and depending on how centrally located the staircase is, it may or may not be worth the effort. Do the stairs inhibit the youngster's access to basic living space? How difficult is it to carry youngster *and* groceries *and* siblings up and down? If you decide it's best just to keep little children away from the stairs, block them off with a baby gate at the top or bottom.

If you *do* want to teach little ones how to navigate stairs, begin by blocking off several steps down from top or up from bottom. This will give the baby a few steps to practice on. Put a rug or foam pad at the bottom of stairs to cushion a fall. If the handrail is high and difficult to grasp, tie a heavy rope below it for children to hold.

Some parents wait until children can walk before teaching them how to navigate stairs, but others teach stair climbing first. Because youngsters are safer on all fours long after they can stand and toddle, those who are already at ease crawling up and down stairs often continue to do so for some months. But those who have just learned to walk, prefer to remain upright when taking on any new challenge, even though it is risky.

Since children go up stairs automatically but must learn to come down, it's helpful to start teaching from the top. Face youngsters upstairs and alternately place their hands and feet down onto the stair below.

While giving instruction in stair climbing, some parents hold children so falls are impossible. On the other hand, fear of falling is a strong incentive to pay attention and learn. Some parents therefore keep their hands just below so, if out of balance, baby will fall several inches into waiting hands. Once youngsters learn to back *down* stairs, climbing up will be comparatively safe.

Childproof Doorways

The front door may not be our only cause for concern. We may want certain rooms to be securely off limits: the kitchen when no one is there to supervise, or the den that holds the new computer. Rather than childproofing everything within a room, it is sometimes easier to keep children out entirely, or let them visit only with adult supervision.

There are many ways to close off a room.

Baby gates come in various sizes, including expandable fences for wide doorways.

Latches at the top of the door are beyond reach even with a chair.

Sock held on doorknob with a rubber band can make a door difficult for anyone to open, and impossible for children. Commercial safety doorhandles from children's supply stores are easier for adults to open.

Screw eye. For sliding glass doors, purchase a burglar lock or drill a hole in the door and frame and tie a screw eye nearby to insert in the hole. See illustration.

Locked in the bathroom? Unless it can be unlocked from the outside, tape the bathroom door lock so children can't lock themselves in.

Cabinets and Drawers

There are several reliable ways to childproof medicine cabinets. For sliding doors, purchase a "showcase" lock. Many hardware stores carry a good selection of childproof locks for standard medicine cabinets. If you can't find an appropriate lock for yours, store medicines in another cabinet that *can* be locked.

Use the low drawers around your house for safe objects like cotton balls and old towels in the bathroom, pots and plastic dishes in the kitchen, clothes to be washed in master bedroom. Drawers can be kept closed with strong elastic bands around two adjacent drawer knobs, with commercial childproofing locks, or even tape on rarely used drawers.

In homes where you visit often with the children (grandparents, for example), you may feel more relaxed if you childproof their medicine cabinets and cleaning closets.

To childproof the refrigerator, stretch an elastic luggage cord around it. To keep the ends accessible while you're opening the door, hang them over magnetic hooks on the sides of the refrigerator. (If an old refrigerator is being *stored,* remove the door entirely so youngsters can't get locked inside.)

Electrical Equipment

Protecting our children from electricity is particularly challenging because the equipment is often low and inviting: bumpy little sockets and cords along the floor, just waiting to be tugged. Nor can the actual danger be seen or safely tested, as hot water might be. In addition, there are all those delightful sounds and whirling blades, which are highly dangerous, delicate, or both.

Electric Fans

Cover the grill with nylon netting, or place a piece of window screening inside the grill.

Electric Outlets

Outlets can be covered with heavy tape, or better yet, buy push-in plastic outlet covers, available in many hardware and baby-care stores. One mother reports that round covers are harder to remove than square ones. Screw-on safety covers, which replace the regular face plates, are available at some hardware and electrical supply stores and deter even ardent explorers.

It's often easy to arrange rooms so the heavy furniture is in front of outlets. Connect extension cords behind heavy furniture or elsewhere out of reach, or tape them as children may pull them apart and put the hot ends in their mouths.

Mix-masters and Power Tools

Disconnect them when not in use. Point out how eggs get smashed between the rotating blades, and explain that that's why we keep our fingers away.

Stand Lamps, Stereo, and TV

These may be barricaded into corners with heavy furniture. Or put tape over dials or switches that aren't commonly used. Tie a wobbly floor lamp to a near-by chair.

Stoves, Matches and More

Jeremy, age twelve months, turned the stove knobs on after his big sister left a chair nearby. Sasha, age two, turned on the burner under a glass coffee pot; fortunately, no one was in the kitchen when it exploded. Sonya, age nine months, couldn't walk but climbed from chair to table top to counter and was discovered crawling across the stove. What can be done for safety?

Potentially dangerous household activities require special planning. Avoid barbecuing unless there are enough adults to supervise. Do the ironing while Junior is entertained in a playpen, on the other side of a baby-gate, or asleep; and cool the iron on the back of the stove or some other safe spot.

One of our early objectives is to teach children the meaning of the word "hot," so they will understand our future words of caution. Some youngsters, however, become confused and engage their parents in months of testing, because they are cautioned "hot" when the oven door, for example, is actually cool. If cautioned only when it *is* hot, toddlers learn to stay away entirely, or to differentiate between when it is on and off. Some parents place the child's hand close enough to feel the radiating heat and repeat "hot." Or they whisk the child's fingertips against a hot oven door just long enough to feel the heat and pull away.

Childproofing is essential to avoiding burns. So a tablecloth of hot food isn't pulled to the floor, pin each corner around behind a table leg. For a floor heater or hazardous wall heater, use a one-by eight-inch board to support a closely set row of one-half-inch wooden dowels well away from the heater, and hold this safety frame in place with wire or angle irons. Avoid excessive heat by taping the household thermostat so little fingers can't push it above the acceptable maximum. Stove knobs can usually be removed and placed out of reach when the stove is not in use. (Controls located behind the burners are safer for toddlers but are a hazard to young cooks who must reach *over* a burner to turn them off.) At times it's a great help to be able to block off the kitchen: Willie's mom locked hers with a padlock after finding him cooking his own early-morning breakfast at age three. Secure a fireplace screen by screwing eyelets into the nearby wall and tying the screen to them. Keep matches up high, and locked away if necessary.

Though we can insist our toddlers never touch stove knobs or matches, we eventually have to teach our preschoolers how to deal safely with heat. Safety rules become, "Unless I am with you, never touch matches, turn on the stove, or put anything in the fireplace because the fire may only *seem* to be out." A child cooking with a parent should stand on a chair with its back to the stove to provide a safety rail. Avoid long, full sleeves; use an apron or clothespin to hold back the billows of a dress; stir with wooden spoons and spatulas, which don't transfer heat; turn pot handles away from the edge of the stove. Tell children what to do if the household smoke alarm goes off, and hold occasional home fire drills once children are old enough to understand without being unduly frightened.

Preschoolers may be especially fascinated with matches and fire if they are never permitted to deal with them. Four-year-old boys seem to be especially spellbound. Therefore, it may be helpful to give children limited exposure to matches and fire in *carefully controlled circumstances and with constant emphasis that this is to be done only with adults.* Lighting candles is a delight and is safe for a cautious, coordinated three-year-old with close supervision. The first opportunity may be during family rituals: birthdays, Hanukkah, or Christmas. Let four-year-olds strike matches and light a small fire of paper and sticks in the fireplace, backyard barbecue, or even a disposable aluminum roasting pan in the driveway.

Sharp Objects

We hardly notice how many sharp things are lurking about until little ones start to explore. Not only are there knives and pins, but sharp corners on the furniture and pretty chips of glass in the street.

If the corners of a coffee table are sharp, parents may choose to pack it away for a few years. Alternatively, purchase corner protectors (now available in some stores), or use foam weather-stripping to pad sharp edges. When youngsters are ready for scissors, get sharp ones with rounded tips, because a dull pair will only cause frustration.

Keeping knives, scissors, and razor blades safely out of reach can be a challenge. If toddlers can open the dishwasher by themselves, keep knives up on counter tops and wash them by hand. Tiny, silent Lori, ten months, had a razor blade in her mouth before her dad even realized she was standing beside the bathtub. Caution: If you discover a child holding a dangerously sharp object, don't panic and grab. Give slow, careful directions.

Geoffrey, age two, was unimpressed when his mother warned him about sharp things. One day, when he wouldn't keep his hands out of her sewing basket, she showed him a pin, and while announcing "sharp," gave his finger a little prick. Knowing the meaning of the word, Geoffrey was more cautious in the future.

Gradually our task changes from forbidding sharp objects to teaching youngsters to handle them safely. Rather than always saying no to youngsters who are fascinated by bright broken glass in the park, some parents teach them to collect it carefully in a paper cup and dispose of it in the garbage. One youngster took the collection home to make bright collages by gluing bits of glass to old cottage cheese lids. When teaching preschoolers to use sharp knives, mark the underside of the handle with red nail polish as a reminder to hold the knife right-side-up. Let them start with easy cutting jobs, such as bananas, and progress as their skill develops.

Household Garbage

Investigating wastebaskets and garbage cans is not only dangerous, but makes a mighty mess as well. How can we prevent it?

Keep garbage in a covered canister, in a kitchen cabinet with a childproof lock, on the counter top, or behind a barricade.

Don't keep separate trash containers in bedrooms, bathrooms, and so forth. Keep all the trash in the kitchen.

Water Safety

Bathtubs and Wading Pools

Filled with only a couple of inches of water, bathtubs and wading pools are fairly safe. Drain the pool when you can't supervise. Two rubber mats will make the entire tub nonslippery, or use extra non-skid appliqués.

Constant supervision is essential when children under age three

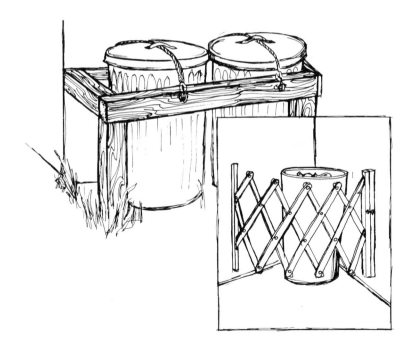

or four are bathing. Be sure all supplies are available before starting. Remove boisterous children from the tub or pool.

Toilets

We've not heard of a child drowning in a toilet, but youngsters have been known to drink the water. When children are little, keep the toilet lid down or put a gate at the bathroom doorway. If you're concerned about sanitation, clean the toilet more frequently—that way you won't worry if little ones splash in it now and then.

Kitchen Buckets

Babies have drowned in buckets! An infant who has just learned to pull to standing can't get back up alone after falling in head first. If you must step out of the room while mopping, put the bucket on a counter top, or close the door.

Swimming Pools

Tanya, an excellent swimmer at age three, drowned in the family swimming pool. She may have ventured in to swim alone, or may have been accidentally pushed in by the family dog. Other children have drowned by falling through a pool cover: Even though they could swim, they were unable to find their way out. Fence and *lock* the family pool.

One family had to rely on repeated warnings: "We lived in an apartment complex with a fenced pool and with a latched, but unlocked gate. Every time we went swimming we told Lee, age fifteen months, 'Never come here without Mommy or Daddy.' "

Water-safety classes are often available for children of all ages, through the Red Cross and other agencies. Such classes, however, never make it safe for youngsters to be near water alone. Pediatricians have different opinions about swimming classes for infants; check with yours.

Miscellaneous Dangers

It's impossible to cover all the potential dangers contained in an ordinary household. We've tried to cover the main areas in the preceding sections; here are some miscellaneous hazards and precautions you can take to meet them.

- *Christmas tree ornaments.* Andrew, fifteen months, ate a glass ornament from the Christmas tree. Buy a small tree and suspend it from the ceiling, or put it in the playpen.

- *Plastic bags.* Eric's mother had discarded all the plastic commercial garment bags marked "Danger! May cause suffocation." But when Eric was two, she found him in the kitchen pulling a grocery store vegetable bag over his head. It had just gotten stuck around his nose, and he was struggling to get it off. She installed a safety latch on the cupboard in which the bags were stored.
- *Playpens.* Roy's mother didn't know he could climb out of the playpen until at twelve months she found him unexpectedly crawling through the house. A playpen with wooden bars is harder to scale than a mesh playpen. Don't put in pillows or big toys that can be used as steps.
- *Sliding glass doors.* Put tape or adhesive designs on them so they are more visible.
- *Toy boxes and piano covers.* Place foam weather-stripping tape or corks at several points, so if the lid falls, fingers won't get crushed. Fasten a magnetic cabinet fastener to the top of the toy box and the wall behind, so the lid will stay open. Install a pneumatic screen door closure, so the lid will close slowly.
- *Curtain and blind cords.* Lee, age one, was found standing on a stool with the venetian blind cord wrapped around his neck. Screw a cup hook near the top of the window so cords can be looped high out of reach.

SAFETY BEYOND THE HOUSE

PLAYING IN YARD AND NEIGHBORHOOD

One reason parenting is such a challenge is that the ground rules continually shift. When we finally become comfortable with fearless explorers living in our houses, they want to conquer outdoor frontiers. As a result, our worries and limit-setting begin all over again.

There are four major factors to consider in setting the boundaries on outdoor play: (1) the children's ages and ability to comprehend danger; (2) the children's temperaments: Are they mischievous? Do they test limits? Is it possible that their misbehavior is due to boredom and a need for *expanded,* not contracted, boundaries? (3) the nature of the hazards in the play area: poisonous plants, cars, places the child might fall from or get lost in; (4) your own level of worry. Without doubt, some of us have an easier job than others. Some have safe, spacious yards, live on quiet streets in safe neighborhoods, and have children who generally accept limits. For others the difficulties are compounded: When youngsters do play outside, appropriate supervision is necessary; and when they can't play outside, we have to tolerate their frustration.

Given this variation in circumstance and individual temperament, it is difficult to set hard-and-fast rules on boundaries for play areas at different ages, but the following provide general guidelines. Some parents permit children to play outdoors earlier than usual because they feel assured that hazards are minimal. Limits also tend to expand earlier for second children, because they play outside with an older sibling.

From crawling to age four or even six, unsupervised youngsters may be kept out of certain portions of the house at certain times, such as kitchen, bathroom, master bedroom, or den.

Beginning between two and three years of age, children may be left alone outside in a safe, fenced yard.

Beginning between three and four and one-half, some children are allowed to play alone in an unfenced yard and some trustworthy little ones may be allowed to include a portion of the block in their play area. Especially at first, indicate the boundaries clearly. A chalk mark or row of rocks may help, or even a stop sign where small, child-propelled vehicles must stop.

No matter what age one settles on as appropriate to let youngsters play alone in the yard, parents are a little worried at first. The following examples show how they handle this common concern.

> I sat outside in the back yard with Adrianna, age two and one-half, for many hours until I felt comfortable that it was safe. I then left her alone for brief periods, checking frequently from the bedroom window.

> Jana, age two, often left the yard to follow the neighborhood dogs. Now we call the dogs to our yard so she gets her fill of loving, hugging, and petting; then we let them out the gate.

> We attached a mirror outside the kitchen window so I can see the children in the back yard more easily.

I installed bright, tall safety flags on the youngsters' big-wheel trikes to make them more visible along the sidewalk.

Living in a small apartment, with a new baby on the way, I knew I'd soon be unable to sit for hours in our unfenced yard so Randy could play outside in the dirt with his cars. Allowing him to play where he most wanted required that he learn to stay nearby. I pointed out the boundaries several times, then for the next couple days sat inside by the window to knit and watch. The moment he stepped beyond the boundary, I brought him back, gave him a quick swat, and pointed out the limits again. On the other hand, if he came and fetched me for a venture beyond the boundary, I went with him. Thus, after two or three days and two or three swats, and several walks at his request, he was reliably staying within bounds. Once the lesson was really learned and he asked me to go for a walk, I could tell him we'd go a little later, and he was able to wait.

Youngsters who wander off to play with a friend without announcing their departure, may have to return home and play alone indoors for awhile as punishment. If repetitions occur, some parents use a swat to emphasize the severity of such an omission.

CROSSING STREETS

Cars are the ever-present, deadly hazard to modern parents that wild animals were to past generations. Emily, age two, dashed into the street when her parents paused to give directions to a lost pedestrian. Anna, age two, ran out of a restaurant and into the street after she burned her finger in the soup. Eric, nine months, found a tiny hole behind a bush in a well-fenced yard; he had *crawled* across the street in the time it took his mother to dash indoors, turn off the gas stove, and return to search the yard and bushes. For these fortunate youngsters, cars were a safe distance away at the crucial moment. But others have not been so lucky.

Before children are old enough to cross the street alone, they must be taught to stay away. Many parents explain to young children on walks and outings that they are never to go into the street by themselves. Others point out objects that have been hit by cars.

When pressed, some parents offer directive choices: If you want to walk, you must walk on the sidewalk. If you walk into the street, I will have to carry you or strap you into the stroller. If you go in the street or in the parking lot, you will have to play indoors. When all else fails, there is physical punishment. A swift, firm swat on the rear may get the message across most effectively when nothing else does.

At some point we want children to learn how to cross the street by themselves. How do we decide on the appropriate age? The most important factors are: (1) Is the child cautious or impulsive? How attentive and reliable? (2) How heavy is the traffic? (3) How fast do cars travel? (4) Are cars rare, but speeding when they do come? (5) What is the visibility?

We haven't met a parent who lets a two-year-old cross the street alone. But an *occasional* cautious and mature three-year-old, living on a quiet dead-end street with good visibility, is allowed to cross. On the other hand, faced with an impetuous youngster or busy streets, solo crossings may not be permitted until age six or later.

Here is a progressive, step-by-step method for teaching safe street crossing: At first the parent is in charge, pointing out crossing hazards and holding the child's hand. In the next stage, the child participates: The parent invites the child to make crossing judgments. They may hold hands or walk close together. When the child first begins to cross alone, the parent should supervise, watching how the child crosses and giving praise accordingly. A child who is finally ready to cross without supervision should be restricted at first to quiet streets, then corners with traffic signals, and eventually other corners. Children may or may not be ready to cross alone until age six; independent youngsters may find it easier to await their added freedom if told, "You will be able to cross this street alone when you turn six."

Traditionally, parents tell children to look "both ways" before crossing the street. But city folks who live with great volumes of traffic and many busy corners often tell their children to look *four* ways before crossing. One mother made up a rhyme to teach stop light safety: If red's on top, it's time to stop./If the light is yellow, wait and wiggle like jello/cause it's no time to race and the curb's the best place./When the light turns green, look for cars that are mean, trying to sneak by without being seen.

STRANGERS AND SEXUAL ABUSE

As concerned parents we think that we *should* educate children to the potential dangers of strangers but worry about burdening youngsters with fears. When children approach school age and begin to venture out into the world without us, this dilemma looms ever larger. Four-year-olds, given the often violent nature of their own fantasies, are apt to be terrified by warnings of kidnappers or mistreated children. Luckily, since children this age are seldom in public alone, we can hold off on their "street education." The five-year-old's firmer grasp on reality makes it possible to discuss the dangers in more specific terms without causing undue fear. Parents often begin to discuss dangers in terms of *their own* worries, a concept with which youngsters are quite familiar. Thus, instead of "strangers in cars will hurt you" children may be told, "If you got in someone's car and I didn't know, I would be worried about you, even if that person offered to bring you home." One mother explained to her five-year-old that *most* people are helpful and caring but a *few* people hurt others.

Most parents discuss certain safety rules with their children and make certain the rules are understood. Decide whom they can accept rides from: for example, grandparents, carpool drivers, but no one else. When can food and gifts be accepted from other people? Decide how far children can go from home and whom they can visit without informing you ahead of time. Where can they go alone, where in the company of a friend, and where must they be accompanied by an adult? Also be sure children know when to open the front door and whom to let into the house.

Most children have a subtle, intuitive sense of the appropriate or inappropriate behavior of others, but we have to encourage them to trust that sense, give them the vocabulary to talk about it, and inform them how to react. For this purpose, the Illusion Theater in Minneapolis developed the model of the "Touch Continuum." All children understand *lack of touch:* wanting a hug when parents are too busy. *Nurturing touch* is snuggling at story time or after getting hurt. As parents, we may be responsible for pushing our children into *confusing touch.* For example, we may let our friends whisk a hesitant youngster into the air, we may require Brenda to accept a kiss from unfamiliar Aunt May, or we may insist that little Carl shake hands when he feels like hiding behind our leg. If we repeatedly require our children to engage in physical contact in spite of their internal sense of discomfort, we teach them to put down and ignore a vital potential warning system. *Forced touch* is when another person won't stop roughhousing, tickling, hitting, or when one is tricked into more contact than one wants. Once given the vocabulary, most five-year-olds can easily come up with specific examples of each category, making it clear that they understand the concepts. One mother remembers being told that her body was "private property." That term made her feel rightfully in control of her own body.

In 80 percent of inappropriate sexual behavior involving children, the teen or adult involved is a relative, family acquaintance, or sitter. Uninformed children generally hesitate to speak up for fear of upsetting others. If, on the other hand, our children have been encouraged to *tell us* about instances of confusing or forced touch, we are in a position to get help. Children also need to know that there is a time to break a promise. If someone made them promise not to tell about touching it is *all right* for them to speak up.

Finally, we can instruct youngsters to shout "No!," to leave if possible, and from whom to seek help if we are not around: policemen, storekeepers, other parents. We can role-play with them what they might do if questioned inappropriately by a stranger in a park, or touched or requested to touch inappropriately while visiting a friend's house. For further discussion of sexual encounters, also see p. 64.

6

Health and Illness

M ost of us take good health for granted before we start a family. During pregnancy, we believe that if we and our indwelling companion come through labor and delivery in good shape, all will be fine. We are not prepared for the amount of time we will have to spend in doctors' offices for routine checkups, let alone for fevers, earaches, stitches, and more, to say nothing of the time we'll spend at home nursing frequent colds and stomach flu. We forget about the hours our own parents devoted to nursing us while we gained immunity to all these obnoxious little germs.

We also have to cope with children's pain, either suffering along with them for each scraped knee or feeling annoyed that they make such a big deal out of every little scratch. Before we go to the doctor, we have to take temperatures, and maybe calm the fear of a youngster who has unpleasant memories of the last such visit. Then, when we return home, Becky clamps her lips tight or spits the penicillin out.

Fortunately, there are some positive aspects to all this. The dreaded "shots" protect our little ones from more dreaded deaths that were commonplace not long ago. Furthermore, we can promote our children's future good health by teaching them about diet, exercise, and more. Occasionally, we find we can read our children's symptoms as we might read a detective story, finding physical clues to emotional needs of which we were previously unaware.

PROMOTING GOOD HEALTH

Promoting good health is more than just a matter of visits to the doctor and providing sympathy and entertainment during colds. As in everything else, children pick up our attitudes toward health, and as the years go by the models we set will become increasingly important and influential. Do we act as though bodies are irreparably fragile, or do we throw caution and common safety to the wind in the assumption that we are indestructable? How often do we put unhealthful things in *our* mouths? Do children see *us* exercise? Do we handle tension headaches with aspirin alone?

Somewhere between pessimistic overprotection and careless abandon, there are constructive health practices from which our children can benefit. From a bedtime anatomy book, Stefan learns how his body works as well as why and how to take care of it. In order to give her youngsters positive images of themselves, one mother tells them intermittently that they have strong, healthy bodies. When a scab falls off, she points out their body's amazing ability to heal itself. Playing the "posture game" in front of the mirror helps another mother point out good posture.

ILLNESS AT HOME

Normal children come down with an astonishing number of illnesses, most of which, fortunately, are not serious and can be treated at home. Unfortunately, such illness can disrupt family life, put us under a good deal of emotional strain, and curtail (or eliminate) our sleep. We have to wrestle with youngsters to take their temperatures and induce them to swallow unsavory medicines. None of this is fun, but there are ways to ease the strain.

First of all, good reference books can lend some peace of mind. We can recommend three: for treating home accidents involving children there is *A Sigh of Relief: The First-Aid Handbook for Childhood Emergencies* by Martin I. Green (Bantam, 1977); for managing illness, *Taking Care of Your Child: A Parent's Guide to Medical Care* by Robert Pantell, M.D., James Fries, M.D., Donald Vickery, M.D., (Addison-Wesley, 1977); and *Parents' Emergency Guide: An Action Handbook for Childhood Illnesses and Accidents* by the Diagram Group (Facts On File, Inc., 1983).

THERMOMETERS AND FEVERS

Temperatures are one of the most important pieces of information in judging the seriousness of an illness and choosing appropriate treatment. A fever of 101 degrees is entirely different from one of 104 degrees and few people can accurately judge such small differences by touch.

Oral thermometers are fine for most three-year-olds, but younger children are apt to bite them so rectal thermometers are generally, preferred. If we take temperature gently with a lubricated thermometer, it won't actually hurt. (When the procedure is done in doctors' offices, children generally cry from fear, not pain.) With experience, we eventually become comfortable with this basic procedure.

Normal temperatures are: 99.6 degrees rectal, 98.6 oral, and 97.6 to 98.1 axillary.

Plastic skin temperature strips available in drug stores are less accurate than thermometers because they are affected by air temperature. They can, however, give a quick and easy estimate so that you know if a regular thermometer check is needed.

Any position that works is fine for taking temperatures. See illustrations. One person may hold the youngster while someone else takes the temperature. A kitchen timer may keep youngsters distracted, and it rings when the time is up.

If the doctor advises baths for high fever, try to keep the child from screaming and struggling, which will create more body heat. A gradual change of water temperature is easier for the child to adjust to. Use comfortably warm water at first, then gradually add more cool water until it is just lukewarm. Cold water is not necessary. Or hold the child on your lap and sponge with a cloth or your hand. Note: Alcohol baths are no longer recommended as fumes may be harmful.

COMMON MINOR AILMENTS

Colds are the most common of all. Give your doctor a call to learn his or her preferred routine.

Teething distress can be eased by teething rings, especially if they have been chilled. An alternative is to tie a frozen bagel within reach on a *short* string, or knot a piece of apple in a damp washcloth. Some parents use a dab of whiskey on the gums, or teething ointment from the drugstore. If the baby is very fussy, but not otherwise ill, some parents use children's or infants' Tylenol® (acetaminophen) at night so everyone can get some sleep. If sucking is painful, express breast milk and give it from a cup, or enlarge holes in bottle nipples for the time being.

Pinworms are fairly common between the age of toilet training and adequate hand washing. The wiggling, white, threadlike worms come out of the anus to lay their eggs in the evening, which can cause bedtime restlessness. If itching is severe, half an Anusol® suppository or a child's Fleet's® enema can give temporary relief until you can get a prescription from the doctor in the morning.

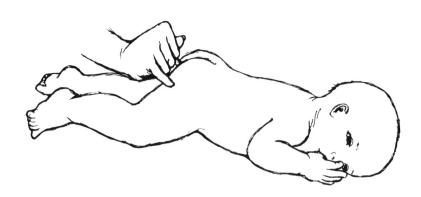

Loss of Appetite

Sick children rarely need to be pressured to eat solid foods they don't want, because appropriate liquids can usually provide sufficient nutrition until appetite improves. If children urinate five to six times in twenty-four hours, they are most likely getting adequate liquid.

CAUTION! If the baby is under six months of age, check with your doctor about diet. Also, cola drinks, because of their caffeine, may cause sleeplessness or increased activity. Fruit juices in large amounts can make diarrhea worse. Depending on the illness, milk and citrus juices may or may not be advisable; ask your doctor if you aren't sure.

Carbonated drinks, especially ginger ale and 7-Up,® are helpful if a child is vomiting. Small children may prefer them "flat" rather than fizzy. Gatorade® replaces body minerals lost in diarrhea and vomiting. Or, make jello water by adding four cups of water to a small package of Jello.® Add extra water to beef or chicken bouillon so it's not so salty. If you serve tea, add sugar for needed calories. As small amounts given frequently are more likely to stay down, some parents freeze some or all of these into popsicles.

Cheer sick children up by making food presentation fun. Serve meals on play size or fancy "company" dinnerware. A muffin tin holds small portions and keeps glasses from sliding. Cut a piece of toast into a puzzle, or serve croutons instead of bread and a lollipop to stir tea.

GIVING MEDICINES AND USING VAPORIZERS

How do we get medicines down children when they don't want to take them, or put them to sleep in a room with a vaporizer when they are frightened of the sound?

First of all, tell children the reason for the medicine or vaporizer as soon as they are old enough to understand. To avoid choking, use liquid medicines for children under age three. If more than one child is sick, make a chart to note when medicines have been given to each child.

Infants may drink medicine if it is poured directly into the nipple of a baby bottle. Medicines can also be given from medicine droppers, syringes without needles, or tiny medicine cups, all of which are less likely to spill than is a teaspoon.

Give a spoonful of jam or other favorite food just after the medicine, especially those with a bitter aftertaste. However, *do not mix medications with essential foods or liquids as youngsters may come to dislike the latter*.

If all else fails, hold the child and drip medicine into the mouth in small enough quantities that it can't be spit out. Pour a little with each scream, or if children clamp their mouths shut for good, have someone else hold the nostrils closed. It may take five minutes to get it all in, and you'll both hate it, but given the choice next time of taking the medicine alone or being held down, many children take it alone.

If the child vomits medicine more than once, call your doctor.

Eye Medications

Eye ointments are more difficult than drops, so if you can avoid them do so. If not, here's how to use: Don't put the medicine into the eye itself, but put a strip along the inner edge of the lower lid.

To administer eye medications, put a baby on the diaper changing table, legs toward you, and knees at the edge. Hold the baby's arms to sides of body with your elbows, leaving your hands free—one hand to hold the head and one for medication. Position a child on his back, with head off the edge of a bed. Kneel with your back to the child. Restrain both arms between your side and left elbow and support the head with your left hand. The other hand is free for applying the medicine.

If the child can't keep his eyes open, drip medicine drops in the depression between the eye and the bridge of the nose. Then put the bottle down and use both hands to pry the eye open and tilt the head so medicine runs into the eye. Ideally, the sterile drops should go directly into the eye, but this procedure is better than no drops at all.

Vaporizers

Vaporizers add moisture to the air and thus loosen mucus, soothe irritated air passages, and help control croup. Doctors recommend *cool mist* rather than hot water models not only because they are more effective, but also to avoid accidental burns. Some are called humidifiers, which is fine, as long as they are designated for sick-room use.

Unfortunately, some children find them scary. You can help by spending time in the bedroom with children until they get use to the sound; or, even though it is less effective in a large room, run it in the living room during the day when you will be nearby.

If the child has a cold, run the vaporizer in the bedroom with the door closed *before* bedtime, then turn it off. The room will generally be sufficiently moist.

One mother overcame her son's fear by the following means:

> Brent, age two and one-half, announced that the vaporizer was a monster and he was terrified. I held him on my lap and asked him to describe the creature, which he did in vivid detail. But then I said he was mistaken about one thing. Such creatures growl. We practiced several growls together to get just the right one. I then pointed out that there was a magic space-ship that makes a whirring sound and puts out magic smoke that keeps monsters away. In fact we had one in our house. As long as he could hear it, no monster could get him. Brent was so convinced that even after his bronchitis cleared up he wanted the vaporizer to scare away the monsters.

THE SICKROOM: EQUIPMENT AND ENTERTAINMENT

A sickroom doesn't have to be the child's own bedroom, especially if this is isolated and lonely. Youngsters may prefer the living room on a sofa, lounge chair, or bean-bag chair. For most childhood illnesses, youngsters need not be confined to bed. Unless your doctor advises otherwise, let them be up and around if they wish. Unlike ourselves, they will usually lie down and rest when tired.

Sickroom equipment may include the following: a plastic waste-basket by the bed for vomiting; a paper waste bag pinned to the side of the bed for Kleenex; a cookie sheet, which makes a neat work table with edges so crayons won't roll off; a covered cake pan to serve as a drawing board with crayon storage inside; you can use an ironing board for a bedside table—turn it partly across the bed for eating. If the child is weak or dizzy and needs help to go to the bathroom, put a bell by the bed to summon help.

To beat boredom in the sickroom, parents include in addition to the usual toys and maybe some extra TV, special activities such as looking at adult art and travel books, family photo albums, or (using a hand viewer) family slides; interesting equipment such as flashlights and magnets; household tasks such as straightening up the sewing drawer; using machines that are usually off limits, such as a typewriter.

Coping with Germs

From the time we first learn about the invisible little germs that cause illness, it's hard not to worry about their potential threat. In fact the vast majority of bacteria are harmless and our bodies are well equipped to protect us from most others.

The body's resistance to infection does, however, vary from time to time. For the first three months of life, an infant's ability to fight off illness is relatively low, so doctors recommend the precautions of avoiding large crowds and, when possible, people who are sick. Throughout our lives, various factors affect our resistance to infection, as shown by the fact that when many people are exposed to the same illness, not all will get it. The strength of the particular germ also affects how many people are likely to become ill.

Another factor in whether germs cause illness is how *many* there are—thus the standard precaution of covering nose and mouth for coughs and sneezes, and hand washing, which decrease the total number of bacteria and viruses in the environment. Getting rid of *all* germs is not only impossible, but unnecessary for daily living.

The myth still pervades our society that a few whiffs of chilly air causes colds. Though *excessive chilling* can lower the body's resistance to infection, it is far more likely that Jeffrey caught his cold because a kid in the grocery store coughed cold viruses in his face than because Mom took him shopping on a chilly day.

Because many common viruses are contagious for twenty-four hours before any symptoms appear, it is impossible to protect youngsters from such illnesses. Babies and toddlers are more apt than preschoolers to pass infections around because they put their fingers in each other's faces and lick each other's toys. (For more about germs and putting objects in mouths, see p. 137). But if we isolated them from their playmates every time someone had the sniffles, they'd rarely see a visitor during the early years. We can, however, take reasonable precautions by keeping youngsters away from friends who have a fever, are acting significantly ill, or—in the case of known bacterial throat and skin infections—until anti-biotic treatment has been underway for twenty-four hours. Isolation is not generally considered necessary for ear infections.

Exposure to the illness of other family members is inevitable, but we can lessen the chances of contagion by such commonsense measures as no kissing or sharing eating utensils with whoever is sick, and proper disposal of used tissues. Isolation in a separate room is generally not necessary or helpful.

Encouraging Positive Attitude toward Recovery

We help our youngsters fight illness with the best of trained medical practitioners and scientific care. And our children fight with their individual wills to survive in good health. But there are ways to strengthen the innate will to recover which are not generally in-cluded in the treatment plans of today's scientifically trained doctors because the processes involved aren't yet thoroughly understood. Parents, on the other hand, are not bound by scientific proof. Many believe that healing techniques involving prayer and forms of med-itation are important *supplements* to medical treatment, despite the skepticism of others. Though many would label such efforts "far out," few would contend that they are harmful.

Here are some of the alternative healing methods that parents report using:

Prayer. When Jennifer, age four, has the flu, I have her close her eyes, relax, "imagine" seeing Mary or Jesus, and ask to get better quickly.

Massage. Sometimes my body conveys love to my sick children more easily than my voice. I give lots of back and shoulder massages.

Energy transfer. When my son, age two, is sick, I sit with him as he drifts off to sleep and get myself into a calm relaxed mood. I then imagine that loving, healing energy, like the warmth from a heat lamp, is flowing in through the top of my head, through my hands, and into his body to heal it.

Images for Improvement. When my five-year-old was sick, I described the white blood cells whose job it is to gobble up bad germs. "You mean like spiders eating bugs?" he asked.

He dozed off to sleep mumbling contentedly about spiders. My daughter, age four, prefers to imagine miniature vacuum cleaners that whoosh up the germs. It may be mere chance, but they rarely stay sick for long.

Personal Involvement in Care. I believe that at some subconscious level, all of us, including children, know something about what we need to feel better. Thus, when my daughter, age four, is ill, I have her close her eyes, relax, and think about what would help. Sometimes it's a bath, or a cup of mild tea, or to hear a particular story. She's never asked for anything outrageous.

COPING WITH PAIN AND INJURY

If only we could isolate our precious little ones in a world of cotton fluff where they would never experience pain! But alas, it would be a dull and lonely existence. Though we do our best to protect our young explorers from injury (see Chapter 5), scraped knees and bumped heads are as much a part of growing up as broken toys. The best of parents will probably make an occasional visit to the emergency room to check out an injury.

There are four basic steps to help children cope with pain.

1. *Evaluate the situation.* We may be as frightened as our youngsters by their first cry of pain. Fortunately, a quick glance usually shows that no serious harm has been done. Then it may be appropriate to scoop them up for a hug or

---

To Pamper or Not to Pamper

Pro. Everyone is emotionally more needy when sick. And people often get sick *because* they are emotionally needy. In either case, pampering is the obvious treatment, and I do it liberally.

Con. I don't want my children to think I love them more when they are sick than when they are well. So I am concerned and attentive, but careful not to overdo it.

wait to see their next reaction. They may get up and go on their way with hardly a pause. Sometimes youngsters scream more in response to our fear than to the injury.

2. *Give sympathy.* Give sympathy when needed with quiet words and a hug to help the child feel understood and secure. "We don't deny Jason's pain," his parents report, "and usually console him with 'That must really hurt,' but we don't dwell on the pain. When his grandmother says 'that didn't hurt,' he screams all the louder."

3. *Give hope.* Explain the pain *will* subside. For example, "The shot will be over before I can count to ten"; "Your knee will feel better after we put a Band-Aid on it."

4. *Direct attention away from the pain. After* giving hope and sympathy, parents use a variety of techniques for focusing children's attention away from the pain of an injury, or from an impending discomfort such as removing a splinter.

Aaron, age five, still had ear pain after returning from the doctor. I asked, "What color is the pain? What does it sound like? What kind of an animal is it like?" It was red like a fire, and wild and angry like a lion. I told him to imagine pouring water on the fire and taking water to the thirsty roaring lion. He did so, and the pain subsided.

When Andy bit his finger and couldn't stop crying, his mother announced, "Andy just had a finger sandwich," whereupon he stopped crying and began to laugh.

I've talked with my son, age five, about all the little wires, called nerves, that go through his body and carry feelings of pain to his brain. We imagine he has lots of switches along the way, so he can turn them off and stop the pain before it hurts. Sometimes we can get so involved in describing the colored wires and how the switches work that he doesn't notice pain. (While taking terrible-tasting penicillin one day, he suddenly announced he could turn off the taste switches on his tongue, and took the remaining course of medicine without complaint.)

A bag of frozen vegetables, a funny shaped plastic glove of ice kept in the freezer, or popsicles for mouth or lips can all help soothe and distract a child.

We offer Jason, age four, the choice of a kiss or a Band-Aid. He usually chooses a Band-Aid, which he loves to put on by himself and have me decorate with a felt pen.

We keep a special little bottle for tears in the medicine cabinet. It's hard to think about the cut on his toe when Byron, age three, is trying to catch his tears in the bottle.

If the pain continues "unreasonably," the injury may be more serious than it seemed at first, so check with your doctor; or the child's reaction may appear out of proportion because the injury may have some additional emotional significance.

When four-year-old Sonya sobbed hysterically despite being comforted for a minor injury, her mother finally said, "This must be a very good pain, because you want to keep it. Tell me what is so good about the pain." The tearful reply came, "I don't have to run the race." Her mother replied, "I love you just the way you are. You don't have to run races with your older brother even if your knee stops hurting." The pain vanished, and Sonya went off to play.

People do perceive pain differently. Just as certain people have more acute hearing, others are biologically more sensitive to pain. Similarly, some children are innately more prone to fear and anxiety than others, and the same pinprick hurts more when one is frightened. Furthermore, children absorb fear from us the way T-shirts turn blue when washed with new jeans. If we feel genuinely frightened by blood, shots and dental drills, then another family member, friend, or health care worker may be able to soothe our youngsters more effectively than we can during medical procedures.

· Removing splinters. Using tweezers on a nervous youngster's hand can be a difficult task. Instead, have your child sit in the tub for a long soak, or apply a piece of ice which may soften the tissue surrounding the splinter and release it. For fine splinters or cactus spines, apply glue liberally to the affected area, and when dry, peel it off with all the splinters.

- Removing plastic bandages. If a bandage is difficult to remove, soak the area in baby oil for a few seconds. The bandage will soften and peel off more easily.
- Picking off scabs. Once a sore is well healed and the scab starts to come off, apply some hand lotion to keep the area moist and less likely to itch, or cover it with a Band-Aid again to keep fingers off.

DOCTORS, DENTISTS, AND HOSPITALS

OFFICE VISITS AND HOSPITAL STAYS

While waiting in the doctor's office, trace your two-year-old's outline on the examining table paper and sketch the parts the doctor will look at. It's a life-size portrait that you can tear off and take home. During exams children's fears may be greatly lessened by our immediate presence. Try holding little ones on your lap for routine exams. Sit near one end of the examining table so there is room for the child to stretch out during the abdominal check. One of the most crucial factors is the confidence we convey to our children, both in their ability to handle what is ahead and in the medical and dental personnel we entrust them to. If *we* are particularly nervous about an upcoming medical procedure, another family member, friend, or health-care worker may provide more comfort and reassurance than we can. A certain amount of fear of the unknown or of pain is inevitable in some medical situations. Since we can't eliminate all our children's distress, it is better to allow them to express it with their tears: "You can cry if you want, but don't move your arm when you get the shot." One mother realized she was pressing her four-year-old to be brave about his ear operation so that *she* would feel less upset when he was wheeled off to surgery.

Fortunately, the days are past when children were told that they were going to the movies, only to end up in the hospital for a tonsillectomy. Today we assure our children's continuing trust in us by being honest about what's ahead. It is, however, possible to go too far the other way and thereby frighten children unnecessarily. We are searching for a middle road between deceit and despair.

Hearing that there is something wrong with their bodies can be a real blow to children's self-esteem. Thus it is important to approach health visits and procedures positively and choose words with care: We see the doctor once a year so she can see how big and healthy you are. The dentist will help make your teeth shiny and strong. The doctor will fix this bad cut on your arm. The doctor will fix your ears so that you won't get so many earaches (i.e., put tubes in ears). Better to state the general facts rather than overloading youngsters with the details of medical procedures which are apt to be misunderstood and therefore frightening. For the same reason, minimize anxiety by discussing unusual medical situations and procedures out of the child's hearing, if possible. Of course we will also give straightforward, appropriately positive answers to whatever questions we are asked. Regarding careful choice of words, children who are told that anesthesia is like slumber may be afraid to go to sleep for days for fear that they will wake up in a hospital again. Better to say, "You will be given special medicine to help you relax and so it won't hurt while the doctor is working. Because of the medicine, you won't remember."

While all agree that children should be prepared ahead of time for medical procedures, authorities differ as to how far in advance. Those who advise preparing a child several days ahead reason that advance warning will give the children the opportunity to rehearse and digest what's coming through familiarity with the steps involved. Furthermore, children may sense our concern, particularly if we make the rounds of medical specialists, and they may be relieved to hear some facts, rather than being left alone to imagine the worst. But, especially for children under five, lengthy preparation may cause a fearful waiting period during which young imaginations magnify every unpleasant detail. Also, time ticks by *very* slowly for youngsters, and what seems to us like a few short days until "minor ear surgery," may seem to a four-year-old like a whole year of dreading that his ear will be chopped off. As a general guideline, the shorter the medical procedure, the less preparation time is necessary. Thus, for shots a moment or two beforehand is fine. For surgery and hospitalization, two- to four-year-olds may be told four to six hours beforehand, and four- to five-year-olds the morning before (not the night before, as darkness and bedtime are difficult enough already).

Honesty is, of course, the basis of trust. We can honestly tell

Brian, age four, we are going to the doctor today, but "omit" telling him about the shot until a minute before. But if he asks about shots on the way, it's better to come out with the truth, even if it makes the whole trip uncomfortable. He'll know he can trust you in the future.

Books about dentists and hospitals and doctor's kits may also be helpful in preparing children for a stay in the hospital. Some hospitals allow children to visit wards prior to admission. When discussing a hospital stay, be sure to include the return home.

COPING WITH THE AFTEREFFECTS

The effects of hospital visits often don't end when the child comes home. Children may be withdrawn, fussy, demanding, clingy, or aggressive for days or weeks after. They may come home with vivid memories of pain, bodily invasion, and fear of desertion. (Fortunately, more hospitals are responding to children's fear of desertion by allowing a parent to stay with them.) Just as we may have fears or nightmares for days after a terrifying movie, children intermittently reexperience fragments of their hospital stay. By going over and over the traumatic experience, we gradually diminish its suspense and terror.

Parents have found unique ways to help children carry out this important work of resolving the hospital visit.

> Several days after his accident, Sandy, age four, was still feeling tense and nervous. He and his dad drew pictures together—of the accident, the visit to the emergency room, and his bandaged foot. Afterward, he seemed more relaxed, and more comfortable as well.

Making a scrapbook is another way of reducing the anxiety of a hospital experience. Collect autographs of doctors and nurses, greeting cards, paper wrapper from a syringe or the first drinking straw after surgery, or a snip of intravenous tubing. Compiling such a scrapbook not only occupies time during the hospital stay, but provides a complete account to review after returning home.

> Bobby was five when he had an ear operation. Each time his dad visited, he took along a special notebook entitled

"Bobby's Hospital Stay." He pretended he was a newspaper reporter, asked Bobby to tell all that had happened since yesterday, and duly recorded it. He made a point of getting it all down: "Tell me again just how that happened," or "How did it feel when . . ." For many days after he returned home, Bobby asked his dad to read the journal.

Other parents tape-record hospital sounds for children as well as complete medical instructions for themselves.

MEDICAL TREATMENT AS PUNISHMENT

Hospitalization is especially difficult for children, because regardless of the circumstances, they assume that what is painful is punishment. Something they thought or did must have caused this painful consequence. Thus, they return home with the crucial but often unexpressed question, "When will I be punished again by being sent back to the hospital?" In the following story that a mother made up, she expresses the unspoken fear, and thereby relieves her son's anxiety.

Once upon a time, Jeffrey had to go to the hospital to have an operation. His mother said his tonsils needed to be fixed. While he was there, they stuck him with needles for shots and blood tests. Sometimes Mommy went away and left him there all by himself. Jeffrey didn't believe his mother that his tonsils needed to be fixed. He knew he'd been sent there for being bad. He had pulled the cat's tail, spilled his milk, drawn on the wall with crayons, waked his mommy when she wanted to rest, and pinched his baby brother.

After he came home from the operation he was very, very good, because he didn't want to be sent back to the hospital. But after three days, he got *so* tired of being good, and he couldn't stand just waiting and wondering when he would be sent back. So he started doing one bad thing after another until his mommy got *really* angry. She swatted him on the bottom, and sent him to his room. Really frightened now, Jeffrey sobbed, "When are you going to send me back to the hospital?" His mother picked him up and hugged him and said, "I'm *not* going to send you back to the hospital, no matter how naughty you are. You didn't go to the hospital for being naughty. We don't take our car to the garage because it is naughty. We take it there because it needs to be fixed. Sometimes it hurts to get fixed. When you are naughty, I may swat you, or send you to your room, but I will *not* send you to the hospital.'' Jeffrey and his mommy gave each other a big hug and Jeffrey finally believed what his mother said.

RELATING EMOTIONS AND HEALTH

Many people think symptoms are either real or fake. Ellen has stomach cramps due to a flu virus, *or* her stomach doesn't really hurt. However, symptoms such as pain can be caused as much by emotions as by physical agents. In both cases, the symptoms are real. Intense emotions, for example, may increase muscle contraction in the head, causing a tension headache, or in the abdomen, causing a stomachache. Stress can also decrease appetite, change breathing patterns, and decrease the body's ability to fight off infection. Furthermore, even if children feel fine but repeatedly pretend they have symptoms, *something* is causing this unusual behavior. Thus, there is no point in admonishing a complaining child, ''Your stomach doesn't really hurt.''

Many doctors acknowledge that a large percentage of adult illness involves the interaction between emotional stress and body physiology. Because there are so many *physical* reasons for frequent illness during the early years, the percentage of emotion-related illness during childhood is probably less than that in adulthood; but exploring mind-body relationships may provide clues to both the cause of a child's illness and its possible cure.

Illness can be like a painting, song, or poem, which publicly displays the inner turmoil of the artist. Behind some symptoms is a need for more love, security, self-esteem, or release of anger. The frustrating thing is that these needs can exist *even though* we are going to great lengths to meet all these basic needs of our children. If there *is* an emotion-related cause, we can treat the illness from two directions simultaneously—physical *and* emotional. We thereby increase the chances of rapid recovery and better future health.

The first clues to an underlying emotional problem may be that standard medical treatments don't lead to improvement, or our own vague inner feeling that there is more to the problem than meets the eye. There are further signals that we can look for.

1. *A symptom which re-occurs for more than two months* for which the doctor can find no physical explanation. At this point, we can either get the opinion of other doctors, including specialists, consider emotions as a possible cause, or both.

2. *A fairly recent, emotionally significant event* in the child's life may show itself in physical symptoms: a move, change in child care arrangements, change in school, loss of a loved one, arrival of a new family member, change in parents' marital relationship, inappropriate sexual stimulation, or a number of other possibilities.

3. *A symptom that curtails normal activities or causes noticeable distress* to the child *or any other* family member may be emotional in origin.

If we suspect an emotional component, what can we do?

1. *Look for a pattern when symptoms occur.* When are they worse or better? If stomach pain always occurs before nursery school, then *something* about going there is stressful. When angry, Brent vomits and Marie scratches her eczema. Aaron wheezed while his parents arranged their divorce, Janna had stomachaches when her grandmother was in the hospital, and Kevin had nosebleeds when his mom was out of town. Greg had frequent colds when his mother returned to work, and Lisa says her tummy hurts when she doesn't want to do something. Do symptoms occur only after eating certain foods, or exposure to particular animals or chemicals? There is a *physical and an emotional* component to many allergies.

2. *Talk with the child.* Often we can help our children talk about and cope with emotionally difficult issues. See Emotional Awareness p. 247.

3. *Look for alternative methods* to provide what the symptom may provide. When our children have symptoms, we may automatically attend to them more lovingly than usual, lower

our expectations of their behavior, or alternatively, cut back the amount of freedom we allow. Thus, the symptom *may* fill a basic need for more loving attention, for relief from our excessively high expectations, or for the security of tighter parental controls, to mention just a few possibilities. If we can discover such a need, and fill it more directly, either by ourselves or with the help of others, the child's health may improve accordingly.

4. *Get more help.* In addition to the above, or because such efforts have not alleviated symptoms, it may be appropriate to discuss with a child or family therapist the advisability of professional help. Also, continue to work closely with the child's physician, especially if new symptoms arise.

Parents also devise their own impromptu methods for handling less serious symptoms. One mother found her son's rectal itching occurred only when she was involved with other family members. She made a rule that he could ask for more time together when he wanted it, but he'd have to go to his room if he complained that his bottom itched. This quickly cleared up the problem.

Another mother describes her program for preventive relaxation:

> I let my son Mark, age five, have a day off when he is well, so he doesn't have to get sick to snuggle, read, and so forth. Once every six months, he gets a TV day when he can lie in bed and watch TV all day if he wants. Mark doesn't need to get sick as he gets his chance to lounge around regularly with our blessings.

Accident-proneness can occur for emotional reasons. Because of their curiosity, lack of experience, and physical instability, youngsters are especially accident-prone from the time they learn to crawl and climb until about age three. However, repeated accidents, especially over age three, may be a sign of emotional strain. Accident-proneness can be handled similarly to other emotion-related health problems.

HOW PARENTS HANDLE THEIR OWN WORRIES ABOUT CHILDREN'S HEALTH

What helps you maintain your children's health? "Luck!" replied one mother. Indeed, there is a great deal of luck. Medical science

180 □ NO-FAULT PARENTING

still doesn't know what reasons, genetic and otherwise, cause some children to be innately more healthy than others. Pediatricians do know, however, that young children are ill more often than are adults. Few of us remember the frequent illnesses of our own early years, so we aren't prepared for repeated sickness of our youngsters. Adults have developed immunity to a tremendous number of illnesses, including many of the one hundred or more cold viruses. Children develop their own immunity only by conquering each individual virus. Furthermore, due to frequent colds and the shape a child's head, youngsters are much more prone to ear infections and only gradually outgrow this susceptibility. Some illnesses persist until subtle allergies are detected. Finally, frequent trips to the doctor are especially common before youngsters have the language to accurately describe body sensations. Despite the best preventive medicine, a certain amount of childhood illness is inevitable. In this age of miracle drugs, there is still no cure for viruses. My doctor says, 'It's just a virus,'' which translates into ''Antibiotics won't help,'' but I still have to nurse a whiny child with a 102° temperature.

Every family will develop its own strategies for dealing with childhood illness. Here are a few that were related to us:

> I simply don't have as much time when the children are ill. For example, when Greg had a cold, he'd nap as long as I was next to him, and cry the instant I tried to slip out of the room. I finally just got a book and sat down to read for the day. The house remained in shambles, and we ate hot dogs for dinner.

> I always forget how long it takes children to recover from illness. Once the fever is down I expect them to be back to normal. But they remain irritable and need special handling for several more days. When I accept the fact that they still aren't completely well, and lower my expectations, things go much better.

If you are worried about your child's health, ask your doctor questions, no matter how minor they seem. If the child, or some other family member, was very sick and you fear this illness is a repeat, ask how to distinguish today's cold, for example, from last month's pneumonia. Also ask approximately when to expect improvement and what symptoms would be cause for further concern.

Worry often increases with isolation. It may help you to talk with supportive friends and relatives and minimize the time you spend alone with your sick child.

Many parents worry because they can't be at home with sick children. Nowhere is the desire to be two places at once more intense than when on-the-job parents have a sick child. Given the normal frequency of illness in the first few years of life, parents who are able to stay home full time or work just part time are able to avoid much emotional strain. In families in which both parents do have jobs, increasing numbers of fathers are taking turns with sick call at home. Some areas, in response to the needs of on-the-job parents, have established centers for caring for sick children or listings of experienced sitters who will stay with them. It is probably emotionally easier on ill children to be cared for at home by a sitter than in a center where both personnel *and* surroundings are unfamiliar, but such centers can be a godsend to parents who lack other alternatives.

Parents are often hesitant to tell youngsters about serious illness of family members, both to protect the child and because they are not sure what to say. However, with or without the facts, children will draw their own conclusions. What children most need to know is how the illness relates to them and their lives. Inform children in simple terms about the medical status of siblings and other close relatives and of the fact that they are not the cause of family illness. The facts we provide may be far less frightening than the fantasies young imaginations invent. Michelle, age four, aware of the distress in her family, concluded that her Daddy had a broken heart until she was informed that her new sister had been born "with a heart that wasn't made right."

7

Travel: Outings, Shopping, and Moving

B efore travel became so "easy," with modern transportation and all its conveniences, few people ventured from home with young children. Our reward for progress is temper tantrums on the superhighway and sleepless youngsters in unfamiliar motels. Before the baby's arrival, we skipped out on errands without a second thought. Now we wonder—How many meals need I take? Will there be another round of diarrhea? Will Lisa run off and get lost again or Edward refuse to return to the car? It takes a lot of practice to broaden our focus from the outing itself to helping our children adjust to a multitude of new rules and strange surroundings, such as the back seat of the car and the local grocery store. When this skill is finely honed, we can contemplate how to entertain a two-year-old on an eight-hour plane flight.

Shopping presents additional challenges. Will there be another scene in front of the candy counter? We have an entire advertising industry to contend with, which cares no more than Junior does that there is a bottom to our bank account. If product X was on Saturday morning TV, it must be essential to life.

Finally, we are a society of movers. We move because our growing families need more space, because of job changes, because the grass looks more lush elsewhere. Moves are hard work for us, and mind-boggling for our little ones. Where, they wonder, is my crib, my kitchen, Dottie who used to take care of me, and where are all my friends? Because young children have few mental resources for dealing with such disorders in their lives, we take up the slack by cuddling clingy youngsters during the day and sleepless ones at night.

With time, however, we automatically pack the familiar contents of the diaper bag. Eventually we find a buying policy for our children that accords with what we can afford. And several months after the move, we have a new routine. Fortunately, in addition to our own ingenuity, we can use the experience of others to help us along.

OUTINGS AND TRIPS

GETTING PREPARED

Whether walking to visit a neighbor with an infant or preparing for a two-week family vacation with our preschoolers, there are many more details to attend to than we dreamed of in our carefree child-less days.

First, what sort of baby carrier to choose? Each has its own advantages. Adequate support for an infant's head and convenience are important factors to consider. It's handy to be able to nurse with minimal readjustment when using a baby pack, and one mother put an infant seat inside her Gerry carrier to provide adequate neck support in the early months. Cloth and aluminum-frame back packs allow more body contact and are easier to manage on public transportation and rough ground, but a stroller puts less strain on one's back as baby grows. Umbrella strollers are also easy to manage on public transportation and they take the least amount of room when not in use, but regular strollers give more versatility—they'll carry packages or a second child on the back. Baby buggies offer better protection against cold weather, and in some models the basket can be lifted off the wheels to double as a bassinet.

If just the baby went along, travel would be simple. But with all the necessary equipment, a quick jaunt to the store becomes an expedition, and an overnighter turns into a safari.

Naturally, there's no single list that is adequate for every variety of outing; but depending on the length of the trip, certain basics will make traveling with little ones easier. Some parents keep a list of supplies in the diaper bag and recheck it before returning home to be sure they have everything.

For Wet Bottoms and Other Messes

- Diapers. Disposables for ease in transit, and extra diaper pins.
- Plastic bags for wet diapers or in case of vomiting. Bread bags are a safe and convenient size.
- Sheet of plastic on which to make diaper changes or to put under an older child prone to bed-wetting.
- Portable potty. Just because youngsters are toilet trained doesn't mean they can get to the next bathroom. Keep a little potty or a jar in the car. One mother even carried an emergency bottle in her purse when in large museums. Other parents return youngsters to diapers for outings, or make inconspicuous curb stops when necessary.
- Bib. The large coverall type for a messy eater in a car or airplane.

· Apron for yourself so you'll arrive unsmudged after feeding baby in transit.

For Hunger and Thirst

· Breast Milk. Don't wean before a trip. You can't beat breast milk for an easy-to-store liquid in spill-proof containers.
· Formula. Formula mixed at home can be carried for several hours if kept cool. Bottled, ready-to-serve formula is more expensive but turns every drug store into a drive-in. Alternatively, to avoid spoiling, mix dry powdered formula with warm water from a thermos just before serving.
· Water. Carry a small or collapsible cup to help toddlers quench their thirst at a drinking fountain. If you carry ''just water'' on car trips, little ones drink less and need fewer stops, and there's no sticky mess when it spills. Or add just a touch of lemon for flavor. Freeze it ahead for a lingering supply of cold water, and serve it in spill-proof containers.
· Snacks. Keep a bottle of dry baby cereal or a crush-proof tumbler of crackers in the diaper bag.

For Comfort and Safety

· Pacifier or other security object.
· Sunscreen for baby's tender skin.
· Plastic bandages.
· Tweezers for splinters on a camping trip.
· Thermometer plus children's Tylenol® (acetaminophen) in case of sudden fever while on vacation.
· Medications the child uses frequently.
· Current safety devices, such as baby gates or electric outlet covers.

For Particular Destinations

· The beach. In addition to sunscreen and hats, an old playpen without a floor provides both safety and sand. A regular one

---

CAUTION: TO AVOID CHOKING IN CASE OF SUDDEN STOPS, do not offer hard candies, nuts, or similar small solid edibles in the car.

turned upside down gives shade. Take a bucket for sand castles, but carry it back to the car with water, to wash off sandy feet. A mesh onion bag keeps toys together and allows quick rinsing before leaving.

· Camping. A long rope clearly defines campsite boundaries for a toddler. A plastic bucket left in the sun solar heats water for evening wash-up.

· Museums. To make museums more interesting to youngsters, go prepared with questions such as the following: What do you think that was used for? How is that job done differently now? What would youngsters have played with after dark? What would have been better about living then? What does this picture show? Does it make you think of a story or a piece of music? What do you imagine you could hear or smell if you were in the picture?

Some kindergartners prefer to wander by themselves, so *if appropriate,* equip them with a pocket timer that buzzes or a watch and meet every fifteen to thirty minutes.

Travel is generally easier if children are prepared emotionally. Describe where you are going with words or pictures, what behavior you expect, and how long you will be gone. You might relieve little ones' distress at being away by reminding them when the trip will be over. One vacationing two-year-old forgot and began to mourn the ''permanent '' loss of friends and familiar places.

HOW TO AVOID LOSING CHILDREN

When traveling with children, there is always the risk that they will run off and disappear.

Here are some practical methods parents have devised to keep track of young travelers:

· Identification. One mother always started bedtime stories with her son's full name and address. He had it down pat by age two and one-half, so she added the phone number. Another mother made up a song containing the vital information.

· Meeting place. When going to a zoo or museum, pick a prominent place to meet in case of separation, such as front of the lion's cage or the gift shop.

· Whom to ask for help. By the time children are three, they should know that they can ask for help from a store clerk, policeman, ticket seller, or mother with a child.

· Bright colors. Children are easier to spot in a crowd when they wear bright and distinctive hats, coats, or swimsuits.

· Name tag. Using a laundry marker, jot name and phone number on a prominently placed Band Aid when attending a crowded event. If traveling by air, attach a luggage tag to the child's clothes or wrist. In addition to name and emergency phone number, include current destination, airline, and flight number.

· Harness. Whether you are traversing a bustling airport or hiking the rim of the Grand Canyon, a toddler harness increases both safety and peace of mind. Rope or sturdy twine will serve in a pinch.

CAR TRAVEL

Some Safety Tips

Whenever little ones travel in the car, car seats and infant carriers are essential for safety. Check *Consumer Reports* for the latest product information, and look for a seat that enables a youngster to sleep in transit.

Seat belts should become a routine matter. Children who have been buckled in regularly from infancy generally resist far less than do intermittent users. Appoint one youngster "co-pilot": to check that everyone is buckled up *before* takeoff. Once her two-year-old could operate his seat buckle, one mother tied it with additional string unless he put it on and left it on.

Parking lots can be even more dangerous than intersections. One mother has a rule that her daughter must either hold her hand or touch their car while in the parking lot.

Car travel can be made more comfortable for young ones in hot weather if you screen them from the sun. Put aluminum sunshades on the window beside a child's car seat, or close the window on the top edge of a diaper. Another diaper tossed over the seat belt buckle will keep it from getting burning hot while the car is parked.

Motion sickness puts a damper on any trip. Avoid large meals just before leaving if the child is prone to this. Often you can prevent motion sickness by ensuring that the child has an adequate view of the passing scene. Sitting in the front seat is an especially good deterrent. Have children avoid looking at books and speeding objects at the edge of the road. If the problem is recurrent, ask your pharmacist about medication. In any case keep a plastic bag handy.

What Kind of Trip?

When planning trips with children, we have to keep our basic objectives clearly in mind. Are we traveling for family enjoyment or because we *must* reach a far destination? Travel is especially difficult from the time infants learn to crawl until about age two and one-half, because during this time physical activity provides the child's prime delight and few youngsters have the vocabulary, imagination, or fine motor skill to enjoy quiet games for more than a minute or two. If long distances must be covered during this period, travel by airplane minimizes travel time. Trains and buses allow children to stretch their legs and have more parental attention in transit. Cars, on the other hand, give personal flexibility for handling the unexpected and privacy for consoling unhappy children.

If you're traveling for pleasure with small children, make life easier on everyone by planning short trips and including frequent stops. If you know you'll be driving much of the day, plan to make several stops of an hour or so to counteract boredom and confinement.

Car entertainment is a must for any long car trip. Make car trips more interesting for infants by taping pictures within view; or place the car carrier in the front seat to allow more interchange with the driver. Use short strings (for safety) to tie toys and teething rings to the safety bar or straps of the infant seat.

Toddlers may travel more contentedly if provided with a box full of favorite things like bottle, crackers, and toys. Attach the box to the car seat for easy access. Keep small children entertained by attaching a steering wheel to the car seat and encourage them to "drive" along with you. As backseat drivers get older, they'll keep busy telling you where to turn and establish a good sense of direction in the process.

Preschoolers love a shoebag or homemade set of pockets that hangs on the back of the front seat, so they can store items of interest. Once they outgrow car seats, prop them on pillows or booster seats before buckling seat belts, so they can see out the window.

Exercise en route eases long sitting. Try jumping jacks or jump rope at gas stations, picnic stops for meals, cooling off in a swimming pool. While in the car, squeeze a fist while counting to five, push palms together and count, make circles with head or shoulders, point toes or push feet against the seat and so forth. Do a "march" or a head and arm dance to music.

Noise and fighting in the car are frequently caused by boredom. Hence the need for plenty of activities. If you need quiet in heavy traffic, slap your hand against the dashboard as a signal for silence. Pulling to the roadside until peace returns is a common solution. Teach children this lesson when they are especially anxious to get to the destination. But one mother just turns up the radio and another keeps a fly swatter at hand so she can reach a troublemaker in the back seat with a quick swat. Some children earn rewards for avoiding fights in the car.

Sleeping in the Car

Comfortable sleeping is helpful on short drives and essential for long ones. Tiny babies can sleep in most any position, but toddlers and preschoolers, like adults, may have difficulty sleeping when their heads flop around. Some car seats recline for easier sleeping, and some allow youngsters to lean forward to rest. Pillows can help provide the necessary head support and comfort. Once car seats are outgrown, youngsters may nap best in the reclining front seat, or buckled lengthwise into both rear seat belts. Some night-owl parents drive mainly after dark to assure peace in the car, and some parents tie a duplicate of the beloved security object to the car seat to invite relaxation.

PLANE, TRAIN, AND BUS

One mother spent two months touring the country by bus and visiting relatives with her youngsters, eighteen months, and four years. "I decided I wouldn't count on time for myself, I'd be having time with my children. I took a huge acitivity bag, which I replenished frequently. One child sat with me for stories and games, while the other played with pillows and dolls on a nearby seat. We all had an enjoyable trip." If only travel worked out so well for everyone!

There's no way to guarantee absolute peace and happiness on long trips involving public transportation, but here are some tips that may help. Choose seats with care: Try to sit near people who seem to like small children and avoid passengers who look askance at pint-sized traveling companions. Take along a pillow or sleeping bag so the child can sit high enough to see out the window. In some planes you can get a bassinet to attach to the wall facing front-row seats. Check with the airline ahead of time.

Changing altitude may cause ear discomfort, which you can help alleviate by encouraging youngsters to suck or chew during takeoff and landing. Offer bottle, breast, gum, or a snack.

Soothe a restless infant by walking the aisles with the young one in a back carrier. Let a toddler play for a few minutes with cups and water in the bathroom. When traveling by plane, soothe yourself with a glass of wine, if necessary. If you're more relaxed, baby may stay calmer. Consider traveling at night so little ones are more likely to sleep.

Under special circumstances, some pediatricians will prescribe a mild sedative for long, confined travel. Or some parents give very active children a dose of cold medicine containing an antihistamine, which generally causes drowsiness. But *be careful!* Children react differently to medications. What relaxes one may hype another. All such medications are dangerous if used in excess.

ACTIVITIES AND ENTERTAINMENT FOR TRAVEL

Keeping children entertained while on the go is a constant challenge. Activities must pack maximum interest in minimal space, without making a mess or risking the loss of irreplaceable parts. However, with characteristic ingenuity, parents have found multiple ways to entertain children in cars, airplanes, restaurants, and doctors' offices, as well as during visits to relatives and while walking.

Books are almost as good as taking a friend along, to keep kids occupied when they must sit for long periods. Workbooks offer an array of mazes, punch-out construction sets, "write-and-erase" activities. A covered cake pan can serve as a portable desk and storage compartment for sketch pads, felt markers, stickers, glue stick, finger puppets, deck of cards, or a felt board. A kitchen storage box with a good seal can hold Lego® blocks or modeling clay, for older youngsters. Keep a songbook or a list of family favorites in the glove compartment.

Block puzzles that make six different pictures hold interest longer and are less likely to get lost than the regular kind; or try a Rubik's cube. Dymo® markers intrigue youngsters who are learning letters, and new slides for the Viewmaster® viewer make great rewards on long family trips.

Bring along a tape recorder with prerecorded stories, or let children record their impressions of the trip. If you have a recorder with earphones, you won't have to listen to ''Snow White'' sixteen times. Family photos are lots of fun: Bring seconds so youngsters can handle them alone.

Get them started on a scrapbook to display trip memorabilia such as maps, postcards, park brochures, and so forth.

There's nothing quite so nice as a present to keep life flowing smoothly. For car and plane trips, wrap small gifts of travel activities to be opened intermittently. Leave a present by the bedside of a child who wakes early in an unfamiliar place—it may enable you to sleep late.

To get somewhere on foot, without youngsters being overcome with boredom, play follow the leader, pretend you are riding on an elephant or water skiis, window shop, greet the flowers and fences, take a pinwheel to encourage speed, carry a collection bag for pretty leaves, or—while you go on foot—let youngsters ride on bikes or in a wagon.

Readily available games include guess what object from pocket or purse is wrapped in a kleenex, penny toss on the carpet of an uncrowded airport, or make rubbings of interesting textures using pencil and scraps of paper. Thinking games don't require any equipment at all, but it does take a certain frame of mind to create something out of nothing, so here are some ideas to get started.

> *Name it.* Name body parts and office equipment while waiting for the doctor; distinguish vans and semi trucks on the freeway; bricks versus cement, and kinds of plants while walking. For older children, play *Word groups.* The first person chooses a category such as flowers, trucks, furniture, and gives one example. Each player follows with another example. After everyone has had a turn, the list continues until anyone chooses to pick a new category.
>
> *Guess what fruit or animal* I'm thinking of. Give hints to little ones and let older children ask yes or no questions.

Rhymes. Make up nonsense rhymes: slop, glop, lop.

Count it. Count chairs in restaurants, driveways while walking, and green cars on the highway. Older children can keep scores on several items.

Alphabet. Count the A's on the menu, or look for the letters of the alphabet on sign boards.

What if. (1) Questions about emotions and values: "What if someone broke your favorite toy, or what if your friend wanted all the cookies in your lunch box?" (2) Questions of logical thought: "What if we didn't stop for gas, or there weren't any waitresses?" (3) Questions for creative fantasy. "What if blue were the only color, or water ran uphill?"

Continuous fantasy. Make up the beginning of a story, and let everyone take turns continuing it.

Silence. All are silent for a few minutes and then report on what they have seen.

If two-year-olds fuss or dawdle on the homebound trip, brighten their prospects by promising that they can ring the doorbell or unlock the door upon arrival. One mother signed her son up for some junk mail so he'd look forward to checking the box.

SLEEPING AWAY FROM HOME

There is tremendous variation in how easily children sleep away from home. Some do best when placed alone in a quiet room with no distractions. Others doze off in the midst of strange new scenery and general commotion. Some parents encourage flexibility by having youngsters sleep in various places at home, rather than always in the same spot. With some youngsters, however, it's so difficult to get them to sleep away from home that it's hardly worth the effort. Have friends and relatives come visit at your house, or leave young ones home with a sitter whenever possible.

As soon as little ones are old enough to understand, explain what is ahead. "You are going to sleep in a different place, but Mommy and Daddy will be near if you wake up or need anything." Sleep generally comes easier with the customary bedtime rituals from home. Because new places tend to be unsettling, parents are often more lenient about bedtime. They are more likely to sing or snuggle children to sleep. It is also more common for youngsters to sleep in the same room or same bed as their parents when the family is away from home.

Porta-cribs or sleeping bags make good beds away from home. For familiarity, let children sleep in them for a while before the trip. One mother took her infant's crib bumpers, so any bed seemed like home. An inflatable pool makes a great bed for an infant, is easy to pack, and doubles as play space and bathtub during the day. Take along a nightlight or flashlight in case youngsters wake during the night. To allow naps in a stroller, tie a pillow over the front tray so a youngster can lean forward in comfort.

Children will have an easier time sleeping in a strange place if they've had exercise during the day. Stop driving early if necessary. If you will be driving past bedtime, put children in pajamas early so you can put them to bed without waking them when you stop for the night.

EATING IN RESTAURANTS

Our objectives for going to a restaurant are obvious, aren't they? Time out from stove and dishpan, time to be served instead of serve, a time of relaxation and restoration with relaxing company. The problem, of course, is that restaurants came to mean all these things *before* we went with children. To take a two-year-old to a restaurant with the same expectations is to court disaster. There will be no stove or dishpan, but we may have to supervise, mop up, and answer so many questions that we leave exhausted. So let's return to our objectives.

If we're looking for a peaceful chance to unwind with great food and adult company, it may be best to leave the youngsters at home. If, however, we want to get the family fed with minimal effort and fuss, then the best choice may be a fast-food restaurant. What such establishments lack in superb food, they more than make up for in speed of service and ease in decision making. If we want to expose our children to the diverse cooking and interesting surroundings that many restaurants offer, we can go when we have the energy to focus attention on the needs of little ones; order one item that can be brought right away to ease the wait, and if necessary take a stroll with restless youngsters while others eat.

If possible, try to avoid particularly busy times when taking children to restaurants. Take infants right after they've eaten so *you* can relax. Breakfast or lunch in restaurants may be calmer than dinner because youngsters aren't so tired. Some parents keep a bib, utensils, and premoistened towelette in the glove compartment or tote bag for spur-of-the-moment restaurant stops.

It's only when we enter a restaurant with a small-sized private investigator that we realize how many "no-no's" there can be. Reduce the chances of commotion and upset by stating appropriate behavior ahead of time. Stay seated? Low noise level? Limits on mustard, etc? Blowing bubbles in milk? Sticking French fries in water glass? (On second thought, maybe we *will* leave Junior at home!)

Because nice restaurants are such a pleasure to us, it's hard to remember that children perceive them as a combined jail cell and china shop. It's hard to understand that our offspring don't necessarily share *our* pleasures, even when it's obvious we don't share all of *theirs*. We will experience much less conflict if we can accept that small children and leisurely dining rarely mix with ease. Even a five-year-old may have trouble with a long formal meal.

Little ones often want to order more than they can eat and rarely choose a well-balanced diet. If children's eyes are bigger than their appetites, some parents insist on a small initial order, then let youngsters reorder or snack off adult plates if still hungry. Other parents order less for themselves and finish off the family leftovers. If a trip requires frequent fast-food restaurants, supplement nutrition by serving fruits and vegetables as car snacks.

Some preschoolers can understand that eating in a restaurant is a privilege: Misbehavior will mean staying with a sitter next time. One family threatened to leave, and did so, when youngsters were out of control. Future outings went more smoothly. Another family purposely parked in front of the restaurant window so when two-year-old Jason was really out of line, he was strapped in his car seat, within sight but beyond hearing. He too did much better next time.

SHOPPING

Our foremothers would be envious of the ease of our lives: ready-made clothes, cake mixes, and umbrella strollers. But as we forage through our shopping plazas, alternately ignoring screams for gum balls and prying bright trinkets from tight little fists, we envy our foremothers who trekked to the bleak country store but once a month or sat home and ordered from the Sears catalogue.

Modern-day shopping is a reality, and fortunately there are ways to make it easier. First of all, a few tips for making shopping easier on ourselves: Minimize stops and the number of shopping trips. Keep a separate shopping list of occasional needs from hardware and drug stores. Wait until you *really* need something, then get everything on the list. Choose the optimal time to shop. Are your kids fresher and in better moods in the morning? When are stores less crowded? Maybe the best solution is to find someone to watch the kids while you shop alone, or else go when Dad can join in as well. To avoid hunger pangs in the grocery store, it may be a good idea to feed children before leaving home, take a snack along, or select a loaf of bread or other package to open in the store.

Strollers keep youngsters from wandering off and beyond the reach of merchandise but they aren't the only way to go. Despite the disapproving looks of strangers, a harness and leash provide more freedom to explore. Some little tykes who disappear behind counters wear bells on their shoes. Some young ones are allowed certain freedom, but are confined to harness or stroller if they don't stay nearby. And certain climbers won't stay in a grocery cart unless strapped in with a harness or an old belt.

It helps to review the rules *on the way* to the store. Remind children ahead of time whether they may touch or just look in a particular store. How close must they stay? Are there ways they can help shop?

Some tips on keeping youngsters occupied and entertained on shopping trips:

Loop a toy on a string to the handle of the grocery cart.

Matching game. Put some picture labels from home in a large plastic envelope and let youngsters watch for duplicates.

Grocery helper. Two-year-olds hold the produce bag to collect your choice of fruit. Some preschoolers fetch items from the shelf, add up the approximate bill on a calculator, and count the items at the check-out counter.

Practice decision making. How many quarts of milk do you think we need? How much do you think vegetables will weigh? What flavor of yogurt shall we buy? Which package costs less?

I allowed two-year-old Eric to choose *one edible* item in the grocery store each week. Such a big decision kept him very busy. When he eventually discovered the candy counter, I kept quiet, believing that because *I* wasn't suggesting sweets, they wouldn't become emotionally significant. For some weeks he stuffed himself on his bag of candy, then delighted in offering the remainder to others. He eventually switched to Danish pastries, then to the ravioli and sugar-coated cereal he'd seen on TV. Once he chose celery because it crunches, and once milk to get another car for his milk-carton train. At five, he requested a lobster, and the budget required a no. Not only was shopping easier, but spin-off included opportunities for generosity and the passing of an obsession for sweets.

CHILDREN'S REQUESTS TO BUY THINGS

There are three underlying approaches for dealing with children's natural inclinations to buy every delightful thing they see.

1. Acceptance. One mother noted, "If I take the boys grocery shopping, I just assume I'll spend a few extra dollars. It's easier than continually saying no." However, those who accept children's desire to buy don't leave the bank account wide open. One way or another, they limit how much children can buy, teach consumer awareness, and may avoid spur-of-the-moment buying as well.

A regular allowance is one of the most common and workable means to limit what children spend. Another is to permit them to select one item, for example, a favorite fruit each week or one purchase from the gumball machine.

When Kenny, age four, asks for things, I suggest he "put it on his Christmas or birthday list." Knowing he might get his wish in the future, he's willing to wait. Items he talks of repeatedly we usually get on the designated occasion. Items he mentions only once are never missed.

2. Face Reality. Another approach is to help our children accept the difficult but inevitable fact that they can't possess everything they lay their eyes on. Teaching this lesson often requires that we

tolerate some tantrums; haul screaming, kicking little bodies from a store on occasion; or leave youngsters with a sitter for a few trips. After repeated tantrums at the check-out stand, one desperate mother parked *within view* and with the next tantrum, strapped her son securely in his car seat to wait by himself. Some parents provide incentive by offering a reward such as a stop in the park or a stick of sugarless gum for hassle-free shopping.

Rather than saying no to everything Mary Ann sees in a store or catalogue, her mother invites her to join in fanciful thinking: "Wouldn't it be nice if you could have it! Where would you put it? What would you like most about having it?"

> Britt, eighteen months, likes to hold an attractive item while we are in the store, then we say "bye-bye" and put it back before going to the check-out counter.

> I tell the youngsters, age four and six, that we don't have as much money as many of our neighbors. I let them know that there are also things I would like to have but can't afford.

3. Avoid Ambiguity. One mother related the following: "I used to occasionally get something for Alix, age four, if she asked for something worthwhile. But it backfired. Soon she wanted something every time we went out. She just couldn't understand getting something only once in a while."

Warning children ahead of time that you're going shopping for certain necessary items and nothing else is the easiest way to avoid ambiguity on any given trip, but life is not always so simple. If, despite our intentions, we are distressed by continual pleas, we may need to question why we find it so hard to say no. Are we tempted to spend on our children to assuage some guilt? Often without being aware of it, we pass on our own attitudes about spending and money. We might do better to examine our own attitudes before setting expectations for our children.

Some of us recall an abundance of luxuries from our own childhood and feel badly that comparable expenditures are impossible for our own children. But it should be kept in mind that our youngsters may not even know they are "deprived" unless we tell them so.

On the other hand, some of us buy today for the deprived inner child of our past. "I want to buy everything for Rochelle that I couldn't have when I was young" is a common desire. If, with such impulses, we feel overwhelmed by the desire to buy something superfluous for our children, we might do better to buy something for *ourselves* instead.

More is at stake than copper coins and gray-green paper. Possessions can come to equal love, because to a certain degree, time equals love. We all try at times to fill our children's requests for loving attention with possessions instead, reasoning, "If I buy this expensive educational toy, Johnny won't demand so much of my time." Unfortunately, many a parent has worked so hard to provide "everything" that some children lack the love that they need most of all. If such parental avoidance is carried to excess, children may come both to exploit our guilty need to purchase their good will and simultaneously to resent that we try to buy them off.

Fortunate indeed are those parents who have both the emotional and economic security to emphasize what their children *have,* instead of what they lack. They neither feel nor convey a need to "keep up with the Joneses." For such parents, the choices may not be easy, but they are clear. As one such mother noted, "With eight children, we buy what the children need for well-rounded growth, not simply what they want."

In the long run, recognizing that much of the conflict is within ourselves, we may shed less of our frustration on our children.

MOVING

To appreciate how unsettling moves can be to small children, we can imagine how we would feel if we went to bed one night and awoke on Mars.

No matter how organized we are, moving is an exhausting business. Not only are there all the arrangements and packing to do, but children need more reassurance than ever. Scared that we're about to disappear forever into some big box, they want us close all the time. And then there's the problem of adjusting to a new home. How do parents reduce the abruptness and mystery of a move?

If the new house is nearby, take a few toys and leave them there for future visits. It shows what moving is all about and makes the new place more like home. Photographs are helpful if you know where you'll be moving and children aren't able to visit first.

Remember when house hunting that babies grow rapidly. Be sure to consider what their needs will be a year from now. If you get harried, stop at a park with the children while a friend or spouse checks out the next apartment or house.

Age-appropriate information ahead of time is vital to decreasing anxiety in a new situation. Stories are especially helpful for two- and three-year-olds. Make a story book about your upcoming move. Will the whole family move? Yes, even disliked siblings and naughty children will *not* be left behind! How will people and possessions get from one place to another? What other people will be part of the move? How long will it take? Pictures from magazines or rough sketches suffice for illustrations. Discuss with children their likely feelings, worries and fears as well as curiosity and excitement. Let them help decide which possessions will go and which won't. We may not be able to accommodate, but it's good to ask children if they have definite wishes about the new house. Matthew, for ex- ample, wanted wood floors instead of carpet so his cars would go

faster. Let youngsters experiment on paper with different arrangements for furniture.

It is often difficult for us to realize that young children's friendships may be as intense as our own. Visits, phone calls, photos and drawings by mail, show that the past is not irrevocably lost. As children become involved with new friends, maintaining past ties becomes less important, but in the meantime, there may be some sad feelings to acknowledge.

When you undertake the chore of packing, give children some boxes to pack with shoes, towels, toys, and other unbreakables. They will probably unpack as much as they pack, but you can work nearby with less disturbance.

On moving day, it is often helpful to give children an opportunity to watch the proceedings. Youngsters who don't watch the moving process may take longer to adjust. Instead of sending youngsters off to a relative or a sitter, have someone come to your house to supervise their care.

When settling in, set up the child's room first for a safe retreat, and for a more homelike feeling, arrange it in the same pattern as it was before, if possible.

8

Parent Care

eligious tradition proclaims motherhood the symbol of unconditional love. Traditional psychiatry blames us for all that befalls our children. Child-development specialists exhort us not to thwart our youngsters' needs *and* to be firm disciplinarians. Our spouses and our children vie for our attention and love. Our children's needs pull us toward home, and financial concerns pull us toward the job market. While a small inner voice tells us that parenting is the world's most important task, Women's Lib implies it is inconsequential compared with self-fulfillment and making our place in the big wide world. Furthermore, all these compelling voices quarrel inside our own heads. To be a mother in today's society is to be torn apart from the inside out and buried amid a hundred conflicting expectations. To parent is to wend our way through this snarled maze of opposing direction markers in order to find the path that best suits our families and ourselves as individuals. We parent from different backgrounds, with different children, in different life circumstances, with different expectations and toward different goals. Thus, no previous map shows the best route for *us*. To parent is to pioneer the depths of our own psyches.

No one expects the kitchen faucet to flow unless it's connected to the water main, or a jet liner to fly without careful maintenance. But we expect ourselves as parents to keep pouring out love and functioning smoothly despite physical and emotional exhaustion. We don't *manufacture* love: We channel it from those who nurture us, through ourselves, to our children. Caring for children *increases* our need to be cared for. Without sufficient inflow, our cistern of love eventually runs dry. Just as our children's problems become our problems, our problems become our children's problems. In order to nurture, we have to recognize and acknowledge our own needs and learn how to get them filled.

We feel alternately frightened by our rage, ensnared by our competitiveness, lonely, and inadequate. At the very time we need more support from spouse or partner, we have more cause than ever for disagreement. Amid feeding schedules, temper tantrums, explanations about why the rain falls, and entreaties for another story, how do we get enough time to develop and sustain a sense of self? To top it off, we've signed on for life as parents of these children. We can fill our commitment either poorly or well, but we can't cancel the contract. No one with experience denies that parenting is a supreme challenge.

OVERCOMING DEPRIVATION

LACK OF TIME FOR SELF

In order to develop a warm, responsive relationship with our off-spring, it is essential that during the many tasks of daily care we pay attention to them: interact with eye contact, words, and mental energy. As crucial as such contact is, we also need some breaks.

Contrary to popular myth, we are not bottomless wells of selfless, loving concern. We have the capacity to put out a great deal for our youngsters, but there comes a point when the accounts are overdrawn, and we resent each further penny's worth of caring for fear of entering emotional bankruptcy.

As one mother of eight put it: "Time for myself doesn't come gift-wrapped on a silver platter. I have to *take* it because getting time for myself is as essential as fixing dinner. Because there are always 20,000 things to do here at home, I make a point of going out to attend a special-interest class once or twice a week. I go away for a weekend with other mothers once a year, and my husband and I get away for a weekend once every year or two."

Another mother realized she'd been so wrapped up in child care for years that it was hard to let the older ones do for themselves even when they wanted to. "Unless I stop myself, I make my life so child-oriented I forget there is a part of me that isn't a mother."

Getting time for ourselves becomes easier after youngsters turn three and are able to take care of many of their own needs, but it still doesn't happen by accident. We need ingenuity, careful planning, and, when appropriate, enough persistence to establish a pattern that youngsters will respect.

Even when children do require our attention, they don't necessarily want or need all of it. Some mothers have found that breast-feeding is a good time for them to sit back and relax or even meditate. One mother set aside twenty minutes each day after the children's lunch for her reading time. She responded only to emergencies; otherwise their requests had to wait. Reading after lunch and snatching moments here and there, she managed to read a book a week. Another mother did her leisure reading by sitting on the floor so her sixteen-month-old daughter could crawl around her. Lori was content, and her mother enjoyed both the physical closeness and the nourishment for her mind.

One mother arranged for both her youngsters to use the same bedroom in order to liberate a den for herself. She could thus leave her sewing projects behind the safety of a baby gate, and work whenever spare moments allowed. Another found it easier to practice piano for fifteen minutes if she first asked her preschooler, "Is there anything you need before I start?"

We all enjoy a certain amount of time watching our youngsters and reveling in their ever-increasing skills. But at times we feel frustrated because *our* lives are slipping away while *they* are making the most of theirs. Thus, instead of simply waiting while youngsters attend a class, Mom may write letters or a personal journal, or sip coffee with a friend. While youngsters play on the jungle gym, she may jog around the playground. While a youngster splashes in the bathtub, Mom may perch on the toilet seat to knit or plan menus, or she may set her hair or clean the bathroom sink. One mother practices yoga at her son's bedside because he wants her nearby while he falls asleep.

Most of us tire of dolls and blocks long before our youngsters do. The next best thing may be to find activities we can actually enjoy with our children. Some parents jog while pushing a stroller in front of them or secure junior in a toddler seat while they get exercise riding a bike. If one is lucky enough to have a content baby, adult activities can be pursued with relative ease and freedom while the child sits or sleeps in backpack, stroller, and so forth. From first walking to age three is the most difficult time. Children at this stage tend to have short attention spans and unpredictable tantrums, and preoccupation with motion and self-determination makes them difficult to relate to except on their own terms. Parks, zoos, nature centers, children's museums, pet stores, may be enjoyably explored together at this time.

As children get older, they will be able to enter more and more into activities that we genuinely enjoy. Children three to five can participate in gardening, play simple card and board games with us, join us in sports and exercise, and even attend short musical programs. From age five up, there are more and more activities that we can share with our children, everything from carpentry to sewing projects to computers.

There comes a point for many of us when taking time away from little ones is the only solution. Many of today's fathers take over so Mom can have a break after dinner, sleep in on Saturday, attend a jazzercise class, or step out for evening coffee with a friend. Some parents arrange that each partner gets at least one day per month without economic or child-care responsibilities. Nursery schools, exchanging children with other parents, or lending them to couples without children are all ways to get little ones out of our hair for awhile. Many parents work out some regular arrangements so that they can rely on an upcoming break.

Television as Babysitter?

Controversy about television will probably rage for years. Some of our children become terrified of it, in their confusion between make-believe and reality. Studies show that children are both more aggressive and more accepting of aggression after watching TV violence. We fear intellectual stagnation and dampening of creativity. Advertising not only pushes junk food and expensive toys, but implies that all life's problems are solved with purchasing power. No wonder some of us refuse to have in our homes an electronic brain washer that promotes sex, violence, and materialism as basic human virtues.

Nonetheless, for most of us TV has become a family member. It is the grandmother, aunt, and uncle of our long-lost extended family. When we are exhausted from lack of sleep, overwork, or endless interaction with our children, the TV provides blessed relief. It is the vivacious sibling of our lonely children who spend many hours in the plush isolation of our homes. There are few family compounds or village squares in our country where children can romp with their age mates under the collective parental eye. In the confines of our small apartments and the privacy of our backyards, we feel the weight of total responsibility for our children and find respite in their electronic companion. Furthermore, we appreciate the tremendous educational value of TV programming at its best.

Television presents a further formidable challenge. The limp doll and battered toy truck that satisfied past generations are poor runners-up for the bounce and glitter of the tube. Today's parents agree that the way to counteract television's attractiveness is to provide better alternatives, so we send children out to ride fancy bikes, we sit and read together, start painting projects, arrange dance lessons, and more. But unlike the parents of yesteryear, we have the weighty task of competing with the best of Hollywood, New York, and Madison Avenue to provide top-quality entertainment for our children.

Managing TV with tots is comparatively simple. But as youngsters reach four, five, and six, stay up later and understand more of the action, their attraction to the tube grows accordingly. While many conscientious parents consider ten hours per week an appropriate amount of TV for children, the current national average is 25 to 30 hours a week, according to an article by Peggy Charren and Martin Sandler, "Is TV Turning Off Our Children?" *Redbook,* October 1982, pp. 68–77. If we find ourselves fighting with our children about television, we must scrutinize our own viewing patterns. Do we use televison for education and intermittent relaxation, or to resolve our bored loneliness, or to shut out the world? Do we want our children to emulate us? One mother noted, "Our kids were hooked on the tube until we *all* went on the wagon five months ago."

Limiting TV watching is a goal of many parents, and here are some approaches they have used successfully:

- No set. Some families choose this approach, especially if parents fear their own sense of addiction, though the drawback is not knowing what children are watching down the street.
- Location of the set. Keep it in an isolated corner where children are apt to feel lonely; in the parental bedroom, which is generally off limits; or in a closet except at prescribed times.
- Black-and-white. Allison seems less interested in TV than her friends, and her parents attribute this fact to their less appealing black-and-white set.
- Simultaneous activities. One family keeps the TV room supplied with blocks, paper, and crayons so less attention is directed to the set, even when it is on.
- The off rule. As soon as the designated program is over, the set is turned off—no sneak previews of the next enticing offering.
- Maximum viewing time. Parent sets the amount of time, and the child decides what to watch. This allows older children an opportunity to evaluate programs for themselves and avoids their feeling overly controlled by parents.

· Choosing programs. Some parents reinforce their young-sters' good choices by watching certain shows (for example, nature programs) with them. On the other hand, some parents sit with their youngsters and teach them to critique violent cartoons and luring advertisements. Choose programs ahead of time from the T.V. schedule, not by random viewing.

LACK OF PARENTAL PATIENCE

Legend suggests that we should be patient and never lose control. We compare ourselves unfavorably with more patient-appearing parents, yet we know that *we* show our most patient selves when others are observing. We watch the calm, pleasant nursery school teachers and feel like raving maniacs by comparison. But *they* don't worry how they'll handle more tantrums at ten o'clock tonight, or whether they and this particular child will like each other five years down the road. With other adults, our youngsters are cautious and maybe even courteous. With us, they feel obliged to crash against every limit to see which one will break. Despite the fact that we all have limited patience, especially with our own children, there are some ways to increase the available supply.

Sometimes our lack of patience signals hidden fears, which are best brought into the open for examination. If Lisa doesn't share her toys with her toddler friends, will she be selfish all her life? If John doesn't eat green beans, will he be a sickly, undernourished child? If two-year-old Patrick pushes another youngster in the park, will he become the high school bully? Once seen clearly, our fears may seem less likely to materialize.

Many parents find it particularly helpful to re-evaluate their own expectations. Impatience and anger often grow out of unrealistic assumptions about how youngsters *ought* to act. We all carry around internal models of the perfect child and the perfect parent, and then feel frustrated when real life doesn't measure up. Many parents feel better after reading books or talking with other parents which demonstrate that neither they nor their kids are so rotten after all. Parents who constantly demand more and more of themselves will eventually reach their limit and snap. More than one parent has discovered that lack of patience means an overly filled parental schedule. If, on the other hand, we have taken care of our own needs, we'll often have more patience for dealing with children. One mother became grouchy and irritable three or four days before her period. Rather than trying to cope when she knew she couldn't, she hired a baby-sitter for an afternoon or left the youngsters with their father for an evening while she set some time aside for herself.

But sometimes nothing seems to help: our patience dissolves in a severe case of "burnout." Much has been written recently about "burnout," and parents are among the high-risk candidates. We work long hours in one of the "helping professions," intensely involved with those in our care. Those of us with the highest expectations of ourselves (and our children) are among the most susceptible to burnout, of which common symptoms include overwhelming feelings of helplessness, worthlessness, depression, physical and mental exhaustion.

Recommended steps toward recovery include the following: (1) Acknowledge the truth: that we are feeling burned out. (2) Review expectations, and adjust them realistically. (3) Separate what can be changed from what can't; work on the former and accept the latter. (4) Take better care of our own needs: Get help as well as time to relax and to pursue other important interests and relationships. (See Getting Help, p. 233; Lack of Time for Self, p. 203; and Lack of Time with Spouse or Partner, p. 224).

Another important symptom of burnout is the feeling that "no one else can do this job adequately." Therefore, concluding "I *can't* take time off" may be the crucial signal to *take* time off. Children may not be as well cared for by someone else, but they will survive, and we will be better able to care for them after we've had a break.

LACK OF POWER

We may face some forbidding personal dilemmas when it becomes clear that endless patience and well-timed rewards are not always sufficient to mold better behavior. Unfortunately, the power to make children behave often comes from punishment of one form or another, yet we are often hesitant to use it.

We are told that our greatest obligation as good parents is to love our children, and we assume that love means patience, forgiveness, acceptance, turning the other cheek. To scream, swat, isolate, and remove privileges is *not* to act in a loving way, and in fact we don't do any of these when we *feel* warm and loving toward our young-sters. Our self-incriminating dialogue may run like this: "When I punish, I don't feel loving. If I don't feel loving, I am not a good parent. Therefore when I punish, I am not a good parent." No wonder it can be so difficult to punish our children even when it is appropriate to do so. In fact, we are always responsible for our young children; but we are not obliged to feel loving toward them all the time. See Disobedience, p. 405.

FRUSTRATION AND GUILT

We feel frustrated when we can't meet our goals and guilty when we judge that we *should* have met them. In parenting, our expec-tations get out of hand as much as our children do or even more so, and the gap between our expectations and reality is measured in units of guilt. We don't expect trees to grow to maturity without weathering winter snows, spring gales, debilitating drought, invad-ing insects, and maybe even a fire or two. Yet, despite our intel-lectual understanding to the contrary, we expect in our hearts that our children will glide from birth to adulthood without a ripple of discontent, either on their part or ours. Despite our better judgment, we *expect* perfect love: Everything will go smoothly and everyone will be happy.

Maybe the wonderful myths, and consequent guilt, are so strong because they are essential to the survival of the species. They keep us going when we wish we'd never had children and just want to get on with the rest of our lives. Unfortunately, the myth traps us into believing that the ideal is possible. *Any* woman will feel like a failure if she compares herself to the mythical super-mom who has endless patience, a sparkling home, exuberant but respectful children, the perfect marriage, and an exciting career.

As Elaine Heffner points out in *Mothering: The Emotional Ex-perience of Motherhood After Freud and Feminism* (1980) when the going gets rough, we assume that either *we* are bad parents or *they* are bad children. We get bogged down trying to decide who is to blame rather than moving ahead to find solutions. Such guilt and a sense of failure can prevent us from seeking help, and from taking better care of ourselves so that we can care for our children more easily. We assume that our feeling of guilt is in proportion to how poorly we parent, but, in fact, we feel guilty in proportion to our unrealistic expectations. Conflict is normal in family relationships: Parenthood *is* problem solving.

When we stop to think about it, even our objectives seem to conflict with one another. We want our children to love us, but don't want them hanging around and bothering us all the time. We want them to be spontaneous, enthusiastic, and assertive, but also calm, obedient and responsive to the needs of others. Fortunately, we don't have to give up one goal or the other. Instead, as if loading a teeter-totter, we aim for a reasonable balance.

We enter parenthood with a great many additional assumptions, in addition to the myth that all should go smoothly, that are far-fetched and fanciful, but ingrained none-the-less. They lurk in obscure, semiconscious corners of our minds, and trip us up regularly, unless we haul them out for inspection. In the stark light of reality, many are ridiculous, and it becomes obvious that we needn't judge ourselves by such standards. Common assumptions are listed below, followed by a more realistic appraisal of parenthood.

- Fatigue. "I shouldn't feel tired because babies and children should sleep through the night." A few babies *do* sleep through the night from two weeks, but night waking is common for months, and intermittent to age three or older.
- Loneliness. "I shouldn't feel lonely because children are my assurance of lifetime companionship." In fact, though children may become good companions in time, they don't start out that way. Staying home with a baby is lonesome until we make adequate connections with other parents.
- Generosity. "I should feel like a more loving, generous person now that I have children because having children turns an ordinary human into a loving madonna." Children *do* change us, but it's for better *and* worse.
- Marriage. "My spouse and I should get along better than ever because a baby brings couples closer together and can even save a sagging marriage." Realistically, a baby complicates and therefore unsettles even the *best* of relationships.
- Self-sacrifice. "I should always put my child's needs ahead of my own because good mothers are self-sacrificing." If we always put our needs last, our children will grow up believing that parents *should be* last. Part of the education

we owe our offspring is teaching them to respect the needs of others, which they gradually learn by accommodating to our needs. The challenge of parenting is continually deciding whose needs to fill at *this* moment.

· Regression. "Children shouldn't backslide or regress because once they slip they may never move forward again." In reality, children regress in order to collect enough energy to move farther ahead.

· Anger. "I shouldn't get angry at my children because good parents always feel loving toward their children." Just because we are always *responsible* for our children doesn't mean we must always *feel loving* toward them. All parents get angry and all parents overreact at times. The way out of this is not to blame ourselves, but to seek ways to reduce tension and accept the fact that a certain amount of frustration and anger is inevitable.

In addition, many parents feel that children's anger and sadness proves they are inadequate. Children's tantrums or tears, however, show how strongly they feel, *not* the quality of our parenting.

· Punishment. "I shouldn't punish my children because to do so means I'm not patient enough and risks that they'll stop loving me." Punishment is part of the upbringing of all children, and it is frequently the only way to get children to behave. "My children," as one mother pointed out, "love me because I am their mother, not because of what I do." Even children who are abused love (as well as fear) their parents. Appropriate punishment builds rather than destroys the parent-child relationship.

· Comparison. "I should raise my children in the same fashion and with the same ease as other parents because all children are essentially the same." Any parent with two or more little ones *knows* how different children can be. *We* know ourselves and our children better than anyone else, and thus, we know how best to raise them. Copying the Joneses won't do anyone any good.

· Mistakes. "I must avoid all mistakes in child-rearing, because one wrong move and I'll ruin my child's psyche for life." In fact, emotional damage is caused by detrimental *patterns*, not isolated incidents.

- Logic. "If I give good *reasons* for what I want my children to do, they will cooperate without a fuss." Although giving explanations to children is important in helping them understand the world around them, they can't necessarily understand what we say because they see life from such a different perspective. No amount of explanation will convince them. Thus, there are times when we *do* have to say, in essence, "You have to do what I say because I am the parent," and then enforce the requirement, despite protests to the contrary.
- Generational improvement. "My children should turn out similar to me, only better, because I won't make the same mistakes my parents made." Experienced parents quickly learn that *some* of the "errors" committed by our own parents were inevitable. Being a parent is a matter of limits and compromises. At best, we can help our children avoid some of our shortcomings and keep ourselves from making the *same* mistakes our parents made. We can't fill all the material, emotional, intellectual and spiritual needs of our children. Hopefully we will support them when they search elsewhere for further fulfillment.

UNREALISTIC EXPECTATIONS OF OTHERS

After each of the children was born, I returned to work full time. But when the youngest turned nine months, I decided to stay home full-time. My husband's expectations skyrocketed. It used to be OK to serve pizza for dinner now and then, and some clutter was acceptable, but now he wants every imperfection justified. He simply doesn't understand what I do with my time.

Because parenting primarily involves *emotional* work, rather than physical work, it is impossible to explain our job to nonparents or semi-involved parents. Their conceptions are as unrealistic as ours used to be. Alas, on a day-to-day basis, there's little to show for our efforts, compared with volumes of paper processed or units of machinery assembled in regular jobs, to say nothing of a heartwarming paycheck. Time has been kind to many grandparents, who seem to forget how difficult life was with little ones. Parents with children unlike our own may not understand that *children*, not just parents, are very different. Even total strangers in shopping malls and restaurants are ready to judge us for being too lax or too severe on the basis of a single observation. Despite the fact that others aren't in a position to judge us fairly, they judge us all the time.

One mother reported that her two-year-old who was jumping on and off a bus stop bench was reproached by a bystander, "You might fall and hurt yourself." At that the mother answered, "It's OK, his Dad is a bone specialist." Randy was too young to interject, "But Daddy teaches school."

Sometimes an effective way to alter the expectations of an unappreciative spouse is to trade places for a day or more. After seeing what life with youngsters is really like, spouse may better understand the time and effort involved.

Often we cut ourselves off from the support that other parents can provide by making unfair assumptions. We look around and decide we're the only ones having difficulty, or we assume that the job of parenting is *supposed* to be easy and fear that we will be judged inadequate if we admit our frustration and pain. Then when things go well, we hesitate to speak up for fear of making *others* feel inadequate. We find ourselves making silent comparisons that are destructive to our children, ourselves, and our relationships with other parents. Rather than spending time worrying whether our children are progressing as well as our neighbors' and friends' children, we would do well to measure progress within our own family. We all have the potential to be the winning parents for our own children; and our own offspring, not our neighbors, will be the final judge.

It's also important to remember, when we are tempted to compare ourselves with others, that some parents have an inherently easier time because of luck, circumstances, and so forth. Children develop at different rates both physically and emotionally; furthermore, current research shows that many character traits are not only inborn, but many persist for a lifetime. A very active, strong-minded, intense child will create more work and exasperation than a quiet, mellow youngster. One who doesn't need much sleep is more exhausting than one who sleeps from 8:00 P.M. to 8:00 A.M. Certain children *and* parents find it innately more difficult to respond to change, so will have a harder time with moves, new friends, new stages of development. In general, everyday pressures are less acute if youngsters are spaced three or more years apart. Parents who experienced abuse or neglect in their own childhood have special challenges in raising offspring of their own. Parents who love helpless infants but are frightened by two-year-old freedom fighters, or vice versa, will find one stage much more difficult than another. The amount of discord with a spouse or partner, on all matters including child rearing, will affect parenting. The size of home and yard, economic pressure, proximity to extended family, family health, and more all affect the ease with which we parent. Rather than putting ourselves or others down, we can heave a sigh of relief if life goes easily or, if our task is more difficult than that of others, we can pat ourselves on the back for coping as well as we do, *and* see about getting more help (See Getting Help, p. 233).

OUR OWN EMOTIONS

LACK OF SELF-CONFIDENCE

Lack of self-confidence is very common among today's parents, what with continually changing professional recommendations on how we should handle our offspring and the fact that just when we've become comfortable with one stage of development, our youngsters grow into another. Futhermore, change is so slow! Sitting down to watch a flower bloom is exasperating, and so is waiting for children to mature. One mother found a problem list was helpful. By listing all the current issues, such as muddy feet, strewn toys, brushing teeth, saying please and so forth, she was able to pick the few most important items to concentrate on. Because she wasn't trying to accomplish so much at once, and because from time to time she could cross something off the list, she felt reassured that progress was being made.

Rather than measure ourselves and our children competitively and often destructively with others, the following questions can help us to evaluate our *own* parenting.

- Are my expectations and responses generally appropriate to my child's individual age, personality, and capabilities?
- Are my children getting reasonable opportunities for growth?
- Am I often able to anticipate what are apt to be difficult situations for my children, and plan appropriately?
- Do my four- and five-year-olds behave worse at home than

away? If they do, they have learned to control their actions, yet are comfortable expressing feelings at home. *That* is progress.

· Do I like my child a reasonable amount of the time and feel genuinely loving at times?
· Have I accepted the fact that difficulties are inherent in each stage of development, or do I still believe there shouldn't be any problems?
· Do I get stuck deciding who is at fault, or get on with resolving conflicts of interest with my children?
· In making decisions, do I consider both my children's needs *and* my own?
· Are there acceptable ways for both me and my children to let out frustration?
· Can I identify signs of significant emotional stress and take appropriate action?
· Am I learning how to keep my expectations for myself and my children within reason?
· Is my capacity to live with uncertainty increasing?
· Am I learning to sort out what my children need now from what I needed when I was a child?
· Do I have sufficient sources of support and can I ask for help without feeling like a failure?

FEAR FOR OUR CHILDREN'S SAFETY

When my first child wanted to ride a trike, I hovered nervously, ready to soothe his little body against my bosom should he fall. When my fifth wanted to ride a trike, I said, "It's out in the back yard." I'd had lots of opportunity in the interim to appreciate a child's will to survive and the ability to recover from the inevitable minor hurts of growing up. For information about protecting children, see Chapter 5.

ANGER AT OUR CHILDREN

The anger that flares at our children can derive from many different sources. Only by discovering the cause can we find an effective cure. Fortunately there are ways both to decrease anger and to handle it more comfortably when it comes along.

One mother decreased her anger by allowing herself sufficient time to make decisions, because otherwise she tended to agree to projects and promises she later regretted. Gradually, she learned to answer certain requests with "I'll tell you in a few minutes," or "after dinner," if it was a big one. Further, many youngsters can respond surprisingly well if we tell them on occasion, "I'm a real grouch today because I'm so tired. Please try not to make me angry."

Much parental anger grows out of the discrepancy between the joy we expected to find in parenting and the mess we now find ourselves in. It helps if we can be aware of our expectations, for only in this way can we modify them. It also helps if we can make ourselves aware of our emotional patterns. The challenge is often to realize our annoyance early on, admit that it's there, and then act to put a stop to the behavior that is causing it instead of waiting until we're so furious we explode.

One mother, with the help of a therapist, came to understand that she wasn't really angry at her children as much as she was angry at traits that reminded her of unresolved conflicts with other relatives. The youngsters got dumped on because they were there. But once the mother understood the source of her anger, she was able to manage and direct it appropriately.

Most of us eventually learn that taking care of ourselves and our own needs is basic to keeping anger at a minimum. As one mother put it, "Feeling good about myself is my biggest aid to being a good mother."

Another mother found that her anger flared as long as she viewed her children as extensions of herself. The reason was that she blamed herself for every imperfection. Once she could accept her children as individuals in their own right, she was able to see them, and her role, in a different light.

Letting Anger Out

There are two schools of thought about how we, as parents, should behave when angry. One belief is that we should always maintain the appearance of calm. This approach may inhibit youngsters who delight in having sufficient power to push our button marked "Scream and Yell." On the other hand, we may confuse children if we appear calm but act in anger. In addition, we have to do *something* with the emotional and accompanying physical tension within us.

Medical science now tells us it is better to get it out safely than to hold it in until it festers into tension headaches, physical exhaustion, accident-proneness, depression, and more.

Finally, what do we want to model to our children? Do we want them to hide their anger when they grow up, or learn from us how to get it out without harming themselves or others?

After a while, one mother reports, I start screaming right along with the kid's tantrums. It feels like giving up the last bit of my power and self-control, and in that sense it is rather humiliating; but things always feel better afterward.

An angry snarl can be a handy way to tell the youngsters we're angry as long as the cause is obvious. It's pure emotion; we don't have to think up the "proper" words to shout. And the *kids* often think the growl is funny, so they move from their anger to a giggle.

Physical exercise and relaxation help release the physical tension of frustration. Some parents do vigorous housework, such as scrubbing floors or kneading bread. Others get regular physical exercise, soak in a warm tub, or get a massage.

Fear of Harming Our Children

When we face the raw anger we sometimes feel toward our children, our objectives are threefold: to protect ourselves from the guilt and regret of going too far, to protect our youngsters from serious harm, and to find safe, realistic ways to deal with our own anger.

About half of the parents in our study said they had had fantasies of seriously harming their infants or children, or had occasionally punished more severely than intended, or had felt genuinely afraid at times of harming their children. Hard as it is to cope with our children's destructive impulses, as parents we have to contend with *our own* as well.

We may resent even our adorable newborns for how much our lives have changed because of them. And our anger can rise to a helpless fury when we are faced with an infant's inconsolable crying, a two-year-old's stubborn negativity, a four-year-old's power plays, a five-year-old's insolence. The violence and rage of our out-of-control youngsters stir subconscious memories of the times we were out of control at their age, which only increases the temptation to use brute force. We fear losing control now, as we did then; and we are terrified by how much bigger and stronger we are than our little ones. Unfortunately, wanting children and loving them dearly is no assurance that we won't wish them harm at times.

Fantasies of Child Abuse

None of the mothers quoted here acted out her violent fantasy. Several of the mothers, who found their fantasies persistent and impelling enough to be really frightening, wisely chose to see a therapist in order to *prevent* potential harm. *It is a relief to know that we don't need to control our fantasies. It is sufficient to control our actions.*

The first week I was home with our new son, confined to bed after a C-section, I had repeated fantasies of dropping him out the nearby window.

When my son was a few months old and we were visiting an oceanside resort, I felt a sudden urge to drop him over the cliff, quickly, before it was too late, before he took over my life forever.

When my daughter was three months old, and crying *every* night, I sometimes wanted to put her on the floor and stomp her out like a cigarette.

My daughter cried continuously for the first six months, unless she was asleep or being walked. More than once I wanted to press a pillow over her face so I'd never have to listen to her cry again. One night I had a dream that I was walking through our apartment with a leopard on a tight leash. I knew that at any time the leopard might kill someone. When I woke in the morning, I knew that the leopard was part of myself, and that my daughter was the potential victim. I decided to see a therapist.

When my five-year-old son teases his younger sister, I suddenly hate him as I hated my older brother. I want to pick him up and throw him against a wall right now, while he's still smaller than I am.

My son, age five, had been whiny for weeks, and I was also having problems with my boyfriend. One day my son came whining up the stairs and I imagined myself picking him up and dropping him down the staircase.

How Parents Avoid Harming Children

During moments of extreme anger, many parents find it best to get away from children momentarily. Put infants in their cribs, youngsters in their rooms or even outside for a few minutes *if appropriate*. Alternatively, we can lock ourselves in bedroom or bathroom or step outside for a few minutes.

Another safety measure is to take time out before reacting to children's misbehavior. One mother takes five deep breaths. Another yells to her four-year-old, "I'm so angry I don't know what to do. Go to your room until I decide what will help." In fifteen to twenty minutes, she's usually ready to face him with rational consequences.

It's much easier for physical punishment to get out of hand when we are really furious. Hit something other than the child! One enraged mother unconsciously grabbed a belt that was lying near her obstreperous five-year-old. Coming to her senses, she lashed the belt against a chair instead of her son, announcing she *felt* like doing it to him. He was duly impessed. Other parents have discovered that a rolled newspaper makes a satisfying whap against a tabletop and many find it helpful to vent their fury with a pillow against a sofa.

Some parents are able to ignore a youngster's antics and do so successfully because they understand that when an obnoxious behavior is ignored, it will get worse before it gradually improves. One father pretends for the moment that his daughter is invisible and a mother pretends that she needs a hearing aid, but has lost her battery.

Essential to coping with anger in the long run is having someone to talk to about frustrations, fantasies, and impulses. An accepting spouse and other understanding parents usually fill this role, though good medical and mental health practitioners are generally available as well. For further discussion, see also Surviving Children's Crying and Tantrums, p. 223; Concerns About the Use of Physical Punishment, p. 390; and Getting Help, p. 233.

SURVIVING OUR
CHILDREN'S EMOTIONS

CHILDREN'S UNHAPPINESS

"To make our children happy" sounds like a praiseworthy objective. But if we call ourselves good parents only when our children are happy, then we are bad parents when they are not. From such a frame of reference, their unhappiness carries a terrible accusation.

We've lived much of our lives trying to make others happy—parents, teachers, friends, spouse—and have measured ourselves by their delight and displeasure. But, often without warning, the rules change.

One of the most difficult things for many of us to accept about parenting is that at times our children *must* cry. They may cry because nothing we do comforts them, because there is a lesson they must learn, or because we have reached the end of our tolerance. Some parents face such unhappiness very early, in the form of a colicky infant. For most of us, the clash between their wills and our limits causes the first, inevitable wails. Maybe time has come to put a night owl to bed earlier, drop a night feeding, or end the domination of a pushy two- or four-year-old. Suddenly we can no longer judge the appropriateness of our actions or our success by our children's happiness. Eventually we learn that we can't measure ourselves solely by *anyone's* happiness, but small children are often the ones who initiate this unexpected reversal of our lifetime assumptions.

No one warned us that *we* would have to introduce our precious little ones to the painful frustrations of life. When we must bear the brunt of their angry disappointment, we feel cheated of our mythical role as the giver of love and joy. Unfortunately, as Elaine Heffner clarifies in her book *Mothering*, our job is not to create a bed of roses for our children, but to help them pick their way through the thorns.

If we always insist that our goal is our children's happiness, one of two outcomes is likely. (1) We will always have to do things their way, and at some point will resent them for it; our children will come to sense our disguised anger, but won't understand it. (2) They will learn to hide their unhappiness from us, pretending they like our way when they don't. Unable to share their discontent and pain with us, they will necessarily become distant. In *The Growth and Development of Mothers* (Harper & Row, 1981), Angela Baron McBride points out that we can often lessen negative feelings, and learn to handle them more effectively, but *we cannot eliminate them.*

To raise our children with the expectation of a lifetime free from problems and heartache would be a sore deception—the same one, in fact, that we as parents frequently suffer from. We can save our self-esteem and our sanity by shifting our objective from "making our children happy" to "gradually enabling them to cope with the inevitable discomforts and disappointments of life."

How much unhappiness we will have to endure from our youngsters will vary tremendously. Researchers agree that some newborns are innately more fussy than others. Basic personality traits can include low responsiveness to soothing, intense emotional reactions, a tendency toward gloominess, and difficulty adjusting to change. The more negatively inclined our youngsters, the more crucial that we not measure our skill as parents by the affability of our children.

CHILDREN'S AMBIVALENCE TOWARD US

Why do our youngsters cling to us so desperately one moment and scream to be left alone the next? Why, when we are enjoying their cuddly loving so much, do they suddenly create such bitter struggles that we can't stand to be around them? Are they *intentionally* driving us crazy?

Mommy is everything to two-year-olds: most beloved being, provider of food and warmth, creator of self-image, life itself. No wonder they cling to her with the determination of a drowning victim. On the other hand, like teenagers, two-year-olds reach the awesome realization that to follow Mommy's every command, to be the ideal child she wished for, means to crush some essential part of their emerging selves. Thus, Mommy is alternately the giver of life and a dungeon from which they must escape in order to explore their own individual identities. One moment they need and love her, the next moment they hate and resent her. In *Oneness and Separateness*, Louise Kaplan refers to this struggle, which is as inevitable as labor pains, as the child's second or psychological birth. It may begin at fifteen months, or not until three years;

and, like labor, may be easy or hard depending on both mother and baby, and on previous experience. It usually starts precipitously and is often at its most difficult about two and one-half. In fact, this birth process takes months and even years of intermittent labor. When at peace with Mommy, the child's sense of personal identity dissolves into the nebulous oneness of infancy. When at odds with Mommy, the child is alone on the great sea of life. Thus, the continual flight from one uncomfortable state into the other! And, as Kaplan notes, "It is difficult for the father to recognize the crazy-making behavior of the 2-year-old is a result of the struggle between essential oneness and separateness of the mother and child, and that the comparative equilibrium of his relationship to the child reflects a different relationship, not basic incompetence of his wife."

Knowing that our young ones' wrenching ambivalence reflects their own internal struggle rather than disregard or dislike for *us* can help us keep our equilibirum during the months of second labor. We *could* avoid much of this struggle by setting no limits and letting them be entirely themselves, but, alas, to do so would create more long-lasting trouble.

CHILDREN'S ANGER TOWARD US

When our child's intense anger is directed toward us, we have both their feelings and ours to manage. At first, they kick and bite. Then they call us names we didn't expect to hear until puberty, and finally they become sophisticated enough to hit where it really hurts: "I'm going to stay in my room for 100 years and make you very sad."

Again we suffer from erroneous expectations. We thought that if we did things right, *our* children wouldn't have tantrums, and wouldn't suffer disappointment like we did. We expected that surely, by the time the youngest reached five, we'd have it all together and family life would be smooth and glorious.

In our saner moments, we realize that the ability to express anger is essential for our children's emotional health, but *we* don't want to be hurt by their outbursts. There are two handholds to help us out of the mire: (1) realizing our children's anger is a statement of strong personal feelings rather than an indictment of our parenting skill; and (2) gradually teaching them how to deal with their anger constructively, rather than destructively.

SURVIVING CHILDREN'S CRYING
AND TANTRUMS

If there are many tantrums about the same issue, such as weaning from the bottle, or if there are hours of crying once newborn colic has passed, we may need to examine whether our expectations are appropriate or whether our own ambivalence is prolonging a struggle. All too often however, children cry even when our behavior is appropriate. We may confidently accept their temporary distress or become mildly irritated, really annoyed, or dangerously angry because of our sense of helplessness. Often, by the time our youngsters have a tantrum, we are ready for one too, having pushed ourselves beyond the limit of tolerance in the name of parental patience. In the long run, we may need to learn to put our foot down sooner, but that resolution doesn't help at the moment. To keep things from getting really out of hand, we need most of all to maintain our sense of control over ourselves and the situation. Sometimes, getting away for a few moments is the best solution.

One of the most upsetting things about listening to our children cry is that they, not we, control how long it will last. And each minute seems an hour. In fact, with an impartial clock to keep track, we may be surprised by the unexpectedly short duration. Furthermore, that which we can predict often *feels* more within our control, even if it isn't. Thus a good place to begin gaining control is to clock the crying time.

Parents to whom we talked found that when night feedings were dropped or when little ones were put to bed earlier or left to cry if they woke, 21 percent cried for less than fifteen minutes and 85 percent for less than forty-five minutes for one to three nights. On the other hand, babies who cried more than forty-five minutes for a number of nights tended to continue such crying for *many* nights. Thus, if babies cry a long time and don't stop within a week, it may be appropriate to consider a different approach.

Many of today's conscientious parents are afraid to let infants cry because we have read that doing so will compromise their sense of security. We have to remind ourselves that it is the long haul that counts, not the immediate incident. Over the course of twenty-four hours a day, seven days a week, twelve months a year, do we *usually* respond to our infant's needs?

As for tantrums, we can predict that few lessons are learned the first time through. There may well be tantrums for *several* days before Nathan accepts that he can't have a cookie before dinner. In general, as youngsters grow older, they have somewhat longer but less frequent tantrums. Most tantrums are over in ten to twenty minutes, though some may last an hour. In order not to *feel* the situation is so much out of her control, one mother tells her two-year-old, "Scream louder. I can't hear you." Another sets the kitchen timer and tells her preschooler that he has ten minutes to be really angry. When the timer rings, he's usually able to stop crying.

Once we know that our children are not in danger, the best solution may be to block out the noise. Some parents sleep farther away from a fussy baby or go to bed with earplugs. Others drown out screaming by turning up the stereo, vacuuming, or taking a shower.

Even the most calm and caring parents occasionally need to get away from crying children. It's better to acknowledge this need and deal with it rather than push ourselves to the breaking point. One mother slept at her next-door neighbor's house for several nights when she'd had enough of nighttime feedings but couldn't stand the thought of the inevitable crying. Dad slept through just fine, and their eight-month daughter was chipper each morning. Another mother went for a drive at her daughter's bedtime and let her husband handle the customary tantrum. And still another mother walked far enough down the block that her infant's bedtime screams were just bearly audible.

LIVING WITH CHILDREN *AND* ADULTS

LACK OF TIME WITH SPOUSE OR PARTNER

Before children arrive, we, as husbands and wives, take it for granted that when we are both at home, we are generally available to each other. As parents, we not only have more to discuss than ever before, and more occasion for discord, but we have less time to talk. Having time for each other is especially important if a baby is very fussy, once a youngster becomes talkative, or (even more so) after the arrival of yet another child. Some parents arrange occasional secret lunches on weekdays, others attend marriage workshops, and many arrange sitters or child swaps with other couples to assure a regular Friday evening or Sunday brunch without the kids. Some couples have the sitter sleep over so they can spend the night in a motel. More than one couple has put off arranging a whole weekend away, for fear they would discover there was nothing left of their precious relationship. Fortunately, such occasions away are usually immensely reassuring.

INCREASED CONFLICT BETWEEN PARENTS

Just as there are more dirty dishes if we have company for dinner, there are more sources of family disagreement once we have children. Dealing with conflict becomes even more difficult once youngsters are old enough to listen in. Two schools of thought have arisen in this area. Because parental argument may frighten children, some parents prefer to disagree in private. However, children who never hear parents disagree grow up without knowing that working through differences is a normal part of every intimate relationship. In fact, whether the disharmony is subtle or obvious, children notice, and assume *they* are responsible for the tension. Thus, they need reassurance to the contrary. Between the extremes of unrestrained abuse and utter silence, there are ways to work on our relationship with our partner without causing undue strain on our children.

In one household, the parents give their preschoolers brief, age-appropriate explanation of what they've been fighting about. Such information makes the fighting less frightening, and reassures the children that they are not to blame. One couple has "dump night," when one sits down and listens without comment to the other's list of gripes. After that, they negotiate what they'll try differently during the following week. Many parents find couple therapy essential to working through the myriad emotional issues raised by parenting.

COMPETITION BETWEEN PARENT AND CHILD

How can it be that the children we wished for as a lasting bond between ourselves and our partner now determinedly chip away at the relationship that conceived them?

Competition between parent and child often starts even before the youngster is old enough to take an active part. A husband may feel more or less cheated when the baby arrives, depending on how much time the baby absorbs, the emotional reserves of the wife, and the husband's own emotional needs. The more actively fathers participate in child care, the less they feel left out, but both husbands and wives can resent the shift of their partner's attention toward the baby. Other family members can suffer as well. Noting that her husband had been unusually gruff with their three-year-old son, one mother realized that the bigger she grew with her second pregnancy, the less attentive she was toward her husband, and he in turn had less patience for their son.

It's understandable that we feel a sense of loss for the closeness we had before the baby; but why do youngsters compound the problem by intentionally driving us parents further apart?

Perceived Loss of Love

We measure love in terms of ultimate concern, but children gauge it by immediate attention. "If Mommy pays attention to me, she loves me. If she ignores me, she doesn't." Thus, when Mommy settles down with Daddy for a few moments of dull conversation at the dinner table, Junior pulls every trick in the book to win her attention back and thinks, "It was so much easier to hold her attention before Daddy came home. How dare that guy barge in on our scene!" After dinner, when preschoolers are basking in Daddy's attention with a romp or a story, he may well be put out if Mom intervenes.

Desire for Control

Two-year-olds want to control everything; and Mommy, the beloved woman in their lives, is no exception. When Daddy (to whom youngsters are usually not so strongly attached because they have spent less time together) attempts to help by getting Sally dressed, she screams "Mommy do it!" She reacts the same way we would if our lover were too busy to be with us, and sent a substitute instead.

The Desire to be Supremely Important

Two- and three-year-old boys and girls want to be as important to Mommy as she is to them. They resent signs that parents share a special relationship from which they themselves are excluded. They may envy the more even-tempered relationship between parents, the bed that parents share, and the hints that parents are emotionally and physically important to each other in a way that children are not. Every child dreams of being the parent's one and only special partner.

Children who are frustrated in their desire and angry at parents for setting necessary limits may wish intermittently that interfering parents would go away "forever," which means until story time. Subconsciously, children assume we know of their secret angry wishes and that we will punish them accordingly. *And* they fear the magical powers of their own imaginations and assume their wishes will come true. Boys seem especially prone to fears that Daddy will punish and send them away forever; maybe even *past* story time. These natural fears are obviously intensified by the fact that we are louder, bigger, and stronger than they. Because such powerful fears about such essential people could be overwhelming if experienced consciously, fear of parents is often projected onto noisy motorcycles, aggressive animals, dangerous little bugs, to name just a few. Youngsters then become terrified whenever these *symbols* of internal distress appear in daytime activities or nighttime dreams.

To Try on Sexual Roles

Four- and five-year-olds like to try on adult life. A son pays close attention to how it is that Daddy captivates Mommy. He sets out intently to copy Daddy's style and do him one better, in order to win over the lady of his heart. A daughter, having failed to monopolize Mommy and realizing that opposites generally attract, shifts her attention from Mommy to Daddy. She caresses his hair and fondles his collar just like Mommy does, but with the hope of doing it better. On one level, we accept this normal attachment to one parent and identification with the other, but on another level we feel uncomfortable when *anyone* woos our spouse in front of our very eyes. One inventive five-year-old suggested Mommy and Daddy get a divorce so *she* could be Daddy's wife. Mommy could come over to their house and cook!

There are as many variations on these basic themes as there are variations in present-day family structures. The scenario varies somewhat depending on the number of adults in the home, whether they are of the same or different sex, how they divide child-care tasks, and the significance of outside caregivers. What does not change is the child's need to participate in loving relationships, both to live in the present and to learn for the future.

To Play One Parent Against the Other

Many five-year-olds become sophisticated enough to ask Daddy for another cookie or for a toy in the supermarket if he's the softhearted one. When Mommy objects, they retort triumphantly "But *Daddy* said I could." Such playoffs increase in proportion to the parents' inability to coordinate their defense.

We can't change the fact that our children will feel distressed by the competition they feel with us, but we can decrease the intensity of their worry by letting them know we understand. It often helps to bring their anxieties out in the open in a way that they can't do. One mother tells of how she helped her son by acknowledging his wish: When Jason, age two, became suddenly frightened of the sailboats on which his father sailed, she told him, "Daddy will come home even though sometimes you wish he wouldn't. Even though you'd like to have Mommy all to yourself, Daddy will come home, and we will all live together as a family." His fear subsided markedly.

When three-year-old Ben acts resentful of the time I spend with my husband, another mother reports, I tell him, "We have only *one* Daddy in this house. Whenever he goes away, he always comes back." Ben seems relieved to hear it.

When Fernando, age two and one-half, tries to push my husband and me apart, I tell him, "It's Daddy's turn. Your turn will be in a minute." If he waits without barging in, he's rewarded with a big hug; otherwise he is ignored. It's important that he not see himself as powerful enough to push us apart and also know that we include him in our love.

Especially during periods when a marriage may be rough, it can take considerable insight and effort not to be lured by children into playing a game of favorites *against* our spouses. One father noted, "It's very flattering to be the father of Lisa, age five, because at this stage in her development, I'm the parent she prefers. It's so nice to finally be the good guy that it's tempting to subtly support her discontent with her mother and let Lisa have her way when I shouldn't.''

Children *do* get jealous at times when parents focus on each other, to say nothing of showing affection. One of the most important things we can do is accord them the dignity of accepting that their desire to be Mom or Dad's first beloved is the same as our desire to be our partner's first beloved. We are very similar, and teasing would be as hurtful to them as to us. Given our greater experience, we know we can love child and spouse equally, but differently. But children just feel painfully aware that they are not number one. Some preschoolers, but not all, like imagining the future when they will have a partner of their own.

SPECIAL CONCERNS FOR FATHERS

Acknowledging the issues is always the first step to improving things; so although there are no simple answers, the concerns outlined here may serve as a basis for fruitful discussion. In homes where Mom is the full-time bread winner, and Dad the full-time house spouse mothers also encountered many of the following problems, which shows that most are related to family role, not sex.

- Edged out. I used to be the most important person in my wife's life, and she was the most important in mine. She's still the most important to me, but since the baby arrived, I feel like a leftover.
- Competition. At work, I am respected for my competence. At home, my wife seems glad when I do the wrong thing with the kids, or don't notice their new accomplishments until after she does. Goodness knows she has a lot more practice than I do, but her competitiveness makes me want to back off completely.
- New rules. One day my son, age four, had a tantrum in the parking lot because I insisted he hold my hand. Later I learned that my wife had changed the rule the day before. I know she's with the kids more and has a right to change the rules, but I feel left out when they change without me, and really angry when I get trapped enforcing obsolete ones.
- Changing social roles. I give my youngsters their nightly baths, spell my wife on weekends, and feel good about my contribution. But when I occasionally miss a poker night

because she's had a really bad day with sick kids or something, I get a lot of ribbing from the guys. If I didn't feel really committed to being an involved father, I couldn't carry it off.

· Refuses help from dad. It was a real problem when Lisa, age twenty months, started objecting when I tried to dress her. We decided it was because I spent comparatively little time taking care of her. Once I began to do more on weekends and evenings, she gradually objected less.

FURTHER HURDLES

In addition to those previously listed, further problems of parenting are mentioned here. There are remedies for some, but others are inherent in the job itself, such as loss of our former freedom, the fact that what our children often want most is our time and attention, and the heaviness of having signed a twenty-one year contract. Often, all we *can* do is tolerate the difficulties. However, clearly identifying what it is that we must tolerate can make the situation less overwhelming.

LACK OF APPRECIATION

We're accustomed to positive feedback for a job well done: a good grade, a word of praise from a client or boss, a task completed with self-satisfaction, a special meal to enjoy after hours in the kitchen. But as parents we are left begging for appreciation. Our childless friends silently (or not so silently) criticize the "misguided" importance we place on our children's needs. We set *appropriate* limits for our youngsters and are greeted with screaming, insults, or pouting silence. Our spouses grumble because we aren't in control as we used to be. Our parents assert that things would go better if we'd only raise our children the way they raised us. Nursery school teachers may tell us we are overly involved with our children or not involved enough, or point out our own children's shortcomings. We turn to other parents and technical experts only to find that in our traditionless society, there are no standards. One generation is told not to be so strict, and the next not to be so permissive. No matter what we do, others condemn us.

All the experts in behavior modification say that people do what brings pleasure and avoid what brings pain. Yet as parents we are barraged from all sides with negative feedback such that *we feel put down even when we are doing well*. How do parents get enough appreciation to keep from drowning? They look for a *few* other accepting parents of similar mind and with sufficiently similar experience that they can exchange support. For more information on where to find other parents, see p. 235.

INTROSPECTION UNLIMITED

No one told us that having a baby would be the equivalent of signing up for psychotherapy; or if they did, we couldn't hear it. Even if we like ourselves just the way we are, and have all the old and painful conflicts locked carefully out of sight, merely living hour after hour in the presence of our infant, toddler, preschooler, and kindergartner unlocks all the cobweb-covered video cassettes of our past. Consciously or unconsciously, ready or not, we review them all again. Some parents resent this forced re-examination of their past. I've managed to grow up once; why do I now have to do it all over again? Others discover that what they learn about themselves as parents helps them in their other endeavors.

In *The Growth and Development of Mothers*, Angela Baron McBride comments, "When you can tolerate your own strengths and weaknesses with good humor (most of the time) then you are well on your way to coping with them in your children." To cope with intense emotional issues aroused by being a parent, some of us find quiet introspection is sufficient. Most bounce inner feeling off accepting friends, family, or support groups. Some find therapy the most effective way to sand down the rough edges of our personalities.

Neither our own parents nor our lovers spent so much time examining the details of our behavior and personality as our own children do. They search for our weaknesses as confined animals search for weak points of their enclosure. Whatever our vulnerabilities, even those we thought were under control (shyness, tardiness, lack of self-confidence, helplessness, jealousy, misguided anger), our youngsters find and expose them for all to see. Alas, we aren't allowed just to work on our children. The bigger part of parenting is working on ourselves.

Our children are also our hope for perfection; the chance to see someone grow up without our own handicapping hang-ups. One mother noted, when I see my shortcomings in my children, I feel doubly defeated: first because my best efforts weren't sufficient to steer my youngsters around them; and second, because my children's behavior reminds me loudly that I have yet to deal with these shortcomings in myself.

Finally, there are many feminine aspects to being a good father and many masculine aspects to being a good mother because children need responsive nurturing and firm controls from both parents. Most of us find that either nurture or control comes to us more easily, but in becoming whole parents, we are required to develop both sides of our personalities.

THE NEED FOR FLEXIBILITY

We can work on some jobs for years with little change in tasks or expectations. But in parenting, both the tasks and expectations are forever changing. Caring for infants and two-year-olds is as different as teaching philosophy and gymnastics.

Intense, moment-by-moment emotional involvement with our infants is essential to their survival, but the same kind of involvement with our preschoolers hampers their growing independence, and leaves us bereft when they fly the nest to kindergarten. To expect our two-year-olds to show spontaneous concern for others is to doom ourselves to a sense of failure; but *not* to expect our five-year-olds to show some concern for others is to doom them to inadequate social adjustment.

We don't expect schoolteachers to be adept with all ages, but as parents we have to be. Just as we are getting the hang of one stage and beginning to feel successful with it, our offspring have sprung to the next. Furthermore, not only stages, but individual children are different. The system that worked so well for one of our youngsters probably won't work with the other. Such emotional and intellectual challenges are exciting when we feel up to them, and exhausting when we don't. Rather than berating ourselves for doing so poorly at a simple job, we are better off congratulating ourselves for surviving so well at an extremely demanding profession.

THE LACK OF "RIGHT" ANSWERS

Throughout much of our own early homelife and our years in school and in the jobs we've held, we lived with the security of many clear-cut rights and wrongs. As parents, on the other hand, only the extremes are black and white. The pros and cons of our day-to-day decisions come mainly in shades of gray. Yet *we* have to make the decisions because *we* have the more mature judgment that enables us to approximately balance our children's individual needs with our own personal needs, *over the long haul.* Lacking *right* answers, we have to rely instead on repeated reevaluation. Fortunately, there is some consolation in the realization that if we can't be entirely right, neither can we be entirely wrong.

THE NEED TO LEARN NEW LANGUAGES

As adults, we are accustomed to relying primarily on words, but as parents, we have to depend on *body* language. We have to go *pick up* an errant toddler, and we have to ignore the defiant "No!" if Susanne is edging toward the destination despite her protest.

In our culture, many of us have been brought up to put our own needs last and thus parenting becomes a fast track to the language of assertion. We tend to *ask* our spouse, "Do you want to go to a movie?" instead of *stating*, "I would like to go to a movie." As pointless as it is to ask, "Do you want to go home from the park?" it is hard for us to learn, "Darryl, it is time to go home."

Finally, most of us cope more easily with the outer, physical world, than with the inner, emotional world. It comes quite naturally to demand, "Karen, stop yelling," but only with effort do we become comfortable enough with the language of emotions to say, "Karen, you must be very angry."

THE NEED TO LET GO

It is terribly difficult to give up the notion that we can cushion our children forever from all the world's pain. Toddlers *will* scrape their knees, preschoolers *will* be rebuffed by playmates, and our youngsters may not be sorry to go off to kindergarten. How dare we be given children so precious, yet have so little power to control and protect them. And how dare we be allowed to keep them to ourselves for such a short time!

GETTING HELP

Most of us have never held a newborn until we go home with our own. No job is more important than parenting, yet it's the only one we start without preparation, previous experience, or a supervised on-the-job orientation. Gone are the days when we could practice on younger siblings, nieces, and nephews. Furthermore, we've been so well trained in independence and resourcefulness that we don't always recognize when we *need* help. As parents, we contend with lack of sleep and the increased physical work of child care as well as the emotional strain of continually encountering the new events, dilemmas, and decisions of childrearing. The frustrations of parenthood are almost always easier to bear when we have moral support from others. Fortunately, there are many sources of help.

HOW TO IDENTIFY STRESS IN OURSELVES

Signs of parental stress include the following: difficulty concentrating, feeling overwhelmed, depression, frequent crying, exhaustion, difficulty sleeping, loss of appetite, diminished sexual interest, persistent fears, increasing doubts about wanting to be a mother or ather, continuous or excessive anger, physical illness, relying heavily on our children for emotional support, or increasing frequency and intensity of disagreements with our partner.

The first step in getting help is trusting ourselves enough to admit that we need it. If we can see asking for help as a sign of mature awareness of our limitations, rather than evidence of inadequacy, we have surmounted one of the biggest barriers to successful parenting. When we are under stress, our children feel the waves as well.

HOW TO IDENTIFY STRESS IN OUR CHILDREN

Tension symptoms among children may include difficulty sleeping, persistent fears, and regression in bowel or bladder control as well as extremely aggressive or extremely passive behavior.

Sometimes, youngsters' tension symptoms become issues in themselves for which parents find a variety of solutions. When Rachel held her breath in anger, her parents found it best to set her down rather than hold her. Sean stopped holding his breath when his parents gently blew against the top of his head. Mom padded the end of Karl's crib because he was banging his head, and Adrianna's mother gave brewer's yeast for teeth grinding as suggested in an article she'd read. When youngsters bite their nails, parents may distract them; purchase a bitter-tasting antinailbiting substance from the drug store; offer the reward of prettily painted nails if they desist; or arrange for more physical exercise to diffuse body tension. On the other hand, some parents accept nailbiting as a sign of temporary stress, for example, when starting a new school, and find that when ignored the symptom goes away as the tension resolves.

If, despite our efforts to deal with them, tension symptoms persist, intensify, or multiply, it is appropriate to seek additional help.

FINDING THE HELP WE NEED

Family

Many of us turn first to our spouse: to share child bathing and night call, to pour out the trials of the day, to snuggle with them when Junior must cry himself to sleep, or to arrange a shopping trip *alone*. In some families, grandparents provide this crucial support. But only in rare cases can families easily supply *all* the assistance we need.

Other parents are crucial as well. Who but another parent is equally fascinated by the ups and downs of living with an eleven-month-old? Whether two or more parents meet frequently over a cup of coffee, or whether they meet at a scheduled time with a designated leader, such formal and informal support groups form essential networks that can restore our self-esteem and provide the strength to pursue our often conflicting roles as parents and individuals. A mothers' group not only provides an excuse to get out of the house, but a chance to honestly share joys and frustrations. It's a relief to know that all mothers go crazy at times. Many mothers find that such get-togethers are essential for friendship, baby-sitting exchanges, tips on child care, and humor.

We can call on other parents while we sit to endure a tantrum or when we fear an excessive outburst of our own temper. One of us can cook dinner in peace while the other bathes the entire brood. Many single parents choose to combine households full-time in order to better manage the demands of parenting.

A word of caution, however. A group of parents may operate under the myth that all children are the same and only parents differ. Thus, some individuals are quick to condemn those who contend with difficult child behavior that they themselves don't have. At times, therefore, we need to seek out those who have similar experiences, such as a colicky baby or a hyperactive child, in order to really feel supported. Similarly, friends from our pre-parenting days may be a mixed blessing. If they don't have children, they may not understand why our lives have changed so much, and if they do have youngsters, we may find differing methods of child-rearing an unexpected source of hard feelings. Thus some old friendships develop and grow, while others peter out.

The frequency of family moves and decreasing numbers of at-home parents can make it surprisingly difficult to meet other parents. Parenting classes, tot's gym classes, the library story hour, nursery schools, and neighborhood bulletin boards are all potential resources. If there's not a baby-sitting co-op in your area, start one and see who shows up. Parents strike up conversations in neighborhood parks, compare notes with co-workers at the office, and even knock on doors because there are telltale tricycles outside.

Books and Magazines

Although information found in books and magazines may be contradictory and may imply that parenting is much easier than it is, such sources may be useful and supportive.

Time Away from Children

An opportunity to shore up our self-esteem and adult relationships, or just to relax, is provided by time away from children. Furthermore, playgroups, child care, and nursery schools allow us to share some of our parental responsibility. Some communities even offer respite care where children can stay for a few days when a family is in the midst of a physical or emotional emergency.

Hired Help for Household Chores

Household help on a temporary or ongoing basis can provide much needed relief. For various options, see p. 116.

Community Resources

Sources of help in the community are becoming increasingly abundant. They include La Leche League for nursing mothers, Parents of Twins, Parents Without Partners, and Planned Parenthood if you aren't ready for another baby! Child care information and referral services (listed under child care in the phone book) help make contacts for parents in need of child care and other child services. More and more communities have telephone services for parents under such names as a Warm Line or Parental Stress to provide or locate assistance. Religious groups, high schools, adult schools, colleges and universities may have a variety of classes and child-care programs. To locate such services, check the telephone book, libraries, your doctor's office, or the public health department.

Therapy

The complexities of raising a family in today's world are mind-boggling. The process of normal child-development is complicated in itself. Our partners in child-rearing usually come from different life experiences, so they have different expectations of themselves, of us, and of our children. Furthermore, becoming parents often sparks unresolved issues with our own parents or siblings. Finally, add changing social patterns of child-rearing, changing family structures, and economic constraints. It's no wonder that family life can become a virtual boiling pot of conflicting opinions and emotions. Many couples manage all these complexities on their own, but it is not surprising that more and more are seeking professional help for themselves, their couple relationships, their entire families. Under a variety of different titles, social workers, psychologists, child psychiatrists, and family therapists can provide short-term help with specific problems or help us work on more complex, long-term interactions, as our situation and our preferences indicate.

Parents generally locate an appropriate therapist through the recommendation of medical practitioners, hospital or county social service departments, nursery school teachers, or their own friends who have been in therapy. An initial phone call or visit is not a commitment to return, but rather an opportunity to consider how the problem might be approached. Certification is only a *minimum* requirement. Above that, sensitivity, warmth, gentleness, idealism, and experience are also important, as well as the essential ability to organize and synthesize new modes of interaction that will be helpful to the individual. Careful choice is especially important for children, for they are at the mercy of professionals, while we as adults can at least evaluate and decide whether to continue with a particular individual. To find a therapist who is genuinely supportive and helpful may take more than one try.

Some parents still struggle with the old-fashioned notion that anyone who sees a therapist "must be *really* sick!" More realistically, however, many of today's parents have found that a few visits during a time of particular difficulty can guide family relationships back toward a constructive track and thus prevent serious problems.

9

Desired Qualities

ur little ones prove from early on that the human race is not innately endowed with selfless concern for others. How do we convert an adamant egocentric into a caring human being? Parenting would be a lot simpler if we had only to *stop* obnoxious behavior such as kicking young visitors and trashing the kitchen. But of even greater concern are our expectations that our youngsters will someday become loving, cooperative, honest, independent adults. And we may harbor other hopes as well: that they might be artistic, or at least appreciate the arts; have a sense of humor; or carry on our religious traditions.

Raising children is rather like learning to type. In the beginning, hunt and peck is the obvious way to go. Only if we *believe* in the ultimate value of touch typing can we tolerate the laborious early discipline. Similarly with children, it is easier to clean up the messes and settle the fights for them than it is to teach them to take responsibility for themselves. When a calm afternoon turns into screaming chaos because we insist that Sonya now entertain herself for awhile or Eric share the last cookie with his friend, we have to believe that this immediate disaster serves an ultimately good end.

This chapter provides inspiration toward the idealism with which we all started our parenting careers. Its purpose is *not* to imply that we should strive every day to instill all the desired qualities. Goodness knows we have enough guilt already. In fact, we found most parents were consciously working on just a few at a time. This chapter, like all the others in this book, is for reference, so that when we *want* to assure ourselves that we are nurturing desired growth or when we need to nudge (or push) our offspring toward being more polite, more respectful, a better sport, or whatever, we can work with the assistance of other parents.

PERSONAL GROWTH

SECURITY

To be secure is to believe that with the strength of our own inner resources, the assistance of those around us, and, for many, the support of religious beliefs we will be able to endure or surmount the difficulties we encounter. When we compare our moments of worry and fear, to say nothing of panic, with those of serenity, we realize how precious a sense of security is.

There are a number of ways in which parents promote their children's sense of security.

Meet the Infant's Needs

One of the most crucial times for establishing a basic sense of security is during the first six to eight months of life. Imagine, after a temporarily incapacitating accident, lying in a hospital bed, unable to move except to push the call button. With the push of the button, a pleasant, attentive nurse arrives instantly to listen and care for every need. On the other hand, imagine a different hospital with totally inadequate staff. The assistance bell brings empty silence for fifteen minutes or an hour. The nurse who finally comes always scowls, shovels in a few spoonfuls of soup, and leaves again before learning that pain, the need to change position, or a faulty TV set prompted the call in the first place. In both cases, we are awesomely aware of our own helplessness; but in the first, help is available and we therefore have hope. In the second there is only hopelessness and anger. Our infants are similarly at our mercy.

Providing babies with a sense of security does *not* mean answering every cry. It means that in the course of a day, a week, a month, we offer help, as best we can, relatively soon, most of the time. Security is the *expectation* that help will come, because experience shows that *most* of the time it does.

Old-wives tales tell us that the more we hold our babies, the more they will cry to be held. Studies show such is not the case. Infants who are held and comforted more in the early months cry less as they grow older.

Spoiling means giving our youngsters what they *don't* need. Under age eight months or so, they are in real need when they cry, whether of food, physical closeness, sleep, new scenery, relief of pain, or something we are unable to discover. We can't always give them everything they need, but we can rest assured that in the early months, no amount we give is too much. As they grow older, we *can* spoil them, by not setting appropriate limits, letting them break rules they need to obey, surrounding them with more toys than they can appreciate, and especially by continuing over the years to place their needs above those of ourselves and others instead of gradually working toward a balance for all. No baby is spoiled by a year of age because spoiling is the result of years of overindulgence.

Manage Separation Carefully

How we manage separation from our children will have a crucial effect on their sense of security. For more information, see Chapter 10, Separation.

Reduce Unnecessary Guilt

From the perspective of children, unpleasant happenings follow misbehavior. Because of their limited experience and because they see themselves as the center of the universe, they assume, "If something bad is happening, I did something wrong." This belief has a positive aspect in that it enables us to teach appropriate behavior through reward and punishment, but it also carries a significant hazard: namely that when something unpleasant happens— routine immunizations, friends moving away, illness or injury of a member of the family, parental disputes, or the arrival of a new baby—children often assume they are being punished for misbehavior. Not sure what they did wrong to cause such dire consequences, they wonder if they are innately bad. Even though such unspoken assumptions may seem preposterous to us, we can boost their endangered self-confidence by reassuring them that they are not at fault.

SELF-CONFIDENCE

Without self-confidence, we come to a tumbling halt. It is both the gasoline that powers our inner drive and the glue that holds our psyches together. If we had to choose among the most important qualities to nurture in our children, self-confidence would be very near the top.

But what about the good old virtue of modesty? Don't the two conflict? We easily confuse "conceited" with "self-confident." Those who are conceited speak too highly of themselves. Those with self-confidence feel comfortable with themselves: They don't need to belittle others in order to boost self-esteem. They have the freedom to appreciate the qualities and accomplishments of others because they don't need to be everything to everyone. People who are self-confident can afford to be modest.

Modesty is not characteristic of three- and especially four-year-olds. Their incessant bragging reflects their lack of confidence.

They are keenly aware of comparative capability: adults and older children are more capable than they in many ways. They protect their fragile self-confidence with wild exaggerations, bragging, and identification with superheros. Unless playmates' feelings are getting hurt, the bragging is probably best tolerated for a year or so, because with the growing self-confidence and relative equilibrium of age five, the conceited tones tend to abate. We can encourage this trend by gently informing our kindergartners that there are appropriate times and places to talk about what they do well. The following six factors are important in building self-confidence.

Set Appropriate Limits

On first thought, it would seem that self-confidence would flourish if children were allowed the free reign of a totally permissive household. Unhampered by outside rules, they would be truly, self-confidently themselves. Such, however, is not the case. In the absence of all restrictions, children's irritating behavior eventually provokes an aura of muted or not so muted disapproval from others, which cuts deeply into self-confidence. Furthermore, we as caring parents can teach more gently than the world at large. Better we curtail their aggression than that they have no playmates. In his book *Parenting,* Ron Norton notes how frightening it would be to drive across a bridge that lacked guardrails. Given the safety of appropriate limits, children become more explorative and more self-reliant. Our children frequently *want* to please us, even when they lack the self-control to do so. Merely telling them that we are angry or hurt by their behavior without finding a means to control it teaches them either to ignore the concerns of others or to feel guilty. Thus, one of our tasks as parents is to provide the necessary external controls until the child can take over with internal controls.

Provide Consistent Rules

We'd all be nervous wrecks if red lights meant stop one day and go the next. Children need enough consistency to predict confidently what will happen from one moment to the next. Realistically, we can't be totally consistent. What upsets us one day may roll off our backs the next. When one plan doesn't work, we need to try another. And sometimes we are just too exhausted to enforce a limit. But we can aim toward consistency without *always* being consistent.

Protection from Perfection

Nothing hurts so much as the awareness that our best efforts are insufficient. If effort leads to disappointment, why try? Therefore, inappropriately high expectations can lead to inertia. Unless *we* can accept our children's less-than-perfect performance, we teach them to be dissatisfied with themselves. As we watch our children's fumbling attempts to butter their own bread, put a new toy together, or whatever, we are tempted to say, "This is how to do it." But there is an important difference between being available when a child asks for help and jumping in because our expectations and standards are naturally higher. Small children who are regularly expected to copy adult methods and outcomes and rewarded for doing so will tend to be less self-confident than those who are allowed to work things through in their own way, at their own pace, and to their own level of satisfaction. Developing adult levels of skill and competence is a long, slow process. Ideally, capability and expectations rise hand-in-hand.

Mistakes will continue to be made by all of us. One mother pointed out, "We try to maintain an atmosphere in our house where mistakes are normal for everyone, and thus no one need feel embarrassed or reluctant to voice a doubt, problem, or mishap."

Careful Comparisons

As adults, we judge ourselves by our own past performance, not merely on the basis of those around us. Children, lacking a storehouse of previous experience, judge themselves solely by a single experience or by the outside world, which is discouraging when you are the smallest, weakest, least coordinated, and least verbal person in the household. The awareness of such differences is hard enough for the child. Far better that *we,* at least, seem oblivious to them and carefully avoid such destructive comparisons as, "Why aren't you careful (neat, helpful, or whatever) like Bobby?" Furthermore, statements such as "You can jump further than Johnny" sound supportive at first, but teach the tension-producing message that in order for one person to be competent, someone else must be *less* competent.

Some youngsters become discouraged because they themselves make comparisons with their surroundings. Thus Mom saved Sasha's art work so she could see for herself how much she had improved over time. When Marie complained about her lack of ability, her mother pointed out, "When your brother was your age, he couldn't ride a bike either." Particularly bright children seem especially prone to comparing themselves harshly with others and they are often frustrated by the gap between their hopes and their abilities.

Activities to Increase Self-Esteem

To be copied is to feel admired. Thus we can greatly build our children's self-confidence by spending even five to ten minutes a day in which they are in the lead. We can build block structures of similar complexity, color with similar precision or lack thereof, follow them on a walk, and even copy their actions detail by detail, much to the delight of most youngsters. Spin-off from such role reversal is that youngsters may be less resentful of the times that they must follow *our* lead.

At bedtime, Dad helps Lisa review her day with such openers as, "Something Lisa felt good about today was . . ." During long car rides, one family plays a compliment game in which everyone gets words of praise from the others.

When children ask to try some constructive new activity that is obviously beyond their capability, our first instinct is to say no, but each time we do, their self-esteem sags a little. Better they try and conclude for themselves that the task is too difficult than that they perceive us as lacking faith in their ability. Better yet, we can ask ourselves, "What modifications or simplifications can I make so my child can safely and successfully try this out?" Even though a two-year-old will undoubtedly lose interest in a too-difficult task in a few minutes, a potentially negative experience has become positive instead.

Toddlers can "help" paint the fence with an old brush and some water, because as the surface gets wet, it will look newly painted. Two-year-olds may gradually progress over the years from applying the undercoat on the baseboards to small areas with finish coat. Bobby, age two, pounds nails in an extra board and Shelly, age three, gives each nail two blows for her Dad. Mom holds the screwdriver in place so Sean, age two, can make a few turns, but Willie, age five, unscrewed the sputtering vacuum cleaner to discover it needed a new fan belt. A two-year-old might fetch the newspaper, a three-year-old might borrow sugar from a neighbor, and some five-year-olds in safe neighborhoods might pick up a few items from a nearby store. Sonya, age five, rides the city bus alone *to* dance class, but not home, which would require crossing a major street.

The flip side of our little ones' urge to participate is their refusal to act: "I can't do it!" Before forcing the issue, we might do well to reevaluate our expectations. Can the child really do the task comfortably and successfully? If so, we may reassure them of their abilities. Some youngsters use such complaints as a means of getting attention. By giving more attention when things are going well, we may help remove their need to be incompetent. Alternatively, some youngsters have learned that it is more acceptable to say "I can't," than "I won't," in which case we might consider whether our expectations and demands for obedience are appropriate or too high.

Finding situations that build rather than diminish our children's self-esteem is often a matter of trial and error. When things don't go as well as we had anticipated on a particular project—with piano or gym lessons or with the chosen nursery school—the challenge is to sort out our own needs from those of our offspring, to reevaluate both the individual child as well as the particular situation, and to make our next move accordingly.

Accept Individual Differences

Many of us have been startled to discover that our children may not acquire their personalities and interests from us, as they do their hair and eye color. One of our greatest challenges as parents is not merely to allow but to encourage our children to be themselves, rather than forcing them into our preconceived mold of what "my children will be like." Not only do academic, athletic, artistic, or social *talents* vary from child to child, but innate *interests* often seem to vary as well. Getting a particular youngster to adore fishing, pottery, or socializing as much as we do may be like asking rain to fall in the desert. Inexplicably, many youngsters seem to arrive with their *own* interests.

Furthermore, research now shows that they arrive with their own personalities as well: some active, some quiet; some intense, some mellow; some generally cheerful and others inclined to be grumpy; some who adapt easily to change, others who do so with difficulty; some who are persistent, others who are more distractible. Our understanding of babies and children has grown far past the old blank-slate theory on which we the parents were believed to imprint everything. Instead, our infants arrive with a set of basic ingredients and the success of the recipe is to be measured by how skillfully we work with the materials at hand. Nothing puts such a crimp in a child's self-confidence as the gnawing fear that "I ought to be someone other than who I am."

Finally, parents have also discovered that it is important to separate, as much as possible, our children's shortcomings from our own. If we see ourselves as clumsy, excessively shy, or whatever, it takes special determination to accept our children's natural clumsiness or shyness at face value, rather than as an indictment of ourselves and our parenting. But unless we *can* separate their faults from our own, we tend to feel disproportionately critical of them and they sense our strong disapproval. By extension, the more we come to terms with our own shortcomings and build our own self-confidence, the more we enable our children to do the same for themselves.

EMOTIONAL AWARENESS

One of the greatest gifts we can give our children is emotional awareness: the ability to recognize, the openness to accept, and the means to communicate their feelings. When we hold our upset feelings in, they accumulate like storm clouds that can block even the brightest pleasures from view. Yet getting our frustration and pain out constructively is still a challenge for most of us as adults.

It is the awareness of our own emotions that enables us, with time, to recognize the emotions of those around us, and ultimately to empathize with others. In turn, empathy is the foundation on which we build close, supportive relationships throughout our lives.

In general, two-year-olds either let out all their feelings, or, in a repressive environment, learn to hold them all in. They aren't able to select and modify certain ones in the name of social appropriateness. But as youngsters approach elementary school, they are beginning to gain control over when and how they express specific emotions. For example, many a four-year-old, having concluded home is the safer place to express frustration, is the delight of the nursery school teacher but falls apart at home. Children manage such control subconsciously. But the greater their *conscious* awareness of their own emotions, the more choices they will ultimately have in how they behave. If learning about feelings is so important, how can we help?

Model Desired Behavior

Even though we may no longer chide our boys for crying, they will learn to hold back their tears nonetheless if they never see their fathers or their heroes shed a teardrop. To hide our sadness from the world is to hide it from those who might comfort us, and to bury it so deeply at times that we ourselves can't find it.

Nor will children talk about their feelings easily unless we talk about ours. We can keep our comments simple and age-appropriate, yet still express our feelings: I'm angry that I have to mop the floor again, or I'm worried that Daddy isn't home yet.

Teach the Vocabulary of Emotions

Teaching children the vocabulary of emotions is essential. We can begin with the words "happy" and "angry." But other feelings always lie underneath our anger, and that is where the real learning begins, often for ourselves as well as our children. Anger is caused by loneliness, disappointment, frustration, fear, jealousy, pain, and more. Surely, we think, such a vocabulary is too complex for a two- or even a four-year-old. Yet children know the meaning of telephone, refrigerator, hippopotamus, and easily communicate with us despite their simplified pronunciation. After all, which is more common in their world, a disappointment or a rhinoceros?

One way to teach children the vocabulary of feelings is to identify their feelings for them, when their reactions to situations are apparent. For example: bored while waiting for a turn on the swing, disappointed that I won't give you a cookie, excited that we are going to visit Uncle Jack, frustrated because the zipper won't work, lonely because Stephanie can't play today, jealous when Mommy and Daddy want to be alone, proud when you learn something new.

We can also identify the feelings of others and ask children their opinions of how others *appear* to be feeling: "Does Jenny look happy or lonely?"

Teach That Feelings Are Not Bad

If fantasy and reality were the same, as young children believe them to be, then to *wish* someone harm would be to *cause* them harm. No wonder our little ones are afraid of the disappointment, jealousy, and rage that make them want to strike out and drop others in their tracks, Mommy and Daddy included. We add to their concern because while we are often upset by the way they *express* their feelings, they assume we are upset by the underlying feelings themselves.

Because emotions that seem dangerous or unacceptable become the most difficult to acknowledge to ourselves, let alone express to others, it is essential that we teach our children how to handle negative feelings in acceptable, nondestructive ways. It will take repeated reassurance over several years before they will understand that *feelings don't hurt other people. It is what you do with your feelings that can hurt others.* Thus, "It's OK to *feel* angry, but it's not OK to hit." Or, "It's OK to *tell* Beth you are angry that she broke your toy, but it's not OK to hurt her feelings by calling her names."

Help Children Get Their Feelings Out

Merely learning the words to describe emotions, essential though this is, is not sufficient. Children eventually need to learn when and how to express surface feelings appropriately and how to get in touch with some of the deeper ones. Our best friends may call us up and declare, "I need someone to talk to," but not our small children. We have to read their signs: increased aggression or whining, fears or difficulty sleeping, tantrums, clinginess, mischief-making, and sometimes recurrent accidents or illness. It takes patience, warmth, perceptiveness, and ingenuity to bring underlying feelings to the surface. In the heat of the battle, or when we are overwhelmed by our own frustration, our efforts often lead nowhere. But once the heat has cooled and we're back in touch with feeling love and concern for our children again, we may be able to learn a great deal about their inner world.

It takes children years to be able to talk directly and fluently about their emotions, even once they learn much of the vocabulary. But the situation isn't hopeless, because the real language of children is play: fantasy with which they automatically weave their own experiences, both of how life is for them, and how they *wish* it would be.

Acting out a difficult situation, especially in front of an understanding audience, can provide children with the same relief we feel when we pour out our heart to a friend. Two mothers report their experiences:

> Beth's dolly, who is two and one-half like she is, gets all the pressure Beth feels from me. Dolly is told not to dump her juice, wet her pants, take too many Kleenexes, and on and on.

> It is difficult for Kier, age three, to talk about his fears and anger with us. Luckily we discovered that characters in picture books can speak when "Kier" can't. Kier *can* describe why the cat looks sad, what frightens the cow, or who upset the dog. He rarely acknowledges verbally that the animals encounter the same difficulties he does. But when we express our understanding of how "the animals feel," Kier's body shows obvious relief. (Other children talk easily about the feelings of dolls, stuffed animals, or toy people.)

Small children can't wander through the emotional forests inside their heads and clearly describe the thornbushes that lurk within. But if, when we are in a receptive and comforting frame of mind, we guess what one such thornbush might be and describe it for them, they can often acknowledge, "Yes, I have one like that!" The knack is to pose our hypothesis in the form of a question that can be answered by a simple yes or a nod: "Do you feel scared when Daddy and I yell at each other?" "Do you wish it would snow so hard I couldn't go to work all winter?" "Do you wish baby Brenda would get carried away by the police car so I could spend all my time with you?" "Do you sometimes start fights so your brother will get in trouble?"

Some parents fear such questions will plant negative ideas in youngsters' heads, but such is not the case, perhaps because mere words mean little compared with the intensity of children's own experience. Other parents expect that answers won't be valid because youngsters will merely give socially acceptable replies in order to please us. Little ones under age four are rarely sophisticated enough to answer falsely. Youngsters age four and over may well say the *words* they think we want to hear, but they haven't yet perfected the poker face. Thus, if we strike a chord that harmonizes with their interior feelings, they almost always flash an instinctive, brief smile of recognition. When four-year-old Jeffey was asked, "Is it fun to scare little Brian?" a devilish little smile flickered across his face just before he stated an angelic, solemn-faced no.

If the answer really is no, youngsters generally give a blank stare of incomprehension, shake their heads, or answer no without telltale signs to the contrary.

This technique is limited in usefulness because it can bring to the surface and confirm only those emotions and motives that we ourselves are capable of surmising about our children. Nonetheless, it can be extremely valuable in identifying with certainty some of the issues with which our children struggle.

As children's language abilities grow, parents find that it becomes increasingly easy to encourage them to talk directly about their feelings. And, in turn, the more readily children discuss their feelings with us, the easier it becomes to offer the sympathy and understanding they so much need.

Communicate with Hidden Personalities

Each child's psyche, like each adult's, is a composite of many different instincts, inherited and acquired traits, emotions and experiences. For the most part, all we ever see or show to others is the surface; the larest part remains submerged, to flash forth on rare occasions. One goal of emotional growth is to develop safe, controlled access to our generally submerged identities so that we can choose when and how to deal with them. This sounds like an awesome task for a child, but if we are responsive and encouraging, children may sometimes surprise us in how open to self-awareness and expression they can be.

One effective means parents have used to contact submerged or hidden personality parts is the imaginary "mental TV screen" (or radio, tape recorder, or record player, if your child prefers). One mother tells of how she introduced this device and how helpful it was both to her and her child in getting to deep-seated emotions:

The first time I tried the imaginary TV, I invited Lisa, age four, to sit on my lap, close her eyes, and imagine seeing a TV set. I told her she could change the channels and watch whatever she wanted. After a moment of silence, she told me she was watching "Sesame Street." Allowing a few moments for her to enjoy it, I then told her there was someone who could tell us why so often she got hurt by her brother. Could she turn to that channel? "Yes, it's channel 8. The girl on channel 8 fights with Brian when she is angry about something." Thus we named the channel 8 personality "Angry Lisa." Lisa and I discussed alternatives for Angry Lisa besides starting fights, such as stomping feet, arranging a pillow fight, getting help, or yelling, and Lisa relayed her preferences to "Angry Lisa." In the following weeks, we had more pillow fights, and yelling, but Lisa started fewer ill-fated tussles with her big brother. With time, we learned more about what aggravated Angry Lisa, and with practice Lisa and her new acquaintance learned to converse even when Lisa was walking down the street with her eyes open.

We are often frustrated when children won't acknowledge their vindictiveness, babyishness, jealousy, dishonesty, or whatever. Rather than mere stubbornness, this may be because the responsive, loving, surface identity is not in touch with the underlying negative identities. Thus Lisa may be as baffled by our pleas that she own up to her shortcomings as we would be if the police sergeant demanded that we confess our neighbor's transgressions.

An alternative to this dead end is to label these various personality parts as they show themselves by behavior or tone of voice, such as Jason and Jealous Jason, who acts out when Mommy and Daddy are together; Charles and Dishonest Charles, who has sticky fingers; Eric and Mouse, a silent little critter who hides in packing boxes after a family move; David and Baby David, who announces himself with baby talk; Ellen and Catch-Up Ellen, whose constant wish is to overtake her older brother. Like traditional villains, these negative identities don't care how much trouble they cause "innocent bystanders." When Angry Lisa starts a fight with big brother, *Lisa* gets hurt. When Dishonest Charlie filches bubble gum from the store, *Charlie* gets punished. Thus, when given the means to do so, Lisa and Charlie are often anxious to induce change in their counterparts and are more successful than we are.

Making contact is not always simple, however. Lisa announced one day that Angry Lisa was away on vacation, indicating that the situation was too difficult to get into right then. Patience, creativity, and a strong sense of warmth and acceptance are the essentials of this technique.

Inner personality parts are not all negative. In one family, youngsters are encouraged to get in touch with "the doctor inside," who can help children get well. In another family, they contact "the answer person," who knows how to get along better with friends, relatives, and school.

CAREFULNESS

We want our children to be careful for many different reasons, but there is no single method to convey so abstract a concept. Many parents have found it useful to hold and guide the hands of their toddlers when showing them how to touch gently. Often they repeat "touch gently" when demonstrating how it's done; and by extension, when youngsters poke or pinch, parents say the words and remove little hands.

Alisha learned that she is pressing too hard on baby brother if her fingernails change color and Bobby learned that he is being too rough if his brother's face begins to pucker. One mother began to teach her son the difference between *touching* and *moving* things when he was seven months. She praised him for touching gently and told him calmly but firmly not to *move* certain books. He quickly learned the difference between these two ways of approaching objects and at ten months he amazed her by touching all the glittering balls he could reach on a Christmas tree, with only the slightest trembling of the ornaments. Another mother taught her eighteen-month-old to differentiate between rough and gentle by letting him play with blown eggs several times a week. When an egg broke, the game calmly ended for the time being, and soon the same eggs were lasting for months.

Making friends with animals is easier if we provide a few guidelines. Basic rules include: Move slowly so animals won't be frightened; let cats and dogs sniff your hand to say hello before you try to pet them; stay away from cats if their tails are wagging, or dogs if they are growling; pet in the proper direction—toward the tail and the toes; and don't hurt animals. Separate pet and child if the rules are disobeyed.

APPROPRIATE SELF-EVALUATION

We want our children to appreciate their abilities without overrating their accomplishments or denying responsibility for their shortcomings. We want to stimulate improvement without engendering fear of failure. Those are tall orders and they are issues with which many of us still struggle as adults.

How our children evaluate themselves is often a reflection of how we, and to a lesser extent other adults, evaluate them. If we are generally critical, they will be more critical of themselves. And if our praise comes at a high price, it may be too discouraging to strive for. On the other hand, if children perform below their capability and we praise their performance as superb, they will bask in the mediocre and see no need for improvement. To the discriminating four-year-old, praise that comes too readily is of dubious worth. As parents, we are once again called upon to consider our evaluation and balance our response, because children learn to accept the limits of their capabilities and maximize their performance through a careful blend of appropriate praise and considerate criticism.

If to make mistakes or to flunk the first attempt is to fail, then we are all failures. Our first task is to establish that imperfection is the norm, and encourage perserverance. One approach is to look at the *intent,* not just the *results* of a child's actions. When Mom found Miranda with scissors and a very ragged head of hair, rather than take away the scissors, she helped her even it up. Parents who freely admit and discuss their own mistakes with children are often gratified by the tolerant attitude their youngsters adopt toward mistakes.

Praise is essential to our children, but like any other parental tool, it can be used skillfully or ineptly, either building self-esteem or causing disillusionment and disruption. Generally speaking, children from birth to about age four don't have a self-concept of their own and tend to judge the worth of themselves and their actions solely on the basis of how adults react. They naively and unself-consciously accept and glory in every word of praise and relish each compliment as a statement about their entire being. Our praise is almost never too lavish.

At about age four, children begin to make their own judgments: how tall they are, how far they can jump, how well they draw, how far they can count, compared with the adults and children around them.

The dawning realization that each is his own judge is an essential step toward eventual independence. Once the process of self-evaluation begins, we can foster its development by stepping back, withholding some of our praise, and helping youngsters evaluate their own progress. In fact, when we do offer compliments during this stage, they may be brushed aside or even criticized. But despite their growing ability to self-evaluate, children still have an immense need for our approval.

Because praise is such a powerful teaching tool, it's important that we use it carefully and effectively. Here are some tips:

- Be specific. Behaviors that are praised are more likely to be repeated. To be effective, however, we must be specific enough that the child knows exactly what behavior to repeat. "You walked quietly and whispered when we were in the library!" "You remembered to give a cookie to Randy before taking one for yourself!"
- Match praise to the child's likely feelings. A further drawback of general praise is that we seldom feel *entirely* delighted with ourselves. This is especially the case with a child who appears very "good" but is actually struggling internally to maintain that illusion. Praise can intensify the tension between outward goodness and inward unworthiness to the extent that the ropes of self-restraint snap. Thus when one mother praised her four-year-old son for being "such a good boy" he ran over and bit her. Better to acknowledge the struggle: "It must have been very hard for you to let Tony have a turn riding on your new fire engine."
- Praise process, not just results. We can unintentionally demand too high a standard if we praise only the results of our children's efforts: so pretty, so far, so fast, so well. Unless

we applaud them at least as often with "you tried it!" or "I see how carefully you are working," we imply that only good results, not effort, count.

· Praise qualities as well as behaviors. To praise the quality that underlies a specific behavior builds self-esteem at an essential level. Thus: "It was generous of you to share your treat with Randy," or "You were very imaginative to think up such a story."

· Second-hand compliments. Sometimes praise is most easily heard when we don't have to respond to it directly. Thus when Mom knows Nate, age four, is listening, she tells Dad, "Nate is a terrific playmate for baby Ivan. He's the only one who can get him to laugh out loud and who can entertain him while he's waiting for a meal." On the other hand, some children prefer to be consulted before their accomplishments are advertised: "Can I tell Grandma that you've learned to ride your new trike?"

Careful Criticism

With two-year-olds, our criticism most often involves *what* children do: Don't unroll the toilet paper, throw the glass, or pull the cat's tail, but do pick up the toy and come to the door. The deed is done or not. But as children approach elementary-school age, we become increasingly concerned about the *quality* of their actions: Did they color within the lines? wipe up *all* the milk? put the toys away *neatly* enough? How we criticize in order to improve performance will either teach children that they are basically inadequate or will build confidence in their growing skills. Here are some ideas for constructive criticism. First, there are times to ignore imperfections: We don't *have* to show Molly that she colored out of the lines or tell little Charlie that he didn't brush *all* his hair smooth. In part, skill develops with mere practice. Sometimes we can avoid direct criticism by giving more precise instructions the next time around: "When you serve soup, please touch the ladle against the inner edge of the pot so it won't drip on the table." At times we can ask if children *want* advice: "Do you want to know a way to saw that board more easily?" At other times we can invite children to look for and correct their own oversights: "Do you see any more milk that needs to be wiped up?" When we do criticize, it is important to be specific: rather than "you are selfish," we can instruct, "It is selfish to play with your trike and not let your friend have any turns." Finally, with some forethought, much criticism can be stated positively rather than negatively: Instead of "You didn't put all the blocks away," we can state, "*All* the blocks need to be put away."

RELIGIOUS AWARENESS

Many of us have two primary objectives regarding religious awareness. One is to teach our children what we value about religion, and the other is to avoid the negativity we may associate with our own religious upbringing. A further concern, both among actively religious parents and those who are laissez-faire in this regard, is how to answer earnest queries about the nature of the universe. One mother mused, "Alix, age four, has been asking all kinds of questions I'm not sure how to answer, about what God looks like, where people go when they die, and what heaven looks like. I don't know how to answer her questions in terms that are sufficiently concrete for her to grasp, yet not so definite they will be a problem for her later."

Avoiding the Negativity of Previous Religious Education

Several parents tell how they try to offer their youngsters a more accepting and creatively flexible religious outlook than they grew up with:

> I grew up with a religious background that declared that God is wonderful, life is wonderful, and therefore everyone ought to feel wonderful. When I was sad, hurt, angry, or whatever, I not only believed such feelings were immoral, but I felt completely alone because I thought no one else had such experiences. With my children, I make a point of talking about all kinds of feelings.
>
> Having been told, when I was little, that God granted all prayers, I prayed for months for a beautiful, expensive doll that never came. For years my religious aspirations were clouded with a deep sense of disappointment. So I have my four-year-old conclude his prayers with "if it be Thy will." I've ex-

plained that just as I don't let him eat all the candy he wants because it isn't good for him, God doesn't always give us everything we ask for because we may not need it or it may not be good for us.

Teaching Religion through Daily Experience

The lessons of religion are often learned best through day-to-day experience. But how do parents make use of this fact?

The respected theologian James Fowler, in his recent book *Stages of Faith* (Harper & Row, 1981), contends that the cornerstone of religious faith is laid along with the security of being cared for by loving parents in the early years of life. To strengthen this connection between parental and divine love, some parents conclude their earliest lullabies with the words, "I love you and God does too."

When children are struck by the wonder of the moon, the beauty of a flower, or the joy of a puppy, some parents point out that each of these was made by God. At Christmas, one family bakes a birthday cake because it helps children understand the celebration in familiar terms.

One family focuses on the religious potential of daily living with the question "What do you think Jesus would do in this situation?" The question may be raised after the five-year-old has had a difficult afternoon with a friend. It is also a part of discussions at the dinner table or on long car trips in which books on "values clarification" provide a basis for considering options in common dilemmas of living.

Teaching through Religious Stories,
Poems, and Songs

For generations, our various religious heritages have been passed down through stories and songs: Today is no exception. Stories, old and modern, about religious people and the lessons of faith are read while parent and child snuggle before bedtime, or when family and friends gather for a seder, to mention just two occasions. Some parents include the entire range of stories illustrating the many aspects of God and religious life, while others, concerned that children might be unduly upset by certain illustrations (such as Abraham's intention to sacrifice his son Isaac), first select those that convey God's love and caring, and later add those age-appropriate stories that teach guidelines for personal behavior. One mother helps her preschoolers and their friends dramatize traditional accounts, while another reads modern stories she believes will be more easily understood. One family keeps bedtime Bible stories on a separate shelf, to emphasize their specialness. Still others use modern technology to bring religious songs, poems, and stories into their children's lives via records and tape recordings.

Answering Children's Questions about Religion

Because children think in concrete terms, it is a challenge to convey religious concepts to them in terms they can understand. Parents may compare God's love to the wind, which can be felt but not seen, or to our breath, which is both inside and outside us. The soul may be compared to the energy that lights a lightbulb but that cannot illuminate a broken or worn-out bulb. But our own lack of knowledge is a hindrance. If Elaine asks where paper comes from, we easily answer that it is made from trees; and if she wants the details we go to the library. But if Bernard asks where souls go after people die, or Alix asks what heaven looks like, we can't answer with our accustomed scientific accuracy.

Our concern about not knowing all the answers is greatly reduced when we stop to realize that in many ways, we and our children are equals when it comes to religion. We have as much to learn from them as they from us. For example, children's belief that thoughts are as important as deeds bears a striking resemblance to the teachings of various religious traditions. Jesus taught that to enter the kingdom of heaven, we must become as little children.

As Edith Hunter so aptly puts it in *Conversations with Children* (Beacon Press, 1979), "the [religious] teacher's most important role is that of midwife to the thought rather than imparter of wisdom." Knowing that we don't have to have all the final answers, we can be more relaxed about both answering and discussing children's questions. Thus, when asked about heaven, we can ask children what *they* think it is like. One little boy answered that there would be an endless supply of Lego to build with. A five-year-old girl asked Jesus, on her mother's advice, to help take away her bad dreams. She closed her eyes and reported that she had talked with

Jesus and seen all his brilliant, white-winged angels. Mom was baffled because as far as she knew her daughter had never heard the angels described, but the bad dreams stopped.

Answering Children's Questions about Death

Children, especially four-year-olds, are as curious about the end of life as about its beginning. They ask about dead bugs, dead pets, and even the unsettling question of our own mortality is subject to their inquisitiveness. Death is discussed here because our own religious beliefs, or lack thereof, affect our answers. What do children want to know?

> *What is death?* Death is when the body stops working for good, like a television set that can't be fixed. A dead person stops feeling, talking, hearing, seeing, or getting hungry. To some people, death is when the soul leaves the body.
>
> *Does thinking about it cause it?* Because angry children fantasize destruction, it can be very reassuring to hear, ''Even if you were so angry at me that you wanted me to die, that wouldn't make me die.''
>
> *Who would take care of me if you died?* This may be the real issue behind children's questions. One four-year-old was relieved to learn that Aunt Roslyn would take care of her.
>
> *When do people die?* When they are very old. —When God says it's time. —When they have lived as many years as they were supposed to live. —When they get very sick or are in bad accidents. Unless a child is facing the early death of someone they know, there is no need to discuss this relatively uncommon event.
>
> *When will you die, Mommy and Daddy?* Unless parents are seriously ill, it is better to reassure children according to what is likely than to worry them about what is unlikely— We are going to live together for a *long* time.
>
> *How do people feel when others die?* People usually feel sad and lonely when someone they love dies, but those feelings gradually go away. People may also be glad that the other person is no longer sick or confined.
>
> *Do those who are dead feel pain?* Children often associate upsetting situations with physical pain. Television probably

adds to their assumption that death is painful. To illustrate the contrary, point out that haircuts don't hurt because the hair is already dead.

What happens to dead bodies? They are put into the ground where they gradually turn into soil. (Sometimes they are burned so they turn into soil faster.)

What happens after death? I don't know. People have different ideas: —The things we like and remember about people keep them alive for us. —They go to heaven where they feel happy and loved. —When our clothes wear out, we get into new clothes. When our bodies wear out, our souls go into new bodies.

"I don't want to stop talking," confided Jason, who was worried about the possibility of his own death. As his mother then explained about death and rebirth in nature, he brightened and interrupted, "Oh, why didn't you tell me that after I die I will start all over again like the trees and flowers!"

Sometimes parents inadvertently create problems for their children through the ways they talk about death. Having been told by parents, "I won't die until you are grown up," children have been known to avoid self-dressing and other similar signs of growing up. And hearing that "death is like sleep" has caused many a sleepless night. Assuming they themselves are to blame when something goes wrong, children need *repeated* assurance to the contrary if someone close has died. Silence is fertile soil for guilt.

Prayer

Some parents select prayers written especially for children, and thus avoid the confusion of difficult vocabulary and intellectual abstractions. On the other hand, many parents teach traditional prayers, of which every religion has a rich supply, knowing that youngsters will gradually come to understand their meaning. Family prayers may be silent or out loud, spontaneous, read by parents, or recited in the form of song or verse. Some families emphasize talking to God through prayers of thanksgiving, petition, praise, or forgiveness; others encourage listening to the Quiet Voice within; and still others invite meditation on, and thus experience of, some aspect of Divine Being. The most common times for prayer are before dinner, after dinner, and at bedtime.

Given children's powerful imaginations, they are often more successful than we in briefly meditating, for example, on a tiny candle that grows to fill the world with the glow of love, or in imagining a prayer as already granted and giving thanks accordingly. In order for them to experience the emotional significance of prayer, however, we need to allow and encourage them to pray about issues that are important to *them*. As they mature, so will their prayers. Thus Liz might feel thankful that her scraped knee stopped hurting, that Daddy took her to the park, that her flower bloomed, or that her brother didn't call her names. Donald may ask for sun so he can play outside tomorrow, or for help to endure his brother's birthday party. And Andy may feel sorry that he dropped Aunt Lisa's dish or mashed his friend's finger in the door.

Rather than saying a traditional grace before meals, one family holds a moment of silence in which the youngsters, age three and six, have been instructed to think about a time they felt especially loved. In another, all sit for several minutes of silence to listen to the Quiet Voice within, then report on what they heard. The immediate reward in both cases is that dinner starts on a more peaceful note.

> Lord, hold me in your arms tonight,
> Just like Mommy, nice and tight.
> Keep my room all safe this night,
> And help me sleep 'til morning's light.

Attending Religious Services

A number of dilemmas confront parents regarding attendance at formal religious services. Advantages of doing so include exposing children to the broader religious community, providing additional models and sources of knowledge, and becoming involved in the support of others. However, these advantages may have to be balanced against the difficulty of taking youngsters to a place they may not want to be, or where they may need to sit quietly for long periods of time. Thus, especially with children under three, some families opt for services at home. Even after that, children being children, very often the highlight of the event for them is the goodies served afterward at the social. How do parents get to services they wish to attend?

One mother explains how she got everyone to attend church peacefully together:

> A friend of mine once told me that when she visited a church in Switzerland, there were little tables set up in the side aisles where young children were encouraged to sit and color. I decided right then that I would take my future children to church with me, so they could be exposed to the atmosphere, even if they couldn't understand everything that went on. When Diana was an infant, it was easy, though I occasionally had to take her out when she cried. When she was a toddler, I took a snack and her blanket, put her in tennis shoes and sat near the back, so she could wander quietly when she needed to. Now, as a preschooler, she takes books, paper, and crayons, and keeps herself quietly busy.

> We've gone to church all along, another parent reports. As infants, they only objected mildly to staying in the church nursery, which had an especially warm and caring atmosphere and was well staffed. And since they've become old enough, they've really enjoyed Sunday School.

Other parents have solved the dilemma by leaving kids with neighbors or having one parent stay home while the other attends either alone or with the older children.

CARES FOR SELF

INDEPENDENCE

When we get right down to it, we want our youngsters to become independent as soon as possible so they won't be such a continual drain on our energy. Still, we don't want them to become so independent that they'll move out and forget about us. We want this attribute on our own terms.

How does the growth of independence normally progress? (The following ages are approximate.)

Birth to Crawling.
How we'd love to be waited on hand and foot, like our infants are—until we think how exasperating it must feel to be totally

dependent on other human beings, who don't understand our language very well.

Crawling to Age Two
Our apron strings grow to about forty feet in length, and our little ones check back every minute or two to be sure we're still on the other end. But they can hold their own crackers and even copy us when we drop clothes in the laundry basket.

Age Two to Three
Youngsters declare their independence, but not in the form we'd hoped for. Their physical independence is hampered by immature coordination, high kitchen counters, stuck zippers, and speeding cars. So they concentrate on freedom of thought, and balk at our every request.

Age Three to Four
This is the year of the physical independence we've waited for so long. They are coordinated and experienced enough to take over a great deal of their own physical care as long as we keep the tasks simple and they are in a mood to put on their own socks.

Age Four to Five
This year most youngsters gain more emotional independence. They can really understand that we love them, even when we are not physically present. Even those who the previous year balked at dressing themselves or using the toilet all the time generally decide to take over much of their own physical care before this year is out.

Age Five to Six
Now our concerns for independence may suddenly reverse. Our children move from our homes into the realm of school bureaucracy and they are often more blasé about that change than we are. Many of us are awestruck by our self-sufficient kindergartners.

Though they may say little about their big new world, most of us hear reports that they are surprisingly mature when away from us. At times we get a sinking feeling that we no longer know them very well. We just wanted them to take care of themselves, but alas, they are rapidly becoming independent.

Ironically, one of the most essential ways in which we help our children become independent is to accept their dependence. True independence develops naturally but slowly out of a pervading sense of security. Children who are pushed into independence before they are ready learn that their basic human need for dependence is unacceptable. To be truly independent is to lead a lonely existence. Ultimately we want our children to become interdependent with friends, co-workers, mates, and with us. To be interdependent requires acceptance of that part of ourselves which depends on others. We also need to accept the fact that children move toward independence at different rates. Jerry may be careening around the neighbor's house, while Daniel, some months older, is still glued to Mom's lap. Furthermore, during periods of family instability or transition, we can expect more clinginess and dependence.

On the other hand, while it is as natural for children to grow independent as for trees to grow toward the sun, it is *not* always so natural for us to let them go easily, especially in this era of very small families. Empty-nest syndrome doesn't drop in on us without warning when our children turn eighteen. It rears its head with each new development in which we become less essential to our offspring. When youngsters go off to school, and there's no younger sibling to absorb us, it's time to take stock of our personal goals if we haven't already. Whether we take up important hobbies, return to work part- or full-time, or become involved in school or community volunteer work is a matter of individual choice. But to remain totally involved with children who no longer need us full time is to give them the message that they can't live without us. We hamper their growing independence if *we* need them to remain dependent.

Just how much independence we provide depends on the circumstances, the child's age and personality, and our own personalities and past experiences. The specific activities we allow are not as important as whether the child's capabilities and desire for independence are fairly well matched with the number of available opportunities. Allowing appropriate amounts of independence not only frees us from some daily caretaking and prepares children for the future but also builds their self-esteem because of the trust we demonstrate in their capability.

A major stumbling block for young conquistadores is our adult-sized world. Thus, after all our earlier childproofing, as youngsters approach age two or three, we start looking for ways to *increase* accessibility. A stool enables Tyler to get his own drink of water and a ''light-switch extender'' that attaches to the wall switch allows Shelley to turn on her bedroom light. The backyard is more accessible with an additional low handle on the screen door and tape or a plastic shield fashioned from an old Clorox bottle, which prevents the high door latch from closing. (To avoid constant reminders to shut the door, attach a spring to the top of it.) When our youngsters want to do something ''by self,'' we can consider whether the request is appropriate and if so, ease their way if necessary.

A major reason we don't let our children do more for themselves is that *we* can do the jobs so much faster and better. Time devoted to developing our youngsters' skills when they are two, three, and four, however, is well spent because given sufficient opportunity, they become amazingly capable five-year-olds. One mother quoted the following rule: If you want to raise independent youngsters, tie your own hands behind your back and let them do whatever they can for themselves, even if it's a mess.

Another good way to encourage independence is to support individual interests. Those of us who assume our children's interests will grow directly in proportion to their exposure to *our* favorite activities may be in for a rude awakening. Helping our children find the classes, books, adults, and other opportunities to develop their own special interests, especially when they don't coincide with our own, proves to them it is acceptable to be independent from us in an essential way.

We can also provide money. There's nothing like a little financial independence to make one feel one has a place in the world. For more about spending money and allowances, see pp. 196 and 312.

Some parents take care to respect their youngsters' privacy. Mothers relate the following:

> Marie, age four, relates every detail of what happens when we are apart. But other than the teacher's occasional reports, I have no idea what goes on when Lee is in school. I ask a few questions so he'll know I'm interested, but basically I feel it is my task to accept his preference for a private life of his own.

Another mother explains:

In our house, a closed door is as good as a wall, unless you bid someone enter. I think it is harder on me than on the kids. Sometimes I want to know what's going on, and it's hard not to barge in, but I think it is important for Amy, age five, to have her own private place.

ENTERTAINING HIMSELF OR HERSELF

Though our offspring need our loving attention as much as food itself, we also want them to entertain themselves because learning how to use time is part of growing up. But we have more immediate and personal objectives as well. If they can't entertain themselves, then *we* have to entertain them. Although recreation director is one basic role in parenting, we also need times to do housework quickly, to bask in our private thoughts, to restore ourselves by conversing with other adults, and to engage in our own adult activities, which interest us more than blocks and trikes. One mother clarifies the situation for her three-year-old: "I will be ready for our time together sooner if you keep yourself busy now."

Up to age two and one-half or so, little ones seem to entertain themselves well for a minute or two at a time, and on rare occasions, even up to five minutes straight. Around age three, attention span seems to increase, and youngsters may often be able to keep themselves busy for fifteen minutes at a stretch. For four- and five-year-olds, fifteen minutes to half an hour is common, and even up to an hour may be possible if there's an especially absorbing activity. There is, however, tremendous variation in attention span from one child to another.

As a general rule, avoid interfering when youngsters are harmlessly entertaining themselves. Anxious to positively reinforce desired behavior, one mother started praising her two-and-one-half-year-old whenever she found him contentedly playing by himself. He instantly dropped whatever he was doing and begged her to join him. After several such episodes, she concluded that the pleasure of entertaining himself was sufficient reward.

Often we assume that when children complain they are bored they mean they don't have anything interesting to do. It took one mother months to figure out that the term means, "I want to do something with you, Mommy." That's why listing a dozen things for Leslie, age four, to do by herself never helped. Other youngsters use the word bored to mean, "I don't want to do this," "I don't understand what I'm supposed to do next," "This is too easy," or "This is too hard."

One mother noted that when she herself is bored, her daughter, age five, more often complains of boredom. When Mom is involved in interesting things, her daughter finds more to do. Another mother noted that because she reads a lot, her boys, ages four, six, and eight, spend a lot of time with books.

Certain toys and activities encourage children to entertain themselves.

> *Dangle bar.* "Before Laurel could sit up or crawl, we tied a three-fourths-inch dowel across her playpen and suspended many objects on *short* pieces of elastic, just long enough that she could reach but not get tangled up. We included measuring spoons, blobs of aluminum foil, wind chimes, and solid glass prisms to reflect patterns of sunlight on the ceiling. Changing items every week or so kept her busy exploring."
>
> *Cardboard boxes* of assorted sizes and shapes make trains, playhouses, robot costumes, beds for dolls, cages for animals, and so forth. As children get older, they spend most of their time cutting and decorating.
>
> *Work space.* When your child is about three, provide a place to work. One family bought a sturdy old table at a garage sale and cut the legs off at convenient child-height. (They saved the ends to reattach later.) Make a simple desk by supporting an old door or piece of particle board on cardboard boxes, or set a square of heavy vinyl on the floor in a corner, and keep the area well stocked with art supplies.
>
> *Butcher paper.* One big roll will last for years. Use it for drawing, painting, and to decorate for gift wrap. Make life-size portraits to color by tracing around each youngster. Children can draw layouts of streets and train tracks, and as they get older make paper costumes and design their own board games.
>
> *Age-appropriate.* One mother, aware that her second son entertains himself much better than her first, realized that Steven, age eight months, had access to many of his brother's more advanced toys, which were more absorbing than reg-

ular baby toys. She was careful, of course, to keep small parts out of reach.

Secret supply. Keep a few new toys stored in a back cupboard to bring out when you really need some time to yourself or set up a toy exchange with friends so youngsters have more variety.

Trash collection. Keep an extra bag beside your garbage can to collect empty spools, meat trays, toilet paper rolls, jar lids, and so forth. Toddlers will stack and sort, preschoolers build and invent.

Playhouse. Put a sheet over a card table or build a playhouse in the backyard. During a long winter storm, one mother pitched a self-supporting pup tent in the living room for her four- and six-year-olds. Once youngsters are safe climbers, most love a tree house.

Water play at the kitchen sink, or on the patio, or in an empty bathtub. One mother used an outgrown baby bathtub as her toddler's wading pool.

Create rather than buy. Marie, age five, wanted dollhouse furniture. Given balsa wood, a coping saw, file, hammer, fine sandpaper, glue, tiny nails, and some help getting started, she kept busy for hours, making her own. To finish it, she decorated her treasures with felt pens and varnished them.

Having read *Nothing to Do* by Lillian and Russell Hoban (Harper & Row, 1964), Mom gave Jason, age three, a polished "magic" stone. When bored, he rubs it, looks around the room, and, amazingly, can then find something of interest. One family keeps an "activity jar" with pictures to indicate games, small household jobs, and so forth, so those who are at loose ends can reach in for an idea. Another family keeps a file box of things to do. When Tanya, age five, complains of boredom, her mother sends her off to sit on the sofa and think about it, or to draw several pictures of things she might do. One mother found her youngsters rarely whined of boredom once she started assigning a household task for each complaint.

Adult Equipment for Children's Use

Adult equipment fascinates children. Even though careful teaching and technical adaptations may be necessary, letting youngsters use the real thing not only swells self-esteem, but also saves the cost of buying a toy to duplicate every piece of household equipment. Increasing numbers of today's preschoolers are introduced to computers at home. On the other hand, one family was unwilling to let youngsters use their delicate stereo, but found a good one at a garage sale for less than a new children's model. The following examples note the youngest ages reported to us; we have included this information not because all children can or should begin at a particular age, but because we often fail to acknowledge when our youngsters *are* capable.

> *Carpentry tools.* Small-size but real tools are much more satisfying than plastic ones. Make sure the child can handle each tool safely. To put things together, first try glue, then roofing nails (their big heads are easy to pound and protect little fingers from the hammer), and large screws. Get wood scraps from a lumber yard or cabinet shop, or let youngsters work with cardboard.
>
> *Calculator.* At two and one-half, Robert liked to push the buttons and watch the numbers flash. At age four, he learned to add; and at age five he loves to ask himself questions, guess the answer, and see if he's right.
>
> *Tape recorder.* Put a smiling face on a piece of tape on the start button and a sad face on the stop button. Sandra started using a tape recorder at eighteen months. Record children's favorite songs and stories on tape and encourage preschoolers to make up and record their own.
>
> *Sewing machine.* When Sonya was four, she started standing beside the sewing machine while her mother was working, and pushing the pedal when told to start and stop. Next, she learned to direct the material while sitting on Mom's lap. Just before she turned five, she learned how to thread the machine. With the floor pedal on a low stool she could reach it so she was using the machine by herself before she turned six.
>
> *Slide projector.* Eric, age four, wanted to run our delicate and temperamental projector. Within fifteen minutes, he'd learned to operate it as successfully as I could, and he loved being the projection master whenever family adventures were viewed. After that he was allowed to use a small and more

sturdy slide viewer and have all the second-quality pictures so he could enjoy them by himself whenever he wanted to.

Is "Busy" Better?

Most of us assume that boredom is bad. Children should be active, not bored, and if they aren't, it is our job to jump in and find something for them to do. Some parents, however, have come to a different point of view, encouraging daydreaming, quiet time, or just plain relaxation. Youngsters who have a full schedule of planned routines and classes gain little experience in inventing activities on their own. One mother, assuming her daughter would need to *learn* how to entertain herself, made a point once a day of feeding, cuddling, then putting her infant down with some toys. Wendy's ability to entertain herself increased markedly over time.

Human beings are social beings. A mother of triplets reports that her youngsters are *never* bored. With youngsters under age three or four, having a friend over may require as much attention from us as a single lonely child, especially while youngsters are getting acquainted. But with time there is a real payoff, because two can entertain themselves better than one. Even six-month-olds are fascinated by watching another baby. One responsible three-year-old was rarely bored once she was allowed to freely visit a playmate down the street.

LEARNING SKILLS

CURIOSITY

We don't need to *implant* curiosity as much as we need to nourish this innate quality, survive it, and ensure that our youngsters survive it as well. Though we justly complain that curiosity is the great mischief-maker, we've also come to respect it as basic to human intelligence. Discovery begins with curiosity. Researchers have found that learning to crawl presents a crucial turning point in a child's ultimate intellectual development. At this early age, youngsters learn from their parents' response whether curiosity is generally acceptable or unacceptable. Those who are allowed space and opportunity to explore tend to develop higher intelligence than those who live in barren environments, spend most of their time confined to playpens, or are limited by an oppressive number of no-no's. In fact, most of today's parents encourage their little ones' natural curiosity by providing ready access to toys and safe household equipment and by letting youngsters explore freely as much as is safe. In order to allow more opportunity to explore, many modern parents avoid a playpen, except for intermittent use. Nursery school and play-groups offer additional opportunities for learning and often give the parents a welcome breather so they have more energy for dealing with curiosity at home.

The second best reward for curiosity is time: time to explore the textures of the food before the plate is whisked away, the gutter before rushing to the store, the glove compartment before leaving the car. The best reward is time plus an attentive parent to listen when young ones want to share new discoveries.

Not merely *accepting* but *encouraging* children's questions is essential to maximum intellectual development. Thus one mother often prefaces her answers with the acknowledgement, "That's a good question." Rather than just pointing out sights, sounds, and smells, parents also ask, "What's that?" Furthermore, parents fos-ter both posing questions and testing answers: "Do you think this toy will float or sink?" Finally, being open to the opportunities of the moment can provide very special rewards, as shown in the following examples.

I encouraged my children's curiosity by letting them play with things that others didn't allow. For example, one day when company was over, Conan, age two, found a roll of Saran Wrap, felt it, listened to it, and unrolled the entire box to make a path. The investigation entertained him for quite a while. The visitors were horrified.

Sonya, age five, stopped to watch sewing machines being unloaded from a truck. They slid down the steep ramp into the freight entrance under the sidewalk. As she peered down the gaping hole, the workman below asked if she'd like to slide down. I held back my bashfulness and training not to bother others, while Sonya slipped giggling down the slide and climbed back up the steep ladder. I've always wondered what those cramped basements look like: Sonya knows.

INTELLIGENCE

Maybe it is because we live in such a technical age that we are inclined to overvalue intelligence in relation to the many other qualities that make for a full and worthwhile life. On the other hand, as we learn about the development of intelligence, we realize that once basic opportunities for intellectual growth slip by, they are difficult to recover completely. Starting with the child's genetic or physical capacity to learn, a number of different factors contribute to maximal intellectual growth.

Strong Parental Bond.
During the first six to eight months of life, infants form an especially strong bond with their primary caretaker. Babies who develop that close, strong bond of love with *parents* seem to learn somewhat more easily than other children as the years go by. Today's child-development researchers therefore recommend that parents, if they are able, be the primary caretakers during those early months so that the bond that forms will be a long-lasting one, rather than one that dissolves when child-care arrangements change.

Language Development.
Much has been written about the importance of talking with babies from their earliest moments, in order that they become accustomed to the flow of language and to encourage them to make sounds. The first step is to make a habit of describing what you're going to do with the child, such as "I'm going to pick you up." The next step in language development is to show our delight when they try sounds and, later, words. Short, clear words and phrases, repeated by us often, will become our baby's first words. Over the coming months and years we can introduce increasingly detailed vocabulary as youngsters demonstrate their ability to understand and use it. Even though toddlers and preschoolers can't copy our pronunciation exactly, if we use correct speech rather than baby talk, they have a better model to aim for. The more we talk *and listen* to our children, the more language becomes a tool for them.

Variety of Experiences.
Encouragement and opportunity to see, hear, touch, smell, and taste in a variety of safe ways help develop the basic senses needed for learning.

Creativity
The world's most creative people aren't necessarily the most intelligent in terms of tests. However, the greater our creativity, the better use we can make of the intelligence we have.

Memory
Some parents purposely encourage memory by asking questions about past events and praising young children when they bring up incidents or facts they've remembered.

Love of Books
In general, the children who like books and are most interested in learning to read are those whose parents read to them at home. Given how basic reading is to learning, fueling our youngsters' enthusiasm for books goes a long way toward their intellectual development.

Attentiveness to the Individual Child
Despite the current national emphasis on early reading, what is appropriate for one child can be detrimental to another. A *few* youngsters pick up books and begin to read on their own at an amazingly early age, but it is a mistake to judge others accordingly. Trying to make children read before their brains are physiologically developed enough to function in this highly specialized way can cut deeply into self-confidence and thus become a lifetime hindrance. Nor is early reading a prerequisite for high intelligence. While some bright youngsters are reading at four and five, others, who are equally bright, are unable to learn until they are well into elementary school, at which time they soon catch up with the early readers.

Throughout all our striving to produce intelligent offspring we have to keep reminding ourselves that our object is not to produce disheartened youngsters who feel they ought to be smarter than they are. Our objective is to enable each child to reach his or her individual potential, whatever it may be, and feel not merely accepted, but appreciated.

IMAGINATION

We have several objectives in encouraging children's imagination and creativity. The immediate reward for us is that imaginative children are more able to entertain themselves. Fantasy is fun, and endlessly expands the mere physical environment that constitutes our "normal" vision. Second, imagination is essential for the eventual development of empathy. We can't truly empathize with other human beings unless we can imagine ourselves in their situation. Finally, in our rapidly changing world, we know our children's lives will be different from our own. To merely pass on what we know without the capacity for creative thinking would be disastrously insufficient, because the wisdom of the past may not apply to the future. The very survival of our planet depends on the creativity with which our children will solve complex, worldwide problems. (Let us hope that we will be imaginative enough to hold things together long enough for them to have their chance.)

Pretend the doll can talk. Pretend the box is a truck. Such examples may seem insignificant or trivial, but creative problem solving starts with the ability to see things in a different light and with the vision that there may be more to reality than meets the eye. Imagination is as innate to children as growing is to seeds, but the capacity fades if it is not nurtured. Our role is to fertilize the soil, avoid stepping on tender shoots, and support the lengthening vines.

Some parents worry that there is something wrong if their youngsters have imaginary playmates. Such friends are especially common among three- and four-year-olds. As long as children also spend plenty of time each week actively involved with parents (and playmates if possible), there is no cause for concern. If a child often *prefers* playing alone in a fantasy world to the exclusion of other relationships, it would be advisable to discuss the matter with your pediatrician or arrange to consult a child or family therapist.

Parents have found they can encourage their children's creativity by making up stories or initiating fantasies that children can pick up and embroider. Most parents join in by pretending to take another part in the child's imaginary play. For example, if Lee is pretending to be a cat, his mother pretends she's another cat, or a mouse. It can also help to ask children what the clouds look like to them, or to invent situations and let them imagine what they might do. For example, if you were out in the woods without a hammer, what could you use instead? Or, what all could be done with a cardboard box?

Time, our children's and our own, is also a factor in creativity.

While we often object to dawdling and daydreaming, we may also discover that silent musing and seeming withdrawal are also the birthplace of creative thought. One mother added:

> I try to generally say yes, instead of giving an automatic no, to the endless projects my youngsters, age four and six, dream up, whether it's to make something out of wood, to plant seeds I suspect won't grow well in our yard, or to invent a dubious new recipe. I believe the opportunity to experiment is important. I arrange time to help and supervise when they want to use sharp knives, candles, the stove, electrical equipment, and so forth.

Some fantasies are best enjoyed in imagination only. But we can also help children turn their imaginings into reality.

> Aaron, age three, loves to have Mom write down the stories he tells me, and read them back to him. Sonya, age five, has mom write down songs she makes up at the piano. When Eric, age five, wanted a robot, Dad bought batteries and tiny lights, and they made a robot with bright eyes out of a few boxes covered with aluminum foil.

Encourage children to use imagination to solve problems. When Laura, age five, wanted to go bowling, and it seemed unlikely she could even lift a bowling ball, her parents asked her to help figure out how to make a bowling alley at home. She chose a ball and empty detergent bottles.

PROBLEM SOLVING

Realistically, life is a series of problems, and many of the ones our children will face in the twenty-first century will be different from our own. Thus, to prepare them for the future, we needn't teach them our solutions as much as we need to teach them techniques for solving problems. One of the challenges of raising creative problem solvers is that they may not come up with the same solutions *we* do. Becky, age four, stands on her bed to more easily pull her blankets up straight.

We need only watch our two-year-olds to realize that problem solving is not easy. The simplest decisions overwhelm them and, in turn, we are driven to distraction by their indecisiveness. Parents survive this difficult era by keeping choices simple, such as "Do you want your egg scrambled or boiled?" rather than "What do you want for breakfast?" When little ones can't decide between a cracker or a bread stick, some parents make the decision themselves, some give a little of each, some say "Let me know when you have decided," and some change the topic to milk. If Annie bites the cracker, she has made her decision. Some days it's easier not to offer choices. Fortunately, there are better days ahead.

Many of the qualities discussed in this chapter contribute to problem-solving ability but three additional aspects are considered here.

Teach the Language of Problem Solving

Those who study the problem-solving process find that good problem solvers often talk to themselves as they work. We can help our children learn this technique by talking to them while *we* solve problems, for example, while putting a puzzle together. "I'm looking for another piece with red on it like this one," or "I'm looking for an edge piece with yellow and blue on it."

We can also help children think their way through problems by asking appropriate questions rather than giving answers. "Is anything stuck under the wheel of the bike that keeps it from moving?" As youngsters approach school age, encourage brainstorming, that is, thinking up a variety of possible solutions, then choosing the most appropriate.

Allow Opportunity

We don't have to go out of our way to find problems for children to solve. We merely have to avoid jumping in too quickly when they encounter a toy that won't work easily, a disagreement with a playmate, or whatever.

Encourage Asking for Help When Necessary

There are times to work by ourselves and times to get help. In this technical age, we'd lead very limited lives indeed without the assistance of the auto mechanic and TV repairman, to say nothing of help from a friend to move the sofa or watch a sick child while we run to the store for medicine.

Parents encourage their little ones to ask for help by responding to their requests; by suggesting help ("You can stand and scream because your zipper is stuck, or you can ask me for help."); by teaching youngsters how to ask so others will be receptive; by encouraging them to ask store clerks and others for help; and by pointing out when and how they themselves obtain assistance.

ARTISTIC

Our objectives are many when we encourage our children in the arts. We want them to sharpen their physical senses, to experience the pleasure of creativity, to have additional means of expressing their emotions, and to develop well-rounded personalities. Some mothers play Vivaldi and Mozart records while pregnant because newborns seem to find such composers soothing, especially if they have become familiar with them in utero. Few of our youngsters will become great artists or musicians, but their lives can be enriched by an appreciation of art. Though many parents will eventually enroll youngsters in a variety of music and art classes, the place to start is with personal involvement. Parents demonstrate how to scribble with crayons, sing to their toddlers, and hold them while they dance. One mother takes her four-year-old to short musical programs and leaves at the intermission of longer ones. Others make brief visits to art musems.

Children are often more interested in music if they have easy access to records and musical instruments at an early age. Music boxes are one way to start. Tape recorders are usually easier for children to operate than record players. As for instruments, look for ones with high-quality pitch and tone, such as bells, finger cymbals, a triangle with a melodious tone, drums with a soft, pleasant resonance, a harmonica without sharps or flats for beginners, soprano recorder, or violin—the only instrument made to one-eighth scale for small players.

One mother chose to play a limited number of records because the repetition enabled Alix to learn the music more readily. Another mother made a game of matching the various tones her preschooler made so Sonya could *feel* the sensation of matched pitches. When Nia was three, her mother began writing down her double meanings and delightful turns of speech with the comment, "This is like a poem." Nia now writes down her own.

What about the visual arts? Free-form design is a great way to begin but some young artists become frustrated when drawings don't look realistic enough. We can help by supplying coloring books, cookie cutters to draw around, or tracing paper. We can encourage our children's involvement in art by displaying their creations in public family rooms such as the kitchen, hall, or TV room. Here are some suggestions for setting up home galleries: magnets on the refrigerator, Fun-Tak® reusable adhesive, ribbons strung from high moldings to baseboards with art attached with paper clips, a net made to support vegetables attached to a wall, or holiday murals of poster paint on the front window.

Acknowledging children's art work is more complicated than first meets the eye. To ask, "What is it a picture of?" deflates the ego of a young artist who is enjoying sheer color or who has failed in the attempt to produce a recognizable object. But our praise *can* generally encourage progress by pointing out improvement. "You colored just inside the lines here," or "You have really learned how to draw a house."

Often youngsters don't want our evaluation as much as they want our involvement, thus "I see you used red *and* blue," or "What tiny little lines you made here," mean more than "How pretty!" To foster enjoyment of art for its own sake, we can teach that the *process* is more important than the *product*. Furthermore, we want our youngsters to eventually rely on their own evaluation rather than ours. Thus when shown a picture, some parents ask, "Was it fun to do?" "Did it turn out the way you wanted it to?" or "Which of your two paintings do you like better?" One preschooler insisted, however, "But Mommy, do *you* like it?"

PSYCHIC AWARENESS

Psychic awareness sounds as strange to many of us today as telephones would have sounded to parents two hundred years ago. However, many people are becoming increasingly intrigued by the apparent capacity of some individuals to transmit thoughts and energy in ways we don't yet understand. Some people believe psychic awareness is as natural to all of us in childhood as the world of fantasy, and that, as with fantasy, most of us leave it behind as we grow up in a culture that places more value on what we can all see, touch, and measure. Some parents, however, believe it is important to encourage their children to develop their potential for psychic awareness. Here they explain what they've done:

> We play games where one person vividly imagines something, or concentrates on a picture or object, and others in the family relax, close their eyes, and describe whatever images come to their minds. It is surprising how often the youngsters pick up the thought. My son, age four, seems particularly good at "receiving" information, and my daughter, age six, especially good at "sending."

> I encourage my youngsters to describe their dreams and fantasies because I believe such mental processes are not only the route to the subconscious mind, but to psychic perception as well.

> My boys, ages five and seven, can often see auras of light around people. I encourage that capacity by asking from time to time, especially in semi-darkness, "What color do you see around so-and-so right now?"

> When my youngsters are sick, in addition to whatever other treatment is appropriate, I touch them and concentrate on an image of healing energy flowing through my hands into their bodies. One day we were visiting a friend who had a stomach-ache. My son, age five, said, "I'll fix it for you." He put his hands over my friend's abdomen while she looked on skeptically. After a few minutes she said with surprise, "I feel better!"

RELATING TO OTHERS

LOVE

This objective is straightforward, at least. We want our children to be able to participate in loving relationships with us, other family members, friends, and eventually with their future partners. What do parents do to lay the foundations for their children to become loving human beings?

First and most important, we can provide a secure, ongoing love relationship. Renowned author and child psychoanalyst Selma Fraiberg declares in her book *Every Child's Birthright: In Defense of Mothering* (Bantam, 1978) that contrary to popular belief, the capacity to love is not innate. It is learned through the experience of being loved.

Love is both precious to have and fearsome to lose. Infants and children who are cared for by an overwhelming array of assorted caretakers or by a series of parents and foster parents conclude that love is very risky. They are apt to find it difficult to form love relationships even in adulthood, and if early childhood bonds were severely and repeatedly disrupted, they may never be able to love another human being.

On the other hand, children who do have an ongoing relationship with their parents and receive high-quality child care when parents are not available, can tolerate the frustration and pain that are inevitable in normal parent-child relationships as well as life in general without losing their basic trust in love.

It is amazing what a boost we can give our young children by being open and expressive around them. Physical contact is crucial to the expression of love, as we absorb love through our skin as surely as we absorb the warmth of the sun. As important as body contact is to us, it is even more important to our infants and children. Many parents believe that it isn't necessary to *tell* children they are loved, because it seems so obvious. But what is clear to us may not be so clear to them, and we all know how much we appreciate hearing that our partner loves us. Some expressions of love seem to be more acceptable than others, however. When one mother tells her boys "I love you," they reply "Yuck!" But when she says, "Wow, I sure am lucky to be *your* mom!" they eat it up.

To love is to experience the warmth of caring, interwoven relationships. Thus we encourage our children to form friendships with their siblings, playmates, and other adults, as they are ready to do so. Sasha posts pictures of her friends by her bed, and she and her mom discuss the value of friendship. As parents, we quickly discover that we can't keep giving love to our youngsters unless we ourselves feel loved (see Parental Sadness and Loneliness, p. 338; and Parents: How They Survive, p. 202).

Parents have made some important observations about love. First, in our culture, pressured by time and surrounded by relative material wealth, it is easy to lose sight of the fact that love has to do with people, not things. One mother noted, "Whenever possible, my husband or I try to be available to snuggle when our boys are tired, ill, upset, or otherwise in particular need of us. We want them to get their comfort from us, not just from blankets, bottles, and teddy bears." Second, in order not to confuse children, it is important to say we love them when we actually *feel* loving. If we tell them with annoyance that they must stay in the backyard because we love them, they will sense *frustration* and equate the word love with restriction. Living with a vigorous two-year-old and a fussy infant, one mother felt calm enough to be aware of loving feelings only when she saw their angelic *sleeping* faces. So she told them of her love just after they dozed off, sure that at some level of mind her message was heard. As they grew past that difficult stage, she found more occasions to tell them of her love. One mother suddenly realized that her four-year-old expressed negative feelings much more readily than positive ones. She had assumed that if she helped him express the former, the latter would come out naturally. She discovered instead that *both* must be learned.

PATIENCE

Although we may worship the clock and the calendar, most children prize the mood of the moment. Why not visit the zoo or Grandma *now* instead of tomorrow morning or Thursday afternoon? We can point it out when others wait patiently and praise our youngsters when they do so, but in part, patience is a quality that develops with age. There are, however, some ways to live more comfortably with our children's *impatience*.

Two-year-olds understand only "now." "Later" seems like "never" and anything past tomorrow is an eternity. Thus, to avoid the anticipation and possible disappointment that often overwhelm a two-year-old, many parents give only last-minute notice of events, unless it's something major like a new baby or a move.

Three- and four-year-olds who can count understand that the trip won't begin for four days or that their friend won't be over for an hour, which is as long as "Sesame Street" lasts. We can help them grasp time more clearly by removing the minute hand from an inexpensive clock. It won't have digital accuracy, but it will show the approximate time of meals and outings. At this age, a large one-week calendar can also be helpful. Draw symbols for regular events like nursery school, clip on pictures for special events and outings, and mark "today" with a big, bright paper clip.

Four- and five-year-olds can begin to grasp that "first will come your birthday, then Christmas, and then way after that we will visit Grandma again." One mother talked to her youngsters about the need for patience on everyone's part, especially during such boring times as standing in line at the store. Both *Mom and the kids* became more patient that year, and once they stopped being so annoyed, discovered songs to sing and games to play at such times.

When we can't have what we want now, imagination is the next best thing. When we're caught in a traffic jam and the youngsters are hungry, it's useless to repeat that there isn't any food. Instead, we can ask, "What all are you going to eat and drink when you get home? How about six glasses of juice? If you could have *any* kind of sandwich, what would it be? How many could you eat? How would it taste?"

COOPERATION

We often say we want our youngsters to *cooperate* when we really want them to *obey*. But "obedience" has such negative connotations today that we feel more comfortable requiring our children to be cooperative rather than obedient. Cooperation is a mutual agreement from which both parties benefit. We need youngsters to pick up their toys and get ready to go even though they can't see any personal benefit. Thus we either have to *make them do what we want* at times, or we have to *make them see the world our way* so they will cooperate willingly. *Having to act* as we wish is far less of an imposition than *having to think* as we wish. Besides, trying to get a two-year-old to think like an adult is a waste of time. In raising children, there are times for cooperation and times for obedience. (See Disobedience, p. 405.)

How do we convey the abstract concept of cooperation to our youngsters? Parents may point out that cooperation is when two movers lift a sofa together or when Emma helps her mother fix breakfast. One mother made up stories about Cora the Cooperator and Sally the Selfish to show how each acted and the responses each received. Other parents teach the advantages of cooperation in the form of "Dinner will be ready sooner if you help set the table," or "I will help look for your doll if you will help empty the trash," or "If you and your brother put your allowances together you can buy the toy you both want (or a nicer gift for Grandma)." One mother realized that because she and her husband always worked out their disagreements in the quiet of their own room their four-year-old had no opportunity to see them solve problems together, so they changed accordingly. Another mother was frustrated by her four-year-old's lack of cooperativeness until she realized that he never heard *her* compromise. She would always answer his requests with a yes or no. Now she tries to think out loud more to let her son hear for himself the mental give-and-take of cooperation.

Realistically, youngsters, like adults, are usually more able to cooperate when they know what lies ahead. When Ben, age five, went to visit his recently widowed grandmother, he knew she would be very sad and unable to pay much attention to him, so he was prepared to entertain himself.

Parents have discovered that children are more likely to cooperate with certain combinations of playmates and adults than others. A certain amount of bickering is inevitable, of course, in learning to cooperate with friends and siblings and the skill comes more easily to some youngsters than to others. But some parents weight the odds by giving stars or other rewards when playtime goes smoothly or when youngsters either offer help to or accept help from a sibling. On the other hand, there are times when even the best of young friends may need a few minutes apart with separate activities.

CONCERN FOR OTHERS

Babies have many endearing qualities, but concern for others is not among them. In the coming years, we want to foster development of concern, but we don't want our children to be so overwhelmed with the need to be considerate of others that they are unable to take care of themselves as well. How do we plant and tend the desired seeds?

Those who study moral development conclude that empathy and altruism develop very gradually. We can teach preschoolers to *act* as though they are concerned about others by requiring and rewarding specific desired behaviors, but to expect them to understand another's point of view or be genuinely concerned without expecting personal gain in return is expecting too much even of five-year-olds. As pointed out in *Moral Development*, Lawrence Kohlberg's studies of moral development can be summarized as follows.

Stage 1.
Birth to about age ten: The child does those things that bring personal pleasure and avoids what brings personal discomfort.

Stage II.
Ages ten to thirteen: The child naturally begins to trade favors, that is, "If you do something nice for me, I'll do something nice for you."

Stage III.
Adolescence: Youngsters choose behaviors *because* they please others. (Unhappily, they may be more interested in pleasing peers than parents, but it is after all their peers, not us, with whom they will spend their future.)

Three-, four-, and five-year-olds *can* also function in the realm of trading favors, which is one stage ahead of themselves, but they *can't skip* to Stage III. They can only do nice things for others if *they* get personal pleasure as well. Praise and appreciation are of course important forms of pleasure but not always sufficient.

Understanding that even our five-year-olds are not able to act out of pure humanitarian concern for others, and won't be able to for years to come, we can set the necessary limits on self-centeredness, plant the seeds of future concern, and delight in their spontaneous kind behaviors, without feeling defeated when their natural self-centeredness shows up again.

True concern for others comes from being able to imagine ourselves in their situation and surmise how they might feel. Children lack both the experience and judgment necessary for empathy. Imagining ourselves in someone else's situation is intellectually more demanding than *remembering* how we felt when we were in a similar situation. To ask a child "How do you think Timmy feels when you call him a name" often elicits a blank stare as if the question were asked in a foreign language. On the other hand, we can ask, "Do you remember how much your feelings were hurt when Sheila called you a cry baby? That is why you aren't to call Timmy names." However, because even our five-year-olds continue to respond in terms of what brings them *personal* pleasure or pain, if we really want this behavior to end, we may need to go a step further and add, "If you call Timmy another name, you will have to go to your room."

Our concept of time is another factor that differentiates between the adult's and the child's willingness to put himself out for others. As adults we expect a return on our kindness in the coming weeks, months, or years, whenever we may be in need. Young children, who live entirely in the present, can't understand that kindness brings return unless the rewards are immediate.

We also have to remind ourselves that much of our children's seeming lack of concern comes merely from a different set of values. Raucous noise is as important to them as restful quiet is to us. Our broken heirlooms mean no more to them than their lost bottle caps do to us. The more they grow into sharing our values, the more they will automatically share our concerns.

Parents help youngsters develop concern by talking about their own concern for spouse, children, other family members, and friends. For example, "I phoned Grandpa today because he has been feeling lonely."

Awareness of the feelings of others begins with the awareness of one's own emotions and then the realization that we all share common feelings. One mother comments: "I show my boys, ages four and six, that they are not alone in their feelings. For example, if they are frightened, I mention a time that I was frightened. I'm careful, however, not to belittle their feelings by recounting a *more* frightening experience." Parents extend the initial awareness of feelings by role-playing situations (such as that of the lost youngster seen in the store that day), by discussing the apparent emotions and probable causes of people in stories and pictures, and by posing hypothetical situations such as "How would you feel if you were the only kid on the block without a Big Wheel?"

Children first learn to be concerned for others by learning to take *our* needs seriously. Therefore we need to restrain them from pushing with abandon past the borders of our reasonable tolerance. As youngsters reach age four and five, they will be increasingly able to respond to our needs if *we* believe we are important enough to be respected.

Sometimes it's a matter of asking them to help when we genuinely need it. This works particularly well when the task is something the child enjoys, such as unlocking the door or answering the phone. One mother notes that when she's upset about something, she tells the children that she's lonely, angry, has had her feelings hurt, or whatever, and usually gives a simple explanation of why she's upset. They listen with interest, as well as relief that she's not upset with them.

Research has shown that another important way to help children develop concern for others is to give them opportunities to care for something or someone. This can begin with partial care of plants or pets and gradually extend to younger siblings and friends as well as to adults in the family and community who are in need of help. The concept we want to convey is that people help others, not merely that adults help children. The rewards for such actions may be a flower that blooms, a warm smile of appreciation, or a star for a youngster's spontaneous demonstration of concern and helpfulness.

Some parents insist that children apologize whenever they hurt another child; others, affronted by the hollowness of an angrily barked "I'm sorry," do not. Some parents ignore the hurtful remarks of child's play as long as the rounds come out fairly evenly; others, especially as children reach age five, begin to teach more about the conventions of social concern. One mother instructed her son that if he hurts someone on purpose, he needs to talk about the problem and work it out. If he hurts someone accidentally, the proper thing to say is "I'm sorry." Another parent requires some form of making amends: fetching a tissue for the tears or some kindly words or a picture to counteract the pain of an insult. If one mother hears especially unkind or unfair things while her five-year-old is playing with friends, she requires a phone call of apology that evening. Though her daughter grumbles, she was delighted to *receive* a call of apology one night.

GENEROSITY

Sharing

What we teach our children about sharing is significantly influenced by our own past experience. One mother recalled, "My neighbor used to hold an entire armload of toys and say they were her son's favorites. And whenever her son whimpered, my daughter had to get off 'his' backyard swing. I vowed I'd never treat other children that way or allow mine to act so selfishly." On the other hand, another mother reported, "I was always required to share *everything,* and I resented having no control over my own possessions." What do we want for our own children?

Toddlers, living in the land of "now," want the red ball when they *see* it, not when another youngster puts it down. The moment we focus their attention on the blue truck however, they will often forget the red ball for the time being. Distraction is less successful in the face of two-year-old determination. Furthermore, youngsters are still figuring out the boundaries between themselves and the outside world so everything they touch may be designated "Mine!" One elder sibling was much more patient after his mother explained that little brother used "mine" to signify "special at the moment," not ownership. Two-year-olds want control of their high chairs, security blankets, and more, as much as we want control of our charge cards. Sharing will not come easily this year, but progress will be clear in the next. Many four-year-olds have some delicate prized possessions that they are realistically reluctant to share, and as four is a common age for petty theft, they may be wise not to trust their friends too far. Sophisticated five-year-olds have the vocabulary and experience to make arrangements for sharing and in several more years they will also develop a genuine sense of fair play. Learning to share is a long, slow process.

From watching our little ones guard possessions on their own home turf, it's obvious that civilization hasn't overcome our basic animal instinct of territoriality. Some youngsters learn to share most readily in the neutral ground of nursery school. Similarly, if the bickering gets intolerable when a friend visits, a stroll around the block or a visit to the park may be helpful. If youngsters take turns visiting each other's homes, they at least experience both sides of the boundary lines.

Whose toy is it anyway? Some of us designate a particular owner for each and every toy, and it seems especially helpful for both siblings to have their own trikes. In some families, youngsters keep individual toys in their own rooms on a private shelf and communal toys elsewhere. One family allows each child to mark two toys as their own, and the remainder are for everyone. Another family avoids much bickering by giving small, perishable gifts for birthdays. They give more substantial toys to *both* children at Christmas or the beginning of summer vacation, even though they know one child will likely play with a particular toy more than the other child. Rather than telling her daughter, "This is your new play table,

Carolyn," one mother explains, "This is our new Johnson family play table, for you and your friends."

Sometimes we inadvertently teach selfishness. When we say "Don't touch Mommy's scissors," we teach that Mommy doesn't share. One mother keeps some sturdy, inexpensive necklaces among her own, which she can willingly share when youngsters ask. Another lets her four-year-old use her expensive colored pencils, but only at certain times and at her desk, as a reminder to treat them with care.

Basic education begins with learning to take turns. Parents point out that *everyone* takes turns at the grocery check-out counter, traffic lights, and while rolling a ball with Dad. The length of a turn can be determined various ways. It may be until Darryl puts the truck down, or three circles around the yard on the bike. Turns may be timed by a large plastic toy hourglass, an egg timer, the kitchen timer, or the duration of a record. As for who gets the *first* turn, it may be whoever gets to the truck first, or whoever didn't answer the doorbell last time. Bobby gets first turns indoors and his sister outdoors. Rosalyn gets first turns before lunch and her sister afterward. On Monday, Wednesday, and Friday, it's Michael's turn to sit in the front seat with Mom, and enjoy any other privileges of the day. His brother gets the other three days, and Sundays are for sharing.

Here are some further tips to help youngsters share.

- When visiting a friend, take a toy to share, and when going to the community sandbox, take one toy "for self" and one for others.
- Before visitors arrive, let youngsters put their most precious things away. Byron wants to put everything off limits, but only three are allowed.
- Let younger siblings investigate the delicate possessions of an older sibling only when a parent can supervise.
- When passing possessions down the line from one sibling to another, clarify the change in ownership by gift-wrapping the old doll, or painting the old crib or bike a new color.
- Keep a doll or truck (which you may have purchased secondhand) in your *own* closet for use when others visit. It adds something different to the scene and helps youngsters feel they aren't the only ones who share.

We will, of course, praise our youngsters when they *do* share their possessions and when nothing else works, we'll move on to stronger measures. Sean, age two, must serve a two-minute time out because he snatched the ball from Beth. The new robot is put out of reach because the youngsters couldn't stop squabbling about it. Lisa, age three, must either let her friend take turns on her bike, or she can't ride it either. Mom holds the new book until the twins, age five, can decide how to share it.

Giving

As for giving things away, there are several different kinds of generosity. First, we can share what we have in abundance, whether that be our time, tomatoes in harvest season, or toys we buy from an ample household budget. Our payment is the pleasure of sharing and seeing the enjoyment of others.

Second is giving with the expectation of return. We give help and consideration to others, and expect the same in return when we are in need, from the same person or from people in general. Or we may give presents to family members and expect reciprocation on the appropriate occasions.

Third, we can give when it hurts: lend a listening ear when we are rushed, give an expensive gift when we don't really have the money, give our energy to a friend or organization when we are exhausted. Such generosity may provide a righteous sense of satisfaction or may leave us feeling taken advantage of and resentful.

Fourth is the generosity of saintliness: to give freely of self and material wealth with spiritual gain as the only compensation. Few of us, even as adults, are able to give this way very often for very long.

It is appropriate to encourage the first and second forms of generosity in our children, but pushing them into painful giving may not be doing them a favor. If *we* give when it hurts, we can monitor our level of resentment and back off if necessary. As for the fourth type, there are few saintly six-year-olds. To expect ours to be one is to court disappointment.

As with most desired traits, the first ways to encourage generosity are to convey objectives clearly and to model the behavior we wish them to imitate. Parents point out examples of generosity so little ones know what they mean by the word. When cleaning out children's rooms, many parents make a point of passing on clothes and toys to give to others who are in need. One mother notes, "When I donate a Thanksgiving turkey to the St. Vincent de Paul Society for the poor, I take the children along."

Children who only receive and never give do not find out how much pleasure there can be in generosity. Thus parents provide opportunities for children to share and feel the pleasure of other people's response. Victor helps Mom do Christmas baking for the neighbors, Jason gets to present the hostess gift when the family is invited out for dinner, and when Steven goes on an outing with another family, his Dad gives him money to buy everyone a treat. One group of preschoolers learned the pleasure of giving by putting together an act for a neighborhood circus and donating their earnings to a children's hospital. When Eric's friendly neighbor teased him one day with "I'm not going to give you anything more because you never give me anything," Eric was always careful thereafter to take Frank a portion of the family's special treats.

Gift-giving sounds like a great way to teach the pleasures of generosity, but sometimes it backfires. If youngsters can't bear to part with a present bought for another child, you may want to make gifts instead, or buy a duplicate of one your youngster owns or shop alone or wrap the present up before your child has the chance to see it and become attached. Often we can enlist a child in decorating a package intended for another. The delightful book *Birthday for Francis* by Russell Hoban (Harper & Row, 1968) clearly expresses the pain of buying presents for a sibling. While children are still young, one family declares birthdays to be family occasions: When Randy, age four, chooses a present for his sister, he gets to pick one for himself as well, and vice versa.

Many parents are disappointed that little ones are so self-centered at Christmas, a time of year for showing concern for others. One mother arranged for her preschoolers to do chores around the house to earn money for buying Christmas presents for their grandparents. Working for the money made the children feel more involved: They selected the gifts more carefully because of limited budgets and watched more eagerly for the grandparents' reactions. Four- and five-year-olds may invest so much energy wondering what they will get for Christmas that they don't notice or care about others around them. Some parents decrease the tension level by avoiding surprises because they see giving, not suspense, as the important message of the season: They tell or show youngsters ahead of time what their gifts will be or even shop together.

Adriana, unlike her twin brother and most other youngsters, has always been unusually generous. Even at age three, if a guest loved one of the gifts Adriana had received, she, *of her own accord,* gave away her new toy. For those of us who live with ordinary children, it's a comfort to know that generosity develops slowly: No one expects fruit from a one- or two-year-old fruit tree. Just because our preschoolers are self-centered doesn't mean they will always remain so. If we can keep our expectations within reason, we can require sharing when appropriate, delight in the occasional display of spontaneous generosity, yet not be disappointed that children aren't saintly.

SENSE OF FAMILY

Family provides a sense of belonging: a fairly predictable and lasting set of relationships that can withstand the vicissitudes of our transient, jet-age job market. Regardless of what else changes, a mother remains a mother, and a brother a brother. Our family connects us not only to other same-age relatives, but also to other generations, both past and future. Family does much for our sense of security, and we want our children to feel it.

Throughout past history, most children have had a handful of siblings and a dozen or more aunts and uncles, to say nothing of endless cousins. Among large, close-knit families there was bound to be at least one close friend for each parent, and at least one mentor for each child. But today's relatives may live so far away our youngsters rarely see them, and because today's families are smaller, with few aunts and uncles, grandparents often bear the emotional weight of being *the* extended family. Furthermore, in our work-oriented society, not only uncles and grandfathers may be too absorbed in their careers to have much family time, but the same may be true for aunts and grandmothers.

When we do get together with our extended family, difficulties abound. First, instead of the fabled open-spaced farms of yesteryear, most relatives today live on city streets and often in homes that aren't childproofed. Thus, visits may be cramped by new rules, lack of space, and fear for the safety of family heirlooms. Second, becoming an aunt, uncle, or grandparent doesn't change basic personality. Relatives who have been critical, remote, or simply don't like children very much won't magically meet our high expectations and form ideal relationships with our children. Third, our parents haven't been around youngsters in years, and our brothers and sisters may have no children of their own. Thus they may feel nervous or uncomfortable, and have their own unrealistically high expectations of small children. We are caught in the middle when things don't go well between our relatives and our children. We often have to take the role of translator or mediator; though at times we can help open more direct lines of communication. Finally, our relatives are often more interested in conversing with *us* than in getting to know our children. Consequently, youngsters may feel ignored by the family we talk enthusiastically about, and act out their resentment accordingly. Sometimes we wonder if it's worth the struggle.

Some parents do have the warmth and support of a close relationship with their respective relatives. Some grandparents have maintained a good relationship with their children over the years and delight in their grandchildren. Other parents suddenly discover common bonds and interests with their own parents, brothers, or sisters in the process of watching the next generation grow. Such families are indeed fortunate. Overall, however, recent generations have witnessed the demise of the extended family. Lacking both the joys and obligations of a troop of blood relatives, many of us are creating our own de facto families from an assortment of friends and acquaintances with whom we share common needs or interests and to whom we feel particularly drawn. Thus the extended family, rather than disappearing, is gradually being redefined. This is indeed fortunate, as a growing body of research is pointing out the value of supportive social ties for the maintenance of both physical and mental health. For places to begin building an extended family, see Parental Sadness and Loneliness, p. 338, and Getting Help, p. 233.

How do we provide our children with a sense of family *and* survive family visits? A sense of family develops over time, through shared memories of obstacles overcome, good times together, and the rhythm of repeated family traditions, whether Thanksgiving turkey or baking a cake for Grandmother's birthday. Some families give youngsters a unique Christmas tree decoration each year, as a visual reminder of their shared past.

Definitions of what a family is will differ depending on needs and circumstances. Some parents stick with the traditional explanation that a family is a group of people related by blood ties. Others have come up with these definitions of family: a group in which people learn to get along with one another; people who always love and take care of each other, even though they get angry sometimes; a group of friends who *act* like family.

Children often feel closer to distant relatives if they can communicate with them in some way. Have them send samples of their art or draw on a letter that you are writing. Better yet, let them dictate a letter for you to write. Phone calls are good for getting acquainted, even if the little ones only listen at first. Tape cassettes and photos provide tangible evidence that these strange relatives are actual people.

Some parents find it easier to arrange family visits in their own homes: Everyone is more relaxed when they don't have to worry about new rules and precious breakables. But if that's not possible, bring along the equipment you need, such as a baby gate, plastic cups, or a lock for the cleaning cupboard to make the visit more relaxed. If Mother-in-law doesn't move an expensive vase, move it yourself.

Planning ahead can often improve family visits. Before her relatives flew in, one mother wrote out a translation list for her toddler's first words: Gaga means cracker, and so forth. Keep a box of old toys at the relative's house to entertain youngsters and help them feel more at home, or take along some surprise activities for self-entertainment. Plan activities in which youngsters can participate during family gatherings. One mother cuts and glues paper collages with her son while she chats with the adults. One family plays charades for awhile. Grownups and youngsters alike can act out and guess simple words.

At times, we have to collect our courage and confront our parents with the reasons that visits don't go well. One mother explained that her son was so obnoxious during visits because his grandparents ignored him. Another pointed out how much her older son felt hurt because grandparents directed all their attention to his younger brother. When such issues are expressed with care and concern for all in-

volved, grandparents are often, but not always, able to respond. One mother told her father that it was his booming voice and over-zealous manner that frightened his granddaughter into tears. At the next visit, he sat without a word, and pulled some irresistible little toys from his pocket. Needless to say, the two were soon fast friends.

Coping with the criticism we get from our parents is a common difficulty of family visits. As new parents, we are often taken aback to find that our parents criticize us as readily now as ever before.

We naively thought that once we became parents we would automatically be accepted as capable adults. In fact, our parents are often the most vocal critics of our child-rearing methods. Furthermore, we are more sensitive to their criticism than to that of anyone else. Each remark about our child's aggressiveness, shyness, jealousy, or fussiness awakens dim memories of similar indictments when we were little. Thus one mother groaned, "I would have been angry if Lee had picked all the green tomatoes off *my* tomato plant, but I was mortified when he picked every single one off my father's tomato plant."

It is often helpful to arrange visits with small groups, so relatives can get better acquainted, or reacquainted, as the case may be. Send Granddad and granddaughter off to read a story together or out for a walk. One grandmother was much less critical of demanding grandchildren once a sitter made it possible to go out for a peaceful cup of coffee with her daughter on occasion. On the other hand, another mother made a point of having a lot of her own friends over whenever the grandparents visited because her friends' support diluted the intensity of critical grandparents. Sometimes more frequent visits help everyone become better acquainted and therefore less critical, but realistically, during certain awkward stages, the best solution may be fewer visits for awhile.

GOOD CITIZENSHIP

SELF-CONTROL

Our small children show only a fraction of the self-control we wish for. We want *self*-control because parental control is so time-consuming and emotionally exhausting. All of us quickly learn that self-control is not inborn, but we suffer nonetheless from the expectation that it should be. We wouldn't expect the zoo's lion to merely eye the meat in the corner of its cage until 4:00 P.M. dinner time, but we expect our two- and four-year-olds not to filch cookies from the cookie jar.

In recent child-rearing history, a number of parents, with the blessing of child-rearing experts, made an effort to free children from the excessively strict parenting methods used in their own childhoods. They let their youngsters run free of parental constraints in the belief that self-control would, in time, develop naturally within the child. Over the years it has become apparent that such is not the case: Children raised in such households grow up with significantly less self-control than others. We now know that self-control develops because adults provide the necessary external controls until children are old enough to adopt them as their own. Thus experience has shown that excessive permissiveness doesn't work.

On the other hand, in our efforts to avoid overpermissiveness, we can burden our offspring with the expectation that they act like little adults rather than children. We can repeatedly ignore their needs or deprive them of the opportunity to express their opposing viewpoints. We can require them to behave "because I say so," rather than teaching our objectives through simple explanations such as, "Wipe your feet so the floor won't get muddy." To command "Do it because I say so" is appropriate in the case of emergency, or when children who understand the rules are toying with the limits, and from time to time when we are out of emotional energy. But in the long run, explaining our intent is important because, as children reach elementary school, those who *understand* the rules show more self-control than those who don't.

If we impose too many regulations, too firmly, too soon, and with too little regard for the child, then our homes can become constricting jail cells from which the unjustly confined will break out in anger. Or, our overzealous restraints may become deeply embedded with the rigidity of a concrete foundation that can limit personal flexibility for a lifetime. We feel trapped: threatened with failure for being either too strict or too lenient. The way out is to set developmentally appropriate priorities so we can concentrate on a limited number of controls at a time. If we accept that innately self-centered two-year-olds *cannot* act out concern for others, and we arrange the environment to minimize physical hazards as well as the amount of mess and property damage they can cause, then we are free to work on curtailing physical aggression: hitting, snatching toys, and the like. The following gives a very rough guideline of when children are realistically able to begin new areas of control. Of course we needn't wait until age five to *talk* about concern for others. It will be months to years before each area is mastered, but if we are making progress along the way, we can afford to keep our expectations and the resulting pressure on our children within reasonable bounds.

Crawling to Age Two.

Children have no concept of rules per se, but learn to avoid specific actions that are repeatedly redirected or that regularly lead to physical or emotional discomfort.

Age Two to about Six.

Children understand clear, simple rules and follow them *if* they are convenient or *if* breaking them will result in personal discomfort.

Age Five and one-half to Six and one-half.

Children develop sufficient self-control to follow rules for their own sake rather than merely to avoid punishment.

Age Eight to Ten.

Children understand that rules can be altered by mutual consent *and* that working agreements require that both parties carry out their part of the bargain.

Thus it is not until five and one-half or six and one-half that we can expect genuine self-control. It's a long time to wait, but at least we needn't give up in despair because our four-year-olds aren't there yet.

In addition to giving simple explanations for our rules, there are other basic ways in which parents of young children encourage the development of self-control.

1. *Repeat the rules.* We have to remember that children learn

by repetition of the rules we taught two minutes, two days, and two months ago. Just because they forget doesn't mean they don't love us or that we aren't good parents. According to Adele Faber and Elaine Mazlish in *Liberated Parents, Liberated Children* (Avon Books, 1975), when asked "How many times do people need to hear the same lesson," famed psychologist Hiam Ginot questioned in turn, "How many times do we have to tune a violin before it stays tuned?"

2. *Supply the necessary control when children are unable to do so.* "Don't hit Johnny. I will hold your hands so you can't hit him," or "put you in your room," or whatever.

3. *Redirect rather than prohibit, when appropriate.* It is much easier to modify our desires than turn them off completely. "You can draw on this paper, but *not* in the book."

The need to redirect our children's boisterous energy is especially apparent at times. Too bad we can't convert their endless vigor to power our cars and electric lights, to say nothing of using it to revive exhausted parents. One mother expressed the wish of many when she sighed, "Many days I'd give anything to turn my three boys loose on a ranch in Wyoming. They need that kind of space. There are lots of great things here in the middle of New York City, but space isn't one of them."

Certainly there are times we need them to sit still, but life is a lot easier if those are the exception, not the rule. First of all, a great deal of routine emotional tension can burn off through physical exercise. Second, most youngsters who are tired from *sufficient* physical exertion settle down more easily to quiet activities, including sleep. Finally, for the sake of life-long good health, it is important to convey an attitude that exercise is acceptable and worthwhile rather than inappropriate and destructive.

With a big backyard or a park nearby, it is relatively easy for youngsters to burn up energy—if the weather cooperates. But to arrange space and equipment for indoor exercise takes a lot more ingenuity. However, just as many modern parents systematically provide equipment for intellectual stimulation, some take pains to design an indoor environment that can dissipate the energy of youthful enthusiasm. We sometimes hesitate to liberate our youngsters' energy for fear they will never slow down again. But we only have to remember the last time we needed them to walk somewhere to realize there *are* limits to their energy. If we involve them in something *really* strenuous they will eventually tire out.

To create more indoor play space, first consider overall household layout. Youngsters may need the space of a large master bedroom more than we do, or a playroom may be more essential than a formal dining room. In one small house, with only one bedroom large enough to hold the parents' king-size bed, that room doubled as sleep space for parents and daytime playroom for youngsters. Lightweight foam sleeping mats can replace children's beds and be hung on the wall during the day, or left on the floor for romping.

Consider a place for youngsters to bounce. Allow jumping on an old sofa or put a secondhand waterbed mattress in the garage or laundry room. A trampoline-like low bouncer, available at home-exercise stores, is great for kids and parents alike. Bouncing for ten minutes is equivalent to jogging a mile. Danny's father put the master box spring and mattress on the floor instead of a frame, and Danny often bounced for as long as an hour.

Encourage indoor climbing on a bunk bed, suspend a trapeze or set of rings from a doorway, or hang a climbing rope from the rafters. One father bolted together an indoor-outdoor climbing structure of plastic water pipe.

Teach youngsters to "drop" not "throw" sand in the sandbox, but indoors, let them toss foam-rubber balls, wads of newspaper, rolled up socks, or an instant beanbag made of rice in a knotted sock. Designate one room as the throwing arena and prolong interest by providing targets and buckets to aim for.

Sometimes the exercise provided by even a short outing is worth bundling up, and it can end with a warm bath if need be. Sign up for winter swim and gym classes, and turn an apartment building laundry room into communal playspace. So youngsters can stretch, make winter visits to the train station, the airport, or large museums. One mother toured large hotel lobbies. When it is impossible to go out, youngsters may accept the news more willingly from the local phone-in weather report or from a thermometer outside the window than from us.

Still looking for games and activities to use up energy? Try: Indoor skating: Slide around on stocking feet on a polished floor; door race: How many times can you run from the front door to the back door before the kitchen timer goes off? Dancing: Start with fast vigorous music and end with something quiet, or do a jumping dance while some popcorn pops, then sit quietly to eat it. Chase: Put two chairs to serve as end posts for children to run around—a race without a finish line. When Lisa catches up to Ryan, she tags him, passes him, and keeps on running. Both children can run their fastest, and both get turns being in the lead. They can exhaust each other in no time. For more ideas, see p. 417.

POLITENESS

Some of us wish we had learned more etiquette at home, rather than through public embarrassment, so we want to teach our children etiquette. Others learned politeness at the cost of suppressing important personal needs and so don't want to place similar burdens on their youngsters. One mother didn't think about politeness one way or the other until a new five-year-old moved in next door—a child who didn't continuously demand food, who said "Yes, thank you," when offered a snack, and voluntarily picked up toys before leaving. Impressed that such social graces made this youngster a delight to have round, she decided it was time to teach her own. Politeness *can* smooth our children's way. We all do better with some of the recognition and appreciation that politeness can engender, and few of us are comfortable when the butter is served with fingers.

Rules of polite behavior are changing as fast as everything else in our world. As polarization decreases between the sexes, we no longer assume "Ladies first." As distance between the generations decreases, some parents prefer to be on a first-name basis with children's friends. And our increased awareness of children's feelings make us less inclined to require handshakes of small children because after all, *we* would feel nervous shaking hands with a ten-foot giant.

Our first task will be to decide *when* and *what* to teach. Before raising children, we don't stop to think how many different polite behaviors we take for granted, many of which are difficult to learn because they occur only intermittently. Parents decide what to tackle on the basis of what is personally important to them, what the child is capable of learning, how much effort it will take to teach at a given age, and how much public censure there will be if the child doesn't learn. One mother observed, "If I required my two-year old to eat politely, *I'd* never have time to eat." But when we are annoyed by the impoliteness of other children the same age as our own, it may be time to teach ours the polite alternatives.

Though there is a tremendous amount of individual variation, the following is a *rough* guideline of when some families begin.

At eighteen months, some parents begin teaching such rote responses as please and thank you, while other families choose to wait. To the amazement of Stefan's parents, he started saying "'cuse me'' all on his own at this age.

At two years, youngsters may learn to take one cookie at a time, and offer one to a friend. What with learning to talk, toilet training, negativity, and mischief to contend with, there's generally not a lot of progress toward politeness this year.

At age three, youngsters may be encouraged to say please and thank you, wait to eat until all are served, not eat all the raisins out of the Raisin Bran, ask to be excused from the table, and begin to wipe their noses on tissues rather than sleeves. Many youngsters enter nursery school at this age, and the mutual reinforcement of home and school teaching can be very effective.

At age four, increasing social assurance makes it easier to learn polite behaviors regarding the outside world, such as greeting guests at the door, shaking hands, offering a chair to an adult, saying "excuse me" after a burp or an interruption, and saying good-bye.

Five-year-olds are more easily able to contain some of their displeasure, rather than declaring, "Yuck, I didn't want *that* for a present!"

Wise parents also acknowledge that different situations call for different degrees of politeness, a concept preschoolers readily understand. One mother notes, "I don't expect Ellen, age four, to say 'Hello, how are you?' to her friends, but I do expect her to greet *my* friends that way." Another mother tells her three-year-old, "It's especially important to say please and thank-you to adults because they really like to hear it."

Once we've decided what to teach, how do we go about it? First and foremost we have to model desired politeness to our children. Unfortunately, modeling is *necessary but not sufficient,* because many a polite parent has never heard please or thank-you pass their youngster's lips.

Most parents assume that reminders will be necessary in the beginning, and for quite some time thereafter. Mom holds on to

Alexi's cracker until he remembers to say thank-you. Other parents ask, "What's the polite thing to say now?" or "What's the magic word?"

Many parents accept gradual progress in the right direction. Thus, a young tot's delighted smile and expression of pleasure may be accepted instead of a specific thank-you. Many parents say thank-you *for* their two-year-olds. When Keith, age three, feels too shy, he whispers his appreciation to Mom and she passes it on.

Impoliteness is sometimes fueled by the need for self-protection. Carolyn, age three, screamed at her grandfather during dinner because she didn't know how else to end his teasing. Her mother supported her by instructing that she say "Please stop!" in the future.

Parents have found ingenious ways to allow youngsters to practice polite behavior in relaxed situations. One mother began postnap tea parties with her eighteen-month-old, speaking the parts of Mr. Teddy and Ms. Dolly, who were regular visitors for orange-juice tea and sandwiches. Weekly candlelight dinners set the mood for some preschoolers to practice etiquette. As she turns into her street from an outing, one mother asks each youngster to say thank-you *and* something each enjoyed about the trip. When one four-year-old appears ready to fall apart some days at the thought of his guest being served first, his mother saves the situation by announcing, "Today, I'll pretend you are the guest."

The essence of politeness, which is to demonstrate our concern for others, is difficult for even five-year-olds to grasp because they are still developmentally self-centered. Children can therefore understand polite behavior more easily if they see how their own politeness can bring personal benefit. Some parents tell children, "People will be more likely to give you things in the future if you thank them" or "Aunt Mary likes kindergartners who shake hands." We can further ease the learning process for our preschoolers by giving them both specific and general information. "Thank Mrs. Jones for the apple because that's what we say when people do something nice."

Because children in fact get little *immediate* personal reward for their efforts to be polite, our continual acknowledgement is especially important. Some parents find star charts are especially helpful for encouraging politeness.

There will come a time when certain youngsters will strenuously resist our demands for even minimal polite behavior. In some such situations, it is helpful for several families to band together and decide which polite behaviors they will require of visiting youngsters, so children don't think it is just their own parents who are peculiar. Though resistance *may* mean our expectations are too high, it may also mean that youngsters just want to find out how serious we are about politeness. Thus Erica, age four, can either excuse herself from the table or stay put. If Ron, almost six, won't call Grandmother to thank her for the birthday present, it will be put away until he does so. If Marie forgets to say thank-you, after various recent reminders, she has to say it five times when she forgets again. If Aaron, age five, snitches food from the serving dish with his fingers, he has to leave the table for five minutes. Children *can* learn to be reasonably polite, but not without effort.

RESPECT

Teaching respect is one of our most difficult tasks. In caring for our newborns, we repeatedly and necessarily put our infants' needs above our own. But if, as they grow, we continue to acknowledge and respect their needs while we put aside our own, we teach our children to disregard us, just as we disregard ourselves. On the other hand, if we continually demand that they comply with our needs to the belittlement of their own, they resent our authority, and rightly so. Between the extremes of overindulgence and overdominance, we must dance a careful pas de deux in order to teach the essential lesson of respect: that people have different needs and that *all* have to bend and cooperate in the interests of personal growth and good will.

Before our little ones reach age four or so, we've long since required them to respect our property, but because they need us so much, we generally believed they had a right to our minds and bodies as long as we were on the premises. Around age four or five, children develop more personal security stemming from an internal awareness that their relationship with us persists even when we are not present. Furthermore, they have become physically quite competent and we may gradually perceive that some of their demands for service are power plays rather than genuine needs. Maybe their emotional and physical development triggers in us a subtle instinct to nudge them away somewhat like the mother bear so we can redirect more of our energy elsewhere. Goodness knows that though our youngsters no longer need us so immediately and intensely as before, we are still frightfully important, and they prefer to keep us at their beck and call as long as we play the willing servant. However, they will not learn to respect the needs of other human beings unless they respect not only their own needs, but *ours* as well.

In teaching respect to children it is important for parents to have and show respect for one another. Thus it's often necessary to work out an acceptable compromise when we disagree with our partner in questions of policy. If one parent blatantly encourages the child to break the rules the other has set down, it undercuts both authority and respect.

One parent found herself wondering about the disrespectful tone she heard her children using to discuss acquaintances and teachers. Where had they learned to be so mocking and critical? Then she began to listen a bit more carefully to how she, her husband, and their friends talked about co-workers and politicians at the dinner table—and she quickly found the answer to her question.

Some parents make a special effort to show respect for the small size and more limited patience of their young children by letting them express their frustrations first during a disagreement and then *acknowledging* their concerns, if not agreeing with them. Naturally, there are many times when even the most tolerant parent doesn't succeed in this endeavor; but the pay-off comes nonetheless, when children are older and have learned to listen to our feelings and those of their friends.

As a general rule, those who respect themselves can more easily respect others. Thus a big part of teaching respect is cultivating children's self-respect. One mother reports, for example, that she has gradually come to respect her children's evaluations of other people. She now admits that they sense more quickly than she does when someone doesn't like children, or is putting them down, or questioning intrusively. She used to try to talk them out of their reactions, but now focuses instead on *when* it is appropriate to talk about such reactions rather than "that's not nice to say." As youngsters approach school age and can respond to delayed discipline, many parents avoid embarrassing corrections in front of others, when possible. Parents have also found that respecting the efforts of little ones to make judgments and decisions, even though they err at times, teaches them a great deal about respecting themselves.

RESPONSIBILITY

While some qualities seem to develop with mere passage of time, this one does not, because irresponsibility is easier. As long as someone else cares for all the people, pets, and plants in the household, spends all the money, picks up all the toys and dirty clothes, pays for all the damaged goods, and settles all the disputes, why be responsible? Children *can* be burdened with too much responsibility too soon, so that they become emotionally drained and bitter. But, if they lead totally carefree lives because we never give them the opportunity to be responsible and always pick up the pieces when they behave irresponsibly, we indicate that their actions and therefore their lives are of little consequence. People of little consequence have no reason to act responsibly.

If we have completely pampered our youngsters for five, ten, or fifteen years, we will be sorely disappointed if we expect them to walk into the kitchen on their own one day and ask, ''How can I help?'' Responsibility begins in little ways at age two or three, with putting some of the toys away, or pulling on one's undershirt. As the months go by, parents add a broader range of opportunities, helping set the table, caring for a plant, or deciding how to spend a dime. Making appropriate amends for accidents and misbehavior is a basic component of responsibility, and the preschool years are as good a time as any to learn. Finally, when a child is around age five, some parents begin to discuss issues of responsibility and teach children to talk about how their behavior affects the world around them.

Just because responsible is a big word doesn't mean that small children can't learn it. One mother tells her two-year-old, ''Good cooks are responsible. They don't throw dough on the floor. You are not being responsible so I don't want your help now.''

Despite our newborns' lusty cries, infants are largely passive recipients of whatever the world has to offer. One of the greatest gifts we can give our children is the realization that they can and do affect the world they live in. We can help little ones make the transition from passive recipient to conscious participant by being clear and consistent enough so that they can understand and *usually* predict our responses. Thus, as they gradually learn to control their own behavior in the preschool years and beyond, they gain the power to control what happens to them. As they approach age five or six, or within the next several years, we can help them start to verbally acknowledge that their action precedes our reaction. As long as they continue to perceive all that befalls them as merely a result of *our* behavior, they will believe themselves unfortunate victims, rather than beings in control of their own destiny.

"Either get your pajamas on before I count to ten, or there will be no story tonight." The easiest way to discipline children is often simply to declare the punishment and carry it out. However, when limits are stated as a choice, children have a better opportunity to learn the effects of their actions. They feel less the victim and more the participant in what happens to them.

"Why did you do it?" seems an obvious way to find out what went wrong, but it is usually a waste of time. Either youngsters don't know why they behaved as they did, or they are afraid to say. "Why" assumes guilt and therefore puts them more firmly on the defensive. Instead, we can state how we think the child was or is feeling: "You must have been very angry at Donna when you hit her," or "You must feel very worried that the vase got broken." Knowing that we accept the underlying, upsetting *feelings,* children often have an easier time relating what happened. With that knowledge in mind, we can gently discuss how similar feelings and situations might be handled more responsibly in the future.

Blaming others comes naturally to children as a means of self-protection. At times the accusations are so far-fetched they are best ignored. Thus when Sylvia blames her Mom for the bad weather, her mother simply replies, "You're really upset that you can't play outside, aren't you?" If blaming is a persistent pattern among preschoolers, however, we might do well to look at our own example. One mother thus changed from "You should have put your airplane away so it wouldn't have been stepped on," to "I'm sorry I stepped on your airplane. I wish it hadn't been left on the floor." Some parents make an effort to clarify the fact that mishaps and misunderstandings often involve more than one person. Thus in the above instance, another mother might have said, "The airplane wouldn't have been broken if I had looked where I was walking. What could *you* have done differently?" One mother helped her five-year-old keep track of the number of times he blamed his sister over a period of several days, so they were later able to sit down and look at the real issues involved. When Brian, age four, has served time out for breaking a clearly understood rule, he must either state why he was punished—"I hit Darren"—or serve his time again.

In their book *Better Parents, Better Children* (Hammond Inc., 1979), Bill and Christina Marshall suggest an alternative to endless repetition of rules. When children reach age four or five, they are talking with ease, have a moderate amount of self-control and a fair degree of understanding, and have already heard most of our rules. At this point, rather than repeating "I've told you not to write on the walls!" we can ask instead, "What happens when people write on the walls?" Or, if Lisa ignores the wide-strewn toys and heads for the front door, we can ask, "What needs to be picked up from the living-room floor before you go out to play?" If she answers "nothing," we can suggest she think about it for a moment, or if she gives an inappropriate answer, we can simply ask, "What else?" By engaging children in talking about the *consequences,* we increase their awareness and understanding of the rules.

To many parents, making amends for damaged property is an important aspect of responsibility. Though we may soothe at times, "Don't worry about it," children instinctively feel guilty when they cause something bad to happen. Some parents respond, "Better that they feel guilty as a deterrent to future carelessness and misbehavior than that they be allowed to buy a clear conscience by making amends." Others contend, "Guilt and bad feelings are all too easy to come by in childhood. Making amends helps decrease it to a tolerable level."

If we do decide the child is to make amends, we must judge what is appropriate based on (1) whether the child knew the behavior was wrong, whether the damage was accidental or intentional, (2) the value of what was damaged, and (3) what kind of repayment the child is capable of. Children up to age six and even older tend to judge the seriousness of a particular act by the amount of damage done, not by whether it is intentional or accidental. To teach them that intentional damage is more serious we need to respond more vigorously when we know they broke something or hurt someone on purpose. While repayment with money helps children understand that expense is often behind our concern about damaged property, some things carry so much emotional significance that monetary payment gravely devalues their worth.

Depending on the circumstances, parents require that children make amends in a variety of ways. Byron, age two, forfeited his usual weekly treat when he intentionally smashed a candy bar in the store. Eric, age three, helps repair book bindings, broken toys, and household items that have collected in the family fix-it drawer. Irene, age four, had to return the armload of flowers she picked from the neighbor's yard. Tracy and Joy, seven and four, contributed some of their allowance to help pay for repairs when they broke Mom's favorite chair. Kelly, age five, dictated to Mom, then copied a note of apology to Grandmother for the vase he broke.

Helping with household chores is one of the most basic means of teaching responsibility. Some children earn stars for their participation, and others earn extra stars for the added responsibility of *remembering* to do their part. For more information see Housework p. 119.

Encouraging children to care for others is a way of teaching the basic elements of responsibility. Caring for others appeals to many children because it is such a grown-up task. Feeding pets is often a relatively easy and enjoyable way to begin. Cleaning pet cages, on the other hand, is a comparatively complex task with which even an animal-loving five-year-old needs help. Children under age six can enjoy and learn a great deal from shared responsibility in caring for other living things, but always remembering caretaking tasks by themselves or taking full responsibility will generally have to wait for several years. Children help in the following ways.

Depending on the animal and the type of food, some two-year-olds feed the family pet from time to time, and because of their own toilet training concerns, they may be fascinated by scooping out the cat box. Some three-year-olds like to brush dogs or cats. Five-year-olds may be given responsibility for feeding, so long as we check up on them. Some children's nature museums loan rabbits, guinea pigs, and other small animals for a week or two at minimal cost. Many youngsters greatly enjoy such pets, and, before committing themselves to buying a pet, parents can see if enthusiasm wanes after the newness wears off. If we buy for our children the dog or cat *we* always wanted to have, we had better be ready to take care of it ourselves.

From about age two, little ones can be involved in caring for plants. They can help dig the soil, plant big seeds in a pot, and even assist with weeding if we teach them to distinguish one weed at a time. Some youngsters love to collect garden snails. So plants don't get washed away by enthusiastic watering, use a fine sprinkler or let them fill cans with holes in the bottom, which have been sunk into the ground. We might do well to advise a two-year-old vegetable picker, "If the tomato doesn't come off easily, it wants to stay on the plant longer," or "Hold the stem with one hand and pull the bean off with the other hand."

Keeping Track of Possessions

Another practical way to teach youngsters about responsibility is involving them in caring for their possessions. At first, of course, it's our job to keep track of special blankets and stray socks. Parents have found a number of ways to ease this chore. Label everything that goes out of the house: toys, clothing, shoes, and each part of a lunch box. Include your phone number in a jacket label. Attach mittens to the jacket with gripper snaps, or to each other, with an elastic cord that passes through the sleeves. Some parents buy lots of identical socks so mates will remain when one is lost, and wash them in an old pair of panty hose knotted at the top. Some parents tie little shoes together when removing them so they have either both or none. If Scotch® tape and fingernail scissors are repeatedly lost, attach a bright ribbon around them or, better yet, tie them in a convenient location.

Around age three, youngsters can start learning to look for misplaced objects. Parents may turn the lost toy into a game of hide-and-seek, especially if they themselves can see the "lost" item and give some clues. Others divide the room or house into sections, and discuss the color and shape of the missing object, to teach children *how* to search. To help youngsters find their boots among the pile at nursery school, put a conspicuous strip of colored tape on them.

We gradually expect four- and especially five-year-olds to learn increasing responsibility for their possessions. If Andy doesn't remember to bring his bike home at dinnertime, it gets locked up for a day. Jason was heartbroken when he lost a favorite ring at nursery school, but his mother resisted the temptation to buy another, and thus he understood her words of caution the next time he wanted to take something tiny. After losing several lunch boxes, Ellen, age three, had to take a bag lunch and drink water at school. When Michael, age four, lost his jacket, he had to wear a less preferred hand-me-down. And when Kevin, age five, lost his second jacket, he had to contribute to the price of a new one.

At some point, we want to extend our youngsters' sense of responsibility to equipment they borrow from us. Thus if Lydia doesn't remember to put the garden spade away, she has to walk it from garden to garage three times when Dad finds it. One mother required youngsters to leave some valued object with her while they borrowed the family scissors.

Financial Responsibility

In financial matters as in all others, we must adjust to our children's continual development. To the toddler, coins are fascinating in themselves and are as apt to get lost (or swallowed!) as spent. Two-year-olds have opinions about everything, including money. They love to feel grown-up by paying for something at the store or, better yet, deciding what to buy with a coin or two. Given the opportunity, five-year-olds may have become quite sophisticated shoppers.

If we buy everything our youngsters want, we teach them that our money is limitless. At the opposite extreme, if we buy only what *we* want them to have, they learn that we don't trust them with money and they have no chance to become financially responsible. Fortunately, there are some intermediate options. (1) Especially in the early years, many parents find it works well to give youngsters a specific amount of money to spend as they wish when on the occasional trip to the dime store or when out at a fair. (2) Alternatively, when children need something, like a lunch box, they may be given money and the opportunity to choose one. This provides good buying experience but may eventually lead to conflicts about what is actually *needed*. (3) Some children earn spending money from household chores, and thus learn the relationship between work and income. If payment for services is carried to excess, however, youngsters expect to be paid for everything they do, and become oblivious to the fact that the family is really a *cooperative* unit. Some parents combine an allowance with payment for *certain* jobs in order to avoid a "business only" mentality. (4)

A regular weekly allowance avoids constant haggles about how *much* children can spend, and gives them an opportunity to plan ahead, save, and budget. Many parents institute an allowance—at age two, four, six, or older—to cope constructively with youngsters' constant pleading to buy things in the store. One mother switched to a larger *monthly* allowance, so more than candy could be readily purchased. Another family kept track of their four-year-old's allowance on paper because otherwise her older brother conned her out of her coins before she got to the store.

Like us, our children will always be enticed by goods beyond their means. Parents handle the situation in various ways. Most obviously, children simply learn to save until they have enough money. Many youngsters are pleased to learn, however, that secondhand buying greatly increases their purchasing power. If the desired object seems particularly worthwhile, parents occasionally pitch in part of the price or let youngsters earn extra money from special chores. For months, Eric, age five, longed for an expensive, unimaginative, but well-advertised toy that his parents refused to buy for his birthday. One day he saw it on sale in the newspaper. To reward his patience and eye for saving money, his parents bought it, and drew a graph of how much he needed to pay them before he could play with it. Six months later, he earned his dream toy. (He tired of it in two months and sold it to his sister for half price, but his parents kept their thoughts to themselves.) But lay-away buying continued for other purchases because the children more easily resisted sweets and glitter in the store when something they especially wanted was waiting on Dad's high shelf.

How children *spend* their money teaches as much about values as how they get it. We can set certain rules and encourage wise spending, but how we spend our money will always be different from the way of our children, just as it is different from that of our own parents, our partner, and our friends. Learning to spend money in order to get the maximum personal value requires experience. In practice, most parents try to strike a balance between discouraging money wasting and encouraging individual decision making. "We talk about value in toys and try to guide our four-year-old out of poor buying, but to some extent, she has to learn by herself. When her money is all gone and she asks for more, we remind her how she spent it and point out that next time she may prefer to use it differently."

While many parents place no limits on what children buy with their own money, others say, for example, that they can buy any-thing *except* candy. Alternatively, one mother won't spend *her* money on sugar-coated cereal, but allows youngsters to do so if they wish. In large part, we can affect how children spend their money by what we *don't* buy for them. Thus when one family goes out for pizza, the youngsters contribute to the sense of a cooperative ven-ture by buying their own drinks. Sonya, age five, feels very grown up when she buys her own barrettes, and was delighted when she saved enough money to buy her own pillow. Youngsters may buy some of their own art supplies or contribute a token sum toward the dance lessons they want. Depending on age and income, they may pay for all or a certain percentage of the gifts they give. Jason, age three, was very proud when he bought a stamp to mail a letter to his friend. Finally, certain families encourage children to con-tribute to charities in order to increase their awareness of the needs of others.

HONESTY

When our sweet innocent children first look us straight in the eye and tell us a bold-faced lie, we are speechless, and they are usually four years old. Honesty may look simple at first glance, but in fact it is an extremely complex issue.

Our aggressive two-year-olds and fibbing, sticky-fingered four-year-olds bring frightful visions of the state penitentiary to our minds. Fortunately, the origins of violence and dishonesty, or, more correctly, their persistence beyond childhood, have been carefully studied. Those most prone to inadequate development of conscience and therefore to serious trouble with the law often share the follow-ing: (1) lack of self-confidence and skills to make their needs known to others; (2) the early necessity to grow much too quickly out of the natural dependency of childhood, and (3) most important, lack of the physical and emotional warmth of long-term bonds with loving caretakers during childhood. Research shows that when chil-dren *do* develop an adequate conscience, temporary removal of love has generally been an important component of discipline. Without love to begin with, there is little to lose through misbehavior and therefore disapproval means nothing.

Modeling honesty is essential to teaching honesty, but that task is far from easy. In fact it is *easier* to lie that there are no more cookies than to tell Danny he can't have another and endure his tantrum. It is easy to promise a trip to the park "later" today or to promise buying that toy "another day" when we know we won't get around to it. It's easy to break a promise of "story time now" when our friend calls on the phone. If, after a disastrous morning, a worried child asks, "Mommy, do you love me?" it's easier to bark "Of course" than to deal with the fact that we don't *feel* loving at that moment. And when the baby-sitter comes to the door, it's easy to bubble, "Why, isn't it nice that Suzanne is here!" despite the baleful glances of our little ones. Being honest is a continual effort, even to the point of telling the waitress that she has undercharged, in order to stress the importance of honesty in everyday situations.

The next obstacle in teaching honesty is that our children live in a world which blends fantasy and reality, and we, appropriately, encourage fantasy because of its importance as a source of creative potential as well as its value in coping with emotional stress. Thus we enthuse about how they take care of their dolls and about the block cities they build. We read about animals who write poems and introduce them to a giant yellow bird who talks from a box in the living room. However, we won't always be the initiators, and we must be willing to join in when our youngsters tell their own tall tales. Thus Dad may arrive home with everything looking as usual, only to be greeted with an urgent story that six houses on the block burned to the ground today. And he just missed the fire trucks! Rather than pointing out that all the houses look just fine, the wiser father asks, "Are you the one who called the fire trucks?" "What did you do while all the houses were burning?" We might as well enjoy these delightful, outrageous fantasies while they last.

To the confusion of many parents, however, children fantasize about many basic issues, *including* self-esteem. Thus when Andrea, who wishes she could tie her own shoes, announces "I tied them myself," we get upset because we saw Uncle John tie her shoes. Or, Jackie points to another's picture on the wall and enthusiastically tells us "I did that!" We will have to teach our children that there are times to fantasize and times not to, but it's a lesson to be learned gently. When Lisa bubbled with delight, "I can read this story," and proceeded to *recite* her favorite book from memory, her mother chose to praise her new accomplishment rather than nitpicking about words. When Bret's mother noticed that he was repeatedly claiming accomplishments that were not his, she looked more closely at the extent to which she was always pushing him rather than letting him progress at his own pace. When she pushed less, he exaggerated less. Some parents acknowledge exaggerated claims with "Won't it be nice when you *can* tie your own shoes"; others explain, "What you do is less important to me than knowing that what you say is true," and still others just give a noncommital "Oh."

Thanks to the work of Swiss psychologist Jean Piaget and others, we have learned that a primary reason for clashes about honesty with our four-year-olds is that their concepts of right and wrong are very different, and will only gradually mature to resemble our own. The preschooler's basic moral code is, "What pleases parents is good, and what upsets them is bad," or alternately stated, "That which is rewarded is good and that which is punished is bad." At age four, with intellectual processes growing rapidly, youngsters suddenly discover a whole new realm of possibility for pleasing us more, namely, to alter the facts and tell a story that is *better* than reality. When his mother noticed him sneaking something, Stefan, age three, responded typically, "Mommy, don't look at me." Three-year-olds aren't yet smart enough to lie. The more sophisticated four-year-old reasons, "Mommy will be angry if I take cookies and pleased if I don't. So I will tell her I'm not taking cookies." Similarly, "I didn't break the glass," and "I didn't hit Josephine, Sally did." To the four-year-old, telling Dad "The teacher said I was the best boy in the class" is *good* (even though it isn't true) because it will make Dad happy. But to tell him "I spilled the honey on the carpet" (which is true) is bad, because it will make him angry.

This new propensity for lying is not malicious in the criminal sense because it comes out of a basic desire to please us. Children are delighted by their new discovery and baffled by our reaction of distress! Our next task is to teach that we are more interested in what really happened than in a story that sounds good, and we can present our viewpoint more diplomatically if we see ourselves as teachers, rather than as victims of a hoax.

Nor is the desire to tell little white lies in order to please others totally alien to us as adults. In fact we *don't* want our children to tell the truth when it will be socially disastrous. If they don't like the present Grandmother just gave, we want them to tell us later in private, rather than truthfully tell all, "I don't want *another* Giant Jim, and I have six already." We can't even settle for teaching total honesty. We gradually have to teach youngsters *when* to be honest.

Once children learn that we are usually upset by untruth, they will still judge the gravity of lies by their own moral code: The more likely a lie is to be discovered (and punished), the worse it is. Thus, to say "I didn't smash the flowers, the dog did," is not so bad as saying "I flew home from school on Sally's purple horse."

The four-year-old's understanding of right and wrong is further hindered by lack of experience and immature thinking ability. Learning rules is not as easy as it seems. It is OK to climb the jungle gym, but not the workman's ladder. It is OK to run in the park, but not in the parking lot. Four-year-olds can recite the rules well enough, but they lack the self-control to abide by them consisently if they are not to personal advantage or if there is no one around to enforce them. Furthermore, they lack the intellectual capacity to apply rules to new situations. For example, until they have a *concept* of not taking from others, they have to learn not to take things from Mom's desk, *or* Matthew's house, *or* nursery school, *or* the store. (When they get the concept down pat, they will ask why we take books out of the library without paying.) It won't be until age seven and up that two important changes will further the development of self-control. First, children gradually acquire the experience and intellect to form concepts on their own so they *can* apply rules to new situations, and, second, they acquire enough experience playing freely with peers to see the *personal* benefits of rules. (Until then, they assume all rules are for *adults*.) Thus honesty tends to become more reliable with age.

Preschoolers don't automatically distinguish between accidental and intentional harm. They judge their crimes by amount of damage, rather than intent. Therefore, breaking six cups while trying to help Mom is worse than breaking one while sneaking a cookie. We've probably helped plant this misconception because when our two- and three-year-olds flooded the kitchen while trying to wash mud off their shoes, we became as irate as when they angrily kicked the dog. Now that we must help our children distinguish this crucial difference, we need to more carefully contain our displeasure with mistakes and accidents. (Fortunately, there are fewer now than two years ago.) We need to be especially self-restrained when youngsters tell us *unpleasant* truths because one of the greatest obstacles to confessing guilt is fear of how we will react. As difficult as it may be to contain our annoyance at times, the reward will be youngsters who aren't afraid to tell the truth. One mother clarified the issue this way. "Mistakes and accidents happen, but lies are wrong. Breaking the dish was an accident, but saying you didn't break it was a lie. In the future, we won't punish you for accidents, but we will punish you if you tell a lie about it." The punishments children imagine are often far worse than those we mete out. Sean said his younger brother has smeared BM all over the bathroom mirror, forgetting that his scapegoat was away for the day. Suddenly realizing he was trapped, he asked if he would be spanked. When reassured that he'd only have to help clean up, he admitted who was guilty. Similarly, when another mother arrived home to find the antique rocking chair broken, everyone denied guilt. Mom kept calm and proceeded to determine what appropriate amount would come from each allowance. Seeing that it was within their capacity to make amends, the responsible parties spoke up. By extension it seems that younger siblings may be more prone to dishonesty because their misdoings meet with so little tolerance from their elder siblings.

One mother reminds her youngsters intermittently that she is much less annoyed if they tell her something has been damaged than if she discovers the mishap on her own. Praise for telling the truth, especially unpleasant truth, is essential of course, but may not be sufficient. If youngsters are still reluctant to admit their mistakes and misbehavior, how do parents respond? There are a number of further approaches.

Sometimes parents avoid the entire issue of identifying guilt. Rather than asking Timmy if he spilled the milk, his mother merely says, "Timmy, please come help me wipe up this milk." Another mother softened her approach by relating, "When I was little and broke something, I used to feel sad and kind of scared. Is that how you felt when this glass broke?" Because our overall personalities are a collection of subpersonalities, there are moments when the left hand really *doesn't* know what the right hand just did. Angry, out-of-control Sonya (not her five-year-old, rule-abiding counterpart) scribbled on a chair. When asked later if she'd scribbled on it, rule-abiding Sonya "honestly" answered that she hadn't. Quickly rethinking tactics, her mother replied, "Well, if *you* didn't, then I think Angry Sonya did. She makes a lot of work for us because we have to clean it up. Do you think you could tell Angry Sonya to do something *else* the next time she's angry?" Rule-abiding Sonya silently instructed her angry, out-of-control counterpart to scribble on paper next time, and she did.

Some parents approach issues of honesty with a light air, asking if a particular story or response was the truth or make-believe. On more serious matters, parents may point out, "It's very important to me that you tell what *really* happened," or they may ask that the incident be described again in detail. A youngster with a dishonest tale will usually falter in the retelling.

Another approach is to be sure youngsters understand the value of honesty. Many parents use the story of the boy who cried wolf, for illustration. Others point out that unless youngsters can be trusted, parents cannot support them in disputes with friends or teachers. Frustrated by continued dishonesty, one mother announced to her almost six-year-old, "I don't believe you. You tell so many things that aren't true that I can't believe anything you say." For the entire day, Mom acted as though everything her daughter told her was a lie. Her daughter was totally frustrated by such disbelief and found that day a turning point.

Issues of guilt are much more complex when there is more than one suspect. A mother of eight relates the following: "I once had everyone sit at the dinner table, but didn't serve food until someone told the truth. It took about half an hour. Now, I don't remember the issue or who was responsible, but it has never happened again." Other parents have sent youngsters to their beds or turned off the TV until the truth emerged.

It is our disapproval of dishonesty that eventually teaches children it is wrong. For some, simple explanations are sufficient, but others need more tangible evidence of our objections. Thus when Randy repeatedly said he'd put his bike away when he hadn't, it was locked up for a day. Lydia said she had brushed her teeth because she didn't want to miss a moment of TV, but lack of minted breath proved she hadn't, so Mom turned off the TV. When Mom heard Alan use unacceptable language that he then denied, his mouth was washed with soap.

With a clear understanding of the development of honesty, we can teach the necessary lessons without a sense of outrage or despair. The chances are that George Washington was ten, not four, when he chopped down the cherry tree.

Stealing

One of the most common and effective ways of coping with stealing is to take youngsters back to the scene of the crime to return the goods in person, or if that's impossible, return them by mail. At times it is good to call ahead, so a soft-hearted friend doesn't make too light of the affair. One family friend thus responded on cue, "Thank you for bringing my lipstick back. I like you very much, but I don't let people visit me unless I can trust them. I hope this won't happen again." The solemn-faced four-year-old was duly impressed. If youngsters have picked up and spent money before it's discovered, the amount may be deducted from their allowance. In one family, stealing gradually became more common, rather than less, so the parents decided to seek therapy before the problem really got out of hand. In the following weeks, they came to see that in their busy lives, stealing was the surest way for their son to monopolize their attention. Once they found more positive ways for him to make contact, the problem gradually disappeared.

GOOD SPORTSMANSHIP

We want our children to be good sports: not to fall apart when they lose, and not to cheat in order to win. That is a tall order for a youngster under six.

When we play competitive games with our children, we tell them that having fun is more important than winning, but it will be a long time before they share our point of view. When children compare themselves with us and their older siblings, they don't measure up as high as they wish. Older siblings, with glee fueled by their basic sense of displacement, often gloat over their intellectual superiority. Thus, playing games tends to become a desperate battle for self-esteem.

Most of us would find it hard to keep our cool if our clothes fell off in public. Despite the bravado of most preschoolers, their veneer of self-confidence slips from time to time. To them, winning a game means "I am capable," and losing means "I'm a personal failure." No wonder they dissolve into tears when the game turns against them. Though four-year-olds may recite the rules, it is generally not until they approach age six or more that they develop the self-control to reliably follow the rules by themselves if doing so means to lose the game.

Because of their fragile self-confidence, they *can't* always lose gracefully. Being a good sport depends on being able to separate our essential selves from the outcome of the game, an ability that develops slowly. Even some of *us* aren't there yet.

What do parents do in the meantime? Look for games that minimize or eliminate competition, such as the *Ungame*®, or those described in Andrew Fluegleman's *The New Games Book* (Doubleday), "For a board game, color the dice and ignore the numbers. If it rolls red, move the red token, and if blue, move the blue one. At the end of the first such game, one competitive youngster gasped, "You mean we were playing just for fun?"

Alternatively, select games such as Winnie the Pooh, where winning is a matter of luck, not superior strategy, or else let younger players get a head start, use more tokens or whatever, to equalize the odds. In checkers, switch sides after a designated playing time so the game is more challenging for the skillful player and less discouraging for the partner. Playing in teams, so one isn't the only loser, can also dilute the sense of personal failure. One mother lets her four-year-old decide whether to play a game "with luck," in which case they follow the rules, or "to win," which allows him to change any rules he needs to in order to win.

Fairness is another loaded issue for little ones. We often confuse our children about fairness. We tell Susie that to be fair, she must share the cupcake equally with Yvonne, give little Jeffy a turn on the slide, and not eat all the cherries out of the fruit cocktail. But when she then complains self-righteously, "Daddy, you took Mommy out to dinner last night so you have to take me out to dinner tonight," or "Danny got a better present than I did," we cut her off with "Life isn't always fair." Sometimes life is fair, and sometimes it isn't. Some sympathy is in order when our youngsters are frustrated by the complexity of it all.

10

Separation

S eparation is the issue we agonize about the most. If we have been with our youngsters for days on end, we yearn for a taste of freedom. But when we leave, we wonder if our little ones are all right and whether we ought to be away. Whether we contemplate going to a movie, or returning to work full-time, many of our concerns are the same. Separation is the supreme balancing act: We weigh the urgency of our need to be away against the quality of child care and our child's stage of development. We weigh children's need to be with us against their need for exposure to others. We weigh their distress about separating against our distress at not separating. We weigh public and personal opinion that says we should go to work against public and personal opinion that says we should stay home. Whatever we do, we will *not* get unanimous support.

Though we ultimately choose the when, where, and how of separation that best suits our own, our child's, and our family's needs, the fact remains that we all deal with separation sooner or later. Baby Danny stays with a sitter, Melissa goes to day care, Andy attends nursery school, Brenda visits Grandma while Mommy and Daddy get a few days to themselves, and Michele enters kindergarten. Once the philosophical haggles are over, we then get down to the practicalities of easing the transition.

DECIDING WHETHER TO LEAVE

Because separation is such an emotionally charged area of parenting, it may be helpful to begin with the basic question: Why *do* so many of us leave our children?

> *Economic necessity.* In recent centuries, productivity has shifted from hearth and farm to office and factory building. Currently, inflation and increasing numbers of single-parent households require that more and more parents get jobs.
>
> *To refuel ourselves.* To catch our breath from the nonstop demands of children and to reestablish our relationships with other adults.
>
> *To raise our self-esteem* in a culture that devalues the homemaker.
>
> *Loneliness.* Many of us feel desperately alone in our isolated

cubicles, so different from the family compounds and village squares of the past.

Too hard a task. Filing papers, troubleshooting a computer, or even teaching children six hours a day may be less taxing than coping all day, every day, with the uncivilized emotions of one's own small children.

Children need playmates. With today's small families, it is increasingly rare to find youngsters of similar age on our own block. So we drive our children to playgroups and enroll them in nursery school in order that they have friends.

To provide "the best" for our children. There's a specialist in every field. We fear we can't socialize or educate our children as well as the professional nursery school teacher. Furthermore, our youngsters thrive on new experiences that we don't always have the energy to provide.

Fear of empty-nest syndrome. Especially if our mothers clung to us when we tried to fly from the nest, or if we saw them in great pain when we flew, we, as young mothers, start plotting our departure as soon as our babes are born to avoid feeling abandoned in the distant future.

EFFECTS OF PARENTS BEING AWAY

Whatever our reasons for leaving, our children's welfare is a primary concern when we do so. We are anxious to know the exact effects of separation from young children, but scientific facts are just beginning to trickle in. The lifetime effects of extreme maternal deprivation are well documented, but long-term studies of day care and working parents are not yet complete. For example, we don't yet know the significance of child-care attachments: Assuming youngsters are primarily bonded to parents, what are the emotional effects of changing from one child-care situation to another, at various ages? Also, many studies talk of "working and nonworking" mothers without making the crucial distinction of how many hours per week parents are away. The information on the following pages is designed to clarify what *is* currently known about children and separation in general, to help parents make a more comfortable decision about whether to leave.

If a young baby is with others more than with parents, *and* is left for long hours with a variety of caretakers (either switched frequently within a single group of caretakers or with many different people over time) such that no strong bond can be formed and sustained with one individual in particular, there can be severe long-term effects. These may include slowed intellectual growth, difficulty developing essential self-control (which grows out of the desire to please a beloved adult), and difficulty forming and sustaining love relationships later in life. Thus, it is crucial in the early months of life that children form a bond with someone who has a long-term interest in their development.

On the other hand, even though youngsters may protest vigorously when left, there is no evidence that children suffer long-term emotional harm because parents take a few hours off per week or an occasional vacation without youngsters. In fact, children can benefit from the parents' renewal. And as far as we know, there is no evidence that being away for a full-time job is harmful to youngsters who begin high-quality day care after six to eight months of age, by which time the sustaining bond with parents has already formed.

Questions to Consider about Leaving Children

From our children's ideal standpoint, we would not leave them at all. We would stay put, and as they became ready they would gradually venture further from us as the years passed. However, there is more to our lives than our children. Given that fact of life, our task is to look for the best available compromise.

The following are factors to consider in making basic decisions about leaving children:

- How many hours will we be away, or, more precisely, what proportion of *waking* hours will little ones spend with us compared to hours spent with others? Essential bonding takes place during the first six to eight months of life and the first three formative years may offer one of the greatest opportunities we will have to be influential in the lives of our children.
- Is this a relatively hard or easy time for the child to cope with separation? Separation is more difficult at certain stages and during periods of family stress.
- What is the quality of the available child care? (The younger

the child and the more we will be away, the more important the answer.)

· How does the child respond in our absence? Is the child left at regular, predictable times, or intermittently? Several hours five days per week may be easier to adjust to than two long days per week.

· How does being away affect the quality of our relationship with the child? Increased self-esteem may improve parent-child relations, or an overly rushed pace of life may diminish them. If we are away because of a job, is earning money necessary?

Naturally, the stresses and rewards of separation will vary depending on the child's age. Let's take a look at the pros and cons of separation during the various stages of early development. (Because of individual differences, all ages are approximate.)

Birth to Eight Months

As already stated, babies during this period develop a deep and significant bond with their primary caretaker and it is important that this bond not be broken. However, most babies are delighted with anyone's loving care at this time in their lives, so, assuming the primary bond is forming, this can also be an easy time for parents to get short breaks. Babies who spend a few hours per week with one particular sitter are much more likely to accept that sitter's care later on, when strangers in general become upsetting.

Eight to Twelve Months

Babies recognize their mothers by sight around eight-months. (They know her by smell when three or four days old, and by voice at three or four weeks.) Eight-month-olds don't look for a toy hidden under a blanket because to them it has simply disappeared. Similarly, when Mom, whom they've just learned to recognize, is gone, eight-month-olds believe her lost forever. No wonder they wail whenever we leave the room! Thus, this period is apt to be an especially difficult one for separating. However, since the baby's bond with mother is normally formed by this age, full-time child care doesn't seem to be damaging.

Fifteen Months to Two Years

By now, little ones know that Mom usually returns whenever she steps away, so they no longer panic. Many children find this a comparatively easy time to establish a relationship with another adult. Nonetheless, they're still apt to protest mightily when Mom leaves.

Two Years to Three Years

Children are learning to think for themselves and trying to control the world around them. Thus they are really put out when we have the gall to leave without their permission. We, on the other hand, may have a greater need than ever to get away from an exhausting two-year-old and restore our own emotional reserves. Youngsters this age enjoy social interaction and can fairly easily expand their sense of trust to adults they already know. However, they are also likely to interpret being left as a punishment, and may need reassurance to the contrary.

Three Years to Four Years

Though children at this age feel separation acutely, they can now contain some of their distress and, furthermore, they have both language and a concept of time to better understand parental comings and goings. They are ready to play with other youngsters, expand their horizons, and explore the world. Nonetheless, don't expect them to separate without protest.

Four to Five Years

Children can now separate without experiencing a loss of "connection." They understand that their *relationship with us continues* despite temporary separation. Therefore, those who start child care at this age tend to cry much less than those who started earlier. On the other hand, resistance *may* reflect problems in other areas, such as jealousy of younger siblings or our own reluctance to let them go.

Five to Six Years

Most youngsters are now ready for separation from home, interaction with others, and the more formal structure of kindergarten. Sometimes they are even more ready than we are. Strong resistance at this age may be due to an inappropriate school situation.

Children's Response to Separation

When we leave our youngsters with others, we not only worry about the effects of separation from us, but we shudder at giving up so much control over our precious little beings. We worry that they won't receive the individual consideration, patience, and love we try so hard to provide. We worry also about their resistance to separation. Resistance, however, is proof of the essential bond between parent and child and does not show, by itself, that the separation is emotionally damaging. How, then, can we tell if our youngsters *are* having *difficulty* with separation?

> *Long periods of crying.* Most youngsters cry for a few minutes at the time of departure. How long does crying continue after parents leave?
>
> *Glum withdrawal* instead of bright participation in activities. Unsophisticated caregivers may praise children who show signs of separation stress because they are quiet and therefore "good."
>
> *Loss of appetite.* "Greg regularly refused to eat at his child care, and waited instead until I picked him up."
>
> *Sullen rejection* of parents when they return. Under age four, seeking parental attention is the normal response to reunion after some hours of separation. After age four, however, youngsters may contentedly continue their projects.
>
> *Increased illness.* Although illness is partially related to exposure to other sick children, emotional stress is known to somewhat decrease the body's resistance to infection. Some youngsters are moved to different child care because they are ill so often. Health may then improve due to higher quality care or because the initial adjustment to separation has already been made.
>
> *Duration of distress.* Signs of upset are more common during the initial adjustment to a new situation, but they generally subside over a period of weeks.

If great stress is being experienced by the child, reevaluate the child-care situation and consider alternative possibilities.

Deciding Whether to Take a Job

A decision to remain at home or take a job can never be explained or understood on rational grounds alone. It is basically an emotional decision. If we liked our childhood, we are apt to repeat the tried-and-true formula and, if possible, choose home or job just as our mothers did. On the other hand, if we didn't like our early life, either because Mom was away too much or resentfully at home, we may try the opposite. Some of us, however, may have grown up lacking both a pleasant childhood and the self-confidence to attempt a different path.

Because we choose according to our own emotional needs, no one else's solution is relevant to us. We can cease our painful efforts to convert others to our plan, and rest assured that under all the rhetoric, everyone else's decision or opinion is as emotion-based as our own. The "logical" arguments are interesting to consider after we know they are of secondary influence.

For mothers who are the economic mainstay of the family, the emotion-stirring reality may be that we have no choice. First things first: money for food and housing.

Some mothers take jobs because we find them more fulfilling than child care. Fortunately, though we are obliged to provide our children with the best care we can, we aren't necessarily obliged to provide it personally. Even babies know when we feel resentfully trapped. If we find fussy, messy infants not only unpleasant but dull, and our frustration with balky two-year-olds far outweighs our enjoyment of all they are learning, our overwhelming sense of discomfort may hamper their opportunities for growth.

We live in an age of specialization. To have others care for our children because we know they can handle part of the job better than we can is one of the ultimate signs of caring. Furthermore, by responding to our own needs and preferences, we give our children permission to care for themselves when they grow up.

Those of us who choose to stay home can't divorce ourselves from the currents within society that put us down for staying home with our children. For better or worse we live in a culture that tends to value physical and intellectual work more than emotional work, intellectual and material wealth more than emotional wealth, accomplishments more than relationships. In addition, our culture idolizes independence: the independent woman, thinker, business person, marital partner. The parent who stays home is accused of being dependent, and fostering dependence in her children.

Thus, the mother who stays home to raise children may have to put up with not only the demands of that taxing job but also the frustration of being undervalued and dismissed as "stagnating" and "lazy." Few parents in years past had options regarding staying home for extended periods. Those who now want to and do so despite pressure to the contrary are surely among the more strong-minded and self-determined of today's parents.

What many parents fail to consider is that the question of whether mothers should return to work is not an either-or decision. In fact there are various possibilities, including:

> *At home, full-time.* Once youngsters require less personal care, mothers at home often become the backbone of a volunteer labor force from which we all benefit—room mothers at school, scout leaders, or the leaders of many community service organizations.
>
> *Back to job, full-time.* Many women return to work full-time as soon as possible. They fill the jobs that glue our system together, and also prove to everyone that women are qualified for the nation's most demanding careers.
>
> *Part-time job.* Such employment increases self-esteem and income, but leaves more time for child care.
>
> *Earn money at home.* Mothers working at home address labels, run small computer businesses, teach sewing classes, do art work, write, teach, care for other children, and more. One mother does after-school care of elementary-age children, which allows her more daytime hours with her infant.
>
> *Extended sabbatical.* Some mothers remain home full-time until children are relatively independent, after age three, five, or older. Offered a once-in-a-lifetime experience, these women say "Why not go for it?"
>
> *Shifting gears.* Many women start out with one plan and change their minds as perceptions and circumstances shift.

WHERE TO LEAVE CHILDREN

Whether we plan to go out for an evening or return to work full-time, there are a surprising number of child-care options. Which is the better choice depends on the circumstances. For example, a toddler in full-time care needs a single, warm caretaker with whom to relate on a regular basis. But if a preschooler who is usually at home goes to nursery school for a "learning experience," the quality of equipment or activities is relatively more important. Staying with an occasional stranger while parents go out for an evening is disconcerting but not damaging, but if parents are away a lot, it is important that the child know the sitter. No matter how carefully we choose, we may see with time that this particular situation doesn't suit our child's needs. We then renew the search, with a clearer idea of what to look for.

OPTIONS IN CHILD CARE

1. Sitter Comes to Child's Home. Child is in familiar surroundings, but there is a lack of playmates for only children.
2. Shared Sitter. Several parents hire one sitter. Care may be at one home, or rotate. Shared expenses allow parents to pay less.
3. Child Goes to Sitter's Home. Sitter may care for one or several children. Provides intimate, homelike environment with fewer other children to adjust to than nursery school or group care.
4. Grandparents and Other Family Members. They may be paid or watch children voluntarily. All may live together or separately. Relatives are uniquely important because unlike other sitters, they have a long-term relationship with and interest in the child. Some, however, may feel put-upon by child-care requests.
5. Own-Home Care. Take several other children into one's own home. This method brings in income, cuts expenses, and allows parents to be with their own children.
6. Play Group. Mothers take turns caring for a group of three or four youngsters on a regular basis. No cost, intimate atmosphere and provides companionship for mothers, especially if two watch children at a time.
7. Baby-sitting Co-op. Parents take care of each other's children when needed and keep track of the hours so the work balances out fairly.
8. Nursery School. A facility that provides organized social and learning experiences. May be professionally run, or

a parent co-op, or a combination. Exposes children to a variety of learning opportunities.

9. Group Care. A facility where children interact with a minimum of organized activity. It is usually available for more hours per day than nursery school. All-day child-care programs may combine mid-day nursery school with group free-play in the early morning and late afternoon.

10. Parent-Partnership. Parents work different schedules, providing both income and child care. Children develop close relationships with both parents. May be difficult for parents to get time together.

11. Male House-Spouse. Father is primary child-care provider and mother earns the money. This method provides the father with a close relationship with children and a sabbatical from regular work.

12. Housekeeper-Sitter. Such a helper may live in or come during the day. This method is more expensive, but because housework is done, it allows working parents more time for children.

13. Live-in Sitter. Someone lives in your home paying a combination of rent and occasional child care.

14. Communal Living. Two or more families live together. Some adults may work and others do child care, or they may work different hours and share child care. Provides flexibility because more adults are available and provides emotional support, especially if parents are single. Cuts living expenses.

What Constitutes High-quality Child Care?

· A high ratio of adults to children such that caretakers can respond to the child's individual needs. Federally recommended ratios for day care are:

three infants per one adult

four toddlers per one adult

seven to ten preschoolers per one adult.

(Some experts recommend four preschoolers to one adult. Those of us who have cared for ten preschoolers know it is impossible to give significant individual attention to each child, as the more demanding youngsters absorb most of the adult attention. On the other hand, though three- to four-year-olds benefit from individual adult attention, they need it less than do younger children.)

· A mother substitute: *one* warm, responsive person in particular who is usually available to your child. The younger the child and the more time spent in child care, the more essential this secondary bond.

· Constancy of child-care personnel. For both adults and children, it takes time to develop trust in others and time to recover from broken relationships. Ideally, one looks for a situation that will be stable for several years, not months.

· A stimulating environment with a variety of equipment and experiences. A child's ultimate intellectual capacity is determined in large part between birth and age five. Once children reach age three or four, some parents look for an academically oriented program that provides an early start toward math and reading. Other parents, who believe there are lots of academic years to come or who fear prereading programs in kindergarten will be repetitive and less interesting after an academic nursery school, prefer a program oriented toward sensory, physical, and social development. Learning the skills of interpersonal problem solving is essential to both social and academic development.

· Similar philosophies about child-rearing. Significantly different ideas about discipline, feeding, toilet training, and so forth, can cause friction and hard feeling between parent and caretaker rather than the *support* that both parties need. Children, of course, feel confused and trapped by such differences of opinion.

· Appropriate number of children. If we feel overwhelmed walking onto a playground with forty raucous four-year-olds, imagine how we would feel if we were half our present height. The larger the group of children, the longer it may take for youngsters to feel comfortable and make friends. The younger the child, the more difficult it is to adjust to large groups.

· An atmosphere that "feels" right to your intuitive sense of what suits your child. Does this situation inspire your trust and confidence, in order for you to feel comfortable leaving your child?

How to Find Child Care

This is a vital concern for temporary or long-term care. Friends, neighbors, relatives, and newspapers may refer you to good sitters, but if these don't turn up the situation you're looking for, try:

Baby-sitting co-ops. Join or create one.

Child-care information and referral services. More and more areas have established such services to help parents and caregivers find each other. (Check the Yellow Pages under child care.) Alternatively, city or county governments may license such facilities and provide lists.

Schools, from high school through college, may list potential sitters. Some parents rely on nursing schools, especially if children are ill or have special needs.

Senior citizen centers have proved to be a valuable resource for a number of parents.

Other parents. For where to meet them, see p. 235.

Information for the Sitter

We'll feel better about leaving, and it will help the sitter, if we make up an emergency list that covers the basic possibilities. Such a list might include: phone number where you can be reached; where to call in case of acute emergency, as well as phone number of baby's regular doctor; number where a friend or neighbor may be reached; and a special-quirks list—things the child especially likes or dislikes. For example, Lori, age nine months, calms down when she's placed by a window where she can see cars passing by. Also provide a schedule of usual actitivies and a vocabulary list of hard-to-understand words when a youngster is just learning to talk.

Sitter Near Home or Near Work?

One mother, faced with a long commute, found a sitter near her job, so she could spend travel time with her youngster.

Another mother uses commuting time to give herself a break, and be ready to attend to her child when they meet.

CHOOSING A KINDERGARTEN

For many of us, the most upsetting thing about kindergarten is giving up the previous control we had over our children's lives, as well as facing the uncertainty of how "the system" will judge our five years of child-rearing efforts. Unlike the selection of nursery school, we may have little choice about kindergarten, but if we do, what should we look for in addition to teacher-pupil ratios and general quality of equipment and program?

- The teacher. Ideally, every kindergarten teacher would be warm and creative as well as able to assess and work with individual needs. But if we must choose, warmth is less important than previously, as kindergartners need a teacher more than a mother substitute. However, the ability to make expectations clear and respond to individual learning needs is crucial.
- Group versus individual learning. Some children work well on their own, while others need more direction from adults.
- Appropriate intellectual challenge. If the intellectual expectations are inflexibly too high or too low, children may face disillusionment with themselves, with school, or both.
- Social versus intellectual orientation. Any good school has both, but may incline more one way or the other. Which do you prefer, and which is more appropriate for your child?
- Continuity. Does this program lead into an appropriate elementary school so that friendships need not be uprooted?
- Location. Near or far? Will ties to other neighborhood children be strengthened or weakened? Other pros and cons?
- Freedom of movement. Many five-year-olds sit easily at desks for an hour, but others do not. Do child and school match?

If children are not ready for kindergarten, there are a variety of ways to spend an interim year. The child who is younger than most and less mature in September can more confidently enter the following year as "one of the big kids."

Such youngsters may benefit from staying home another year, starting nursery school, or remaining in their previous school for another year. Daniel attended a relaxed private kindergarten one year, and moved to the more structured public one the next. Some parents teach home-study kindergarten via correspondence courses. Check with your local library for more information.

COPING WITH OUR OWN FEELINGS

FEELING GUILTY FOR LEAVING

It's hard enough to leave our little ones when we see them content and well situated, but what about when we must wave good-bye amid their sobs? How do parents minimize their qualms?

It is essential to feel we can trust the sitter or day-care program we've chosen. It also reduces strain all around if we try to make sure the child is comfortable and familiar with the situation ahead of time. "I feel better," one mother reports, "when I know I'm not asking my daughter to cope with more than she can handle."

The moment of parting is often a very difficult time, not only for the child but for us as well. One mother waits outside the door until the crying has stopped, usually about five to ten minutes, so she can leave with a free conscience.

As in so many situations, it helps to think positively. Keep in mind the activities youngsters enjoy in nursery school, the pleasure they derive from new friends, and the pleasure we derive from time spent alone with our friends, work, or whatever.

Some parents note that the possibility that they might die while vacationing or otherwise away from children is a source of anxiety. Those who force themselves to make arrangements *in writing* (and witnessed) find it a relief to know children will be assured the next-best home.

Not all children have difficulty adjusting to separation. When Alix was thirteen months old, her mother returned to teaching half-time and found a woman who cared for three other toddlers. Alix smiled on arriving the first day, and didn't complain when Mommy left. When Alix learned to talk she asked to go more often because she liked being with the other children in her "second" family even though she had plenty of warm attention at home. Unfortunately, not all parents are so lucky.

When children are upset about separation, there is nothing contradictory about their intense angry sadness when we leave and boisterous happiness a few minutes later. Just as a child's knee hurts intensely when it is scraped, *and* feels better once covered with a Band-Aid, so it is with separation. It *does* hurt to see parents leave, but once they are out of sight, attention generally shifts to others things. We have to accept our children's momentary distress as much as we have to accept our need to be away from them. When possible, we take into account their personality, stage of development, and recent emotional strains, and at times we can change our plans in response to their needs. But we *can't* always avoid separations just because they are difficult.

Nor can we make child-care arrangements without the awareness that they may not work out and may need to be renegotiated. Finding care in the first place is rather like buying clothes. Despite how they look on the mannequin and how the labels read, we can't be sure they'll suit us until we try them on. Regardless of careful screening, our child may not "click" in a particular situation. Or, once all is settled, we or the perfect sitter or the ideal teacher may move. Furthermore, youngsters outgrow the age limits of various caregivers. If children are even *temporarily* away from child care due to illness or vacation, they may need time to make the transition back again.

Sometimes all we can do is let youngsters complain and try to be understanding. We can also keep in mind that many children show their most difficult feelings to us. Often the tantrum subsides minutes after we leave and the sitter reports that the child spent the time playing contentedly.

Realistically, it is rare to find a situation that is ideal in all respects. But if we have looked carefully, we can rest assured that we have found the best that is available under the circumstances. And there are times when the best we can do for a child isn't very good. When marriages dissolve or parents are undergoing crises, child-care arrangements may have to be made quickly and not always satisfactorily. It's senseless to pile guilt feelings on top of our other worries at times like these. We do the best we can and improve the situation when we're able to.

FEELING GUILTY FOR STAYING WITH OUR CHILDREN

Some of us prefer to be with our children, but are made to feel it is inappropriate to do so. Narrow-minded nursery school teachers and opinionated relatives and friends may insist that children will never adjust socially unless they separate *now*. One mother took her child out of a nursery school because the older children frightened him; the teachers accused her of being overprotective and said Matthew would never learn to cope with the real world. "Yes," the mother reports, "I knew he'd have to learn about the cruel world someday, but I also knew he'd be better equipped to deal with it later." She formed a small playgroup with a few other mothers and Matthew loved it.

On a broader level, many parents wonder whether nursery school is really essential. Much has been said, and appropriately so, about the importance of a stimulating environment for young children, and the value of the opportunity to socialize with others. However, many people have therefore concluded that two-, three-, and four-year-olds *ought* to be in nursery school, no matter what. Though children from disadvantaged homes often benefit intellectually from *high-quality* group care after six to eight months of age, in middle-class families, studies indicate the intellectual difference between those who do and those who don't attend nursery school are minimal to nonexistent.

PARENTAL SADNESS AND LONELINESS

Separation is difficult because we are not only the parent leaving the child, but also, from dim memory, we are the child being left. We respond intensely to our child's pain because it stirs similar distress in us. Realizing the source of the pain helps us decide how to cope with it.

Three mothers relate their experiences and tell how they coped:

> I used to spend all my effort taking care of my two-year-old when we were separated, such that I never had time to get in touch with *my* sadness about leaving him. After I finally sat down quietly, let my feelings surface, and had a good cry, *he* was able to separate from me more easily. It's almost as though he had been acting out my sadness for me.

> I felt my youngsters' separation distress most intensely when I was feeling lonely myself, when I was "out of sync" with my husband or my friends were away, so I didn't have my usual support system. The solution, I learned, was not to avoid

leaving the kids, but to cultivate a larger support network, so I wasn't so subject to loneliness. When I'm feeling good about myself, the youngsters protest less when I leave them.

I was separated from both my parents for long periods when I was little, and separation is still scary for me. When my kids protest at being left with a sitter or at nursery school, I remind myself that their distress in being left is less than my distress in leaving them, because, fortunately, they haven't experienced prolonged separation.

Few of us cope well when we are lonely. When we become new parents, we may be far from our own families and may also lose contact with our former friends who are in school, on the job, or have older children on different schedules. We have to look for new friends with interests and time schedules similar to our own. Once we *do* establish new ties, they are interrupted by illness and impossible weather. Many a family is uprooted by a move to another neighborhood or city. Even if we are lucky enough to stay married and in the same locale, the most carefully constructed friendships can dissolve when others move on to new homes, new jobs, new schedules.

Many a spouse goes out of town on business and leaves Mom with the kids. It's time to simplify life. Try leftovers, TV dinners, and fast-food restaurants, or ask over *helpful* friends and relatives for dinner-time companionshp. Some parents, who don't like staying alone at night, invite friends to sleep over, or pack up a child and go sleep elsewhere. One mother asked her husband to bring home postcards instead of more expensive souvenirs so *she'd* have money to hire a sitter and catch her breath while he was away.

The strains of modern living shatter many a marriage, and require a new beginning in the isolation of single parenthood. Fortunately, we need not hide our frustration and sadness from our children, as they will pick up on our emotions anyway and have such feelings of their own as well. We and our children can to some extent work through our feelings together. Support is essential whether from family, friends, other single parents, or all combined. Bookstores and libraries contain a variety of books to help us and our children work through the complexity of ambivalent feelings. *If possible*, it's a time to minimize other changes: to maintain the same house, nursery school, or schedule, at least through the early months of adjustment.

When our partner is away, whether for a late meeting at the office, a business trip, military duty, illness, estrangement, or divorce, our children will assume *they* are the cause of the separation and will require reassurance to the contrary. They need more from us at the very time *we* are missing the support of a basic adult relationship. It is very difficult to nurture children when we ourselves are starved for companionship. If we lack nearby friends and extended family, we have to continually build our own support systems in order to make our way from draining isolation to refueling friendship. Few partings are easy and often the frayed ends of previous separations painfully clog our psyches as well. The aid of family and friends may not be sufficient to get us through such a critical period. Depending on the duration or distress caused by separation, it may be wise to seek temporary professional help for ourselves, our children, or both.

Finding time to make friends, let alone keep them, can be a challenge with young children. Because brief visits may still leave long lonely hours, some mothers move into one or the other's house for the day, so they can chat and share housework while little ones intermittently fuss, nap, and play. One mother writes letters to her friends while her youngsters play in the park, and another perches her typewriter on the kitchen counter so she can add a few lines throughout the day.

The telephone is often our only connection to the outside world, yet the moment we pick it up we are besieged with noisy youngsters. Keep a special box of toys nearby, and if possible, include a toy telephone that talks. If baby chews on the cord, attach a teething ring to it. At times we declare, "Either play quietly here or I will put you in your room," and at other times we ignore the noise with closed eyes and a finger in one ear. The problem gradually fades when preschoolers learn to interrupt for emergencies only. In the meantime, leisurely calls may most easily be made when youngsters are asleep.

Children, of course, want *their* turn on the phone. With toddlers, keep the phone out of reach, or tape down the receiver buttons so they can play without making calls, or just figure they won't make contact very often. We're more likely to have the phone to ourselves if youngsters get a moment to listen first. If little ones are inclined to talk nonstop, advise your caller ahead of time to ask for you in a moment. Verbal two-year olds love to answer "Hello, who is it?" Four- and five-year-olds delight in making their own calls if we post pictures of friends with their phone numbers. Include the local emergency number, and the library telephone story if there is one.

Longed-for contact that it brings, the telephone is also an annoying intruder, waking us from precious naps and interrupting bedtime rituals. Rather than "I can't talk right now," some parents cover the phone with a pillow, disconnect it (and leave it in an obvious place to hook up again), or invest in a message-recording device.

MAKING THE TRANSITION

PLANNING AND PREPARATION

Mom asked Sonya, age four, to draw a picture about how she felt while Daddy was away for a week. She drew a small stick figure under a large one, and gazed intently for a moment. Next she scribbled over both figures and sighed, "I feel crossed out." A child without a loved one is like a person without a name. Children see themselves reflected from the adults who love and care for them. Without the reflection, they cease, in part, to exist. No wonder they need all the help we can give them with separation.

However, depending on the child's age and personality, transitions may be easier or more difficult. Though we certainly don't choose our children's personalities, and may not be able to pick an "ideal" age at which to leave them, we usually *can* decide how best to make the actual transition when we will be away. There are often three components to separation: (1) unfamiliar surroundings, (2) a strange adult, (3) Mom or Dad's disappearance.

A smooth transition is usually a gradual transition. It's often helpful to visit together first, so youngsters become comfortable with new locations and people, *before* they have to cope with separation. Even during the latter part of the first year, when babies are especially prone to stranger anxiety, experiments show that gradual introductions reduce stress. If handed directly to the sitter, the baby is much more apt to cry hard than if Mom and sitter chat for ten minutes, sitter then plays near the baby for another ten minutes, and sitter next holds the baby while Mom leaves. Despite the protest of well-meaning teachers, several parents insisted on staying at nursery school for *weeks* until their particularly shy youngsters were ready to stay by themselves. The result was a peaceful transition. Once they are comfortable, we can leave youngsters at the sitter's for increasing periods of time, or gradually cut down our own visiting time at playgroup or nursery school. As youngsters grow older, more experienced, and more verbal, we can *talk* about new situations, including likely rules and expectations. Thus a kindergarten visit with parents is nice, but less crucial than for nursery school.

Little ones fear our *disappearance* even when we don't go out of the house. They squall when we step through an open door. They are sometimes reassured, however, if we maintain voice contact from the other room. Landon, seven months, is content with his dad, unless he sees his mother in the morning, so she keeps out of sight until breakfast time. Until assured to the contrary, Jason, age two, was suddenly afraid to go to his room to fetch a toy for fear a sitter would replace Mom in his absence.

There are many techniques for helping youngsters handle their separation from us. Which ones we choose depend on the individual child, the length of separation, and where youngsters will be staying.

No time is too early to begin a habit of telling youngsters that we will return: Long before they can ask for themselves, they will hear our answer. Even our earliest games of peek-a-boo are lessons that we will come back. One mother made up a song about going and coming home which she sang regularly on the way to day care to emphasize that the pattern would be repeated. It helps older children to know *when* we will return. "Soon" or "in a little while" is far more difficult for them to understand than "for dinner," or "in the morning." If we're going to be away for several days, three- and even some two-year-olds may be reassured by marking off the days on a calendar. One mother made a booklet of the special activities that would take place at Grandma's during the week, and ended, of course, with a picture of the family reunion.

It's also important to explain *why* we will be away. Believing the world revolves around them, young children often assume parental absence is punishment for real or imagined misdeeds. We can diminish such concern by saying they are not the cause and by explaining our absence honestly: because of work, the need to earn money, or the desire to visit friends or get out of the house alone.

Preschoolers find it helpful to know where we are when we are away, and a personal tour of our work place make a much stronger impression than mere description.

Other relationships, when available, can also be supportive in our absence. Damon, age three, and his brother Ryan, age eighteen months, sleep together when there is a sitter because they get to sleep more easily. Allison started nursery school easily because her friend was starting too, and Elena because her big sister was already there.

Most children find it helpful to have a reminder of us. Early on, that's a bottle or security blanket, and later it may be a snack from home to share with the gang. Danny, age two, goes to sleep more easily because his mother puts a dab of her regular cologne on his pillow before the sitter comes. Ben, age three, carries a picture of Mom and Dad to nursery school. Rebecca, age four, was allowed to wear her mother's watch during her hospital stay.

Lee, age two and one-half, was surprised when Mom informed him that Daddy loved him even while away for long hours at work. Such a possibility hadn't occurred to Lee. So they made a phone call to check it out, and made such calls again from time to time.

The question of whether to phone becomes more complicated when we are away on a trip. Some parents prefer not to call at all: "We need some time off. If things aren't going well, we don't want to hear about it until later, unless someone calls us for a real emergency." On the other hand, some parents call the sitter to reassure *themselves* that all is well, but don't talk to youngsters for fear of upsetting them. Yet, such phone calls don't really *cause* sadness, but rather provide opportunity for underlying unhappiness to come out. Even if they cry, children still like to know they haven't been forgotten.

We can also help our youngsters get more in touch with the emotional tie that binds us even when we are apart. Mother described to Jason, age two, a magic cord that connected them, and through which love could always flow. Jason was delighted with the idea, and described in turn the colors and bells that decorated it. A few days later he announced that a similar cord connected him with his dad. As he became increasingly independent over the coming years, his interest in the cord diminished.

Another way to ease the strain of separation is to sit down together and act out the partings and reunions with dolls or other figures, either before or after the fact. Such play can be as releasing for children as our release in reading an apropos novel. Other youngsters find it helpful to keep a journal. They dictate onto tape, or have their sitter write down experiences they want to share with us later, and include drawings as well. In the meantime, the process helps them feel more in touch.

Some parents record favorite songs and stories so youngsters can hear their voices, despite the absence. Just before Landon turned three, his parents went on vacation for ten days and left a tape reminding him that: Mommies and Daddies need time together sometimes; they would miss him; he would probably feel sad and angry that they were away, but it was OK to feel that way; and when he felt lonely, he could ask his grandparents for a hug. Landon asked to hear the tape at least once a day, and requested frequent hugs as well.

When away, parents may also leave some gifts to be doled out, as reminders of their continued love. If sending postcards, leave one in the mailbox to assure quick delivery.

When separation seems particularly difficult, there are various factors to consider. First is the individual child. Adrianna, unlike her twin brother, screamed all the time her mother was away, whether for half an hour or three. Thus her mother didn't leave her very much until the problem disappeared at age two. With some children, evening outings are easiest, because they spend more time asleep than lonely. Others are most easily upset by strangers at bedtime, so parents try to be home then if possible.

Molly, age three, was more content to return to nursery school after a few days home to observe that her new sister just slept most of the time, rather than cooing and snuggling with Mom. Stefan, it turned out, was upset about one of the car-pool drivers, not nursery school.

Understandably enough, if we threaten to leave as a form of punishment, children will undoubtedly find separation more frightening. And if we haven't worked through *our own* sadness about leaving, children will sense our distress and react more strongly to partings.

Children also miss others besides ourselves. One little girl sorely missed her grandmother while vacationing with her parents. And another was reluctant to leave home because the family dog had recently died and her grandmother was seriously ill.

Despite the fact that we treasure our own close friends, we are often surprised by the intense attachments among our preschoolers. In our mobile society, youngsters suffer as much as we do from losing friends. For ways parents can help, see Moving, p. 198.

HOW TO SAY GOOD-BYE

There are four common forms of parting.

1. Parents leave without warning, after youngsters are engaged with the sitter. This saves *us* the distress of witnessing our youngsters' sadness and anger, but *they* may be left to search helplessly for us when they notice our absence. They are also apt to be more clingy at other times and feel less secure around new people and places, as they are never sure when we are going to take off.
2. Parents say a friendly but firm good-bye at the door and leave, despite the screams. Although it *is* hard to leave our little ones in distress, they generally keep crying only briefly.
3. Parents falter with their children's wails and attempt to soothe them before leaving. It's rarely possible to calm youngsters at such a time. Seeing our ambivalence about leaving, children are apt to become even more concerned, or learn to manipulate us into staying longer.
4. Parents move into the background as youngsters become absorbed in some activity or engaged with another person, and then, as previously announced, say good-bye and leave. This technique works smoothly with some youngsters but others still cry at departure time.

Here are some variations on the above. Separation is easiest for Mom and Timmy, age two, if she notifies him clearly an hour ahead, then leaves without a good-bye after he is involved with the sitter. Because of his strong attachment to Mom at this age, Damon, age two, separates more readily at nursery school if *Dad* drops him off. Monica, age three, goes to day care more easily since her mother suggested she look each morning for a lonely child to comfort.

REUNITING

Just as our lives are an ongoing series of separations, they are an ongoing series of reunions. Youngsters return from nursery school, parents return from work or from a needed vacation away from the kids. We expect reunions to go well, but often they don't.

Upset with separation varies in direct proportion to dependence. We don't care if Joe Blow moves out of town, unless he's the only one who can issue the family paycheck. It's because our children need us so much that they are so upset when we leave, and may still feel angry when we come back. They may greet us with an icy stare that declares, "If you don't want to be with me, I don't want to be with you either." They may demand our exclusive attention as reassurance that they are still loved, or may act out their anger directly.

When his parents returned from a ten-day vacation (during which Landon, almost three, stayed with his grandparents), he left no trick unturned to vent his anger. He banged cupboards after being told to stop, and wrote on the walls. He dissolved in hysterical sobs when put in his room for punishment. When Mom asked, "Are you afraid I'll leave while you are in your room?" Landon replied insightfully, "If you *don't* put me in my room I'm afraid you'll leave." Suddenly Mom realized how much Landon needed to know that his anger wasn't dangerous. The more she tried to be patient, the more he sensed her rising frustration and feared she might leave. Not being old enough to contain his own anger, he needed her to contain it for him. He calmed down considerably when his mother started telling him, "No matter how angry you are at me, or I am at you, I will always come back."

MAKING THE TRANSITION
FROM WORK TO HOME

This is often a difficult time of the day. On-the-job parents, whether mother or father, often need a few minutes to themselves to shift gears, but children want immediate full attention from the parent they haven't seen. Furthermore, if Mom (or Dad) has been home with the youngsters all day, she looks forward to some relief when her spouse arrives. Instead, she often winds up taking care of children *and* spouse by keeping youngsters out of his hair *and* getting dinner on the table. Thus, her job gets harder rather than easier when Dad gets home. *She* feels resentful and *he* wonders why he gets a cold shoulder. Smoothing the work-home transition is crucial because it sets the tone for the remainder of the evening together. The key is to find an acceptable way to meet the varying needs of the individuals involved.

Parents describe what works for them:

> I park the car for ten minutes before driving all the way home, or get off the bus early and walk the last blocks so that I have a few minutes to myself before I walk in the door.

> I used to drive right home after nursery school and start putting away groceries or fix lunch while Kenny frantically tried to get my attention. Now I stop in the park for a few minutes together first. If I've been shopping, I leave refrigerator items in an ice chest in the car.

> Brian does best on the days he comes home from kindergarten and goes off to his room for a while. He needs a little time to get himself together after the effort he puts out at school.

> I watch fifteen to twenty minutes of Sesame Street with my son when I get home from work. He's content to snuggle on my lap and I can be with him physically while letting my mind relax.

> When I get home, my daughter and I sit on the sofa and play a tape recording of songs and stories we have previously made up together. She gets closeness, and I can relax.

> I generally take the kids for a walk just before five when my husband arrives so he can get a few minutes to himself. Then he watches the kids while I fix dinner.

> I try to get the children absorbed in a TV program just before my husband arrives. If the kids ambush him for attention the moment he comes in the door, he gets really annoyed.

> I hated never knowing whether my husband would get home at five or six. This summer I arranged to eat dinner in the park

with two other families every other night. We talk, take turns jogging while the kids play, and eat potluck leftovers from the night before. Because I have company, I don't care whether my husband is early or late.

My husband and I get home about the same time. He prefers the relative quiet of cooking dinner, so I spend time with the kids until it's ready.

11

Siblings

A few siblings arrive by accident, but for the most part we have another child to complete our sense of family, or perhaps because we wished for a sibling when we were little. A sibling will provide a future extended family and, long before that, a live-in playmate. However, if the latter is our only reason, we may find it easier to import a neighborhood playmate when needed than to care for another child day and night.

No matter how good our reasons and delightful our fantasies, there will still be another set of diapers to wash, additional loudly voiced opinions, and, as the years go by, endless discussions about what is fair. Elementary school math suggests that two children would be twice the work of one, but depending on the ease of the new baby as well as the age and personality of present family members, we may need four times the emotional energy.

When, how, or if sibling rivalry becomes a problem varies tremendously. A few parents shrug, "We haven't seen much of it." Certain difficulties in sibling interaction, however, tend to vary rather predictably with family structure and children's stages of development. Some youngsters feel significantly displaced in the latter months of pregnancy as Mom's lap shrinks ever smaller and she increasingly focuses on the upcoming delivery. Others are more upset when she deserts them for the hospital. Many are disappointed when they realize the little attention-guzzler has settled in to stay. Others do fine until baby begins to crawl, walk, or talk, thereby threatening both possessions and sense of superiority.

Generally, children under age three have more obvious difficulty with a new sibling, not only because they are still very dependent on us, but also because of their limited self-control. They act out, rather than merely contemplate, the displeasure of displacement. Many parents choose longer spacing in order to avoid caring for more than one child under three. On the other hand, some mothers manage just fine with two easy-to-care-for youngsters eighteen months apart. There are no simple answers. Some of us, who were four or six years old when younger siblings arrived, can still remember feeling painfully less significant to our parents. Others regret age discrepancies so great that even as adults a parent-child relationship persists between siblings.

Firstborn children, who have been the center of our focus all their lives, tend to resent a new baby most of all, even though they may have begged for a brother or sister. Second children not only shared our attention all along, but have an elder companion if a new baby arrives. In coming years, however, middle children may fight a special battle for self-esteem as big sister's projects are often off limits and copying little brother's behavior may be frowned on. While we enthusiastically wait for our firstborn to grow up, the baby of the family may be unintentionally pressured not to grow up *too* fast. Younger siblings struggle with the ambivalence of their elders' support and teaching plus teasing and bossing. The capabilities of older brothers or sisters are constantly before them, enticing yet frustratingly out of reach. Each sibling has different hurdles to contend with.

One mother pointed out, "I'd be really upset if my husband brought home a second wife. And if he said he wanted another because he liked me so much, I wouldn't be impressed." Children are unlikely to grow up without feeling pushed aside, resentful, or outdone by their siblings from time to time. It's unlikely that we'll eliminate sibling rivalry entirely, but fortunately there are many ways to lessen its intensity, many valuable lessons to be learned, and, ultimately, many joys to experience as well.

ON THE ORIGIN OF BABIES

Though many children ask us about the origin of babies, some do not. We must either raise the topic ourselves or take the risk that they will be misinformed by their peers.

Here are some guidelines to the kind of information children want to know and can understand at various *approximate* ages. Two-year olds are prone to confusing food, bowel movements, and babies, so it is important for them to know that babies grow in the uterus or womb, not the stomach. Three-year olds, wondering how babies are manufactured, are interested to learn that father's *sperm* and mother's *ova* combine and grow. Ann Bernstein in *Flight of the Stork* recommends these terms because talk of seeds and eggs seems to cause confusion. Especially if Mother is pregnant, youngsters also need to know that the baby will get out through a stretchy, socklike tunnel, without causing harm. Four-year-olds wonder how sperm and ova meet. Thus parents talk of father's penis in mother's vagina, of intercourse as a special way that adults express their love, and of the option of birth control. Four-year-olds may also ask the *philosophical* question, "Where was the baby before it was in the uterus?" Depending on personal beliefs, parents may answer that it was always within their own bodies, that it was in heaven, or that they don't know where it is.

PREPARING FOR A NEW SIBLING

Modern parents are accustomed to giving simple but honest explanations about many difficult topics, like where babies come from, upcoming separations, and routine immunizations; but we tend to shy away from discussing the emotional realities of baby's home-coming for fear of putting negative ideas in children's heads. If we remember back to days of blind dating, we realize how our spirits sagged or swelled as we instantly compared our expectations with the reality of the person who arrived on the doorstep. Realistic information insulates us from disappointment. The baby *will* take a lot of parental time and will *not* be a playmate for a long time. To a three-year-old, a playmate is another three-year-old. We can give clear information without dwelling on dismal facts. By mentioning both potential difficulties and likely pleasures, we can avoid casting a spell of foreboding doom, or building hopes that will be abruptly dashed. There are many ways to prepare for the arrival of a new baby so that older children will feel part of the planning and emotionally more ready for what lies ahead.

In *Raising Cain and Able Too* (Wyden, 1980), John McDermott points out, not suprisingly, that the stronger and more exclusive the bond between mother and child, the more disruption a new sibling is likely to cause. If several other people, including Dad, sitter, grandparents, friends, are closely and actively involved well before the baby arrives, youngsters will feel less bereft when Mommy is occupied with infant care.

Some youngsters help choose a name, make baby announcements, and open shower presents. Others attend pre-natal visits, hospital previews, and even the birth. While some find the birth exciting and heartwarming, others are frightened despite preparation. Sensitivity to the child and the circumstances is essential.

Incorporating a "baby" among your child's toys can also ease the transition greatly. One mother had her two and one-half year-old son pick out the "baby" of his choice at the toy store. "Baby

Alice'' became his constant companion through the end of pregnancy and the early months of the real baby's life. Through Alice,
he talked about his fears, worries, anger, and positive feelings.
Another mother used a teddy bear to teach her daughter ahead of
time how to handle the new baby gently. And another let her preschooler play with all the new baby clothes, then ran them through
her washing machine just before her due date.

It's also a good idea to talk about the feelings our children are
likely to have during this trying period. Ask if they miss having a
big lap to snuggle on and if they find us tired and grumpy. Talk
about how the new baby is likely to act, how difficult the crying
can be, how much time will have to be spent feeding it and what
an older sibling can do at such times. We can also talk about the
jealousy children are likely to feel and reassure them that we will
still love them as much as ever.

Older siblings are prone to feeling excluded from the moment
baby arrives, and especially so when visitors shower the little one
with praise and presents. Being an older sibling is definitely second-
rate unless parents make definite plans to the contrary.

We can reduce the elder siblings' sense of exclusion by calling
them first when the new baby arrives and letting them spread the
news to other relatives. A Polaroid photo may be cherished for the
moment and later destroyed with a vengeance. Some small but well-
timed gifts "from the new baby" can also reduce the strain. One
mother lets her daughter lead the way to the nursery, another introduces the newcomer as "Justin's new baby," and another lets
her son pass some celebration mints to visitors. If guests talk endlessly about the baby, bring the conversation around to older siblings, so they can share the limelight.

If *we* were once displaced by a younger sibling, old wounds may
be reopened when we contemplate a similar fate for our firstborn.
Thinking about what we wish our parents had handled differently
can help give us the insight and strength to smooth the passage for
our own offspring.

THE ORIGINS OF SIBLING RIVALRY AND HOW TO DECREASE ITS INTENSITY

We love to imagine our children playing together joyfully, listening
to each other respectfully, helping each other lovingly. It's a won-

derful fantasy, and, in fact, at times it comes true. But to expect such behavior routinely is to set ourselves up for disappointment, because a certain amount of conflict is inevitable. As one mother summarized, "My eldest was not a very gracious sibling."

Anthropologists tell us that sibling rivalry is not universal. For example, in a study of one village in India, three factors were identified as responsible for the absence of rivalry: (1) Large, extended families lived around a central courtyard and ate together. Because there were always a number of youngsters of various ages, no infant was the unique firstborn. (2) Youngsters were cared for regularly by a variety of women and girls within the compound, so they were never solely dependent on their mothers for nurture. (3) Other than being carefully fed and washed, babies were generally ignored. Because social interaction was minimal, there was little to inspire the older children's jealousy.

Given our cultural background, few of us would be willing or able to pay the necessary price to avoid sibling rivalry completely. However, there is much we can do to decrease its intensity.

STAGES IN RIVALRY, FROM THE PERSPECTIVE OF THE OLDER CHILD

There is no single answer to issues of conflict, because progressive development creates a variety of problems that require different responses. Because of the age and capabilities of the younger child, the older child perceives sibling rivalry in five distinct stages: (1) displaced by a baby, (2) invaded by a little monkey, (3) harassed by a two-year-old, (4) pressured by a preschooler, and (5) cheated by a fabricator.

Such an overview clarifies a major pitfall of raising more than one child. In the beginning, older siblings push and pinch, but as the months go by, younger children are equally or even more likely to instigate trouble. Because of the younger one's endearing sweetness and our instinct to protect whoever is smaller, it often takes us a while to recognize the shift. An elder sibling falsely accused of *starting* trouble when in fact he or she merely *reacted* to intrusions or unfairness can feel justly resentful.

As the younger approaches age three, siblings are increasingly able to play together, so although sibling interaction becomes increasingly complex, conflicts are interspersed with periods of genuine companionship. There follows a discussion of how parents deal with problems in the five stages.

Stage 1: Displaced by a Baby

The challenges of this stage are the older sibling's sense of loss and consequent anger, as parental attention necessarily shifts to include a newborn. Furthermore, the older child must learn how to relate to this tiny, new stranger. This important transition will flow more smoothly if we reassure older siblings that they are still loved; make feeding time companionable; involve older children in baby-care activities; discuss feelings of displacement and anger; halt direction aggression; and expect regression. Here are some suggestions for how we can accomplish these goals.

Reassure Older Siblings
From the child's perspective, time equals love. If Mom spends more time with the baby, she loves the baby more. Parents cope with this logical but painfully incorrect conclusion both by assuring adequate time with the older sibling and by attempting to broaden the child's understanding of love. According to John McDermott, in *Raising Cain and Able Too,* this newborn period greatly affects the intensity of sibling rivalry *over the coming years.* The more demanding the new baby, the less the available help at home, the more exhausted the mother, the more the older child is likely to carry feelings of resentment.

Though baby's naptime is the most common opportunity for time with the older sibling, it's not the only possibility. Jason and Mom go out on Saturday morning while Dad stays with the baby, and Beth's mom hires a *baby*-sitter on Thursday afternoons. Mom wakes Nate up early so they can have thirty minutes of "secret time" before the baby is up. If the new baby is unusually fussy, time away with the elder sibling can be especially helpful and we need to let the baby cry at times so big brothers or sisters don't always feel on the bottom of our priority list.

What children fear most is that they have lost our love, and parents have found many ways to offer reassurance. Lisa likes to hear she is special because she is the *first* child. Jason was delighted when told that his parents had loved him for three years, and Alexi for only one month. Ricky was reassured to learn that he had the same high priority treatment when *he* was a baby. Carol's mother pointed out that even while eating hamburgers, he still loved ice cream, and similarly she still loved him even when she was helping his brother. After strangers stop her on the street to comment on the new baby, Stefan's mother turns to an imaginary stranger and exclaims, "Look at this nice little boy!" Benji and his mother made up a play in the swimming pool: She left him momentarily on the side, then returned to carry him around the pool, noting that boats and sails need each other to travel well, just as Moms and big brothers need each other too.

Physical situations also affect feelings of exclusion. Terry was much less resentful of his baby sister once she no longer slept in the parents' bedroom, and Sheila could snuggle more easily with Mommy once baby was moved from a front baby carrier to a back one.

Make Feeding Time Companionable

As we all know, babies spend a *lot* of time eating. Finding means to include older children is therefore essential. Try feeding the baby on the sofa, where there is room for everyone. One mother held her preschooler and infant on her lap simultaneously and another let her two-year-old nurse *after* baby sister was full. Youngsters may also listen to a story while baby nurses, help feed the baby, or enjoy a treat of bottled baby food.

Involve Older Children in Baby-Care Activities

Our youngsters need not only closeness to us, but also access to their new sibling. The praise and appreciation children receive for helping can boost morale, make parent and child a baby-care team, and teach positive ways to interact with the new arrival. One mother compliments her two-year-old on how well he takes care of "his baby." On the other hand, another mother is careful not to ask her five-year-old to fetch things, as she doesn't want the baby to seem a burden to him.

Elaine, age three, can see her baby brother now that the crib mattress is lowered, and a stool by the diaper table allows her to hold his feet while Mom pulls up the rubber pants. Equipped with tissues and tape, Katie diapers her doll while Mom does the baby. Lee loves the backpack Mom made, which allows him to *carry* Teddy, just as Mom carries baby. Nate is too small to carry Ivan, but he loves to *pull* him around the house on a blanket. Older siblings may also be able to brush baby's hair, zip zippers, and help give a massage, especially if *they* get one afterward. In addition to winding up music boxes, they can draw and cut out pictures to post over baby's changing table, make faces, and tell stories.

Discuss Feelings of Displacement and Anger
Attention-winning pranks, clinginess, aggression, regression, and accident-proneness can all be signs of the older child's lonely sense of displacement. We can deal more successfully with such reactive behavior if we first acknowledge the emotional strain our children are under. Once feelings and wishes are in the open, they are no longer so frightening, and relieved of the burden of keeping terrible secrets, children sometimes improve their behavior without further ado. Though some parents fear that talk of angry feelings might cause aggression, this is not the case when our teaching conveys the difference between thought and action. There's nothing like being understood by loved ones to melt feelings of alienation.

Occasionally, mother and child have a good cry together, remembering how cozy life was back in the good old days. Some parents can reminisce about feelings of displacement from their own childhood. At bedtime, one four-year-old quietly sings to his tiny sister all the things he would *like* to do to her. One mother gave her daughter permission to express negative feelings by asking, "What would a bad guy do to baby Emma?" A bad guy, it turned out, would take her to the zoo and feed her to the alligators.

Halt Direct Aggression
Evelyn pinches the baby when no one is looking. Eric takes a swat at his sister as he walks past her crib. Larry attempts to push over the baby swing. And helpful Anna drops her baby brother. Our first goal in coping with sibling rivalry is to assure that everyone survives with minimal physical injury. It helps to remember that older siblings are *not* really angry at the baby. They are angry at *us* for allowing this intruder into the house and taking up so much of our attention and energy. But they wisely take out their resentment on the little creature who is insignificant to them, and defenseless, rather than on Mommy, who is both powerful and desperately needed. Thus one mother recognized, "About every three or four days,

Benjamin, age three, needs a full undivided hour of my attention. If he gets that, he is much more gentle with his younger brother.'' And another mother tells her daughter firmly, ''If you are angry at *me*, you are not to hurt the *baby.*'' For further information, see How to Stop Unacceptable Aggression, p. 422.

Expect Regression
After the arrival of a new sibling, Alisha, two, returned to diapers; Matthew, three, screamed for a bottle; Kier, four, wouldn't feed himself; and Ben, almost five, refused to pick up his toys. Regression isn't universal, but it *is* common. Because helplessness is apparently rewarded with our loving attention, we'll make little progress these months by exhorting our offspring to act like big boys and girls. For the most part, parents accept such backsliding as part of the adjustment process. In time, youngsters gradually regain their previous accomplishments.

Stage 2: Invaded by a Little Monkey

In some families, rivalry appears for the first time when newborns begin to crawl. With new mobility, younger siblings attempt to play with older ones, but they don't know how. Older siblings suddenly face the difficulty of protecting their projects from exploring little hands. When asked about handling interaction at this stage, one mother sighed, ''I watch them like a hawk.'' A further concern for older siblings is how quickly babies develop compared to themselves: They fear the loss of their seniority. Brian, age four, was afraid his toddling sister would turn four on her next birthday. How do parents help?

**Safeguard the Older Sibling's Need for Freedom
from Interference**
Older siblings need a lot of help interacting with little ones. Dad encourages Joshua to loan his brother the ball when he wants it, because a toddler's short attention span assures it will soon be free again, but an airplane model is different. Jessica has been instructed to call for help when her brother grabs her dolls, and when Alexi, eighteen months, knocks down the blocks on his brother's side of the table, Mom takes Alexi elsewhere for diversion.

Protecting children's special projects and possessions from a crawling infant can do much to prevent angry retaliation, and allows cooperation to develop gradually in less-threatening situations. Let older children work their puzzles and do drawing on tables or counters, or even in the playpen or highchair to be out of reach of toddlers; set aside a drawer that only older child can open; or, if you have the space, create a "private den" by blocking off a section of a larger room with furniture or boxes for several months. One family built a loft for their older son—he could climb up, close the hatch, and play undisturbed.

Demonstrate Activities Youngsters Can Play Together

Toddlers' efforts to interact with older siblings can lead to disaster unless we guide both children into activities that accommodate their differing physical abilities. The easiest way to initiate such games is for us to begin playing with the younger child, then let the older join in, taking over our role.

Try these activities for more and less skilled. Blow bubbles to be chased, mould Play-Dough blobs to be squished, build block towers to be toppled and Lego trucks to be driven. In the sandbox, fill containers to be emptied. Give wagon rides or "horseback" rides. Build caves and tunnels of pillows and sheets and "read" books.

Easy interactive games include puppets, rolling balls, dancing, and singing games such as Patty Cake or Ring Around the Rosey. Play chase or hide-and-seek, on hands and knees.

Reassure Older Siblings of Their Seniority

After periods of coping with her brother's new physical independence, Allison found it a relief to push him around the house in the stroller, wherever *she* wanted. At this stage, Ronald was delighted to acquire some goldfish to help care for because they stayed where they belonged. One family encouraged their daughter's pride in the baby's new accomplishments by announcing, "Emily taught Seth to crawl," and "Emily taught Seth to walk." Brian's mom drew a time line to show that he would always be three years older than his sister.

Talk about Feelings

After a heart-to-heart talk about the difficulty of living with an intrusive toddler, Mom overheard Brian, age four, explaining solemnly to his little sister, "It's *hard* to live with an eighteen-month-old."

Stage 3: Harassed by a Two-year-old

Lori, sixteen months, tries to drag her older brother off Mom's lap. Sonya, twenty months, sidles up behind her brother and smacks him with a tambourine. Jeremy, two and one-half, attacks his big sister with a wooden spoon. Beth, almost three, talks a blue streak so her big brother can't get a word in edgewise. Most two-year-olds want to dominate and seek to be as independent of older siblings as of us. They tend to resist sharing and cooperation on all fronts, siblings included. Furthermore, they want as much parental attention as possible, and are smart enough to get it. Some can regularly start fights in such a way that big brother or sister looks guilty. In fact, the younger child's competitiveness for parental attention is sometimes the first sign of sibling rivalry. One mother commented, "Many mornings start with a big attention grab to see who can get the biggest piece of Mom before she blows up." Two-year-olds strike out with feet and fists, and muscular superiority is often the only language they respond to. Yet we generally forbid older siblings the use of physical force. Given how difficult it is for *us* to deal with rebellious two-year-olds, and how much we rely on our greater strength to pick them up and tote them when necessary, it's no wonder four- and five-year-olds can't always cope constructively with such troublemakers.

To make matters worse, little siblings, unlike friends, never go "home," so there's no escape from the ongoing conflict. This stage, more than any other, brings out the irrationality of both parents and children. If we don't put some curbs on aggression, we'll end up with family free-for-alls. The best thing about this stage is that it passes.

Stage 4: Pressured by a Preschooler

Sibling interaction enters a new era once speech is fluent and two-year-old rebelliousness blows over. Siblings can begin to resolve their own conflicts, though it will be a long slow process during which they will need help and support. At the same time, three- and four-year-olds' increasing comprehension of their environment makes them acutely aware that older siblings are much more skillful than they are. Appreciating the privileges we allow their elders and the praise we bestow for accomplishments, younger siblings make a giant effort to catch up. Older children's fear of being outdone is rekindled. In some families, complaints about a little copycat may signal the arrival of this phase. Our challenge as parents is to build our children's self-esteem on the basis of personal progress rather than interpersonal comparison.

One mother tells her youngsters, "I love you no matter what you can do or cannot do. I love you because you are *you*, not because you are more or less like your brother." Supporting each child's self-esteem does much to cushion the effects of sibling rivalry. Sometimes that means enabling little ones to do activities similar to those of their elders: One mother keeps a special supply of coloring books to be used while older sister is doing homework. At other times we encourage younger ones to strike out on their own rather than push after a sibling who resents a constant tagalong.

Much of the struggle between siblings may be to establish a personal identity more meaningful than merely being the oldest or the youngest. Each of us needs the individual recognition that comes from having a special place in the family. Our task as parents is to do our best to assure that the positions our children strive for are positive.

All too late, some families realize a self-fulfilling prophecy has evolved whereby one child is "good" or "hardworking," and another "lazy" or "the troublemaker." Even though labeling one child the artist and one the intellectual sounds positive enough, such *general* labels may discourage each child from exploring an entire realm of possibilities.

We can help by being *specific* and *positive* in characterizing children. Molly loves to climb, Dennis is fascinated by bugs, Brent loves to paint, and Lisa especially likes storybooks. Helping youngsters pursue their own personal interests, whatever they may be and for however long they persist, in itself leads many siblings away from competition.

Stage 5: Cheated by a Fabricator

As discussed in Chapter 9, four- and five-year-olds are often prone to dishonesty: to cheating at games and breaking household rules if they can get away with it. But elder siblings may now have moved on to a stage of genuine concern about fairness and achieved sufficient self-control to *act* fairly. Having so recently made the effort to become more honest, they are infuriated by dishonesty. Our demanding task is to support the older child's developing sense of justice, yet deal both firmly *and* patiently with the younger child's infractions.

FURTHER CAUSES OF RIVALRY

Just as family interaction is far more complex than mere stages of development, so there are additional factors in rivalry. One mother kept track of fights and their causes for several days in order to look for a pattern. Others intermittently ask children what is difficult (and nice) about their siblings. Having youngsters draw a family map, with a circle representing each family member, may show by size and position the inner feelings about relative importance and relationships of family members.

If we are frustrated by our children's inability to cooperate, we might investigate how competitive *we* are with our partner. Or, if Dad is away more than usual, girls may look to their brothers for attention they usually get from Dad, but they may not ask for it constructively, and brothers may not be willing or able to give it. The opposite may happen if Mom is away. Younger siblings may resent elder siblings who have too much parentlike authority and older children may bristle from too much responsibility for their juniors. Youngsters who believe parents have favorites are more apt to resent those siblings both in childhood *and* throughout their lives. Thus it is important to avoid talking down to a child by comparing one child to another. It is also important to distribute your time with each sibling more or less evenly, if possible.

Some youngsters start fights to get more physical contact, so instead we can encourage horseback rides and so forth. If one child is more self-contained than the other, we can help the social one discover *positive* means to entice the other into more involvement.

One mother suddenly realized that the intense rivalry between Eric, age seven, and Sonya, age five, might date back to the intensely difficult colicky period of Sonya's arrival. When she and her son reminisced about those heart-rending days, both became teary-eyed. The next time Sonya cried, Eric grabbed Mom's hand, as agreed upon during their discussion, led her elsewhere, and climbed into her lap with a sigh, as he'd been unable to do years ago. After several weeks he no longer requested the special cuddling when

Sonya cried, and the fights with his sister became less bitter. It felt as though a deep wound had knitted.

WORKING WITH CONFLICT BETWEEN SIBLINGS AND PLAYMATES

Whether we are trying to help playmates or siblings get along more smoothly, the techniques are often the same.

HOW TO PREVENT IMMINENT FIGHTS

Some parents have a knack for sensing tension in the air, and making adjustments *before* the screaming and tears erupt. In many households, boredom and fatigue are the customary preludes to fights. Parents intervene and separate youngsters, read to them, or present quiet activities. One mother found that the direct approach is effective in preventing fights: When she feels tension brewing she tells her three boys, "We can either have a miserable day or we can cooperate with each other and have a good day. What can each of us do to help the day go well?" It helps them shift gears to a more positive direction.

Fights frequently erupt when one child has a visitor and the other feels left out. This might be a good time to do a special project with the other child, let him or her join parental activities, or maybe call up a friend so everyone has a visitor. Then, if necessary, restrict each pair to a different section of the house.

DECIDING TO STEP IN OR STAY OUT OF CHILDREN'S FIGHTS

Learning the skills of civilized social interaction is challenging, whether children are dealing with siblings or playmates. When two newly acquainted mothers heard blood-curdling screams from the bedroom, they looked in to see Lee, a large two-year-old, and Willie, a small three, engaged in a tug-of-war at opposite ends of a fire truck. The mothers left silently, returned to their coffee, and the noise soon subsided. In the following months, Lee and Willie became fast friends and played together in relative peace. Unfortunately, things don't always work out so well. Some authorities advise intervention. What is the best answer? Or *is* there a *best* answer? Consider the following guidelines:

A certain amount of rough-and-tumble is to be expected at any age, and two youngsters of similar strength can be given a fair amount of latitude to discover for themselves that force doesn't solve conflicts as long as they don't use the building blocks as weapons. On the other hand, does one child *regularly* dominate through physical strength, verbal aggression, or sheer force of personality? If we stand by and watch, youngsters assume such behavior is acceptable. Therefore adults may need to step in and even out the balance of power not only by curbing the aggressiveness of one, but by encouraging assertiveness on the part of the other.

There are three traps to avoid. First is that *all* children can learn with time to use conflict as a means of getting attention. Are we continually sucked into children's arguments? Do children fight more when we are within sight or when we've been too busy to interact with them as much as usual? If so, fights may be a bid for attention. The second trap is that if we usually blame or punish the same child, the other may quickly learn to take advantage of our bias. Third, we must teach ourselves to gradually step back as youngsters become more verbal, and allow them increasing opportunities to solve their own conflicts.

WHO STARTED THIS FIGHT ANYWAY?

Generally, this question is greeted by a chorus of accusations that the *other* party is guilty. A mother of a two- and a five-year-old reports, "I've become resigned to two systems of justice, one when I see the beginning and another when I don't." Another mother, with four youngsters between three and ten, always punishes the older child for hurting a little one, even in response to provocation, and has thereby minimized physical fighting. In another home, the same approach would cause understandable resentment because four-year-old Toni screams as if mortally wounded when her older brother so much as flicks her with a feather. What do parents do?

> *Listen to both sides.* I ask each child, ages four and six, to tell me their story. Given the two different versions, I guess as well as I can about what probably happened, and punish or set things right accordingly.

Punish both. If Jenny, age five, and her friend are bickering continually, I tell them it takes one to start a fight and one to continue it, so they get equal punishment.

Talk to the older child. I sometimes take Ron, age eight, aside and ask him what happened because he generally gives me a straight answer, including admitting when he started the fight. His brother, age four, always says it was Ron's fault, so at this stage I don't necessarily ask for his viewpoint.

When Alice pushes a fellow toddler in the playgroup, she is momentarily restrained on a parental lap. Toys that become weapons are placed out of reach. Donald, age two, has to take time out and Sally must go to her room for hitting. Common sense and ingenuity often add to the success of punishment. If Laurel and Darryl are fighting over *his* special firetruck, putting it out of reach punishes him more than her, so Mom also puts aside Laurel's bike or turns off her TV show for a similar length of time. When Sheila calls Debbie a hurtful name, she can either apologize and tell one of Debbie's positive attributes or she has to take time out. When Danny, age five, calls his sister "stupid," he has to sit on the sofa until he describes the situation more clearly, such as "She didn't tell the truth." When one mother senses her preschoolers are fighting to get her attention, she pretends she must go to the bathroom as soon as the battle erupts, as they settle their disputes more quickly when she is not around. A combination of punishment and reward tamed Matthew's response to his younger sibling. If he hurt his brother, a single swat sent him to his room for a few minutes, but if he refrained for an entire morning, he earned a little plastic car. Brenda's mother pointed out, "If you make your little brother cry, you will have to sit on a chair while I comfort him. If you can get along with him, I can have time together with both of you." Some youngsters earn stars or an ice cream cone for smooth interaction throughout a long car ride or long holiday weekend.

Ultimately, although we can decrease the intensity of children's rivalrous feelings and put an end to a particular fight, we cannot do away with the fact that children's differences will frequently erupt into arguments and bickering. As one mother puts it: "I've gradually come to realize that progress in sibling rivalry doesn't mean no more fights; it means fighting in new ways, about new issues."

TEACHING YOUNGSTERS
HOW TO RESOLVE CONFLICT

Once children reach age three, they can begin to learn how to resolve their own differences. The most basic components of this process are knowledge of the negotiating process and opportunity to practice. It will be a number of years before they will develop sufficiently to add the third component, the ability to see the world from the perspective of others. Not surprisingly, just as we adults sometimes need lawyers and negotiators, children will continue to need our help from time to time.

Teach the Process of Negotiation

Negotiation does not come naturally to our small children. Those who study moral development assure us, however, that there is a developmental progression from 1) the preschooler's total self-centeredness to 2) the mid-elementary-schooler's acceptance of fair and square trades, to 3) the teenager's grasp of altruism. Youngsters can understand concepts *one* stage ahead, but not *two*. Thus, preschoolers don't naturally trade, but they can comprehend the notion of trading favors or taking turns having their own way. Altruism, however, is still completely beyond their understanding. One mother summarized the essence of negotiation for her five-year-old with the words, "You have to find an answer that works for *both* people."

Weekly family meetings are one way to teach young ones to talk through problems. During the week, anyone can put problems on the agenda. Children are often more able to negotiate solutions during the meeting because the heat is off. The next week, check to see if any revisions of the plan are necessary. Because young children may have difficulty stating their concerns, some are allowed to invite one parent to represent their point of view to an older sibling or to the other parent.

Provide Opportunity to Try

According to the mother of three boys, ages four, six, and eight, her hardest job is to allow her youngsters to work out their own conflicts when she knows that she could settle them more quickly herself.

Parents take various roles in helping youngsters learn to resolve conflicts. They may alternately clarify each child's concerns and proposals. They may provide an incentive to settle the matter: "Either find a solution in three minutes or you will each go to your rooms." Some parents require a cooling off period: "Go to your rooms for ten minutes and think about a solution." When the time is up, youngsters have either fallen asleep, forgotten the problem, or come up with ideas for negotiation. One mother occasionally tape-records youngsters' arguments so they themselves can analyze what goes on. At times the most constructive role is to stay out completely. A mother of three girls ages eight, five, and three notes that "if I don't rush into their conflicts, even when I hear sobbing and screaming, they usually find a solution on their own. Sometimes they don't realize the extent of hurt they've caused until they see the other child's full reaction. Then they often make amends on their own."

Help Children Understand the Issues

In addition to talking about sources of conflict, role-playing is another useful tool with preschool age and up. In one nursery school, children took turns acting out what they might do when they wanted to ride a trike that was already in use. At home, Lisa and Bobbie were invited to switch roles and then act out common ways in which fights began. Next, they tried acting out different responses to provocation.

PARENTS IN A BIND

TRYING TO BE FAIR

The wish to be fair to each of our children plagues us from the moment the second one arrives. All too soon, our offspring learn to turn a knife in this tender spot. One mother sighed, "Albert isn't even three, yet from time to time he accuses, 'Not fair, Mommy.' " We *can't* give our children the same life experience. Older siblings *do* have to contend with the encroachment of younger siblings. Most of us *are* more hesitant with and more protective of our first-born, and waiting excitedly for each new step in their development, we unwittingly pressure them. On the other hand, we can't give younger siblings the same timeless, undisturbed, eye-to-eye contact or the hours of one-to-one babbling we enjoyed in our less busy days. Second-born children will undoubtedly have more hand-me-down clothes and skimpier notes in their baby books. But who is to say which is better: more attentive parents, or more accepting ones? Furthermore, during the neonatal period, times of illness or family stress, we necessarily focus our attention more on one child than another for a time. And, finally, our children don't need the same things from us. As one mother put it,

> I try to be fair, not necessarily equal. Amy, age six, needs a lot of cuddling; while Aaron, age three, quickly feels smothered by physical closeness. But he *does* need me frequently to be the attentive admirer of his building projects. For Amy, I need to arrange lots of playmates; for Aaron, supply lots of building materials. To treat them the same would be absurd. The goal is to be similarly attentive and responsive to the individual needs of each child, and I must evaluate my success over the long run, not the short run.

Children's Perceptions of Fairness

Our two-year-olds feels maliciously taken advantage of whenever they don't get their own way, and there is little we can do to modify their viewpoint. To a preschooler, fair means identical. If baby goes to bed at nine instead of eight because she naps in the afternoon, it is still unfair because she gets to stay up later. If little brother doesn't have to clean his place after dinner because he can't yet reach the kitchen counter, it is still unfair because less work is required of him. It is not until age ten or twelve that children easily comprehend that what is fair varies with circumstance. In the meantime they will be understandably annoyed with many of our decisions.

To develop our youngsters' sense of trust and self-confidence amid this double standard of justice is indeed a challenge. Fortunately, there are some ways to alleviate the fear of being the perpetual underdog.

Some parents institute an alternating "privilege day," when one particular child gets to sit in the front seat, open the packages that come in the mail, and so forth. Each child, thus, has a regular chance to feel special. A baby book is another way to show young-sters that things are generally fair. Parents can check back on chores or privileges and show the complainer that big brother was accorded similar treatment at the same age. For all of us though, there are times we can only sigh that fairness is not always possible.

Acknowledge Parental Prejudice

We feel morally obliged to be fair to each of our children, but inclinations to be unfair spring from the intense emotional depths of our past experience. We may sympathize more easily with the older sibling's displacement or with the younger sibling's vulner-ability, depending on which *we* were. We may automatically side with male or female children according to our own gender. We may find it much easier to understand the youngster whose personality resembles our own, or we may be involuntarily repulsed by char-acteristics that remind us of relatives we don't like. We may harbor continued resentment of the child who came unplanned or be less patient with the elder child, whom we expect to act more grown up.

The most important means to ensure fairness to our offspring is to acknowledge and gradually work through our inclinations to be unfair. We may be able to do so in the privacy of our own thoughts, or with our partner, our friends, or the assistance of a good thera-pist. Otherwise we are likely to burden our children with our prej-udices.

Finding Time for Each Child

Given the time shortage after the arrival of a new family member, some parents make the most of routine chores such as diapering, bathing, dressing, and feeding to regularly focus brief but exclusive attention on the new arrival. Rather than individual time with their toddlers, these parents may emphasize shared activities such as rolling cars on the carpet with the younger while watching TV with the elder, or all playing dolls, blocks or looking at books at the same time. Such togetherness, which encourages a sense of family unity, may be easier to manage before the youngest becomes an avid talker, and is more apt to continue if youngsters have similar interests.

Other parents arrange individual time with the youngest child while big brothers or sisters attend school, watch TV, play with friends, do special projects, or sleep. A few families set the kitchen timer and take turns with each child. Some parents attend gym or other classes with one child or another. Other families set up a special outing once a month, for shopping, sightseeing, or a meal, in which each child alternately has a turn with parents while siblings stay with a sitter or a friend. Such individualized time, parents report, can build self-esteem, encourage exploration of individual interests, and personalize the relationship with parents. Which approach is most satisfactory depends on age, personality, interests, and time available.

PRESENTS AND BIRTHDAY PARTIES

The pleasure with which we anticipate family celebrations and gift giving can be deflated by the pressure of intensified sibling rivalry. What can be done to help?

Choosing presents, once youngsters are old enough to care, is no longer a simple matter. We want to give the gift that is most personally suited to a particular child. Unfortunately, however, preschoolers don't necessarily value presents according to suitability or price as much as size or number, especially on the day they get them. Gifts are generally perceived as visible measures of parental love. Thus, if Joey gets two presents, and Sally only one, Mom and Dad love him more. Or if Byron gets a little present, and Lydia a big one, then she is the more loved. Really good things don't come in small packages unless sister gets a smaller package. Realizing all this may help us minimize disappointment, but a certain amount of upset is inevitable.

Parties are also sources of pain for those who are not the center of attention. There seems to be nothing quite so humiliating as watching a sibling in the limelight of a birthday celebration. Many children react by whining, pushing limits, or whatever mischief-making will assure them a share of the attention. How do parents avoid disaster?

> *Taking turns.* "Before each party, we explain to the other youngsters that their turn for a party and presents will come. The older ones, now seven and nine, can understand that, but it's still hard for Todd, who is four."
> *Secret helper.* Whoever is not the birthday child is allowed to

help plan and prepare for the party. Thus there is something special for each child.

Half-birthdays. Children who have winter birthdays may feel cheated because they have to wait so long between presents because their birthday is close to holiday season, compared with the sibling with a summer birthday. Some families therefore celebrate a half-year birthday in the summer.

Chaperon. Ask Grandma to chaperon whoever *isn't* having the party, to assure a full measure of attention.

New guest. "With some encouragement, Michelle, age five, pretended she was a guest at her little brother's party. She knocked at the front door and introduced herself as Mary Bell. Because she pretended she wasn't Donald's sister, she didn't feel so jealous."

Special friend. "We let each child, ages four and seven, invite one friend to their sibling's party, to ensure an enjoyable time for all."

Birthday children are apt to feel in the dumps after the excitement has ended. Some families start planning the next party right away, while others make miniature cakes of Play-Dough and sing "Happy Birthday" as long as interest and candles last. One three-year-old announced a series of birthday parties for his teddy bear and his relatives, which the family tolerantly celebrated with sandwiches and little gifts from around the house.

12

Social Adjustment

I t's a terrible shock to watch the metamorphosis of our wide-eyed gentle infants. We believed they would emulate our warm, loving consideration for others in general, and for them in particular. But suddenly they kick and bite, and before long they holler indiscriminately, "I hate you, you dumb-dumb."

We try so hard to be positive and encouraging. We offer rewards fearfully, however, wondering about the difference between a prize and a bribe, worrying that sweet rewards will make our youngsters fat and pennies make them materialistic. We thought punishment went out with the era of authoritarian parenting, but despite our gentle dissuasion, Stephanie hits Antonio, Geoffery throws blocks, Natalie interrupts continuously, and Peter runs the other way when Daddy calls. So we also punish fearfully, afraid that we may be too harsh, and we worry about what we'll do next if this doesn't work. How *does* one change unacceptable behavior?

To parent is to encounter culture shock. The junior tribe, with its bouncing energy, impatience, indecision, and selfishness has taken over our peaceful homes. They are a different breed—surely very *distant* relatives of ours. Given how hard it is for *us* to get along with children, it's not too surprising they have difficulty with each other. What with temper tantrums, tattling, teasing, and testing, to say nothing of constant demands, dawdling, and outright disobedience, no wonder we feel haggard. We worry if they are too aggressive and worry if they are too passive.

Yet we are acutely aware that life is not easy for our little ones, who lack size, strength, coordination, and power compared with us. It becomes obvious that frustration and its consequent anger are inherent in family living, but how to deal with them is not so obvious. So much for our idyllic visions of life at the hearthside. Medical scientists now tell us that high blood pressure, depression, tension headaches, and many more physical symptoms are caused in part by inappropriate channeling of anger. How can we teach our children to handle anger constructively when we aren't even sure how to handle it ourselves? How much physical and verbal aggression is appropriate? Somewhere between repression and destruction there are appropriate outlets for anger, but they aren't always obvious.

If we expect social sophistication from our two-year-olds, we will be sorely disappointed. But as our preschoolers approach kindergarten, we will be impressed by how well they get along with the parents of their friends, if not always with us.

CHANGING BEHAVIOR: THE USE OF REWARD AND PUNISHMENT

Which is better, reward or punishment? Behavior-modification psychologists tell us we all naturally repeat what brings pleasure and avoid what brings discomfort. Theoretically, then, children can learn either by punishment for undesirable behavior or reward for desired behavior. We needn't be psychologists to see that teaching with rewards is more enjoyable for all, and more readily promotes a sense of self-esteem. When Brenda, age eleven months, toddles toward the stereo, and we distract her with a bright toy, we are in fact rewarding her for bypassing our delicate possession. We're making use of the wise old saying, "You catch more flies with honey than with vinegar."

However, some children are more persistent than others, and all of them have to stay out of the street whether or not we have a reward to offer. Thus in many circumstances we necessarily ally ourselves with the child's intense instinct to avoid discomfort.

Learning to use rewards and punishments effectively is more difficult than first meets the eye, because it takes imagination to reward the good and determination not to reward the bad. We expect our little ones to talk quietly and resist the urge to snatch toys, though such achievements have no intrinsic reward for the child and we rarely think to offer one. At times, we inadvertently reward the bad and punish the good: Tanya gets constant attention while she dawdles into her pajamas; then when she finally climbs into bed, she is punished by our departure. Furthermore, children may have their own ideas about what constitutes a reward. Ron becomes increasingly outrageous until Mom starts screaming at the top of her lungs, whereupon the glimmer of a smile at the corner of his mouth shows he's gotten *exactly* what he hoped for: proof that *he* has control of her buttons.

Realistically, rewards are more effective in some situations and punishment in others. Alternatively, learning may be most efficient when we simultaneously propose the choice of a reward *or* a punishment. The following pages are designed to help with the arduous process of learning to use rewards and punishments effectively.

ARE REWARDS REALLY NECESSARY?

Children have a tremendous number of things to learn, some of which are easy and some very difficult. They don't *naturally* urinate in the toilet, eat with forks, wipe mud off their shoes, say thank-you, brush their teeth, offer cookies to their friends, talk quietly in libraries, pick up dirty clothes and avoid interrupting. *We* do many of these so automatically that we forget we had to learn them.

Rewarding desired behavior provides incentive to learn and therefore makes our job easier because we team up with the child's natural inclination to do that which brings pleasure. Young children, having little experience with the world at large and no capacity to see life from the perspective of others, see *themselves* as doing all the accommodating. They are blind to our efforts to adapt to them until the awareness-expanding elementary school years. Thus they are around age six before they truly understand that the family is a cooperative venture. In the early years, rewards make it easier for them to put up with the frustration of "always" doing things Mom and Dad's way.

Finally, by rewarding children's efforts, and by gradually inviting them to join us in the process of making decisions about rewards, we teach them how to reward themselves. We thus provide them with a basic tool for persisting in their own future endeavors.

Parents who wonder why rewards are necessary at all—why children can't just do things because they are supposed to—should remember that most of *us* need rewards of one sort or another for the work we do. Children may be less subtle and more in need of immediate, tangible return, but the basic principle is the same.

Guidelines for Effective Rewards

Whether rewards are effective depends on a number of factors.

1. *Age-appropriate expectations.* Rewards won't bring about changes unless the child is developmentally ready. Stars for using the potty had no effect when Lisa was two and one-fourth, but succeeded when she was two and three-fourths. Similarly, reward didn't help Erin overcome shyness at age three, but did at age five.

2. *Gradually increasing expectations.* In the beginning, children need rewards for even small steps in the right direction. Terry, eighteen months, gets praise for carrying his teddy bear toward the toybox. Brian, age four, gets a star for picking up all the blocks. Sandy, age five, gets an extra star for picking up without grumbling, and Robert, also five, for picking up without a reminder.

3. *Awareness of the reward ahead of time.* Some parents fear that a reward announced ahead of time becomes a bribe. However, we don't consider a paycheck a bribe just because we expect it. In fact, knowing what the reward will be gives children the strength and determination to carry through. A bribe is payment for doing what is wrong; reward is a payment for doing what is right.

4. *Enticing rewards.* Even good things get boring with time, which is why praise and affection alone don't work so well with four-year-olds as two-year-olds. If we are nagging youngsters to earn their rewards, it's time for a change; but those who own every toy in town may show little interest in working for more. The key to continual incentive is to keep up with changing interests as rewards are only effective in proportion to how much children want them.

5. *Appropriate timing.* The younger the children, the more immediate rewards must be in order to provide incentive. At age two, that means now! One mother offered her four-year-old a superhero sticker for each ten stars, and a small Lego set for ten stickers. She bought the Lego set ahead of time so it would be on hand the moment Jason earned it. Some five-year-olds earn stars for weeks on end in order to reach the desired goal.

6. *Parental follow-through.* Youngsters will balk at doing their part unless we do ours, but follow-through isn't necessarily easy for us. We have to choose rewards we are willing to give and can afford, on a long-term basis if necessary. If we want to go to the beach only once a month, we're in trouble if we make it possible for Joshua to earn such a trip once a week. It's also important not to overextend ourselves by offering rewards for six behaviors when we have the energy to keep track of only two. Finally, if we are more

anxious to get to the library than Danny is, we'd best not make the trip contingent on *his* good behavior.

7. *Gradual tapering off.* For efficient learning, rewards are generally given for every instance when teaching a new behavior, but as the desired behavior becomes fairly easy and automatic, we can gradually taper off rewards. Fortunately, unlike punishment, which *must* be doled out most every time to work, rewards are generally more effective if given intermittently after the initial learning. We increase the number of times Alice must urinate in the potty before the reward is due, or the amount of clean-up Jennifer must do. If the desired behavior stops when the reward decreases, it hasn't yet been sufficiently learned. We need to reward more often for a while longer. Once the present concerns are really under control, youngsters can continue earning rewards by working toward *new* goals.

PROS AND CONS OF PARTICULAR REWARDS

Deciding which rewards to use gives us cause for careful consideration. A family, we say, is not a business. We do things for our children because we love them and want the same from them. However, children up to about age ten are still basically self-centered. When the plumber fixes the sink and the grocer gives us flour, they expect something in return, right then. In fact, the world of early childhood has more in common with the marketplace than it does with the freer-flowing give and take of mature relationships.

Whatever we reward our children with, whether dill pickles or dollar bills, takes on the glow associated with our acceptance, approval, and love, and therefore affects our children's ultimate sense of values. Youngsters who are rewarded primarily with sweets are apt to feel deprived and unloved when sugar is not available. Those who are rewarded only with possessions are more likely to become materialistic. If children are given money for every household chore and family favor from age two to twenty-one, they will believe they ought to be paid for everything. Many critics therefore contend that food, money, and material goods should never be used as rewards.

Whether a child in fact develops an insatiable sweet tooth or becomes overly materialistic probably has a lot more to do with how *much* such rewards are used rather than *whether* they are used. Especially if they are frequent substitutes for needed parental love, attention, and concern, we can anticipate trouble. Realistically, there are pros and cons to every type of reward. The practical answer seems to lie in using a *variety* of rewards for the many behaviors we want to reinforce. The rewards listed here can be used singly or in combination.

Affection

Love and affection—smiles, hugs, warm voice, eye contact—are what our children need most. Affection adds power to any other reward and builds self-esteem in a very basic way. But, unless it is reinforced with more tangible rewards from time to time, it loses its power, especially when the lesson to be learned is difficult or the tasks to be done are very tiresome.

Praise and Appreciation

Mom and Dad clap their hands when they are pleased, or they enthuse, "I like . . ." "Thank you for . . ." "Your teeth thank you for brushing them."

Not only can this sort of reinforcement build self-confidence, but it is always available despite shortages of time or money, or even when we aren't feeling affectionate. However, like praise, it loses its effect with time, especially when the going is rough.

Activities with Parents

These may include reading stories or talking together; games, craft projects, getting pushed in a swing; helping in the kitchen or running family errands; outings to the park, library, beach, or a movie, according to the child's particular interests. The advantage is that they are instinctively desired by children and place value on family togetherness. But rewards of this type do require parental time, which may be in short supply. If activities with the parent are *only* available as rewards, children are apt to value themselves only for what they do or accomplish, rather than perceiving themselves as innately lovable human beings.

Activities the Child Enjoys

Any activity the child likes becomes a reward if we require the necessary task beforehand. Jeremy can take his book to day care *if* he gets dressed before the timer rings. Lisa can have a friend sleep over *after* she cleans her room. Robert can stay up late *if* he doesn't fight with his brother. Our children's natural desires supply an endless array of rewards, as long as we are sufficiently on our toes to take advantage of them.

Food

Repeatedly plying children with sweets when they need our affection—bottles when they need to cry out their frustration, or snacks to make them sit still—can lead to craving for sugar and to becoming overweight, because we have taught them to eat when they are lonely, angry, or in need of exercise. But occasional food rewards have their place in the parental repertoire and need not always be sweets, as youngsters may also love popcorn, fruit juice popsicles, raisins, stuffed olives, and more.

Purchased Goods

There is much in the marketplace to provide worthwhile incentive: art supplies, toys, and clothing. Careful planning and shopping can keep the cost within reason, especially if we arrange for youngsters to *earn* a few of the things we would willingly give them. But if forced to earn too many things, they'll feel personally undervalued, or if we regularly give things *instead of* love, we incline them toward excessive materialism.

Money

Flexible both in terms of size of reward and what can be purchased, money can have the same disadvantages as purchased goods.

Star Charts

A star chart is generally a means of accumulating sufficient points to earn other rewards: activities the child enjoys, purchased goods, or money. (Some youngsters, however, are delighted merely to collect stars.) The chart itself may be a calendar or piece of paper on which checks are marked, or stars or stickers are pasted. Some families keep track with beads or poker chips.

This very flexible system allows parents to reward small behaviors and the child to earn a significant reward over a period of time. Star charts generally aren't effective until age three or four because they involve delayed rewards. Also, it can take considerable time and effort for parents to keep track and carry through, though some preschoolers reliably keep track on their own.

IS PUNISHMENT NECESSARY?

Most of us fantasize a harmonious household where everything will work out through empathy and concern for others; our children's love for us will automatically tame their appetites for noise, mess, and instant gratification. It's therefore difficult to accept the fact that punishment is a necessary teaching device for young children. Though it need not be cruel, sadistic, or overly harsh, it is punishment nonetheless, of the sort that brings screams of fury and wails of despair from our beloved offspring. To believe that if we loved them enough and they loved us enough punishment wouldn't be necessary is to load ourselves with disappointment and guilt every time we enforce appropriate limits. The more successfully we have developed our youngster's self-confidence, the more determinedly they may push to do things *their* way. They can't yet understand that we have not only our interests, but theirs as well, in mind.

It is easier for us to carry out needed punishment when we realize that children *expect* and *need* penalties for their misbehavior. The only way children learn what is appropriate is through our response. To accept misbehavior is to teach that misbehavior is acceptable. Furthermore, they naturally perceive the world from the viewpoint of "an eye for an eye and a tooth for a tooth." Punishment washes away guilt the way a bath washes away grime. It is the means by which one buys one's way back into favor with the universe. Forgiveness is a concept beyond their emotional grasp. As pointed out by Ronald Duska and Mariellen Whelan in *Moral Development: A Guide to Piaget & Kohlberg* (Paulist Press, 1975), if young children are not punished by parents, they assume that the sidewalk that "trips" them or the dog that frightens them is now meting out deserved punishment. In fact, youngsters sometimes accumulate so much fear of impending punishment that their behavior becomes more and more outrageous until we *do* punish them, and thereby lighten their guilt-laden consciences. Add to the expectation of a penalty the fact that children lack the self-control to follow rules, and the picture gets rather frightening. Far better that the penalty be immediate and tempered with parental wisdom than that the child creep around wondering when the axe will fall.

Several misconceptions make it difficult for us to punish. First, we fear that punishment will cause emotional harm, when in fact it is *repeated, inappropriate* punishment that is harmful. Second, the belief that we should always be tolerant is just plain erroneous. Third, behavior doesn't have to be ''bad'' in order to be punished. Repeatedly pouring water on the kitchen floor isn't bad; it's an unacceptable nuisance, and punishment may be the only way to stop it. Finally, many of us assume our children's complaints and tears mean *we* are too impatient, self-centered, or unfair. Realizing, however, that *their upset more often measures the difficulty of change and learning* rather than our ineptness enables us to listen to their protests with sympathy rather than guilt.

Purposes of Punishment

Those who believe punishment serves only one purpose underestimate the complexity of the parent-child relationship. Parents can, however, handle the current situation more successfully if we identify the immediate goal. Common objectives of punishment include the following.

> *To change children's behavior.* We provide negative incentive when necessary in order to teach them to act differently.
>
> *To let out parental frustration.* Small children don't understand logic and *can't* see the world from our point of view. (As Jean Piaget observed in *Piaget: With Feeling,* by Philip A. Cowan (Holt, Rinehart and Winston, 1978), preschoolers literally cannot sit on one side of a table and describe how a simple scene would look if viewed from the opposite side.) Thus *we* often display our extreme frustration with them in our own temper tantrums, the only language our youngsters understand. Our screaming and yelling doesn't change their behavior very effectively, but it's an immense relief to let

our feelings out. We needn't feel guilty about our outbursts, because it is better to get our feelings out than to swallow one razor-sharp annoyance after another.

For parents to get time off. This job has no coffee breaks or restful lunch hours. Sometimes banishing kids to their rooms is the only way for us to get a breather.

For children to make contact with parents. It's been called the soggy-potato-chip theory: Better a soggy potato chip (punishment) than no potato chips (being ignored) if there are no crisp chips (enjoyable attention) to be had.

Guidelines for Effective Punishment

Sometimes punishment works, and sometimes it doesn't. What makes the difference? Individual children respond differently to identical punishment, but there are other factors to consider as well.

Repetition and consistency. Physical or mental discomfort *eventually* stops misbehavior. Not surprisingly, undesired behavior stops sooner if it is punished most every time, rather than just occasionally. *Repetition is generally necessary for learning.* Thus several short time-outs are more effective than one long one. (Some parents, in their effort to be consistent, are afraid to change their minds and try a new approach. Consistency means trying something the same way as much as we reasonably can, until the problem is solved *or* until it becomes clear that we should change tactics.)

Disapproval. A frown, stern voice, and especially direct eye contact effectively convey our disapproval. To punish light-heartedly engenders confusion. Our ranting and raving, however, don't usually add to the effectiveness of punishment. If we want to keep our cool, it helps to remember that young children's apparent *refusal* to control behavior often signifies *inability* to consistently control behavior.

Teach desired behavior. Some forms of punishment, such as making amends, teach desired behavior, but others, such as physical punishment or isolation, only teach what *not* to do. Once the storm is over, be sure youngsters have a chance to learn *what to do instead of misbehave.*

Use appropriate timing. Two-year-olds expect punishment to follow the misdeed immediately. If Wayne digs up the flowers, then plays in the sandbox, and *then* gets punished, he'll assume he wasn't supposed to play in the sandbox. (If you don't find him right away, show him the flowers again before punishing.) Four-year-olds, on the other hand, can understand a delay of an hour or two in punishment. Thus Brian, age four, gets a mark on his wrist for dashing away from Mom at the grocery store, and receives his punishment when he gets back home.

Use sufficient punishment. Putting Mom in a panic by banging on the window with a broomstick may be worth sitting on a chair for four minutes. When one four-year-old repeats the same misbehavior after he's just been punished, his mom proposes an increased penalty and asks, "Will this be enough punishment?" Sometimes he says it isn't, so she figures out a greater deterrent.

Punish the child, not the parent. It can often happen that the punishment we administer hurts us more than the child. Skipping a family outing that *we* were looking forward to enjoying with our child gives the youngster too much power over our own happiness. Thus, an essential key to effective punishment is discovering what punishes the child more than us.

Follow-through. Words without actions are useless for teaching children. See enforcement of various punishments, p. 386.

Using Choices to Enhance Rewards and Punishments

The use of choices can be helpful in a variety of ways.

First, if we offer a reward *and* a punishment simultaneously, we make the difference between acting appropriately and inappropriately much more obvious. If Elaine picks up her toys before the timer rings, she is rewarded with a star. If she doesn't, she is punished by having to stay inside until her toys *are* picked up and doesn't get a star. If Pat is in bed by 8:30 he is rewarded with a story. If not, he is punished by Dad's leaving the room at that point.

Second, some older children may be able to cope with punishment more easily, and thus be less apt to fall apart, if they can choose one of two punishments. Choice allows them to maintain some control over the situation. For example: "Either give back the toy you took and apologize, or give it back and sit on the sofa for two minutes." Either pick up the papers you threw when you were angry, or I will pick them up *and* I'll put your building blocks out of reach." "Either wipe up the milk you spilled, or go to your room for a rest."

Third, we can encourage the development of responsibility in four- and five-year-olds by letting them help plan punishments. When Dennis stole some money from his mother's dresser and spent it, they decided together how much would be deducted from his allowance each week. We imagine that children, when given such opportunities, would propose insignificant punishment, but such is not generally the case. In fact, they are inclined to suggest severe punishments just as we are inclined to purchase the more expensive gift if we need to buy someone's good will. We often need to temper their choices with our broader concept of appropriate values.

Must the Penalty Match the Crime?
Punishment versus Consequence

There is an important way in which the punishment *does* need to match the crime with young children. They learn to judge the severity of their misdeeds by the severity of the punishment. If Rita, age two, is sent to play in her room for two minutes after running in the street, and spanked for spilling her juice, she learns that it is worse to spill juice than run in the street. Thus we need a hierarchy of more and less severe penalties to teach the significance of various misdeeds.

Rudolph Drikurs, widely acclaimed author of *Children: The Challenge* (Dutton, 1964), recommends disciplining children through natural and logical consequences rather than "punishment." If Byron, age five, refuses (or forgets) to carry his lunch to school, the *natural* consequence is hunger. If he goes hungry one day, he'll be more inclined to carry his lunch the next day. With *logical* consequences, parents select a response that bears a direct, logical relationship to the child's misdeed: "Because you threw your peas, you must be finished eating, so I am putting your food away." "You aren't dressed so you will have to wear your pajamas to nursery school."

Natural consequences have several drawbacks. First, as Drikurs points out, they may be hazardous. Putting fingers in the flame is a dangerous way to learn it is hot. Second, natural consequences may distress *us* more than our children. Rochelle's bedroom will be knee-deep in junk if she hasn't picked up for a month. But when it's time to visit the doctor, *Mom* is more upset that shoes can't be found amid the clutter. Logical consequences also have two significant drawbacks. First, we can go crazy trying to think up a logical consequence for every two-year-old antic. What is the logical consequence of Lisa's peeling wallpaper off her bedroom wall, or pouring Aunt May's perfume on the cat? Second, to be effective in changing behavior, natural or logical consequences must be *unpleasant* for the child. One youngster was the hero of his nursery school when he showed up in his Superman pajamas. If we select *unpleasant* consequences, we are, in the language of behavior modification, choosing *punishment.*

Natural and logical consequences teach more about how the grownup world functions than a slap on the hand or isolation. But the first thing we must teach our two-year-olds is what is acceptable and what is not. Young children are not logical beings in the same sense we are, and therefore our punishments need not always be logical. By age eight or ten, our youngsters' developing sense of justice generally obliges us to choose penalties that relate to the misdeed, and fortunately to do so is much easier with older children. Consequences *do* have an important place in the discipline of young children, but to tell ourselves we shouldn't punish unless we can think of a logical punishment is to tie our own hands needlessly. In the following pages, some consequences are listed separately, and others are included under such punishments as ignore the child, withhold privileges, make amends, and so forth.

Another important consideration, also attributed to Rudolph Drikurs, is that of matching our responses to the *emotional value* behind the crime. Very often we can ascertain a child's true motive by examining our own emotional response.

> *If we feel annoyed,* children probably want attention. Therefore, maximize attention for good behavior and minimize attention for misbehavior.
> *If we feel angry and defeated,* children want to win power. Therefore, step out of the power struggle by calmly enforcing consequences.

If we feel hurt, children want revenge because they feel so hurt. Therefore, avoid punishment and deal with the child's underlying pain.

If we feel helpless, children are feeling inadequate. Therefore, support their self-esteem.

KINDS OF PUNISHMENT AND HOW THEY WORK

Verbal Punishment

Toddlers pause out of instinctive fear of loud noises, but gradually learn to ignore *our* loud noises unless "No!" and "Don't . . ." are consistently followed with distraction or punishment such as time-out, withholding privileges, physical pain. Our ranting, raving, and lectures are a safe release for our own inevitable frustration as long as we avoid telling children that they are bad, stupid, clumsy, or whatever. In general, we need to avoid insults and shout out our own feelings instead, such as "I *hate* cleaning up all the messes in this house!"

Natural and Logical Consequences

Barry's finger hurts because he touched the hot oven door, Jeff's ball is gone because he left it in the park, Lisa is carried to bed because she won't walk, Greg is late to school because he wasn't ready, and Julie has no money because she spent her allowance yesterday. For natural and logical consequences to be effective, Drikurs emphasizes the importance of children's learning from *personally experiencing the results* of their behavior (when it isn't dangerous to do so), rather than being badgered ahead of time by threats, or frightened or humiliated afterward by angry parents. Thus carrying out consequences requires a certain detached frame of mind, or at least the appearance thereof. We have to detach ourselves from direct personal control of many behaviors and from our role as "protector of children." Instead, we have to endure the distress of their pain, and not cave in by giving Jeff another ball this week. Allowing children to learn from the world at large frees them from learning everything from us.

Ignoring the Child

This is an especially effective punishment when the main purpose of the child's misbehavior is to gain parental attention. For example, when Aaron has a temper tantrum, Mom pretends to read a magazine. When Melissa asks for another sip of water after bedtime, Dad pretends he can't hear.

In order to enforce this means of punishment, parents need the willpower to keep from responding, despite the fact that behavior which is ignored automatically gets worse *before* it gets better. This approach *will not work* if the child's activity is inherently rewarding, such as scribbling on walls or snatching toys from younger children.

Isolation

Allan, age two, has been in repeated mischief, so he is put in his room and let out in twenty minutes. Wanda, age three, is having a tantrum, so is carried to her room and told she can come out when she has finished. Jennifer, age five, keeps interrupting Mom and Dad, so they go to *their* bedroom to talk, and lock the door.

Some parents persistently carry youngsters back to their bedrooms until they learn to stay on their own. Others use a baby gate or resort to putting a childproof doorhandle on the inside of the door, reversing the doorhandle so the lock is on the outside, or installing a hook-and-eye latch. Some parents install a chain lock so the child can see out, but not get out. Some children will stay in voluntarily once they learn that the alternative means they will be locked in for a while.

A few children become fearful of their bedrooms if confined there for punishment, so more problems are caused than solved. Other youngsters delight in playing with their toys and thus encounter little incentive to change their previous behavior. In the latter case, parents at least get a fifteen- or twenty-minute breather. Many youngsters will experiment with trashing the room, so it's helpful to plan a strategy beforehand. Some parents pretend nothing happened and pick up by themselves after youngsters have gone elsewhere. Some require youngsters to clean up the mess alone and others pick up together once the air has cleared. If the problem persists, a well-childproofed hallway, laundry room, or bathroom may be necessary to make the point.

Time-Out

Bonnie, nine months, reaches for the electric plug again, so is placed in a playpen. Karl, age four, hits the baby, so must sit on a chair. Sarah, age five, is screaming because the peaches are all gone, so must stand in the corner.

Time-out differs from isolation in that children are confined to a small, *dull* location for *brief* periods of time. A general rule is one minute per year of age. Thus a two-year-old gets two minutes; a four-year-old four minutes, and so forth, with the kitchen timer to keep an unbiased count. A firm word from parents usually keeps youngsters where they belong, though in the beginning being hauled back or even a slap on the wrist may be necessary.

Sitting on a chair requires that children contain the physical energy that naturally accompanies frustration and anger. Such restraint may be harmful in the long run *unless* youngsters get adequate exercise at other times. The advantages of time-out is that it can be used at home or away, is short and simple enough that parents find it relatively easy to carry out, and most children dislike it intensely.

Physical Exertion

Examples: Lee, age five, rocks backward on the dining-room chair despite being told not to, so has to do ten pushups. Marie, age four, is screaming in anger, so has to hit the sofa with a pillow ten times.

Enforce this punishment by preventing the child from doing anything else until the task is carried out. It's a great way to disperse excess physical energy, but requires parental attention to be sure it is carried out.

Withholding Privileges

Examples: Bobby threatens to hit Jeff with the truck, so Dad puts it out of reach. Lisa can't play outside because her toys aren't picked up. John can't eat lunch because his hands aren't washed. Allison can't watch Captain Kangaroo because she isn't dressed. Anna's doll is taken away for the day because she deliberately kicked the cat's dish, which broke. [NOTE: Removing security objects is *not* recommended, as their value lies in being available when the child is in emotional need.]

This is effective punishment when you want the child to *do something constructive,* not just stop being destructive. It is extremely flexible, protects both people and property, and works well to enforce other punishments. It may, however, require that we plant ourselves in the doorway so the youngster can't leave before the task is done.

Making Amends

Examples: Laura, age two, took a toy from Cindy, so has to give it back. Larry, age three, spilled his milk, so must wipe it up. Danny, age five, deliberately smashed Glen's toy, so must buy another out of his allowance. Theresa, age five, didn't pick up her toys before school, and Mom had to do the work before guests arrived. Therefore, that night, Theresa owed Mom a backrub.

This method teaches responsibility, but requires parental time and attention. Enforcement is usually by means of withholding other activities until amends are made.

Positive Practice

Timmy, age four, dropped his jacket on the floor, so he has to take it back and forth to the closet five times. Enforce this one by withholding privileges, that is, no other activities until it is completed. It helps teach new habits, but requires parental time and attention to enforce.

Retaliation

David, age two, pushes over Tony's block tower, so Mom allows Tony to push over David's tower.

Children immediately experience the discomfort of their offenses. The negative aspect of this punishment is that it may create resentment and vengefulness, especially after children are old enough to work out disputes more intellectually.

Physical Restraint

Barry, age two, won't walk a safe distance from the curb, so he is strapped in his stroller. Lisa raises her arm to hit the baby, so Mom grasps her arm and holds her firmly for a moment. Most children dislike restraint, and all it requires is the physical means to carry it out.

Physical Pain

Examples: Shereese, eighteen months, returns repeatedly to the stereo, so Mom slaps her hand. Melissa is spanked for climbing the railing on their second-story balcony. Brad, age two, pulls a handful of Mom's hair, so she squeezes the muscle at the top of his shoulder until he lets go.

The advantage of physical punishment is that it is quick and gets through to the child on a basic emotional level. There are, however, some potentially serious drawbacks. 1) It models physical force as a means of solving problems. 2) Parents may hurt children more than they intend. 3) Excessive use of physical pain not only increases aggression, but also causes fear that undermines self-confidence and the parent-child relationship. *If physical punishment is not working, do not hit harder or longer.* Instead, try other kinds of punishments and rewards.

CONCERNS ABOUT THE USE OF PHYSICAL PUNISHMENT

We are presently caught in the swing of a pendulum. Fortunately, beating children with belts and sticks or otherwise harming them is no longer acceptable. However, many of us have moved to the opposite extreme in the belief that *all* physical punishment is emotionally harmful and therefore bad. One mother recounted, ''I remember being so hurt and humiliated by my father's spanking that I vowed never to strike my own children.'' Many of us feel guilty even when we use physical punishment appropriately. At times we end up not punishing at all because our instinctive swat is forbidden and we can't think of what to do instead. Though physical punishment *can* be overused, it has its proper place in our repertoire of teaching methods.

In fact, depending on the child's age and personality, as well as the circumstances, a quick swat may cut through resistance, make the point, and clear the air more quickly and painlessly than a long harangue, or isolation. Whether we use occasional physical punishment is less important than whether children generally feel loved.

Many parents wonder if hitting teaches children to hit. The answer is probably not. Anyone who watches toddlers and two-year-olds left to play on their own soon concludes that physical force is instinctive. Our task is to use and teach more civilized methods of problem solving as children become able to *understand* and use them. Thus the need for physical punishment is gradually outgrown.

Fear That We Will Punish Too Harshly

In moments of fear or desperation, many of us tread a thin line between punishment that is harsh and that which is too harsh. A *pattern* of overly severe punishment cannot only cause serious physical and emotional harm, but is potentially deadly. Child abuse is more likely when we are emotionally isolated or under excessive stress, when we are physically exhausted, overwhelmed by unrealistic expectations of our children, or if we ourselves were abused as children. Intensely fussy youngsters and very active, strong-willed children are also more likely to push us beyond control. *If we feel afraid that we might really harm our children, or if we repeatedly break our resolutions not to punish so harshly, we need help; the sooner the better. Tragedy can be avoided.* For alternative ways to handle our own anger, see Surviving Children's Crying and Tantrums, p. 223. Also see Getting Help, p. 233; Fantasies of Child Abuse, p. 218; and Anger at Our Children, p. 215.

Nearly all parents run up against occasional situations in which they find themselves punishing more severely than they had intended. Parents gave the following examples of *rare* extremes in punishment:

- I was so terrified to find my two-year-old in the street that I spanked him hard, many times, before I came to my senses.
- One day my two-year-old intentionally smashed her head into my nose, and without even thinking, I slapped her across the face.
- I looked at the sandbox just in time to see my two-and-one-half-year-old push his six-month-old sister over backward and prepare to pour a bucket of sand into her open mouth. In horror, I snatched him up, turned him over my knee, and spanked repeatedly before I was able to stop.

The parents' responses in these situations are understandable because of the severity of the circumstances. So long as situations like these remain infrequent and we stop ourselves before we inflict real physical harm, we are within the realm of acceptable parenting.

Guidelines for the Use of Physical Punishment

There are three situations in which physical punishment can be constructive. Such limited use assures that we will rely on other forms of punishment *most* of the time.

1. *To avoid repetition of life-threatening actions.*
2. *To enforce other punishment,* as when youngsters leave time-out too soon.
3. *To counter deliberate pushing of limits,* as a youngster who keeps a sidelong eye on Mom while trying to climb over the back gate again.

John McDermott, M.D., author of *Raising Cain and Able Too,* suggests that a slap to the "offending part," such as the foot that kicked Jessica, or the hand that touched the stereo, seems appropriate to a young child's sense of justice. Because pain is the moving force of physical punishment, a swat on the hand is apt to be more effective than a slap on a well-diapered bottom. And because children are different, what causes one to wail will merely elicit a look of surprise from another. An alternative technique is to use thumb and middle finger to flick a child's hand.

A husky, six-foot-tall father was afraid he might really hurt his son with a single swing. So he kept an extra flyswatter handy instead.

James Dobson, author of *Dare to Discipline* (Tyndale, 1977), recommends squeezing the muscle where the shoulder joins the neck. Unlike a slap, a shoulder pinch may be modulated to apply just enough pressure to get the necessary response.

We are better off avoiding physical punishment if we are so angry that we might possibly harm the child, or if the child is becoming increasingly resistant, aggressive, or fearful. More than one parent, when angry or frightened, has given a "moderate" slap and then been startled to see a red hand print appear on their child's skin. Furthermore, what works with one child doesn't with another. Some tough-minded youngsters put on a stiff upper lip that declares, "I'll make sure this hurts you more than me," and don't change their behavior despite repeated infliction of pain. In such cases, try other forms of punishment, as well as rewards for good behavior, or *get help.*

Age is an important factor in physical punishment. It's essential to avoid such punishment altogether in infancy, a time when serious injury can easily occur and no positive learning can result. Much physical punishment can be avoided in the toddler years by child-proofing. Two-year-olds come in for their share of physical punishment because of their negativity, self-determination, and inability to understand our needs. Because it may be difficult to pick up and carry a resistant four-year-old, parents are apt to resort to an occasional swat. As children gain more self-control and greater intellectual capacity, over the next several years, physical punishment normally seems to taper off.

No matter what the age, avoid the following physical punishments:

- *Slapping the face*, which is extremely humiliating and can damage hearing in extreme cases.
- *Shaking the child*, which may cause neck injuries, such as whiplash, and even brain damage in extreme cases.
- *Weapons*, such as belts, wooden spoons, ropes, electric cords, or closed fists, as they are apt to cause physical injury.

DIRECT DEMANDS FOR MORE PARENTAL INVOLVEMENT

CLINGINESS, DEMANDING ATTENTION, INTERRUPTING, AND NAGGING

Setting Parental Objectives

Expecting to be perfect parents, we naively imagine devoting hours of loving attention to our precious little ones. But idyllic dreams collapse amid soggy bottoms and hungry mouths, lost sleep, disgruntled spouses, and feuding siblings. We scrub spit-up off the living room carpet, search for shoes, and plan individual menus.

CHILD ABUSE

Any punishment that leaves bruises, scratches, or burns, or otherwise causes physical damage to the child, constitutes legal child abuse.

Through it all, children cling to our legs, yank the drapes, and interrupt our every thought. Lacking a nanny, a housekeeper, a cook, a chauffeur, and several attentive relatives, we cannot possibly give youngsters all the attention they would like.

We know the frustration of half-attention: a dull uh-huh from someone whose eyes remain glued on TV or the newspaper. Given how little of our full attention children actually get, that is, when we aren't simultaneously trying to clean up, shop, fix dinner, and so forth, it is not surprising they go to outrageous lengths to get more.

Separation from the womb is a gradual process. Like the first moon-walkers, toddlers *look* self-contained but repeatedly return to us, their base, for a replenishing pat or hug. One mother, who couldn't concentrate enough to write a letter to a friend, put a check on her paper for each interruption. Because there were fifteen checks in half an hour, she at least knew she wasn't suffering from an obscure brain disease. Approaching age three, and more confident of their physical well-being, youngsters play further away for longer, but maintain contact via looks or voice to be sure the emotional connection is still secure. "The problem," sighed a father who cared full-time for a two- and a four-year-old, "is not that kids take half your time, it's that they take five minutes out of every ten."

Dealing hour after hour with demanding youngsters is surely one of parenting's most difficult aspects. One mother commented that four-year-old Nate "is either a real saint, or a genuine, rotten brat." Another explained, "Things always seem to fall apart around 3:30, no matter how well the rest of the day has gone. If I'm feeling like super-mom, we go for a walk, but when I'm not, I usually end up putting Kenny, age four, in his room for awhile."

There are many causes for unusually demanding behavior in addition to the basic need for attention. Youngsters may be tired, teething, ill, bored, lonely, jealous, frustrated by the inability to crawl or walk, or reacting to an emotionally demanding child-care situation. They may also be responding to added emotional strain in the household such as upcoming or current travel, a move, a new sibling, house guests, parental exhaustion, or any other emotional upset of other family members. Unfortunately, youngsters often need the most attention when we are least able to give it. At times, getting help is the best solution, and at times, even that is not possible.

One place to begin may be to consider how much undivided attention our children actually get. It's unlikely to be the hours we had fantasized. Parents commonly report *undivided* attention for as little as ten or fifteen minutes a day (or even an hour once a week) up to forty-five minutes or an hour per day in several segments. When we do claim even the minimum amount of quality time for our children, the results are often dramatic, both because we have responded to their basic needs and because we have temporarily cleared our guilty conscience. Even when we have company or are visiting with others, excusing ourselves to spend a few minutes with our youngsters may well be well worth it.

In addition, if we allow children to participate in our activities in some way, they often move on more contentedly to their own activities. Raymond helps cook, Sasha converses with Mom's friends when they first arrive, and Barry can either snuggle on Mom's lap while she talks or go to his room.

As soon as youngsters are old enough to understand, it is important for us to clarify our expectations. One mother explained to her two-and-one-half-year-old that bad attention such as hitting or breaking things made her angry, and good attention, such as cuddling and reading, made her happy. She instructed him to *tell* her when he needed attention. When he then asked for " 'tention, Mommy,'' she dropped everything to spend two to five minutes with him. Once he had learned that her positive involvement was available, she was able to finish short tasks before time together. Not only did his acting out decrease dramatically, but he rarely asked for " 'tention,'' more than twice a day. Before friends visit, another mother tells her children, ages three and five, that she will want to be left alone because "talking is my playtime with my friends.'' She discusses what youngsters might do while she is busy, and asks if they need anything beforehand.

One couple sets the kitchen timer for ten minutes during which they are not to be disturbed by their three-year-old. One mother wears her bright "company apron'' when "emergencies only'' are allowed. And another taught her son to take her hand, rather than burst into the conversation, so she can attend to him at the next appropriate pause. Realizing that Timmy usually acts out when bored, his mother sends him to listen to a record, or to run to the corner and back a few times.

Children quickly learn to nag if it assures the results they want.

One mother finds it easier to stand firm on decisions if she gives herself time to consider them adequately; thus she may answer "I'm not ready to decide," and youngsters must wait five minutes, till after dinner, or whenever. Another approach to nagging is to shift from the limited physical world to the realm of imagination where everything is possible. Thus if Justin can't go to the park because of the rain, Mom has him draw pictures of what he would do if he *could* go.

Ultimately, there comes a time to say, "I have heard you, but there is nothing more I can say or do," and then ignore what follows.

TALKING TOO MUCH, YELLING, AND MAKING NOISE

Within eighteen to twenty-four months after the first babbled "mama" or "dada," we may be astonished to find we live with a talking machine that spews out reams of trivia, interspersed with scientific queries of stunning proportion. "Mommy, kitty is licking her tail. Her tail is black. Why don't I have a furry black tail? (Answer this question in fifteen words or less.) My friend Davie has black hair. And he has a baby. I like babies. Davie calls me a crybaby. I am not a crybaby. He broke my doll. When are you going to fix my doll, Mommy? Mommy?! Why aren't you listening?" And when their vocabulary is not the problem, often their *volume* is. A certain decibel level jangles our nerves even if the message is "Mommy, I love you."

There are five basic reasons for talking loudly, and each may best be handled somewhat differently.

First, it may be the family pattern. One mother reports, "I yell when I'm upset, and I don't mind if my children do. Better we holler than draw blood." If parents routinely speak in loud voices, children may also.

The second reason may be to improve communication. Children who have a hearing disability naturally speak loudly, in the unconscious hope that others will do so also. Children may respond *similarly* if parents normally speak softly or indistinctly. Pay attention to how you speak or arrange a hearing test if appropriate.

The third reason may be to get attention, especially if we tend to ignore quiet bids for attention. We need to more carefully reward quiet requests for attention, and ignore or otherwise punish loud ones.

The fourth reason may be lack of awareness of loud and soft. One mother played the "loud-soft" game with her two-year-old, in which they alternately shouted, spoke quietly, and whispered. He enjoyed the game immensely and when she asked him to lower his voice at other times, he knew what she meant. Other parents differentiate between a loud "outdoor" voice and a soft "indoor" one. One mother marked the TV and children's record player with tape to show the maximum allowable volume. If Lisa slams the front door, she has to close it quietly three times.

The fifth reason may be to vent the normal excitement and exuberance of childhood, as well as express anger and frustration. Some parents handle this inevitability with soundproofing: plastic rather than metal kitchenwear on low shelves for toddlers, carpets on stairs and floors, corkboards on children's doors. They also select toys that if loud are at least pleasant, not obnoxious. If youngsters can't go outside to be noisy we may be able to settle them into a quiet project. They *may* quiet more readily if first allowed to make as much noise as they like for the duration of a record or for a few minutes ticked off on the kitchen timer. It also helps to assure adequate opportunity to work off physical energy (see pp. 299 and 417). When a family argument has turned into a screaming match, the noise level may drop dramatically if parents start to whisper. See also Temper Tantrums, on p. 398.

We know that language is the key to intellectual development. Linguists tell us that preschoolers ask several hundred questions a day. Our answers not only provide the data base for their understanding of the world, but also determine their basic attitude toward learning. What an awesome responsibility!

On the other hand, we can't converse pleasantly and intelligently while we simultaneously decipher a recipe, navigate a new freeway, plan how to avoid a sibling's imminent tantrum, or take a much-needed mental time-out for ourselves.

We must let our children know we are often but not always available for conversation.

What do parents do when they can't listen anymore, or are frustrated by an endless series of questions?

Some try the direct approach: "My mind needs a rest now." "I can't listen while I'm reading this recipe." "You can keep talking, but I can't listen right now."

One mother found she could turn off her child's strings of questions without turning *her* off by asking some questions instead of always giving answers: "Where do *you* think the doggie might have gone?"

Another offers this anecdote about the secret issue behind her son's questions:

Randy asked in sequence, "Why does Daddy go to work?" "Why do we have to have money?" "Why do we have to eat?" I finally realized my answers weren't getting to the real issue. Then it dawned on me to ask, "Do you miss him?" He nodded, and I had some sympathy for his feelings; he was then able to go off and play.

TATTLING

Some tattling is best encouraged, and some discouraged. We do want our children to responsibly report dangers, and at times they really do need help with social situations they can't solve by themselves. However, if we are forever drawn into arguments on the basis of tattling, or if we regularly punish whoever is tattled on, chances are our attention and response are encouraging the behavior.

When tattling is inappropriate, some parents ignore it entirely, give a noncommittal "Oh," or respond, "I'm sure you two can solve the problem on your own." A mother of twins, age four, discusses the situation with both parties and, when appropriate, adds, "If you see your brother do something wrong, you can tell him to stop, not just watch until he's finished." One mother ended the problem by giving the same penalty to the tattler as to the other culprit.

RESISTANCE TO PARENTAL CONTROL

TEMPER TANTRUMS

A few parents declare that their children don't have tantrums, but in most households, such outbursts are as common as spilled juice and broken toys. Tantrums are especially common at age two, not only because youngsters meet more frustrations at this age, but also because they haven't yet developed more constructive ways to deal with anger. The average two-year-old may never again meet so many incomprehensible and insurmountable barriers and be so poorly equipped to deal with them. During such difficult periods, some days seem like one prolonged tantrum. From age two and one-half, generally the most difficult time of all, the frequency of tantrums *gradually* decreases, over the next several years, but we all have to survive in the meantime.

The immediate cause of a tantrum is often the necessity for youngsters to do something *our* way. Some parents adeptly use humor to rescue the tone of events: for example, when a cookie is denied, "Did you see Wilbur the white mouse ride his bike down the hall toward your bedroom?" Sometimes we can stave off a tantrum by letting youngsters know we understand their feelings: "I bet you wish you'd never have to get in this hot, sticky car seat again." In general, the more we and our children can communicate with language, the less need there will be for incoherent tantrums. However, there may be some underlying factors to consider as well.

Possible Reasons for Tantrums

1. Fatigue or hunger may be a cause, especially if tantrums occur about the same time each day. Be sure snacks are available when needed, and minimize pressures when youngsters are tired. Changing bath time or story time may ease the pace of the afternoon and evening.
2. Frustration from learning new skills. Whether it's zipping zippers or learning to talk, learning *is* frustrating. Allow sufficient time for youngsters to speak, avoid pressuring for correct pronunciation, and if particular words cause confusion, practice them in quiet moments. Other than keeping our expectations within reason, our task with learning frustration is often to wait and sympathize because youngsters may not want our help.
3. A power play to get one's own way. If we often buckle under the pressure of a tantrum, any smart youngster will be quick to press the advantage. Frequently our child's main objective is to test our limits. Rebecca, age two, wants to play with several

cups and we give them to her willingly. She pleads for another and we oblige. She demands still another. Her attention has now shifted from playing with cups to the fascinating question, "Will this lady keep giving me cups forever?" Giving more cups at this point leaves her question unanswered and prolongs the uncertainty for everyone. We will eventually run out of cups (or patience, or whatever), and at that point there will be a tantrum. The further down the road the limits are met, the longer it takes the child to figure out where they are, and the more frustrated we become in the process.

4. A reaction to emotional strain. When the general strain of family living was getting out of hand, Michelle's parents took her to her room (or their room) for a few minutes to collect herself. Because they took her in order to allow her some space of her own, rather than as punishment, and led her with concern, rather than anger, Michelle learned to say she needed to go to her room. Not surprisingly, tantrums are more common with a change in housing, family structure, child-care arrangements, or any other emotionally draining situation.

5. Concern about a family secret. Frustrated by repeated tantrums, and suspecting a possible cause, Landon's mother asked guardedly, "Do you know anyone who is going to take a trip?" Landon replied that Mommy and Daddy were. He had apparently overheard suspicious tidbits about their upcoming vacation without him. On the other hand, Sasha's mother had no idea what the difficulty might be. "There seems to be an Angry Sasha living here. Do you know what she's upset about?" Sasha responded that the problem was a baby in Mommy's tummy. Her mother was amazed because she was sure Sasha had not overheard a word about recent attempts to become pregnant. Once these secrets were out in the open, tantrums decreased markedly.

Possible Responses to Tantrums

Depending on both child and parent, there are a variety of ways to handle tantrums. What works in one family doesn't in another, or what feels appropriate one month may not the next.

In the midst of a tantrum, Lisa becomes enraged at the sight of Mom or Dad, and David prolongs the show as long as there is an audience, so they are best left to themselves. One mother used to send her son to his room; then, since he wouldn't stay, she put a lock on his door. When he broke the lock, she just let him kick and scream on the living-room floor while she busied herself nearby, and he calmed down much more quickly. Some children do best with physical contact. Thus Mom holds Emily while she sobs. Justin is too big to hold, so Mom carefully straddles his thighs and rubs his back while he kicks and pounds the floor.

Though ignoring tantrums is often recommended, it isn't always easy. Keven, age four, screams lustily, "I'm dying. I can't breathe." When Mom leaves the room, Allison scrambles off the floor to follow her and continue in the next room. Andrea's first tantrum came when she was four, and lasted several hours. Nor does ignoring one tantrum necessarily prevent the next one. The reason is that tantrums for children, like sex for adults, release physical tension and thus provide rewarding relaxation.

It's probably not until age four or five that most youngsters have sufficient conscious control to *stop* tantrums in mid-course. Only then is the firm choice "Calm yourself or we will leave the swimming pool" apt to be effective. At age five, Sasha gets a star for putting the lid on a tantrum. Jeremy gets a time-out for a tantrum, but his time doesn't start until he stops crying. In the meantime, with younger children, we can send them to their rooms until they eventually calm down, or pick them up and carry them to the car or wherever. Spanking, though used by some parents, is generally not recommended because tantrums are neither dangerous nor destructive.

A difficult concept for many of us to grasp is that we can accept the fact that children *feel upset* without doing things *their* way. To listen sympathetically to the child's viewpoint doesn't mean to abide by it: to tolerate a tantrum doesn't mean to give in to it. Things must often be done our way because of our broader viewpoint and more mature judgment. That fact is difficult for children. For more about how to put up with the noise, see Surviving Children's Crying and Tantrums, p. 223.

Once the tantrum is over, children need the reassurance that they are still loved. Awkwardly, young children are often ready for friendly hugs before we are. Some youngsters need more time, and some less, to be ready to make up. One mother said of herself and her son, "Once we've both calmed down, we talk for as long as necessary, to feel like friends again."

NEGATIVITY

Some days it seems as if no is the only word in our youngster's vocabulary. For the majority of children, the most intense period of negativity comes at age two or two and one-half, but for some it starts months earlier, and for others not until age three or more. During the previous stage of development, we could distract or sweet-talk them into doing things our way. But now, they call us on our manipulation. The practical question of this negative period is how to balance the needs and desires of two strong-minded people in such a way that neither loses face more than necessary.

Those who study infants tell us that newborns, flesh of our flesh, cannot tell where their bodies end and ours begin. And in the first months of a child's life, though physically separate, parent and child function as one psychological unit. If this intense state of oneness continued, our offspring could not grow to feel and think for themselves, or develop sufficient independence to lead their own adult lives.

Much is written about the difficulty of the child in making the transition to psychological separateness: This central struggle accounts for negativity, indecision, and tantrums. And the wrenching can be just as difficult for us. Our dream of an ever-loving, cooperative child is rooted in our longing to have the primal oneness continue forever. We probably couldn't manage the transition at all if not for the fact that it comes in stages: negativity at two, off to school at five, rebelliousness at thirteen. In preparation for eventual separation, we and our children must come to grips with the painful fact that our needs and theirs do not and will not always coincide. *Unless we allow our children to say no to us, they cannot say yes to themselves.* Our children's dilemma is the same as ours. Either one bends to the will of the other and feels united, but somehow stifled; or each follows his own inclinations and feels separate from the dearly beloved. That it is possible to *go* one's own way, *endure* the separateness, and *return* again to warmth and closeness is one of the most important lessons we and our children can learn.

The difficulty of this period is not only that our children are negative, but that we must be negative too. We must often curtail their adventures or proceed with our business despite their protest. If we usually do things their way, but resentfully, they sense our anger and are frightened by their personal power to create such antagonism. If we always do things their way, willingly, they can't learn that others have needs too. It is through their relationship with us that they gradually and *unwillingly* learn that the luxurious self-centeredness of infancy necessarily ends.

The answer to developing both independence and responsiveness to others lies in balance: in dovetailing our needs with our children's. We will each gain some and lose some in the back-and-forth of daily living. In matters of safety and concern for others, we will often require them to bend in our direction. In matters of independence and learning, we will often bend toward theirs. It's a relief to know that who comes out ahead in any particular issue is far less important than overall balance.

As for dealing with the current negativity we can begin by avoiding questions that invite no for an answer. It's better to say, "Time to go see Dr. Jensen." than "Let's go see Dr. Jensen now, OK?" On the other hand, a carefully phrased question or invitation may be better accepted than a command, for example, "Now that you're finished playing, where does dolly belong?" instead of "Put your doll away." Sometimes singing or chanting direct requests gains more compliance. When possible, redirect, rather than prohibit: as in "Wipe your fingers on your napkin," instead of "Don't wipe your fingers on your shirt."

When we don't *really* care about the outcome, reverse psychology may ease the course of events. Thus, while plodding home from the store, Mom says with a smile, "Walk very slowly, Danielle. Don't run." When Marie is bypassing vegetables on the plate, her father kids her, "Don't eat any of those carrots. I don't want you to get as big as I am." Contrary children often can't resist a lighthearted invitation to self-assertion. It's important to keep up the spirit of the game, however, lest children be confused by our unusual response.

Because self-control is the issue behind negativity, choices are often helpful in that they allow a certain degree of self-determination. Thus, Dad asks, "Do you want a last turn on the slide or the swing before we leave the park?" Here are a few guidelines to keep in mind when using choices:

- Limit choices appropriately. Too much choice can take one's breath away, especially when you're only two. Thus, "Do you want to paint or do a puzzle?'' is easier to answer than "What do you want to play with?" Sometimes choices of any sort are too difficult for either parent or child to cope with.

· Give choices about the means, not the end. As the parents, we must determine the *end* of many daily interactions. But letting Lee choose the *means*—whether to walk or be carried to his room—meets our need that he get there *now* and his need to participate in the decision. One day Lee reached for more control by proposing a different means. He wanted to be pulled, so he lay on his back with his feet in the air and giggled all the way. As long as the new means is an acceptable path to the desired end, we can encourage such a creative beginning toward the art of negotiation.

· List your preference last. If you'd somewhat prefer that Sandra wear her blue shirt, try asking "Do you want to wear your yellow shirt or the blue one?" Some two-year-olds instinctively say no to the first option, and therefore choose the second, whatever it is.

· Remember who the parent is. Sooner or later, some youngsters try changing roles. Eric, age three, announced, "Mommy, you can either buy me an ice cream cone today or tomorrow." And Allison, age four, threatened, "Either let me do what I want or I will scream all day." Because these plays for power were unacceptable, Mom told Eric no, and Allison's mother ignored the proposition, as Allison was unlikely to scream *all* day.

Various factors can influence the intensity of negativity in any given household. Some children are intrinsically mellow and fairly easily blend their needs with those around them. Others, single-minded and feisty, assume everyone should bow to their decrees. More friction is inevitable in the latter case. We might also check on how often we are saying no to our negative youngsters. One mother was awestruck when she actually kept count. Finally, one family noted increasingly angry negative behavior in their five-year-old, a time when conflict often softens. They opted for family therapy, and found that as issues between parents resolved, so did their youngster's negativity.

DISOBEDIENCE

We feel like tearing our hair when the children ignore or disobey us, but "obedience" is rather out of vogue these days. We associate the term with unquestioned authority, and we are acutely aware of the hazards of blind obedience. We therefore feel ambivalent about using parental power to curb disobedience.

But we do want Lucy to take a bath, Paul to get in the car, Dean to stop smashing flowers, and Jessica to stop hitting Benjamin. In short, we want our children to question authority, but not necessarily *our* authority. Our fantasy, that our children will do what we ask because our requests are *reasonable* and because our children love us, usually crumbles around the second birthday. We face the stark realization that they do things our way only because we are bigger.

To require obedience does not mean adopting an authoritarian style of parenting, as many people fear. We don't have to choose between despotic power and unstructured chaos. We can use rewards as well as punishment, let our children express themselves, take their concerns into consideration, explain our decisions, *and* require children to obey appropriate rules.

In deciding whether to be tolerant or to require obedience, we generally face situations in the following categories.

1. Matters of urgent safety. We don't wait for compliance when youngsters reach for the electric socket or run toward the street; we physically stop them.
2. Conflict with immediate parental needs. Mom has to fix dinner, but Jenny doesn't want to leave the park. We will meet parental need by leaving now, and Jenny's by returning another day.
3. Conflict with parent's ongoing concerns. Ray wants to eat crackers, but Mom doesn't want crumbs all over the living-room rug. In these situations we can look for solutions that meet the needs of both: Ray can eat crackers, but only in the kitchen.
4. Testing limits. When Dad calls, John runs the other way. Unless we generally enforce compliance in such situations, children can become abusive of their power over us.

We realize that our two-year-olds often can't comply, and thus we tolerate a good deal of unsocial behavior. But because four-year-olds understand many household rules and have a great deal more self-control, we expect more compliance from them. Though their resistance is less frequent, it is often more sophisticated, more accusingly intoned, or more deliberately outrageous. One four-year-old taunted, "I'm trying to annoy you," and another threw a handful of rocks at her mother. The former was sent to her room, and the latter got a spanking. Many parents feel an instinctive need to be firmer when youngsters reach age four or five.

As our youngsters grow, we can increasingly involve them in negotiating rules and establishing rewards and punishments. As they progress through elementary school, they will even develop sufficient self-control to abide by the rules they help make. But for now, whether we make the rules single-handedly for our two-year-olds, or cooperatively with our five-year-olds, *we* are responsible for enforcement.

It is always difficult to know if studies of animal behavior are relevant to people, but the following research report has fascinating implications. One researcher found that when puppies were punished as they approached a certain food, they learned to avoid it in the future. Other puppies who were punished *after* they ate the food continued to eat it on future occasions, but guiltily hung their heads and tucked their tails between their legs when the trainer then entered the room. This may mean that we can decrease the amount of guilt our children experience by preventing misbehavior, rather than punishing it after the fact. Better to punish Laura when she threatens to hit Roger with a block than after he has a goose-egg.

Having accepted the necessity of obedience, we naturally ask next: How can we get children to do what we need them to do?

1. *Make clear, specific requests.* Repeat the same phrases slowly and clearly enough for toddlers to learn what they mean. Make specific rather than general requests. For example, "Don't stamp your feet," instead of "Be good!" "Ask me before you take something out of the cupboard," instead of "Cooperate!"

2. *Don't just speak, act.* G. Ron Norton, in his book *Parenting* (Prentice-Hall, 1977), contends that it is not until children are about three that they respond to the *meaning* of words. When Susie, age thirteen months, reaches toward

the stereo, she pauses from instinctive fear of loud noises whether we shout "Yes!" or "Don't touch." With time, she either learns that our voice is mere bark, which can be ignored, or she learns that unless she heeds the voice, something else will happen: She'll be physically removed, given another toy, or, ultimately, get her hand slapped. Avoid commands you aren't willing or able to back up. One mother clarified the issue in these words: "With my first two children, I usually repeated myself three times before I acted. With the last two, I jumped after the first request. Needless to say, the latter ones are more obedient."

3. *Set time limits.* For example, "Before I count to ten, come to the door." "Before the timer rings in five minutes, put these toys away."

4. *Give positive information as well as negative.* When we tell children to stop, they have to figure out what to do next, and we may not like their alternative. By also telling them what they *can* do, we help them direct their interests and energies in acceptable directions: "Stay on the sidewalk" or "Ask *me* to turn on the stereo for you."

5. *Clarify the need for obedience.* Mom tells Ken, age four, "This is a time to obey, not negotiate." Another says, "Do what I say now, and I'll explain later."

6. *Reevaluate.* Consider the following questions: a) Is the child able to comply, physically, emotionally, and intellectually, at *this* point in time? b) Are the child's basic needs being met for love, attention, exercise, interesting activities, and an appropriate amount of self-determination? c) Do you feel ambivalent about expecting obedience in general, or expecting compliance on this issue in particular? Resistance is bound to continue as long as parental ambivalence does.

Are we setting double standards? Do we expect children to be more considerate, more patient, or more polite than we are? If so, resistance is inevitable.

Creative rewards and punishments are useful here, as anywhere else. One mother got a box of her son's favorite crackers and called him frequently for a few days. When he came, she said "I just wanted to give you a hug and a cracker because you came right away.'' Because of her pregnancy, one mother didn't want to carry her two-year-old home from the park just because he chose not to walk. So she carried him, but a little *too* tightly so that he preferred to walk. For more rewards and punishments, see Changing Behavior: The Use of Reward and Punishment, p. 374.

DAWDLING

There's nothing quite so frustrating as waiting six minutes for a child to get one sock on, or making the homeward traverse of the park with a grass-blade inspector. Dawdling often seems like simple orneriness, but the motivation may be more complex.

The Child Has a Different Concept of Time

For all of us, time moves at different speeds. One mother confided, ''I find it all too easy to linger over my coffee and morning newspaper, and then expect Alex to make up the time by collecting things for school in a flash.''

Furthermore, we and our children perceive time differently. We have a strong sense of what *we* mean by the word ''now,'' but we seldom convey our precise meaning to our children. For example, when we ask them to do something ''now,'' we tell them when to *start* moving toward the door or picking up toys, but not when to *finish*. Clarifying the finishing time can be a great help. Thus, Alice must get her shirt on before Dad counts to ten or *he* will pull it on. Beth gets one star for picking up her toys, but earns two if she does so before the five-minute timer rings.

One mother taught her son the word ''hurry'' by describing his own behavior: ''You are in a hurry to get home and eat.'' Then she pointed out times when she was in a hurry and began to differentiate between ''hurry trips,'' and ''no-hurry trips.'' Understanding her vocabulary, it was much easier for him to cooperate.

The Child Doesn't Want to Stop the Current Activity

Parents have found various ways to ease this awkward transition. Warning ahead is crucial: ''We will leave in five minutes,'' or ''after one more turn on the slide.'' In some families, the parental ''one more ride,'' is countered by ''I want three more,'' and then everyone settles for two. Anya gets out of the tub more easily if she tells it ''bye-bye.'' Ben leaves the house more readily if he can take his current project to the car. While leaving the park, families may discuss what was the most fun, imagine what it would be like to *never* have to leave, or pretend they are horses galloping toward a water trough by the car.

The Child Is Bored with the Present Activity

Dawdling often sets in when the walk home, or whatever task is at hand, is dull. Imagination is often the answer. See How to Make the Work Emotionally Easier, p. 127; and Activities and Entertainment for Travel, p. 190.

The Child Is Indifferent to the Upcoming Activity

Sometimes youngsters would rather stay home than attend the dance or art class *we* arranged for them. Or they may prefer to play at the house of a friend than accompany us on errands. Thus dawdling may call for reexamination of our plans with more attention to the interests and desires of our young ones.

When youngsters drag their feet to nursery school or home from the park, one mother initiates the "I hate . . ." game. She may declare, "I *hate* to go home and have to wash the dishes," and each youngster adds another objection. Soon they are stomping onward at a good clip. Later, they may discuss the issues that came up and even change routines accordingly.

On the other hand, youngsters may not know how much they value something until they miss it. Rather than pushing to leave on time, Mom left home when Andy was finally ready, and arrived late at gym class. After that, Andy was ready on time. Beth was delighted to miss her car-pool ride to nursery school until she discovered that Mom was too busy to play with her all morning. The next day she got ready with one reminder.

Child Feels Overwhelmed by the Upcoming Activity

We are frightfully fast and efficient compared with our little ones. John, age five, told his mother she rushed him so much his stomach hurt. Even at their best, youngsters need a lot more time than we do. In fact, it's often tempting to do everything for them because we can do it so much more quickly. But we stifle their curiosity if we always travel at our pace, and smother their self-confidence if we always do *for* them. Furthermore, what's the point of working if the response will be that the bedspread isn't straight enough, the clothes don't match well enough, or the blocks are in the wrong box? Better to dawdle and delay the criticism.

Thus we need to temper our expectations, and allow sufficient time whenever possible. When time *is* short, the best solution may be to lend a helping hand ourselves, or have elder siblings help younger ones. In addition, a big task is less discouraging if divided into smaller segments, and even little tasks go more easily when one is rested and well fed.

The Child Is Using a Power Play for Attention or to Get His Own Way

If children are getting sufficient attention at other times, and have appropriate opportunities for independence and self-determination, it's time to look for ways to end a power play of dawdling. Because we aren't going to leave youngsters behind, and talk of doing so is frightening, such threats are generally best avoided. However, if we walk a little ahead, *some* youngsters will scurry along. Alternatively, one mother who *was* willing to carry through told Stefan he could go to the doctor naked or with clothes. He preferred to get dressed. Having once gone to nursery school in pajamas, some youngsters choose to dress more quickly. For more about getting dressed on time, see p. 89. One mother ignores the dawdling and seats herself by the front door with a magazine. If Karen is ready early, Mom will read to her until leaving time. Another mother loads her youngsters and their clothes into the car because they dress more quickly in the nursery school parking lot. After repeated struggles about getting to nursery school, one mother dropped her son at a sitter instead, and because he missed his friends, he was ready to go more willingly thereafter. When another youngster missed his car pool, Mom sent him in a lonely taxi, which he didn't want to repeat.

WHINING AND COMPLAINING

Depending on what mood we are in, a child's whiny voice may seem like an irritating drippy faucet, or like the spine-tingling scrape of fingernails on a blackboard. In desperation, one mother put a piece of tape over her whiny son's mouth. "He took it right off, but he got the point." What's the whining all about?

The first thing to check out may be how much *we* whine and complain around our youngsters. Secondly, do children understand what tone of voice distresses us? One mother praised her youngster for using a "strong" voice, and another made up a story about Complaining Carla who was so unpleasant to have around that she wasn't invited many places.

Whining is often more common when some immediate but basic need is unmet. Youngsters may need a rest, a snack, or help getting started on an interesting activity. A brief walk, a bath or story, or a few minutes joining in our activities may provide some needed attention.

A sense of discouragement or defeat can also lead to these grating sounds. Sometimes all we need to do is sympathetically acknowledge the child's feelings. Or, we may need to consider whether our expectations are too high on the one hand, and whether we are not allowing sufficient opportunity for growth on the other. Aggressive youngsters seem more inclined to yell and stomp when upset, and mellow children more prone to whining: We may have to live with a certain amount of one or the other.

Another cause is emotional strain. Children may be reacting to *our* worried tone, adjusting to a change in family circumstances, or adapting well to the outside world but letting their hair down when safely home again. A certain amount of such whining may be inevitable. One mother plays the "crabby game" in which she joins her daughter's mood by announcing, "I feel crabby right now." After a few minutes of crabbing together at the world in general, both feel better because they have gotten the feelings out *with,* instead of *against* each other.

Finally, whining can be a tear-jerking power play to wear us down. The more often we give in, the more whining and complaining we are apt to hear, in which case some form of punishment may be the most effective solution. See Changing Behavior: The Use of Reward and Punishment, p. 374.

AGGRESSION: PHYSICAL AND VERBAL

WHAT ARE OUR GOALS?

Not only is learning to handle aggressive impulses as complex and time-consuming as learning to read and write, but how we teach our children to channel the inevitable anger of daily living is among the most important decisions we make as parents. One mother summed up the basic task this way: "There are two parts to helping my daughter deal with anger. One is to help her put the lid on when it is out of control and the other is to teach her how to get it out constructively. Thus I tell her it's OK to say she's angry, but it's not OK to hit."

Youngsters *can* learn to contain their physical and verbal anger, but to hold in too much, especially at too young an age, has significant drawbacks. First, toddlers and preschoolers who are expected to control the *expression* of anger more firmly than they are able may learn instead to suppress their underlying *feelings* of anger in order to avoid punishment. To suppress excessive amounts of anger is to suppress the basic underlying needs that caused the anger, and to live with many unexpressed needs is to live with deprivation. Second, young children, it seems, have difficulty suppressing just *one* emotion. They let anger, sadness, joy, and excitement all explode into view or learn to hold all their feelings in. Third, suppressed anger often leaks out in other ways. For example, several mothers reported their children became more accident-prone after a new baby arrived. These older siblings were trying to hold in more anger than they could manage, so their ire surfaced in a different direction, namely bumps and bangs accidentally inflicted on themselves.

Finally, just as all fires create heat, all anger creates energy. Even when verbal skills solve problems, they don't dissolve the physical tension created by conflict. When the physical component of anger is regularly suppressed, rather than burned off through physical exertion, the underlying energy tends to persist as muscle tension throughout the body. Current research in stress management indicates that if such tension, rather than being discharged, accumulates over the years, it can evolve into tension headaches, high blood pressure, and a multitude of other physical ailments. Leftover physical anger may well be the leading cause of national ill health. If we want our youngsters to outgrow physical aggression and tantrums without adversely affecting their long-term health, we need to provide alternate physical outlets. Overall, a child who necessarily suppresses a great many feelings may be easier to live with, but the ultimate price can be very high.

On the other hand, if, whenever Donald rages, he gets what he wants, we teach him that we are afraid of his anger; and he, being smaller, will be even *more* afraid of his rage. Children perceive that anger can be dangerous, and correctly so. To accept their anger generally does not mean to take away the cause of their anger, though *sometimes* that is appropriate. To accept anger means to accept both *their need* to express it and *our responsibility* to teach them how to express it nondestructively.

Whether we ourselves grew up in the confining isolation of unexpressed feelings or whether we experienced the physical and emotional pain of unbridled anger will greatly affect our automatic responses to our children's anger. Coming to terms with our past experience is often the first step toward dealing appropriately with our children's anger. A number of parents find that therapy is a useful tool in this regard. If you feel unsure about how much anger is "normal" at a given age, discuss the matter with a parent support group, nursery school teacher, or pediatrician.

Whether to let youngsters use toy guns as an outlet for aggressive feelings is a controversial subject among parents. Some straightforwardly forbid guns, "because they don't solve problems." Alternatively, others buy guns in the belief that this phase will pass and that if youngsters don't have toy pistols, they will use their pointed fingers anyway. Some parents make their point by refusing to buy such toys, but allowing youngsters to spend their own money to that end if they wish. Certain parents allow fanciful ray guns, but not those that look like the real thing, and one mother instructs her boys, "If you want to play games about danger, you can play fireman, mountain rescue, or emergency room doctor." Finally, some limit the *use* of toy guns with such rules as "No pointing them at people," "No playing in the house," "No playing except with those who *want* to," or "No playing if the game gets overly rough."

Limiting hurtful physical aggression is fairly clear-cut. We want to avoid pain, scratches, bruises, and so forth. On the other hand, limiting verbal aggression is much more nebulous, as each of us has personal feelings about particular religious, excretory, sexual, or otherwise derogatory terms as well as teasing and bossiness as means of expressing anger. Our ultimate goal is to teach children to express and take reasonable care of their own needs with minimal distress to others.

Because reaching our ultimate goal will take years, we need to keep not only the destination in mind, but the process as well. For the most part, we are doing well to contain our two-year-old's physical aggression. Following the advice of the experts, many parents ignore the early ventures in bathroom language, which usually disappears as soon as it is no longer hilarious to playmates.

The father of a three-year-old, however, was horrified when his daughter called the janitor in his office a "poo-poo head." Thus as youngsters enter the world at large where we and they will be judged by their language, many parents begin restrictions. Families may distinguish between words for public and private use, or may differentiate vocabulary that is appropriate to use with playmates, siblings, parents, or other adults. Given the complexity of the decision making involved, one mother opts for a double standard, and thus tells her four-year-old, "I can swear because I am a grown-up. When you are grown-up, you can swear too." Other parents limit their own vocabulary to words they are willing to have children repeat. After years of teaching "You are not to swear because we don't," one couple finally eased up on themselves when their son turned seven, only to have him correct their colorful vocabulary.

Exploring language is a favorite pastime of four-year-olds, and by this time, they have usually graduated from mere bathroom language. Nate swears like a sailor for the pleasure of shocking others, but rarely does so at home because no one notices. Many parents ignore the choice words and taunting among peers, as it causes little distress and it *is* progress from pushing and hitting.

But while two-year-olds use colorful language playfully, and three-year-olds innocently, four- and five-year-olds eventually learn the art of sophisticated and calculated verbal aggression, with insults, teasing, bossiness, and words that intentionally color *our* faces in public. Just like a punch in the stomach, insults can reduce playmates and siblings to tears of rage, to say nothing of ourselves, when *we* are the victims: "My cookie is bigger than yours," "You can't come to my birthday party," or "Mommy, you don't love me." Given the powerful effect of the new aggression, it may not diminish if ignored.

As parents, we react differently when attacked by our sharp-tongued youngsters. One mother comments, "I don't care if my five-year-old tells me she hates me. I know it's temporary and I'm glad she can get her feelings out." Other responses include, "You are not to tell me I am a bad mother because it hurts my feelings,'' ''Sometimes Mommies *have* to be mean,'' and ''I don't care what you call me in your head, as long as you don't say it out loud.''

The very value we place on verbal problem solving may lead us to expect too much too soon. We wish that instead of slugging his playmate, two-year-old Jeffery would propose, ''Let's take turns, Donald.'' And we explain the reason behind every roadblock in hopes of allaying our little one's anger: ''We can't buy this toy because we don't have enough money.'' Unfortunately, our logic is nonsense to our little ones. Though our explanations provide information they will *eventually* understand, expecting them to *respond* to logic is like expecting the deaf to use radios. Verbal problem solving requires a fluent vocabulary, a concept of time, an understanding of cause and effect, and an awareness of where the other person is coming from. Because these abilities evolve slowly, the inclination toward physical and verbal abuse diminishes slowly. Even at age six, although our young ones are making real progress, they are not yet accomplished in clearly describing what upsets them and working toward solutions that are acceptable to others as well as themselves. Nor can we blame them, as many of us aren't yet accomplished in this arena either.

WHAT CAUSES AGGRESSION?

The origins of childhood aggression fit into four broad categories: (1) basic personality, (2) innocent exploration, (3) an instinctive reaction to pain, and (4) a bid for power. To begin with, some youngsters have strong, aggressive personalities and therefore require more persistence to restrain than their mellow counterparts. Second, our babes and toddlers may poke, pinch, and tug as a means of exploring, without realizing they are hurting others. We can best help by teaching them to explore gently.

Aggression is our *instinctive* response to physical or psychological pain, and frustration and fear are among the most common forms of the latter. Due to their instinct for self-preservation, children often direct their aggression toward someone smaller and less important than their parents. Thus, some of the inevitable fighting and bickering among youngsters, is, in fact, a way of venting the frustration and disappointment they feel with us. We tell Ellen, ''No cake for breakfast,'' ''You can't go naked to the grocery store," "Don't write on the walls," "I'm too busy for time together now," and she necessarily gives in. Then when Marilyn gets onto the swing first, Ellen may erupt with all the fury of her anger at us. A new babe in the house is an especially likely target for the painful realization that Mom is no longer so attentive as she used to be.

At other times, we are the safest target for our children's frustration. The nursery school teacher or friend's parents may rave about the little darling who is a demon at home. The better we succeed in conveying our overall love, the safer our offspring feel in venting their disappointment and upsets on us. Ironically, in these early years, their misdirected anger is a compliment! Learning how to direct anger appropriately is a long, slow process. Many of *us* are still learning how to express anger at the boss instead of dumping on our spouse, or how to express anger at our spouse instead of dumping on the kids. The more self-confidence we instill in our little ones, the more appropriately they will eventually be able to handle their frustration in the big wide world.

Lionel's mother, on the advice of her doctor, started spending fifteen minutes a day playing with him: letting him choose the activity and take the lead, while she paid attention and gave praise, but refrained from suggestions and criticism. Given this much-needed attention, and a consequent rise in self-esteem, his aggressiveness markedly decreased.

When Martin, age four, became *increasingly* aggressive at nursery school, therapy revealed a number of contributing factors. He was afraid of some of the bigger, stronger boys; he missed several good friends who had moved during the summer; he was concerned about his parents' marital difficulties; he was adjusting to a new sibling; *and* he was worried about his mother because he had feared she might die when she had the C-section. Once the issues were in the open, it was possible to work with them, and combined with transfer to a more comfortable school, his aggressiveness faded.

When Andrea felt isolated from other children, she teased them. Once her mother instructed the playmates to ignore the teasing and helped Andrea find ways to join in their play, there was no need for further teasing.

One four-year-old was unusually aggressive until a hearing problem was diagnosed, and another improved his behavior when parents stopped using excessive physical punishment.

Finally, aggression can be a bid for power. It may be the surest way for youngsters to get what they want, and may allow them to monopolize our attention as well. For more about lack of parental power, see p. 208.

TEACHING APPROPRIATE OUTLETS FOR AGGRESSION

Expecting our little ones to emulate us, we spend months nurturing our adorable infants with gentleness and love, yet our example seems to go unnoticed. Suddenly, between eighteen months and three years, they turn into hitting, biting demons. Nor do they show patience and tolerate setbacks just because we so often do. We avoided generalizations such as "bad" or "naughty," and labels like "stupid" or "ugly," but they return from encounters with other "nice" children with language that makes us gasp. When our little ones turn brutal, we despair for ourselves, our children, and the future of world peace. Modeling alone doesn't work.

Though our two-year-olds seem oblivious to many of our actions, our offspring *will* pay increasing attention to how we handle anger as the years go by. Kevin, age five, watched closely when an irate, off-the-wall neighbor stomped over and started cursing at his father. Dad stood quietly through it all, then went to the park to shoot some baskets. Afterward, Kevin's parents discussed the fact that in this case, yelling back would only have made matters worse, and exercise in the park worked off the frustration of the encounter. We have just a few short years to figure out what we want to model regarding the expression of anger. This awareness may be the incentive we need to clear up our own dirty fighting, express our own needs more assertively, learn more efficient problem solving, or practice more fully dispersing the physical energy produced by anger.

We, of course, are not the only models for our children, especially if they are in child care. Furthermore, some playmates seem to induce more cooperative play in our children while others seem to produce more hostile interactions. At this age, we can still select our children's companions if we feel it is appropriate.

In addition to modeling desired behavior, we can also discuss the disadvantages of direct aggression and certain vocabulary. We tell our two-year-olds that hitting hurts others. Our four-year-olds not only realize that words hurt feelings, but can learn that name-calling doesn't solve problems: "I want my turn too," is more useful than "I hate you." One mother tells her son that some adults don't like children who use certain words, and another made up a story about a little girl who didn't have any friends because of her teasing and name-calling. These lessons are of course, learned better in friendly discussions than in the heat of a shouting match.

The key to helping our children handle anger safely, is not to prohibit its expression, but to direct it, and parents have discovered many attractive and effective games to accomplish this end. With some youngsters, it is possible to redirect their anger at the moment they are upset. Others can do so only after the initial outburst and some time to calm down. Some will try such games only when they are no longer upset. Fortunately, it doesn't matter which, because they learn the techniques in any case and after-the-fact games can effectively dust out accumulated emotional grime.

To tell children to go play an angry game is not nearly so effective as to invite them to join *us* in one. We have to show them how to play, how to channel their feelings. One mother noted, "When I'm angry, I remind myself not just to raise my voice, but to stomp my foot as well, to show Elise, age twenty months, that we can both express anger in similar ways." In fact, given how frustrating it is to live with young children, many parents find it a relief to discover safe ways to vent their own feelings.

When Shauna starts to bite, her mother grabs the nearest rubber toy, bites it, growls, and says how good it feels. She then passes the toy to Shauna.

Hit a store-made punching bag, or fill an old pillowcase with wadded paper and suspend it from a doorway. Beat the bed or sofa with a pillow, a wooden spoon, or a plastic baseball bat. Buy a toy cobbler's bench, or hammer on a board. Pound bread dough or Play-Dough. Swat flies with a flyswatter. One mother purchased a doll for her son when the new baby arrived. When Benji stroked his doll, his mother cooed. When he hit it, with a devilish little smile on his face, Mom gave a loud "Waaaa." Benji loved it.

What can one do with angry feet? Evelyn and her mother stomp on the floor, declaring in turn, "You're not mad, *I'm* mad." When Sean has a tantrum, his mother chides, "Don't kick a hole in my rug!" Sean kicks harder of course, and wears himself out sooner. Fill a shopping bag with wads of paper and tape it closed: Angry four-year olds will kick it "until its guts fall out." Kick an old milk carton around the house or go for a rainy-day puddle stomp.

For those who like to tear things, supply old newspapers and magazines. For things to smash, save old broken toys or provide some macaroni. If plentiful, pine cones take a lot of energy to destroy, and once youngsters calm down, cracking nuts is great. For those who like noise, slamming certain doors is loud and harmless: "I can slam my door louder than you can slam yours!"

Controlled fighting not only works off frustration, but can be safe and fun as well. When Britt, eighteen months, is frustrated, Mom invites her to play "Patty Cake." If Aaron, age two, isn't too angry, Mom tickles him, which evolves into a wild giggling session. When Alix, also two, won't stay in her room for misbehavior, she and Mom have a tug-of-war on opposite sides of the door. For a pushing contest, entrants put hands on each other's shoulders and try to shove their opponent across the end lines. Stronger players must stay on their knees or push with only one hand. Pillow fights work most easily with long, lightweight pillows, and may require some rules, such as no hitting above the neck, or stronger players have to hold on with just two fingers. Kids love it when parents quake in fear and "fall dead." Alternatively, try a pillow spanking, in which each person takes a turn lying still while the other spanks with a pillow for the agreed-upon number of times. Once youngsters are verbal, add to the challenge and usefulness of the game by requiring a statement about how the recipient causes aggravation, to accompany each swat. In summer, have a family water war, with squirt bottles and water balloons, and in winter, try the same with wads of newspaper.

In order to burn off the energy of anger, activity need not be directed toward another person, it just needs to be strenuous. For more ways to let off steam, see p. 299.

Paper provides another outlet for frustration. Scribble out angry feelings, or draw an ugly picture of the enemy and, if so inclined, take the matter one step further by positioning it on the wall as a bean-bag target.

Just as physical aggression can be redirected into nonharmful physical outlets, verbal aggression can be similarly directed so that children get their feelings out without inflicting emotional bruises. We can gradually teach youngsters that the purpose of angry words is to let others know we are upset. Thus, Tim cannot call Lisa stupid or a crybaby, because it hurts her feelings, but he can call her a "lousy liver lover." Informed that his current choice of words was unacceptable, one four-year-old invented the word "Shitz-ka-bob" for moments of great frustration. One mother discovered that growling was a great way for her and her son to express anger, because it allowed them to get their feelings out without having to think of acceptable words during moments of fury. In the angry word game Yes-No, one person shouts no, and the other yes, each changing sides whenever they feel like it. Four- and five-year-olds love the game in which everything means the opposite, so it's OK to shout, "I hate you."

LEARNING TO EXPRESS FEELINGS AND NEEDS CLEARLY WITH WORDS

Bad words and aggressive acts are apt to persist as long as upset feelings smolder. In order to deal constructively with anger throughout our lives and form close, fulfilling adult relationships, we have to be able to describe our feelings and pinpoint our needs. Potentially destructive emotions often melt away with a sense of healing relief when we are able to express them to an understanding spouse, parent, friend, or therapist. Teaching our children how to talk about frustration and anger is one of our most important jobs as parents, and, often, the larger part of that task is to teach *ourselves* how to listen.

Active listening, as described by Thomas Gordon in his book *Parent Effectiveness Training* (McKay, 1970), means to relate back to the child the feeling that seems to underlie the hitting and name-calling. Thus we say, "You looked angry when you hit David," or "You must have been *upset* about something when you teased Lisa." And when Beth spins out a tale of woe about what happened at Larry's house, report back to her the *emotional essence* of what she said: "You were really frustrated that everyone else could reach the rope ladder but you couldn't." Finally, even when a youngster is raging at us, we can sometimes keep our cool sufficiently to reply, "You are really disappointed that I won't let you go play at Marcia's house right now." Active listening is a valuable means of inviting children (and adults) to explore their feelings if they want to, without our taking over responsibility for their problem. Active listening not only conveys our understanding of the child's predicament, but also teaches the vocabulary that will eventually enable them to talk about their own feelings. For more about teaching the vocabulary of emotions, see Emotional Awareness, p. 247.

Play to children is like therapy to adults, and thus it is often through play and imagination that children first express their feelings. Some parents discourage youngsters from naming a punching bag after baby Jennifer or smashing a blob of Play-Dough named brother Barney, for fear that loss of control and actual physical harm might follow. In fact, imaginatively blowing off steam teaches the means of *limiting* expressions of anger and thereby *decreases* the likelihood of actual violence.

Games of imaginative anger not only help children express their feelings, but also help them differentiate between thoughts and actions. Small children fear that what they think in anger will actually happen. That's pretty scary if the wish that "Mom would go away and leave me alone" holds the silent threat that she really might disappear for good. Imaginative games, especially when played with the emotional support of parents who participate as fellow actors or as an appreciative audience, help children experience the fact that their play-acted fantasies don't really happen.

One mother relates how her son acts his negative feelings out with make-believe:

> I encourage Danny, age three, to use his little toy people and make up plays about situations I know are difficult for him. Once he gets into the spirit of the thing, he has a wonderful time. He tells me the front door is locked so the Mommy can't go to work. If the Mom and Dad want to go out for the evening, he sends them to their room instead. He tells them they have to eat with their fingers, and that they can't eat at all unless their hands are dirty.

When one brother and sister started discussing good-humoredly how they would like to get rid of each other, it sounded like a page from Edgar Allan Poe. Marie, age five, giggled, "I would chop Lee up into little pieces and decorate a cake with them. Then everyone would sit around and sing, 'I'm happy Lee is dead.' " Lee's version was equally gruesome. But having so vividly expressed the intensity of their feelings, they got along more smoothly in the following days.

Children may need our help in transferring their new vocabulary from play to real life. Thus, during the moment of annoyance, or once Daniel, age four, has calmed down, Mother may say *for* him, "I hate staying inside when it's raining," or "I wish you'd never go away and leave me with a sitter." At age five, self-control is still precarious, but is on the increase in many realms. Angry outbursts still occur, of course, but not *every* minor incident triggers one. Our five-year-olds are learning that they can *choose* how to express anger. Mom points out to Kier that he can take a big breath and *decide* what to do next. Sasha discovered that she can hold back a tantrum if she makes ugly faces. Sonya likes to dictate to her mom and then illustrate in her "Angry Book" events that upset her.

HOW TO STOP UNACCEPTABLE AGGRESSION

Early on, we may put up with our little ones when they lash out at us in anger, but there comes a point when it's time for them to learn an alternative. If repeated isolation or time-outs aren't sufficient to stop physical aggression, parents may resort to punishment with physical pain. When Tina pinches, Mom manipulates her hand so she then pinches herself. If Barry pinches his dad, Dad pulls on his hair until he lets go. Karen gets a finger flick on the chin for biting. (More than one parent has accidentally bitten back much harder than intended, so it's not a recommended technique.) When youngsters hit, some parents grasp little wrists and tussle hand-in-hand while energy lasts. Others offer to play "hitting back," warning clearly that each time the parent will hit a little harder than the child. Most youngsters tire quickly of *this* game. When attempts to divert spitting at people to spitting in the bathroom sink failed, one mother resorted to finger flicks on the chin, and another made her son sit in a corner until he had accumulated a tablespoon worth of weaponry in a medicine cup. It took a surprisingly long time, and didn't have to be repeated.

One mother terminates inappropriate language merely by intoning, "If you don't know what that word means, don't use it." When explanations, isolation, and time-outs fail to end the unacceptable language of a five-year-old, more than one parent has resorted to swiping a bar of soap across clenched teeth.

For more information about stopping aggression between youngsters, see pp. 363 and 366 and for more about changing inappropriate behavior, see Changing Behavior: The Use of Rewards and Punishment, p. 374. If efforts to understand, redirect, and limit excessive aggression are not reasonably successful, a consultation with a therapist can help point the direction toward further solutions.

BOSSINESS

Just as name-calling is a level above hitting as a form of aggression, bossiness is another, more sophisticated way to gain power over others. With this technique, youngsters ally themselves with more adult behavior, copying the way *we* necessarily boss *them* around. We sympathize with the lack of control they have over their own lives and thus may tolerate a certain amount of bossiness, especially if playmates are able to work things out fairly evenly among themselves with an acceptable amount of hassle. But if the play of our four- and five-year-olds erupts into constant turmoil as youngsters struggle for supremacy, we look for other alternatives.

The place to begin may be with ourselves. Do we allow our children the independence they are capable of? Do we encourage older siblings to use too much parentlike authority over younger ones? Playing games of parent-child role reversal for a few minutes several times a week helps many youngsters feel less resentful of the times we are necessarily in charge.

Discuss the ins and outs of power. When her friends are *not* around, Jenny's mother points out that they may resent her excessive bossiness and therefore not want to play with her as often. To Adrianna's mother, bossiness indicates leadership potential, but she tells her daughter that if she is going to boss others successfully, she must take their wishes into consideration.

Some parents arrange for youngsters to have a variety of older *and* younger playmates, so they experience both sides of the power line. Games like Simon Says and Red Light–Green Light give all children an opportunity to be in control, as does a kitchen timer set for fifteen-minute ''turns to be in charge.'' Finally, if the power struggles become excessive, it may be time to direct youngsters to separate activities for awhile, or send them off to different locales for a few minutes break from the pressure of cooperation.

WITHDRAWAL

FEARS

As our children move out into the busy complex world, there are more and more potential hazards. Youngsters are appropriately fearful of exuberant dogs as big as themselves, and understandably frightened after falling off a swing. But often their panic seems to spring from nowhere: Suddenly they become terrified by a distant airplane, the vacuum cleaner, the little bug on the sidewalk, and imaginary monsters. Unfortunately, they rarely become so fearful of the things we want them to avoid, such as streets and hot stoves. In trying to understand their dread, it helps to consider six likely origins of fears.

Fear Resulting from a Painful Experience

When a child has had a painful experience such as falling in the bathtub, treatment involves a very gradual reintroduction, with praise and maybe even tangible rewards for each brave step. At nine months, Ivan liked dogs and slept comfortably with a visiting one. At thirteen months, he was knocked down by a large barking dog. He became terrified even of little puppies, and he'd tremble and cry even if he saw a dog on TV. I just picked him up and held him whenever a dog was around. When he turned two, we got two puppies, and for a month he was in a panic whenever they were out of their enclosure. Gradually he became used to them. Then I bought some *long* dog biscuits that he could feed to them. At two and one-half, Ivan saw a large dog while we were out walking. He told his big brother to go pat the dog, and after observing that it really was safe, Ivan patted it too.

Painful experiences can be in the realm of the physical or the imaginary world. One little girl of two and one-half became fearful of getting into the family car. Months later, with improved language ability, she explained she was afraid her car would crash again. Her parents pointed out that *her* car had never crashed. But the little girl insisted it had. Accepting her fear, the parents said she must have had a bad dream about being in a car accident and it must have been very frightening. Assured that it was a dream of the past, and that her parents would drive carefully, her fear subsided.

Sometimes, in the effort to respond to our children's distress, we unintentionally increase their fear. For example, when Don, age one, closed the door on his finger, his mother consoled him, then led him off to another activity. But Ryan's mother consoled her and then took her back to the door and helped her close it painlessly. Don associates the doors with pain; Ryan associates it with pain *and* successful control. She will likely reapproach the door more easily than Don.

Fears Learned from Parents

If we ourselves are terrified of creepy-crawly things, heights, or drowning, it may be all to the good if we can arrange for other adults to introduce our children to insects, climbing structures, or swimming lessons. Just because we have our own fears, we needn't necessarily pass them on to our youngsters.

Misunderstanding of Physical Laws

Two-year-olds perceive the physical world very differently from the way we do. To them, a vacuum cleaner that can wisk up dust balls, can gobble up kids as well. We can demonstrate that even the teddy bear is too big to fit up the hose, but it may take repeated demonstrations and *time* before scientific proof is given more credence than magic.

Misunderstanding of Language

One little girl became terrified whenever the family car headed for a bridge, and only later did her parents learn she feared they would "dive over" rather than "drive over." In *The Magic Years* (Charles Scribner's Sons, 1968), Selma Fraiberg mentions a little boy who was terrified of the upcoming family airplane trip until reassured that it was OK that he himself couldn't "fly." Given the complexity and color of the language we speak, be alert for possible confusions.

Fears That Express Internal Conflict

Children may suddenly become frightened of a routine sound or object, *when they unconsciously choose it as a symbol to represent internal worries*. For example, the noisy coffee grinder may come to symbolize the loud, angry parent. For more about understanding and working with such fears, see Nightmares and Scary Creatures, p. 68, and Competition Between Parent and Child, p. 225.

Fears of Unknown Origin

Despite our detective work, the origin of many concerns will remain a mystery. No matter how ridiculous such fears seem to us, they are as intense to the child as our fear of toddlers' dashing into the street. Thus, our sympathy is in order, and sometimes we can help youngsters gain some measure of direct or indirect control over what frightens them. Mom warns Jason to go to another room before she turns on the Osterizer. Ben became terrified of the animal pictures on his wall, so his mother removed them for several months. During thunderstorms, Alice and her mother clap their hands to drown out the frightening noise. Dad gave Scott a fly swatter and helped him kill the spider that frightened him. Because he was afraid of a loud buzzer at school, Andrew's mother let him experiment with the car horn. And Alix, who became terrified of wolves, was reassured by having a small toy wolf, which was obviously harmless. If our efforts bring no relief, time generally will. However, if children's fears intensify rather than diminish over the course of some months, or if little ones become frightened of more and more things, consider seeking the assistance of an expert in child behavior.

SHYNESS AND PASSIVITY

Clarify Parental Objectives

Anyone in his right mind would be cautious if surrounded by unfamiliar giants and unpredictable playmates, as our youngsters routinely are. Some parents mistake prudent caution for unacceptable shyness. However, it is also true that some youngsters are innately more cautious than others, and need more time to warm up to new situations and new people.

Furthermore, while some youngsters are doers from the day they first crawl, always the hub around which the action rotates, others tend more to be observers: They watch and enter in only when they are sure they understand what's going on. These divergent personality traits tend to last a lifetime.

In general, we tolerate the common shyness of two-year-olds, just as we tolerate a number of their other less social characteristics. In the coming years, we can help our shy children develop self-confidence in many other spheres besides the social arena (see Desired Qualities, Self-confidence, p. 242). As needed, we can teach some self-assertion skills, and when the time seems appropriate, some rules of polite encounter (see Desired Qualities, Politeness, p. 301). Equipped with such awareness, most youngsters are noticeably more at ease in social situations, especially familiar ones, by age five. Patience plays a major role.

Shyness and passivity take two basic forms. The first is shyness around other adults, which becomes an issue when we want to leave the children with other caretakers, or when they are meeting unfamiliar adults, especially relatives. The second is passivity around other children, in which one child may tend to be taken advantage of by others.

Arranging a less demanding social environment where quiet children feel naturally comfortable can be far more conducive to social growth than letting them struggle in situations that are overwhelming. They may do better with younger playmates, or in a smaller nursery school.

If youngsters are ill at ease with unfamiliar relatives or family friends, a trip to the zoo, rather than a visit at home, removes pressure for verbal interaction. Or, let children invite a friend of their own on such visits. Some parents make a point of arriving early for birthday parties, so shy youngsters can adjust to the scene before the crowd arrives. Some children want to stop by only long enough to drop off the present, and others will sit on the parental lap for the duration of the party.

Early on, adults rather than our children may need instruction. One mother tells her overenthusiastic friends to sit on the floor and soon Stephanie, eighteen months, will come to investigate. When Lori ducks behind her father's knee, he introduces, "This is Lori, she feels shy right now." But when Robbie was almost five and still very shy, his parents chose a coveted toy and let him earn points toward acquiring it. His first points were for saying "Goodbye" at the end of a visit, and then for "Hello" on arrival. Later he could earn extras points for eye contact. Gradually, he became more confident and socially at ease. When Allen, age five, balked again at attending the usual family gathering, his frustrated mother declared he could either come in and greet his relatives or sit in the car by himself. (She correctly judged that he wouldn't choose the latter.) Rather than a mere downcast "Hi" to Grandma and Granddad, he not only greeted everyone, but shook hands as well!

Those of us with shy children don't have to worry about what to do when our youngsters attack others, but we do have to decide how to handle the situation when our children are threatened or harmed by others. There are four possible responses to aggression from others.

1. *Withdraw from the conflict.* Our peace-loving side may wish our children would withdraw when other youngsters start to fight. What truck is worth a goose-egg? Unfortunately, children who succeed through aggression become more aggressive. In addition, they learn *which* children they can take advantage of. Therefore, instructing our children to withdraw from every conflict teaches them to become the victims of aggression.

2. *Seek help from adults.* We restrain the hand that would snatch tiny Michael's cookie or smash him on the head, and our little ones instinctively toddle to us for protection. But if, as the years go by, we handle all their conflicts, they will never learn to resolve them alone. Gradually, we have to change our role.

3. *Verbal defense.* Even two-year-olds with limited vocabularies can often be encouraged to defend themselves successfully with "No! Don't!" But just as determined children don't always listen to *our* verbal commands, aggressive tots won't necessarily respond to their playmates' words.

4. *Limited physical defense.* Because two-year-olds understand the concept of taking turns, some parents reason that they can understand the difference between hitting first and hitting back. Thus, they discourage the former by isolation and encourage the latter with discussion and praise. One two-year-old learned to push the aggressor away. Parents find that young children *can* distinguish between initiating versus responding to aggression.

Many parents have discovered that passive youngsters don't need us to fight for them as much as they need us to teach them how to stand up for themselves. The place to begin is often to practice ahead of time with parents. After being intimidated by a neighbor child's angry growl, Eric and his mother practiced growling. Dad instructs Sally to hold on tight when he tugs at her toy. When Mom lifts her hand in mock battle, Darryl practices saying "Don't hit me," and when she shoves, he pushes back. Most youngsters thoroughly enjoy such practice sessions.

Once back in the real world, youngsters may still need some coaching: "Go get back the doll that Wendy took!" or "Tell David it is your turn." Because Rebecca has had ample opportunity to practice, she must either try to stand up for herself against playmates, or go to her room.

Parents take various approaches with the verbal attacks children will encounter. One little girl was taught to say to *herself*, "No matter what you do or say, I am still a good person today." When her son complains that he was called a crybaby or stupid, his mother replies, "I don't think you're stupid, do you?" or "I think it is OK to cry when you are upset. What other people say doesn't matter." And another mother playfully practices name-calling with her daughter and finds she is less sensitive to the words of her playmates.

LACK OF FRIENDS

Several five-year-olds in our study complained repeatedly that they didn't have any friends. There are several important factors to consider in evaluating such a complaint.

> *What is a friend?* How children define the term "friend" makes a difference in how they feel. Instead of saying, "I don't have anyone to play with now," Randy, age five, says, "I don't have any friends." Diana, age five, thinks that whoever isn't her "best" friend isn't a friend at all. From time to time her mom tells her that people can like lots of different friends just as they like lots of different foods.

> *Changing neighborhoods.* Today's neighborhoods are no longer packed with a variety of youngsters among whom there are bound to be playmates of similar age and interests. Not only are there fewer children in each household and each neighborhood than there were generations ago, but many of those who do live nearby are in child care. Indeed, youngsters who have several friends within walking distance are fortunate. Children are more and more dependent on adult

transportation for the development and maintenance of friendships, many of which are formed in school or elsewhere rather than with kids down the block. Thus children may need our help in making and maintaining friendships.

Composition of playgroups. A youngster who feels left out in one social situation may thrive in another.

Possible difficulties in social adjustment. If a four- or especially a five-year-old hasn't made at least *one* friend, despite adequate opportunity to develop friendships in various circumstances with different children, discuss the matter with teachers or your pediatrician.

Bibliography

COMMUNICATION TECHNIQUES

Ginott, Haim G. *Between Parent and Child*. New York: Macmillan Co., 1965. How to understand and talk to children more clearly.

Gordon, Thomas. *P.E.T. Parent Effectiveness Training* New York. New American Library, 1975. Excellent for improving communication with children as well as adults.

Simon, Sidney. *Caring, Feeling, Touching*. Niles, Ill.: Argus Communications, 1976. The importance of touch and how to assure it as youngsters grow.

CHILD-CARE CONCERNS

Alloway, Thomas, et al, eds. *Attachment Behavior: Advances in the Study of Communications and Affect*. New York: Plenum Press, 1975.

Caldwell, Bettye M.; Wright, Charlene M.; Honig, Alice; and Tannerbarum, Jordan. "Infant Day Care and Attachment." In *Social Issues in Developmental Psychology*. Edited by Helen Bee. New York: Harper & Row, 1974.

Fraiberg, Selma. *Every Child's Birthright: In Defense of Mothering*. New York: Bantam Books, 1978. The importance and characteristics of high-quality child care.

Robinson, Halbert B., and Robinson, Nancy M. "Longitudinal Development of Very Young Children in a Comprehensive Day Care Program." In *Social Issues in Developmental Psychology*. Edited by Helen Bee. New York: Harper & Row, 1974.

Yarrow, Marian Radke; Scott, Phyllis; de Leeuw, Louise; and Heinig, Christine. "Child Rearing in Families of Working and Non-Working Mothers." In *Social Issues in Developmental Psychology*. Edited by Helen Bee. New York: Harper & Row, 1974.

DAILY LIVING TIPS

Lansky, Vicki. *Best Practical Parenting Tips*. Deephaven, Minn.: Meadowbrook Press, 1980. Many practical hints collected from parents.

Pinkham, Mary Ellen, and Higginbotham, Pearl. *Mary Ellen's Best of Helpful Hints*. New York: Warner B. Lansky Books, 1979. Helps and timesavers for home and children.

DEATH

Brown, Margaret Wise. *The Dead Bird*. Reading, Mass.: Addison-Wesley Publishing Co., 1965. Children find a dead bird and bury it with gentle concern.

Grollman, Earl. *Talking about Death: a Dialogue between Parent and Child*. Boston: Beacon Press, 1976. Designed to help children deal with the normal, but conflicting emotions which accompany the death of a relative.

Kubler-Ross, Elisabeth. *A Letter to a Child with Cancer*. Available from Shanti Nilaya, P.O. Box 2396, Escondido, Calif., 92025, 1979. Although written to a cancer patient, this is a hopeful answer to any child's question "Why do people die?"

DESIRED QUALITIES: INDEPENDENCE, HONESTY, CONCERN FOR OTHERS

Berman, Eleanor. *The Cooperating Family, How Your Children Can Help Manage the Household for Their Good as Well as Your Own*. Englewood Cliffs, N.J.: Prentice-Hall, 1977. Discusses older children, but principles apply to younger as well.

Brearley, Molly, and Hitchfield, Elizabeth. *A Guide to Reading Piaget*. New York: Schocken Books, 1966.

Cole, William. "Friday's Child—Your Loving, Giving Toddler." *Parents Magazine*, June 1980. On the innate inclinations of youngsters to be concerned for others.

Duska, Ronald, and Whelan, Mariellen. *Moral Development, A Guide to Piaget and Kohlberg*. New York: Paulist Press, 1975. A short book, slow reading, but extremely useful in clarifying how children perceive and develop moral values, especially honesty.

Gould, Shirley. *How to Raise an Independent Child*. New York: St. Martin's Press, 1979.

Katz, Lilian G. "The Truth About Lying." *Parent's Magazine*, Jan. 1981.

Weinstein, Grace W. *Children and Money: A Parent's Guide*. New York: Charterhouse, 1975. Basic objectives and practicalities of money management for children.

DISCIPLINE TECHNIQUES

Dobson, James. *Dare to Discipline*. New York: Bantam Books, 1977.

Dreikurs, Rudolf. *Children the Challenge*. New York: Hawthorne Books, 1964. Theoretical basis for using choices and logical consequences, with practical examples included.

Hammer, David, and Drabman, Ronald S. "Child Discipline, What We Know and What We Can Recommend." *Pediatric Nursing* 7 (May/June 1981).

Marshall, Bill C., and Marshall, Christina Mae. *Better Parents, Better Children: A Workbook for a More Successful Family in 21 Days*. Maplewood, N.J.: Hammond, 1979.

Norton, G. Ron. *Parenting*. Englewood Cliffs, N.J.: Prentice-Hall, 1977. Excellent description of how to use behavior modification effectively.

EMOTIONAL DEVELOPMENT

Berne, Eric. *What Do You Say after You Say Hello? The Psychology of Human Destiny*. New York: Bantam Books, 1973. The effects of childhood perceptions on adult personality.

Brazelton, T. Berry. *Infants and Mothers: Differences in Development*. New York: Dell Publishing Co., 1983. Contrasts the differences between average, quiet, and active babies.

Fraiberg, Selma H. *The Magic Years: Understanding and Handling the Problems of Early Childhood*. New York: Charles Scribner's Sons, 1959. A wonderful introduction to how children see the adult world.

Kaplan, Louise J. *Oneness and Separateness: From Infant to Individual*. New York: Simon & Schuster, Touchstone, 1978. A sensitive description of a young child's growth toward independence and consequent effects on the family.

Kennedy, Wallace A. *Child Psychology*. Englewood Cliffs, N.J.: Prentice Hall, 1971.

Klimek, Paula. "Befriending Our Children." *New Age Journal* 5, no. 6 (Jan. 1979): 30–45.

Nicholson, Luree, and Torbet, Laura. *How to Fight Fair with Your Kids and Win*. New York: Harcourt Brace Jovanovich, 1980. A practical guidebook for handling the inevitable frustrations of living together.

Young, Leontine. *Life among the Giants: A Child's-Eye View of the Grown-Up World*. New York: McGraw-Hill Book Co., 1965. Pap., 1971.

GAMES AND ACTIVITIES

Fluegelman, Andrew. *The New Games Book*. Garden City, N.Y.: Doubleday & Co. Inc., 1976. Describes many physically active, non-competitive mes.

Gregor, Carol. *Working Out Together: A Complete Fitness Program for Partners*. New York: Berkeley Books, 1983. Doing calisthenics in pairs. This book for adults describes useful physical exercise for children as well.

Hoban, Russell. *Nothing to Do*. New York: Harper & Row, 1964. A delightful children's story about how to find things to do.

Leishman, Katie. "The Music Makers." *Working Mother*, March 1980. Choosing good-quality musical instruments for young children.

"Sammy Is Climbing His New PVC Trapezoid." *Sunset Magazine*, May 1981. How to construct your own indoor-outdoor climbing structure.

GENERAL

Ames, Louise Bates, and Ilg, Frances L. *Your Two-Year-Old Terrible or Tender*. Gesell Institute of Child Development. New York: A Dell Publishing Co., Delta, 1980.

Dodson, Fitzhugh. *How to Father*. New York: New American Library, Signet,

1974. Similar to *How to Parent* but geared specifically to fathers; covers through adolescence.

———. *How to Parent*. New York: New American Library, Signet, 1970. Detailed yet easy to read; an excellent introduction to physical, emotional, and intellectual development in the early years.

Ilg, Frances L., and Ames, Louise Bates. *Child Behavior from Birth to Ten*. New York: Harper & Row, 1955.

Kelly, Marguerite, and Parsons, Elia. *The Mother's Almanac*. Garden City, N.Y.: Doubleday & Co., 1975. Practical advice for daily living plus many activities for children.

Olness, Karen. *Raising Happy Healthy Children*. Wayzata, Minn.: Meadowbrook Press, 1977.

Spock, Benjamin. *Baby and Child Care*. New York: Simon & Schuster, Pocket Books, 1976. The updated version of the old standby gives advice on both medical and behavioral concerns.

Whiting, Beatrice. *Six Cultures: Studies of Child Rearing*. New York: Wiley, 1963.

HEALTH AND SAFETY

Arena, Jay, and Bacher, Miriam. *Child Safety Is No Accident*. Durham, N.C.: Duke University Press, 1978. How to avoid the most common childhood accidents and injuries.

Campbell, Claire. *Nursing Diagnosis and Intervention in Nursing Practice*. New York: Wiley Medical Publications, 1978.

Frazier, Claude A. *Parents' Guide to Allergy in Children*. New York: Grosset & Dunlap, 1978.

Green, Martin I. *A Sigh of Relief, The First-Aid Handbook for Childhood Emergencies*. New York: Bantam Books, 1977. A quick, concise, easy-to-understand reference.

Kilmon, Carol, and Helpin, Mark. "Update on Dentistry for Children." *Pediatric Nursing* 7 (Sept./Oct. 1981):41–44.

Pantell, Robert, et al. *Taking Care of Your Child: A Parent's Guide to Medical Care*. Reading, Mass.: Addison-Wesley Publishing Co., 1977. Step-by-step information on what to do when children get sick and when to call the doctor.

Rader, Nancy; Bausano, Mary; and Richards, John. "On the Nature of the Visual-Cliff Avoidance Response in Human Infants." *Child Development*, 51 (March 1980):61–68.

Simonton, O. Carl. *Getting Well Again*. J.P. Tarcher, Inc., 9110 Sunset Blvd., Los Angeles, Calif. 90069, 1978. Though this book deals specifically with cancer, it clarifies the relationship between emotions and illness and tells how to use mental visualization as an aid to healing.

Surveyer, Judith A; Halpren, Judith. "Age Related Burn Injuries and Their Prevention." *Pediatric Nursing* 7 (Sept./Oct. 1981):29–34.

Vaughan, McKay, and Behrman, Nelson. *Textbook of Pediatrics*. Philadelphia: W.B. Saunders, 1979.

White, Mary K. "Breastfeeding and Dental Caries." *La Leche League News* 20, May/June 1978.

————. "More on Breastfeeding and Dental Caries." *La Leche League News* 21, March/April 1979. 9616 Minneapolis Ave., Franklin Park, Illinois 60131.

Wong, Donna L. "The Paper Doll Technique." *Pediatric Nursing* 7 (Nov./Dec. 1981):39–40.

Wynder, Ernst L., ed. *The Book of Health: A Complete Guide to Making Health Last a Lifetime.* New York: American Health Foundation, Franklin Watts, 1981.

HYPERACTIVITY

Brazelton, T. Terry. *Toddlers and Parents.* New York: Dell Publishing Co., 1974. In addition to providing a chapter about a hyperactive toddler, this book discusses working and single parents, sibling rivalry, and the general struggle of children toward independence.

Feingold, Ben F. *Why Your Child is Hyperactive.* New York: Random House, 1974. Hyperactivity as an allergy to certain natural and artificial chemicals in foods.

Rapp, Doris J. *Allergies and the Hyperactive Child.* New York: Simon & Schuster, Cornerstone Library, 1979.

Rosenthal, Joseph. *Hazy. . ? Crazy. . ? and/or Lazy. . ? The Maligning of Children with Learning Disabilities.* Kaiser-Permanente Medical Center, 280 W. MacArthur Blvd., Oakland, Calif. 94611, 1973. Hyperactivity and learning disabilities as inborn variations in brain function.

Smith, Lendon. *Improving Your Child's Behavior Chemistry.* New York: Simon & Schuster Pocket Books, 1977.

INTELLECTUAL DEVELOPMENT

Board of Cooperative Educational Services of Nassau County. *While You're at It; 200 Ways to Help Children Learn.* Reston, Va.: Reston Publishing Co., 1976. Educational activities that can easily accompany parental housework.

Cowan, Philip A. *Piaget: With Feeling, Cognitive, Social and Emotional Dimension.* New York: Holt, Rinehart & Winston, 1978.

Gerber, Magda. *Resources for Infant Educarers.* Resources for Infant Educarer, 1550 Murray Circle, Los Angeles, Calif. 90026, 1979.

Hendricks, Gay, and Roberts, Thomas. *The Second Centering Book.* Englewood Cliffs, N.J.: Prentice-Hall, 1977. Activities for children in communication, fantasy, intuition, and meditation.

Jackson, Jane, and Jackson, Joseph. *Infant Culture, The First Year of Life—What Your Baby Can See, Hear, Feel, Taste, and Learn.* New York: New American Library, Plume, 1978. An easy-to-read compilation of research findings.

Montessori, Maria. *The Montessori Method.* Translated from Italian by Anne E. George. Schocken Books, 1964. On the evolution of Montessori's work and the importance of developing the five basic senses as a first step in intellectual growth.

Moore, Raymond. *Better Late than Early.* New York: Reader's Digest-McGraw Hill Book Co., 1977. The importance of waiting to teach the complex task of reading until children are old enough to learn it with ease.

"Museums: Examining Old Objects Inspired New Ideas." *Gifted Children*

Newsletter, 1, no. 8. Gifted and Talented Publications, 530 University Ave., Palo Alto, Calif., 94301, Oct. 1980.

Pushaw, David. *Teach Your Child to Talk, a Parent's Guide.* New York: Dantree Press, 1976. Activities for encouraging language development, from birth to school age.

Silva, Jose. *The Silva Mind Control Method.* New York: Simon & Schuster, Pocket Books, 1978. Based on a widely taught course for adults in the development of intuition and psychic awareness, the techniques are adaptable to children.

NUTRITION

Bowes, Anna de Palanter; Church, Charles; and Church, Helen Nicols. *Food Values of Portions Commonly Used.* 10th ed. Philadelphia: J.B. Lippincott Co., 1966.

Duarte, Harriet, et al. *Breastfeeding–1:1 Counseling.* Childbirth Education League of the Monterey Peninsula, Inc., Box 6628, Carmel, Calif. 93921, 1980. Troubleshooting problems in breastfeeding.

La Leche League International. *The Womanly Art of Breast Feeding.* Franklin Park, Ill.: 1963. The most widely used handbook on breastfeeding.

National Academy of Sciences. *Recommended Dietary Allowance.* 9th ed. Washington, D.C., 1980.

Pipes, Peggy L. *Nutrition in Infancy and Childhood.* 2nd ed. St. Louis: C.V. Mosby Co., 1981.

Pryor, Karen. *Nursing Your Baby.* New York: Harper & Row, 1963; Simon & Schuster, Pocket Books, 1973.

Robertson, Laurel, et al. *Laurel's Kitchen: A Handbook for Vegetarian Cookery and Nutrition.* Berkeley, Calif., Nilgiri Press, 1976. An excellent reference and cookbook for those who do not eat meat.

Williams, Sue R. *Nutrition and Diet Therapy.* 4th ed. St. Louis: C.V. Mosby Co., 1981.

PARENTING: THE PERSONAL EXPERIENCE

Faber, Adele, and Mazlish, Elaine. *Liberated Parents–Liberated Children.* New York: Avon Books, 1975. A parent support group in action.

Heffner, Elaine. *Mothering: The Emotional Experience of Motherhood after Freud and Feminism.* New York: Doubleday & Co., 1980. A look at the double binds in modern parenting.

Marzollo, Jean. "When Can Parents Be Alone?" *Parent's Magazine* 57, Oct. 1982.

McBride, Angela Barron. *The Growth and Development of Mothers.* New York: Harper & Row, 1973.

Pines, Alaya M., and Aronson, Elliot. *Burnout: From Tedium to Personal Growth.* New York: Macmillan Publishing Co., Free Press, 1981.

SEX EDUCATION

Bernstein, Anne. *The Flight of the Stork: What Children Really Want to Know about Sex and When and How to Tell Them.* New York: Dell Publishing Co, 1980.

A delightful and informative account of what children can understand at different ages.

Hennepin County Attorney's Office. *Child Sexual Abuse Prevention Project: An Educational Program for Children.* Sexual Assault Services, Office of the County Attorney, 2000 Hennepin Government Center, Minneapolis, Minn. 55487. A non-threatening course for home or school use, to help young children protect themselves from inappropriate advances.

The Study Group of New York. *Children and Sex: The Parents Speak.* New York: Facts On File, 1983. How contemporary parents handle the questions and issues that arise in daily living.

SIBLING RIVALRY

Fishel, Elizabeth. *Sisters: Love and Rivalry Inside the Family and Beyond,* New York: Wm. Morrow & Co., 1979. From interviews with sisters both famous and obscure, Fishel reflects on this fascinating family relationship.

Hoban, Russell. *A Birthday for Francis.* New York: Harper & Row, 1968. A children's story that sympathetically portrays the difficulty of enduring a sibling's birthday.

McDermott, John E. Jr. *Raising Cain (and Abel too): The Parents' Book of Sibling Rivalry.* New York: Harper & Row, Wyden Books, 1980. Stages in sibling rivalry from birth through adolescence.

SINGLE PARENTS, DIVORCED PARENTS, AND STEP-PARENTS

The following titles are excellent books and self-explanatory.

Galper, Miriam. *Co-Parenting. A Sourcebook for the Separated and Divorced Family.* Philadelphia: Running Press, 1978.

Gardner, Richard A. *The Boys and Girls Book about Divorce.* New York: Science House, 1971. With an Introduction for Parents.

Grollman, Earl A. *Talking Divorce: A Dialogue Between Parent and Child.* Boston: Beacon Press, 1975.

Hope, Karol. *Momma Handbook: The Sourcebook for Single Mothers.* New York: New American Library, 1976.

Klein, Carole. *The Single Parent Experience.* New York: Avon Books, 1973.

Visher, Emily, and Visher, John. *How to Win as a Step-Family.* New York: Dembner Books, 1982.

Wallerstein, Judith, and Kelly, Joan B. *Surviving the Breakup: How Children and Parents Cope with Divorce.* New York: Basic Books, 1980.

SLEEP

Anders, Thomas; Emde, Robert; and Parmalee, Arthur, eds. *A Manual of Standardized Terminology, Techniques and Criteria for Scoring of States of Sleep and Wakefulness in Newborn Infants.* U.C.L.A. Brain Information Service. Los Angeles: BRI Publications. NINDS Neurological Information Network, 1971.

Apley, John, and Mackeith, Ronald. "Sleep Problems." *International Journal of Early Childhood* 1 (1969):34–39.

Bax, M.C.O. "Sleep Disturbances in the Young Child." *British Medical Journal* no. 6224 (1980):1177–1179.

Brazelton, T. Berry. "Why Your Baby Won't Sleep." *Redbook,* Oct. 1978.

Caudill, William, and Plath, D.W. "Who Sleeps by Whom? Parent-Child Involvement in Urban Japanese Families." *Psychiatry* 29 (1966):344–366.

Coons, Susan, and Guilleminault, Christian. "Development of Sleep-Wake Patterns and Non-Rapid Eye Movement Sleep Stages During the First Six Months of Life in Normal Infants." *Pediatrics* 69, no. 6 (June 1982):793–798.

Hanks, Cheryl, and Rebelsky, Freda. "Mommy and the Midnight Visitor: A Study of Occasional Co-Sleeping." *Psychiatry* 40 no. 3 (Aug. 1977):277–280.

Harper, R. M., et al. "Temporal Sequencing in Sleep and Waking States During the First Six Months of Life." *Experimental Neurology* 72 (1981):294–307.

Hoban, Russell. *Bedtime for Francis.* New York: Harper & Row, 1960. The true-to-life tale of a youngster who procrastinates at bedtime.

Kales, Anthony. ed. *Sleep Physiology & Pathology: A Symposium.* Philadelphia: J.B. Lippincott Co., 1969.

Kaplan, Stuart, and Poznanski, Elva. "Child Psychiatric Patients Who Share a Bed with a Parent." *Journal of the American Academy of Child Psychiatry* 13 (March 1974):344–356.

Luce, Gay, and Segal, Julius. *Insomnia.* Garden City, N.Y.: Doubleday & Co., 1969.

Myers, Wayne A. "Clinical Consequences of Chronic Primal Scene Exposure." *Psychoanalytic Quarterly* 48, no. 1 (1979):1–26.

Oleinick, M. S., et al. "Early Socialization Experiences and Intrafamilial Environment." *Archives of General Psychiatry* 15 (1966):344–353.

Ozturk, Maulla, and Ozturk, Orhan M. "Thumbsucking and Falling Asleep." *British Journal of Medical Psychiatry* 50, no. 1 (March 1977):95–103.

Pagins, Naomi, and Schachter, Joseph. "A Study of Sleep Behavior in 2-Year-Old Children." *Journal of the American Academy of Child Psychiatry* 10, no. 3 (1971):464–480.

Perkins, J. *Possible Causes of Crying and Frequent Nighttime Nursings.* Minneapolis: La Leche League, 1972.

Rosenfeld, A. A., et al. "Sleeping Patterns in Upper-Middle-Class Families When the Child Awakens Ill or Frightened." *Archives of General Psychiatry* 39, no. 8 (Aug. 1982):943–947.

Schumann, Mary Jean. "Neuromuscular Relaxation—A Method for Inducing Sleep in Young Children." *Pediatric Nursing* 7 (Sept./Oct. 1981):9–13.

Thevenin, Tine. *The Family Bed—An Age Old Concept in Child Rearing.* La Leche League: Minneapolis, 1976.

U.S. Dept. of Health, Education and Welfare. *Parent Ratings of Behavioral Pattern of Children, United States.* National Center for Health Statistics, series II, no. 108 (Nov. 1971).

SPIRITUAL DEVELOPMENT

"Babies and Toddlers at Church." *Leader/Teacher Manual for Sunday School and Church Time.* Glendale, Calif.: G.L. Publications, 1979.

Fowler, James W. *Stages of Faith: The Psychology of Human Development and the Quest for Meaning.* San Francisco: Harper & Row, 1981.

Hunter, Edith. *Conversations with Children*. Boston: Beacon Press, 1961.

Jones, Olive M. *Inspired Children*. New York: Harper & Brothers, 1933. How children use personal prayer in daily living.

Sanfrod, Agnes. *Let's Believe*. New York: Harper & Row, 1954. A modern presentation for children of the practical uses of prayer.

TOILET TRAINING AND BEDWETTING

Azrin, Nathan, and Besalel, Victoria. *A Parent's Guide to Bedwetting Control: A Step-by-Step Method*. New York: Simon & Schuster, 1979. A detailed and useful book.

Azrin, Nathan, and Foxx, Frichard: *Toilet Training in Less than a Day*. New York: Simon & Schuster, Pocket Books, 1974. A multifaceted and practical approach, though many parents found the title proved overly optimistic.

Narveson, Jean Wallace. "A Young Mother's Story. Last-Resort Toilet Training: What Worked for Us May Work for You." *Redbook*, Aug. 1981. Using rewards with a 3½-year-old.

Parenting Center. *Toilet Training Your Child*. P.O. Box 471, Brea, Calif. 92621. A pamphlet with practical tips.

Zaleski, Anne; Gerrard, J. W.; and Shokeir, M. H. K. "Nocturnal Enuresis: The Importance of a Small Bladder Capacity." In *Bladder Control and Enuresis*. Edited by I. Kolvin; C. MacKeith; and S.R. Meadow. Philadelphia: Spastics International Medical Publications, J.B. Lippincott Co., 1973. Technical material written for pediatricians.

TELEVISION

Charren, Peggy, and Sandler, Martin. "Is TV Turning Off Our Children?" *Redbook*, Oct. 1982. Why and how parents regulate TV viewing.

Goldsen, Rose K. *Show and Tell Machine: How Television Works and Works You Over*. New York: Dial Press, 1977.

Schramm, Wilbur; Lyle, Jack; and Parker, Edwin. *Television in the Lives of Our Children*. Stanford, Calif.: Stanford University Press, 1961.

Two excellent sources of ideas from parents are "Parents Exchange," a regular column in *Parent's Magazine,* and "Tricks of the Trade," a regular feature of *American Baby Magazine.*

Appendix

A COMPREHENSIVE LIST
OF PROBLEM-SOLVING APPROACHES

While our children present us with an endless array of problems, types of solutions can be divided into five basic categories. The following techniques are based on a careful analysis of how parents solved numerous day-to-day problems. These same approaches are summarized inside the front cover and form the underlying organization of the book. By presenting this detailed list, we hope to provide a foundation from which parents can develop still more creative, individualized solutions to problems of family living. Any one of these approaches, or combination of approaches, may provide escape from a well-worn rut.

1. CLARIFY OBJECTIVES
    Decipher the child's objectives in order to better understand the situation.
    Clarify *specific* parental objectives. (What is your goal in this issue?)
        Evaluate whether objectives are appropriate and practical.
        Sort out ambivalent and conflicting goals.
        Coordinate objectives with other caretakers to avoid different messages.
    Convey parental objectives to children.
        Model desired behavior. (For example, they won't say please if you don't.)
        Point out appropriate and inappropriate behavior in others.
        Teach necessary vocabulary.
        State rules slowly, clearly, and with eye contact at the child's level.
        Use visual cues for reinforcement. (For example, post a picture list of the bedtime routine.)
        Tell stories that highlight desired behavior.
    Remind youngsters of rules ahead of time. (For example, "Remember to talk quietly in the library.")

Teach specific examples *and* general rules, when appropriate. (For example, "We don't take gum without paying for it, because it is wrong to take things that belong to others.")

2. CHANGE THE ENVIRONMENT

Add, modify, or label equipment for easier use.

Ask yourself, Is there a better location for this activity?

Alter the social environment, such as the number of playmates.

Decrease the amount of general emotional stress in the environment, if appropriate and possible.

Change the time, duration, or frequency of the activity.

Consider food or chemical allergies that may contribute to the problem.

3. CHANGE ATTITUDES

Many things can change *our* attitudes:

When sufficiently fed up with the status quo, it may finally be worth the effort to instigate change.

More information from our children, other parents, books, or professionals may change our perspectives.

Reviewing childhood memories and present emotions may affect present attitudes.

If we change our expectations, our attitudes change accordingly. (For example, recognizing that it is normal to be less patient and efficient when short of sleep, we feel less disappointed in ourselves.)

There are many ways to change *children's* attitudes.

Change the mood with humor and/or games.

Acknowledge the child.

Listen carefully and acknowledge underlying emotions, as "feeling misunderstood" may be a major frustration.

Negotiate solutions with the child's participation.

Use fantasy.

Switch roles and act out different parts.

Make up stories that acknowledge feelings which children find hard to express. (For example, a child might be fearful about an upcoming trip.)

Make up stories that teach the value of different behavior. (For example, "Wilson is invited to interesting places, but Whiney Wilber isn't.")

Use fantasy to put the child in control of fears. (For example, "This flashlight turns nighttime monsters into stone.")

Have youngsters imagine a TV screen in their heads with personalities who will clarify the situation or help. (For example, "What does the angry kid on channel 3 have to say?" . . . "How about turning on Mr. Rogers to see what he thinks would help?")

Use positive programming.

Encourage the positive, rather than point out the negative, whenever possible.

Sleeptime suggestion: Repeat at bedtime that things are getting better.

To reduce fears and build self-confidence, reintroduce fearful situations very slowly, step by step.

4. CHANGE PARENTAL RESPONSE

Act, don't just talk.

Move the youngster and provide distraction.

Redirect, rather than prohibit, unacceptable behavior whenever possible. (For example, "Drop the sand, don't throw it.")

Respond to parental needs.

Set firmer limits.

Choose acceptable ways to blow off steam.

Take some time off—everyone needs it.

Pursue a personal interest, for a few minutes a week at least.

Make time for your relationship with your partner.

Get help from family, other parents, professionals, hired household help.

Respond to the child's needs.

Is the child hungry or tired?

Is the child in need of more comforting or attention?

Does the child need more physical exercise or less pressure to perform physically?

Is the child getting excess or insufficient intellectual stimulation?

Does the child lack opportunity to feel in charge? (Allow age-appropriate decisions and opportunities to play the leader.)

Reward good behavior.

Punish unacceptable behavior.

5. ADOPT TOLERANCE

Accept inborn differences in body rhythms and personality traits.

Recognize individual differences in interests and abilities.

Recognize that many behavior patterns will be outgrown. Accept that children inevitably suffer disappointments. Conserve energy for more important issues and let this one slide.

Experiment: Back off and see if the problem goes away.

Look for ways in which you too may benefit from the status quo.

If there are no alternatives, put up with the situation.

Index

Bowel movement: baby confused with, 84-85. *See also* Toilet training
Bragging, 242, 243
Brainstorming, 277
Brearley, Molly, and Elizabeth Hitchfield: *Guide to Reading Piaget, A,* 381-82
Breast milk, 9, 15; expressed, 4, 5, 163; quantity of, 8, 14; reaction to, 43
Breastfeeding, 2-6, 14; and co-sleeping, 57; milk supply in, 8, 14; as mother's time for self, 203; and overfeeding, 15; and sleep disturbances, 48; tips for, 3-6; during travel, 185
Buckets; safety concerns, 152
Burnout, parental, 208
Burns, 149
Burping, 7, 9
Bus travel, 188, 189-90
"Business," 271
Buying things, 196-98, 312; as reward, 379

Cabinets: childproofing, 146
Caffeine, 43, 165
Calcium, 12
Camping, 186
Car travel, 187-89; safety tips, 187-88
Carbonated drinks, 165
Carefulness, 253-54
Caring for others, 309-10
Caretakers, 281. *See also* Nursery schools; Sitters
Caretakers, primary, 66, 68; bonding and, 273, 324-25, 326
Cause and effect: understanding of, 415
Caution, 426
Change: and fears, 67; minimizing, in family crisis, 339-40; and sleep problems, 47
Changing table, 144
Character traits, inborn, 213. *See also* Personality
Charren, Peggy, and Martin Sandler: "Is TV Turning Off Our Children?", 206
Cheating, 361
Cheese, 12
Chemicals: and fussiness, 42-43; hazardous, 139

Child abuse, 211, 214, 391, 393; fantasies of, 217, 218-19; fear of, 216-19
Child care, 236, 281, 394, 417; adult/child ratios in, 332-33; age for, 327; finding, 334; need to renegotiate, 337; options in, 330-36; quality of, 325-26, 332-33; for sick children, 181
Child-care information and referral services, 236-37, 334
Childproofing, 117, 137, 139-40, 141-43, 393; and burns, 149; cabinets and drawers, 146-47; doorways, 146
Child-rearing (theory), 237, 240, 297-98; change in, 20, 23; and choice of child care, 333; comparison in, 211; happiness as goal in, 220-21; punishment in, 390-91 390-91
Children: accept and need penalties for misbehavior, 380-81; appropriate quantity and quality of foods for, 8-19; assume they are at fault for whatever happens, 108-09, 181, 225, 242, 261; fear power of magical thinking, 227; helping with housework, 119-33; involved in baby care, 355-57; reaction to separation, 325, 326, 327-28, 344-45, 346; spacing of, in family, 213 (*See also* Family structure)
Children: The Challenge (Drikurs), 384-85
Choice(s), 277; in cleanup, 132-33; in financial responsibility, 312; in handling negativity, 403-04; in household rules and restrictions, 118-19; in learning to cross streets, 156; offered in tantrums, 401; in reward and punishment, 374-75, 383-84; in teaching responsibility, 307
Choking, 137; avoidance of, in giving medicine, 165; prevention of, 25, 185
Christmas tree ornaments, 152
Circumcision, 105
Cleaning chores, 116
Cleanliness, 73-109; household standards of, 112, 120, 128
Climbing, 143
Clinginess, 107, 265, 357, 393-96
Clothing, 73-109; checking, in sleepless-

ior); deciding whether to take a job, 328–30; distress at sleeplessness, 46, 47; effects of being away from home, 324–30; emotional difficulties of, and co–sleeping, 62; fears of, passed on to children, 425; loneliness, 63, 210, 323–24, 338–41; lovemaking, 65–66; as models of good health, 161; overcoming depriva- tion, 203–14; prejudice toward children, 369; as primary caretakers, 273; rejec- tion of, after separation, 328; self- examination in handling aggression, 423; and sibling rivalry, 367–71; sleep deprivation, 35, 47, 58, 71–72, 137, 162; as source of information on child care, 334; taking care of own needs, 207–08; as target for children's frustration, 416; time to themselves, 67, 113, 203–07, 223, 224, 382; who suffered child abuse, 213–14; worries about children's health, 179–81. *See also* Expectations; Marital difficulties; Objectives

Parents, working, 324, 325, 328–30; cop- ing with own feelings, 336–41; work- home transition, 346–48

Parents' Emergency Guide (Diagram Group), 162

Parents of Twins, 236

Parents Without Partners, 236

Parking lots, 187

Passivity, 306–07, 426–29

Patience, 282–83, 427; lack of, 207–08, 223

Paying for chores, 131

Pediatric check–ups, 8. *See also* Doctor, visits to

Pediatrician. See Doctor

Peer pressure: and giving up security objects, 55

Perfection, 244

Permissiveness, 243, 297

Perseverance, 254

Personal growth, 240–63

Personality(ies), 221, 337; and aggression, 415; effect of harsh toilet training on, 84; hidden, 251–53, 318–19; and indepen- dence, 265; individual differences in,

246–47, 426; and tolerance for messiness, 119

Pets: caring for, 287, 309

Physical contact: crucial to lover, 281; as response to tantrums, 401

Physical exertion: as punishment, 388; to work off anger, 412–13

Physical laws: misunderstanding of, 425

Physical punishment. *See* Pain as punishment

Physical relaxation: for sleepless- ness, 44–45

Physical restraint: as punishment, 389

Piaget, Jean, 316, 381

Pinching, 422

Pinworms, 163

Plane travel, 188, 189–90

Planning ahead: for family visits, 294; regarding housework, 115–16; in self- feeding, 26

Plants, 139–40; caring for, 287, 311

Plastic bags, 153

Play, playing, 249, 317, 327; fighting in, 423; with siblings, 354; therapeutic value of, 421–22; in yard and neighborhood, 153–56

Play–Dough, 114–15, 359, 371, 418, 421

Play groups, 236, 272, 324, 338; as child care, 331; composition of, 430

Play space: indoor, 300

Playing doctor, 105

Playmates, 281, 283, 324, 417, 426, 427; and bossiness, 423; imaginary, 275; working with conflict among, 363–67. *See also* Friends, friendships

Playpen(s), 114, 136, 185–86; avoidance of use of, 272; safety concerns, 153

Pleasure: in moral development, 284, 285–86

Poison control center, 140

Poison emergencies, 140

Poisons, 137, 138

Politeness, 301–04

Porta–cribs, 193

Possessions: protection of, from younger siblings, 358–59; protection of valued, 140–43; responsibility for, 311–12

while eating, 9-10; during illness at home, 167; mental, 250-51; safety concerns, 148
Temperament, 24, 153
Temperature, 162-63; normal, 162; when to take, 9
Tension: from anger, 216; created by conflict, 412-13; reduced through tantrums, 401; symptoms of, in children, 234-35; use of praise and, 255
Therapist, 275; choice of, 237
Therapy, 64, 416; for bed-wetting, 88; couple, 225; in emotion-related illness, 179; for emotional issues aroused in parenting, 231; family, 404; for help in dealing with anger, 413; for help in stopping aggression, 423; for masturbation, 103-04; in parental prejudice, 369; for parents, 237-38; play as, 421; to prevent child abuse, 218; for stealing, 320
Thermometer(s), 162-63, 185
Thirst, 15; during travel, 185
Thumb(s): as security object, 51, 52-53, 54, 55
Tics, 64
Time: for children, 395; concept of, 286, 327, 408, 415; curiosity and, 272; factor in creativity, 275-76; individualized, 369-70; learning to use, 267; needed by children, 409-10; for parents to themselves, 236, 325, 326, 378; relation with love, 355; spent with older siblings, 355-56, 362
Time-out: as punishment, 386, 387-88, 422; for tantrums, 401
Timing: in punishment, 382-83
Tiredness. See Fatigue
Tobacco, 138
Toddler harness, 187
Toilet, 117; safety concerns, 152
Toilet flushing, 77, 81; concerns about, 82
Toilet paper, 117
Toilet training, 74, 76-85; basic approaches to, 78-79; common problems in, 82-85; guidelines for, 76-77; resistance to, 82; timing, equipment, clothing, 77-78
Toilet Training in Less than a Day

(Azrin), 79
Tommee Tippee® spoon, 28
Tommee Tippee® training cups, 8
Tooth alignment: thumb sucking and pacifiers and, 53
Tooth brushing, 99-102
Toothpaste, 101-02
Touch: confusing, forced, nurturing, 158
Touch Continuum (model), 158
Toy boxes: safety concerns, 153
Toys, 129-31, 241, "baby," in preparation for arrival of new sibling, 352-53; impounded, 132; ownership, sharing of, 288-89; for self-entertainment, 268-69; storage of, 126-27; for use when parent telephoning, 340
Trading favors, 285, 366
Train travel, 188, 189-90
Training pants, 77
Training seats, 77
Travel, 182-93, 394
Trust: in love, 281; sense of, 327
Truth-telling: parental reaction to, 317-19. *See also* Honesty
Tupperware sipperseals® drinking cups, 8
Tweezers, 185
Tylenol® (acetaminophen), 163, 185

Ungame®, 321
Unhappiness, 220-21

Values: of children, 286; rewards and, 377; and work outside the home, 323, 329
Vaporizer, 50, 165; fear of, 166-67
Vegetables, 13
Verbal aggression, 419-20
Verbal defense, 428
Verbal punishment, 386
Vickery, Donald, Robert Pantel, James Fries and: *Taking Care of Your Child*, 162
Viewmaster® viewer, 191
Violence, origins of, 314
Visiting other homes, 137; childproofing for, 147
Visiting relatives, 292-96
Visual arts, 279